Transgender
RIGHTS

Paisley Currah
Richard M. Juang
Shannon Price Minter

EDITORS

University of Minnesota Press

MINNEAPOLIS · LONDON

The University of Minnesota Press gratefully acknowledges financial assistance provided by the Gill Foundation for the publication of this book.

Chapter 8 was first published in *New York Law School Journal of Human Rights* 17 (2000).

Published by the University of Minnesota Press
111 Third Avenue South, Suite 290
Minneapolis, MN 55401-2520
http://www.upress.umn.edu

Library of Congress Cataloging-in-Publication Data

Transgender rights / Paisley Currah, Richard M. Juang, and Shannon Price Minter, editors.
    p.   cm.
  Includes bibliographical references and index.
  ISBN-13: 978-0-8166-4311-0 (hc : alk. paper)
  ISBN-10: 0-8166-4311-3 (hc : alk. paper)
  ISBN-13: 978-0-8166-4312-7 (pb : alk. paper)
  ISBN-10: 0-8166-4312-1 (pb : alk. paper)
  1. Transsexuals—Civil rights. 2. Transsexuals—Legal status, laws, etc. 3. Sex and law.
I. Currah, Paisley, 1964–   II. Juang, Richard M.   III. Minter, Shannon.
  HQ77.9.T716   2006
  323.3'26—dc22   2006014106

Printed in the United States of America on acid-free paper

The University of Minnesota is an equal-opportunity educator and employer.

12 11 10 09 08 07 06   10 9 8 7 6 5 4 3 2 1

Contents

Acknowledgments

A project such as this is both a collection of ideas and a collective effort of friends, activists, colleagues, institutions, and families. We drew our energy from the deep river of support that they created.

The editors would like to thank the institutions that supported this work in its early stages. The Center for Lesbian and Gay Studies (CLAGS) hosted the Transgender Law and Policy Roundtable in 2001, where many of the contributors to this collection first met to hash out some of the ideas presented here; the Astraea Lesbian Foundation for Justice provided essential funding for that meeting. The National Center for Lesbian Rights provided key technical support for this project. The editors are indebted to Camila Gomez-Salgado for her speedy and efficient translating, to Claudia Isler Mazur for her help with copyediting, to Paula Dragosh for her fastidious work, and to Richard Morrison for his patience, good judgment, and, most important, his willingness to take on this project.

Paisley Currah's work on this collection was supported by the Wayne F. Placek Award of the American Psychological Foundation and a research grant from the Professional Staff Congress of the City University of New York. He would like to thank Monica Barrett, Kylar Broadus, Maria Carosone, Donna Cartwright, Fraser Currah, Kelly Currah, Chris Daley, Megan Davidson, Carrie Davis, Zillah Eisenstein, Doreen Grant, Jamison Green, Peter Hegarty, Courtney Joslin, Mara Keisling, Maureen Kelly, Kelsang Kunden, Jennifer Levi, L. Maurer, Robin Gilbrecht-Minter, Tara Montgomery, Lisa Moore, Lisa Jean Moore, Lisa Mottet, Ruthann Robson, Joe Rollins, Franklin Romeo,

Liz Seaton, Dean Spade, Mark Ungar, and Stephen Whittle for their support of this work. He is deeply indebted to his colleagues on staff at CLAGS— Preston Bautista, Sara Ganter, Megan Jenkins, Lavelle Porter, Jordan Schild-crout, Chun-Ping Yen—for their patience, and to his students at Brooklyn College for their insights and enthusiasm.

Richard M. Juang's work on this book would not have been possible without the support of the English department, the women's studies and LGB studies programs, and the Human Sexuality Collection of Cornell University; the students, faculty, and staff of Oberlin College; the Department of English and Creative Writing and the School of Arts, Humanities, and Communications at Susquehanna University; the National Endowment for the Humanities; the Phil Zwickler Memorial Research Grant; and the Feminism and Legal Theory Project. Richard thanks the participants, speakers, sponsors, and organizers of the 1998 TransPositions conference in Ithaca for the energy that sparked this project. Richard is indebted to Kathy Abrams, Laura Brown, Loren Cameron, Debra Castillo, Terry Castle, Martha Fineman, Jack Halberstam, Brenda Marston, Biddy Martin, Ramon Saldivar, and Shirley Samuels for their intelligence, warmth, and patience. Many kinds of thanks go to Mara Keisling and the National Center for Transgender Equality; to Nora Balfour and Margie Montfort for their shady home and warm dogs; to Morgan, Willy, and Nohemy, who remained steadfast; to Nancy Boutilier, Sven Brandenburg, Jennifer Bryan, Christa Champion, Stacy DeMarco, Sue Elkevizth, Thamora Fishel, Felix Giron, Jennifer Good, Tyrell Haberkorn, Jana Hassan, Cid Isbell, Kimari Johnson, Maureen Kelly, Jennifer Lewis, Hanna Markusson, Lis Maurer, Lauren Miller, Noelle Morrissette, Sharon Osterloh, Elizabeth Palmberg, Anna Parkinson, Rafael Reyes-Ruiz, Debbie Rozelle, Rachel Safman, Sarah Simpkins, Carter Smith, and Tami Loos, all of whom made things meaningful. Richard's deepest thanks go to his family— George, Gloria, their children, and Amy and Kuo-Sheng Juang—thank you for a sense of justice.

Shannon Price Minter would like to thank Robin and Alia Gilbrecht-Minter, Marta Ames, Marcus Arana, Lena Ayoub, Ray Bernstein, Ken Choe, Chris Daley, Jon Davidson, Karen Doering, Beatrice Dorhn, Phyllis Frye, Prado Gomez, Alexander John Goodrum, Jamison Green, John Hammond, Courtney Joslin, Michelle Kammerer, Michael Kantaras, Kate Kendell, Vernie Ruth Kimmons, Geoff Koors, Jennifer Levi, Kerry Lobel, Jody Marksamer, Martha Matthews, Sharon McGowan, JoAnne Miner, Natasha Minsker, Kay Minter, Chris Newfield, Tiffany Palmer, Jack Reardon, James Reardon, Shirley Samuels, Liz Seaton, Steve Shiffrin, Lia Shigemura, Sterling Simmons, Susan Stryker, Janis Walworth, Shannan Wilber, and Riki Wilchins.

To have had the time and resources to create this book was a luxury that few have, in or outside the trans community. We wish to close these acknowledgments by giving credit for this book to the many trans activists and civil rights and social justice activists who, over decades, survived, spoke, loved, fought, sometimes died, and sometimes triumphed, and so paved the way for this work.

Introduction

Paisley Currah, Richard M. Juang, and Shannon Price Minter

In the past thirty years, the transgender movement in the United States has gained surprising visibility and strength. In the legislative arena, transgender advocates have successfully fought for inclusion in nondiscrimination and hate crime laws in several states and dozens of municipalities. More than two hundred employers, including some Fortune 500 companies, and more than sixty colleges and universities now include gender identity in their non-discrimination policies. In 2004, overturning decades of prior case law, a federal court of appeals ruled for the first time that transgender people who are discriminated against in the workplace are protected under Title VII of the Federal Civil Rights Act of 1964, which prohibits discrimination based on sex. Trans activists have formed hundreds of social service and advocacy organizations, such as the Transgender Law Center in California, the Sylvia Rivera Law Project in New York, and the International Foundation for Gender Education. In several cities, trans activists have created community gender identity centers and clinics to counterbalance the power of doctors, therapists, and psychiatrists. Every major LGB national organization has changed its mission statement to include transgender people. In higher education, trans people are no longer simply an "object" of study in abnormal psychology textbooks. Rather, transgender issues have become a topic of serious and respectful inquiry in virtually every scholarly field, from medicine to political theory, and scholarly works by trans authors are now widely available.

At the same time, violence and discrimination against transgender people persists in daily life. In 2003 Gwen Araujo, a transgender teenager from a small town in Northern California, was murdered by a group of young men who beat her to death with a shovel after discovering that she had male genitalia. The attorneys representing the young men argued that their clients' actions were justified by Gwen's "deception" in not disclosing her transgender identity to them. Far from an isolated event, Gwen's brutal murder was one of thousands of similarly lethal hate crimes against transgender people that have been documented by the community Web site, Remembering Our Dead. While this epidemic of actual violence goes largely unnoticed by the mass media, it is an ever-present reality for transgender people—and especially for transgender women, who are most often the victims of such crimes. This vulnerability is amplified in prisons and jails, where transgender prisoners typically are housed by their birth sex and where transgender women are particularly vulnerable to rape by both fellow prisoners and guards.

The legal status of trans people in other arenas is equally precarious. In the past few years, appellate courts in Texas, Kansas, Ohio, and Florida have ruled that transsexual people are prohibited from marrying; in three of these cases, the courts held that marriages of many years' duration were null and void, simply because one of the spouses in each case was transsexual. In 2002 a federal court in Louisiana ruled that it was not discriminatory for Winn-Dixie to fire Peter Oiler for occasionally cross-dressing outside work. In prior decisions, federal courts routinely have excluded transsexual people from any protection under federal nondiscrimination laws, thereby leaving employers free to fire transsexual workers at will. In many states, obtaining a driver's license or birth certificate that reflects one's new gender is extremely difficult; in some, it is impossible.

In short, while the gains won by the U.S. transgender movement are impressive, most transgender people still are deprived of any secure legal status. In the eyes of the law in most states, they are nonpersons, with no right to marry, work, use a public bathroom, or even walk down the street in safety.

The Movement

What does transgender mean? Since about 1995, the meaning of *transgender* has begun to settle, and the term is now generally used to refer to individuals whose gender identity or expression does not conform to the social expectations for their assigned sex at birth. At the same time, related terms used to describe particular identities within that broader category have continued to evolve and multiply. As new generations of body modifiers and new social formations of gender resisters emerge, multiple usages coexist, sometimes easily, sometimes with much generational or philosophical tension: *transvestite, cross-dresser, trannie, trans, genderfuck, genderqueer, FTM, MtM, trans men, boyz, bois.* Transgender is an expansive and complicated social category.

The term *transgender* offers political possibilities as well as risks. Any claim to describe or define a people or a set of practices poses the danger of misrepresenting them. The danger is not trivial; distorted representations lead readily to misguided advocacy. The term can, at times, mask the differences among gender nonconforming people and risks implying a common identity that outweighs differences along racial and class lines. Nonetheless, there is also considerable value in a term that can draw together people who believe that individuals should have a right to determine and express their gender without fear, stigmatization, marginalization, or punishment.

One particular area of tension is the inclusion of intersex people in the definition of transgender. Intersex activists argue, rightly we think, that being intersex is not the same as being transgender. Being intersex denotes, according to Alice Dreger, "a variety of congenital conditions in which a person has neither the standard male nor the standard female anatomy."[1] The attempt simply to assimilate intersex identities and political interests within a transgender rubric too often has meant ignoring the urgency of ending the surgical mutilation of intersex children. In this collection, we hope to make some connections visible without erasing the specific concerns of the intersex movement. So while this collection is titled *Transgender Rights,* we have included an important court decision about an intersex child and a critical introduction to the case. We do so on the grounds that, while transgender and intersex politics refer to different constituencies and have significant differences in their goals, the materials we are publishing here nonetheless grapple with questions of autonomy and gender self-determination. In doing so, we hope to acknowledge the specificity of intersex rights without abandoning an awareness of the interconnections between the interests of transgender and intersex peoples.

Ultimately, the effectiveness with which the transgender movement addresses the diversity of its constituents will depend less on finding a satisfactory vocabulary and more on how actual strategies for social change are implemented. The same is true for creating effective connections with people who do *not* see themselves as transgender. Put simply, the movement's effectiveness will depend heavily on who benefits from its successes.

Ultimately, *transgender* refers to a collective political identity. Whether we have psychological features in common or share a particular twist in our genetic codes is less important than the more pressing search for justice and equality. *This book is not concerned either with supporting or with refuting any claims about why we exist.* It is a matter of fact that trans people conceive of themselves in many radically different ways: as transsexual women and men who have always known that they were female or male; as genderqueers living in an existential rebellion against the biopolitics of the dominant society; as butches who move complexly among lesbian and transgender identities and communities; as quietly androgynous femme boyz. Despite their profound differences, these groups all share a common political investment in a right to gender self-determination.

In practice, *transgender* is a useful term in many contexts, yet insufficiently inclusive or too imprecise in others. Many activists organize directly under the transgender rubric: the National Transgender Advocacy Coalition, the National Center for Transgender Equality, the Transgender Law and Policy Institute, and the Massachusetts Transgender Political Coalition. Other activists have embraced what appears to be a more universal term, *gender:* the International Foundation for Gender Education, Gender Education and Advocacy, the Gender Rights Advocacy Association of New Jersey, and Gender-PAC. Still other groups such as FTM International and American Boyz use more gender-specific labels to describe their constituencies. Nonetheless, when these groups seek justice and equality for people whose gender identity or expression contravenes social norms, they become facets of the same movement.

The Work

This collection evolved out of the contributors' ongoing intellectual and activist projects. Responding to the realities of transgender political work, these essays implicitly reflect many of the goals and principles enunciated by the International Bill of Gender Rights (IBGR). Produced in 1993 by the International Conference on Transgender Law and Employment Policy, the IBGR offers an important public articulation of the aspirations of transgender people. Written in the discourse of civil and human rights, it begins by declaring that "all human beings have the right to define their own gender identity regardless of chromosomal sex, genitalia, assigned birth sex, or initial gender role." The IBGR goes on to call for the following freedoms and rights: freedom of gender expression; equal employment opportunities; freedom from involuntary psychiatric diagnosis and treatment; freedom to form sexual, familial, and marital relationships; freedom to control and change one's own body; access to competent medical and professional care; access to gendered space and activities; the right to have and adopt children; the right to nurture and have custody of children. We provide the full text of the IBGR in this book as an appendix.

To many nontransgender people, such aspirations might seem surprisingly ordinary. However, this collection implicitly argues that the radical dimensions of the transgender movement arise neither from simply claiming that trans people are "normal," which we certainly are, nor from claiming that we are "exceptional," which we also are, but from arguing that being transgender is eminently compatible with all else that comes with being human, the ordinary as well as the extraordinary.

Law

Until recently, nondiscrimination laws did not define sex or gender. Consequently, it was left to the courts to decide whether discrimination against trans people should be recognized as a type of sex discrimination. The judiciary's record on this issue has been poor. The exemplary case in this area is *Ulane v. Eastern Airlines*, a 1984 case that is still binding precedent. In *Ulane*, a federal appellate court found that the plaintiff, a transsexual woman, was not discriminated against on the basis of sex. Rather, the court explained, "it is clear from the evidence that if Eastern did discriminate against Ulane, it was not because she is female, but because Ulane is a transsexual—a biological male who takes female hormones, cross-dresses, and has surgically altered parts of her body to make it appear to be female."[2] The court's evasive logic has seemed weak even to people equipped with only a dictionary's definition of transsexuality; after all, it seems hardly an affront to reason to think that, if it is wrong to fire someone for being a woman, it is equally wrong to fire someone for becoming a woman. Nonetheless, this decision, and scores of others exactly like it, is symptomatic of the broader patterns of exclusion and misrepresentation faced by transgender people in the law.

Trans activists have put their energies into changing both laws and cultural perceptions. Perhaps the most visible strategy used to counter judicial hostility has been to ask legislatures to define sex, gender, or even sexual orientation within nondiscrimination laws so as to explicitly include trans people, or to add a new category, usually gender identity. At the same time, trans advocates have drawn on the tools provided by other civil rights movements to change the judiciary's understanding of who counts as a person deserving of protection. In "Gender Pluralisms under the Transgender Umbrella," Paisley Currah examines how, in both legislative work and litigation, trans advocates have worked to counter the dehumanizing legal decisions that construct the gender of trans people as outside the realm of legal protection. Trans advocates have made strategic choices, he argues, to frame rights for types of persons, rather than rights for particular practices (such as speech), in order to place gender nonconforming people firmly within the compelling legal and cultural logics of the civil rights tradition.

Cases involving marriage and other gendered legal arrangements may demand other modes of advocacy. In "The Ties That (Don't) Bind: Transgender Family Law and the Unmaking of Families," Taylor Flynn observes that "we live in a highly gendered society where sex distinctions have significant legal consequences, particularly within the realm of the family—these distinctions affect issues including whom you can marry, whether you can inherit your spouse's estate, or whether you provide an 'appropriate' role model for your children." Taylor explains that in cases involving marriage and child custody, trans advocates largely have stayed within the bounds of the existing gender paradigm, arguing that trans men *are* men and that trans women *are* women, rather than attacking the state's ability to define one's legal gender.

In "The Roads Less Traveled: The Problem with Binary Sex Categories," Julie A. Greenberg argues that the law's role in gender assignment is multifaceted and contradictory. Reviewing both legal constructions of sex and current medical data, Greenberg argues that the legal assumption that sex is fixed and binary is fundamentally at odds with current medical knowledge and practice. Greenberg's work lays the groundwork for reversing the commonly held assumption that the body provides a much simpler, more clear-cut, and secure foundation for legal sex classification than gender self-identification.

Challenging medical models in which differences are pathologized has been central to transgender politics. In doing so, activists have followed a critical path opened up by the disability rights movement. Jennifer Levi and Ben Klein provide a detailed exploration of that intersection in "Pursuing Protection for Transgender People through Disability Laws." For decades, disability rights activists have suggested that the problem for people with disabilities lies not in their bodies but in the social architectures—legal, physical, normative—that turn a physical or cognitive difference into a disability. Similarly, transgender activists have targeted the physical, legal, and social structures—from sex-segregated bathrooms to legal sex-classification systems—that prevent trans people from functioning as equal economic, social, and civic actors. At the same time, some trans people and trans allies have felt profoundly uncomfortable with the use of disability rights laws for trans advocacy. This is a consequence, ironically, of having fallen prey to the stigmatizing discourse surrounding disability. Levi and Klein ask that trans persons reconsider their reluctance; while the fear of reinforcing our own pathologization is not to be dismissed lightly, such a fear stems from a fundamental misunderstanding of contemporary disability rights advocacy.

Workplaces can be precarious for trans people. Kylar Broadus, who was forced to leave his own job after transitioning in the workplace, explores the evolution of employment discrimination case law for transgender people from the vantage of both an attorney and an unsuccessful litigant in his own case. In addition to describing the emergence of a new judicial receptiveness to sex discrimination claims by transgender people, Broadus addresses the personal significance not simply of winning or losing but of finding one's humanity either mirrored or occluded by the law. For transgender people, the law often has been a source of terrible disempowerment and loss; conversely, Broadus argues, the emergence of a new recognition and respect for transgender people in the courts can be a source of great political power.

While trans advocates argue for the centrality of gender self-determination, intersex activists are engaged in a related struggle to give intersex people the right to self-determination and to resist surgical mutilations that attempt to produce, as the intersex activist Cheryl Chase notes, "normatively sexed bodies and gendered subjects through constitutive acts of violence."[3] At present in the United States, there is no substantive right to bodily autonomy and integrity for intersex infants and children. In a groundbreaking 1999 decision, however, Colombia's highest court ruled that the interests of intersex infants and children should be weighed. We publish here, for the first time, selections in English of this decision, translated by Nohemy Solórzano-Thompson. Morgan Holmes frames these selections with her essay "Deciding Fate or Protecting a Developing Autonomy? Intersex Children and the Colombian Constitutional Court" and outlines the significance of the decision's emphasis on autonomy and consent. Holmes also reckons with the limitations of the precedent, observing that "the ruling does not actually recognize intersexuality as an integral feature of one's being." What remains to be affirmed is a substantive right to bodily autonomy and integrity.

History

Transgender civil rights struggles arise within a complex historical context in which the transgender movement is visible as both an important social movement in itself and part of a broader fabric of struggles. In "Do Transsexuals Dream of Gay Rights? Getting Real about Transgender Inclusion," Shannon Price Minter reminds us of the historical interdependence of transgender and lesbian, bisexual, and gay communities. He identifies the key question raised by our interlocking histories to be "not whether transgender people can justify their claim to gay rights, but rather how did a movement launched by bull daggers, drag queens, and transsexuals in 1969 end up viewing transgender people as outsiders less than thirty years later?"

In "Transgender Communities of the United States in the Late Twentieth Century," Dallas Denny, the founder of several major transgender organizations, traces an often-overlooked genealogy of formal and informal community building by gender nonconforming people. In an effort to track the emergence of transgender self-identification and community, Denny offers a portrait of tumultuous interactions, from uneasy compliance to the outright refusal by trans people of pathologizing and criminalizing discourses. In Denny's essay, the development of a medical understanding of transsexuality is only one branch, and by no means the dominant one, of transsexual and transgender history. Her work makes visible a fuller palette of networks, writings, groups, and gatherings.

Transgender organizations develop in the midst of larger social changes: Willy Wilkinson offers an account of community organizing around the AIDS crisis. The vulnerability and marginalization of trans people in the public health arena were brought into stark relief by the epidemic's disproportionate impact on trans women. It became an epidemic that demanded a community response. In "Public Health Gains of the Transgender Community in San Francisco: Grassroots Organizing and Community-Based Research," Wilkinson offers a case study of how trans people successfully engaged with nontrans researchers and policymakers to document the specific health-care needs of trans people and create changes in service provision.

Politics

Transgender discrimination is not simply a consequence of private distastes; individual acts, from instances of employment discrimination to hate crimes, are made possible and channeled by public ideologies and a host of social and economic structures. In turn, the politics of the movement must address broader structural realities. Dean Spade, in "Compliance Is Gendered: Struggling for Gender Self-Determination in a Hostile Economy," expands the work of feminist theorists who have explored the impact of welfare regulation on women and shows how such regulations enforce gender conformity and magnify the economic marginalization of trans people. Spade notes that mainstream LGB organizations have tended to focus too narrowly on the needs of middle-class constituents. An effective trans movement, he argues, must be grounded on antipoverty work, the widening of economic opportunity and redistribution, and the decriminalization of poverty.

Similarly, in "Transgendering the Politics of Recognition," Richard M. Juang argues that discrimination against people of color and discrimination against transgender people are, in fact, "two faces of one ideological coin." Through an analysis of the rhetoric associated with two historically pivotal deaths, Tyra Hunter and Vincent Chin, Juang argues for the importance of a politics of recognition that addresses both racial and gendered forms of discrimination.

While this collection cannot fully represent the political concerns of transgender people across the globe, it is important to note that the United States is neither alone nor at the "forefront" of transgender activism. Indeed, a rich critical dialogue has emerged in national and transnational settings in which the United States is only one locale among many. Many U.S. activists are aware of the recent decision of the European Court of Human Rights in *Goodwin & I v. United Kingdom,* which held that the UK's refusal to permit transsexual people to obtain new birth certificates or to marry in their new gender violated the European Convention on Human Rights. As a result, the UK passed in 2005 the Gender Recognition Act, which allows transsexual people to apply for legal recognition of their new gender, including the issuance of new birth certificates.[4] The development of transgender rights in countries outside the United States and Western Europe may be much less familiar to activists here. In an effort to bridge that gap, in "(Trans)Sexual Citizenship in Contemporary Argentina" Mauro Cabral and Paula Viturro analyze the ideological conditions within which transsexual and transgender people have emerged into legal visibility in Argentina. To an extent, the compromised status of "(trans)sexual citizenship" that Cabral and Viturro identify in Argentina is similar to the constraints faced by trans people in the United States. However, Cabral and Viturro also explore the specific and in many respects quite unfamiliar legal and ideological demands placed on transsexual and transgender persons within the context of Argentinian law.

Drawing the collection to a close, Judith Butler and Ruthann Robson explore the meaning and risks of a politics of normalcy. As Butler observes in "Undiagnosing Gender," the diagnosis of gender identity disorder (GID) remains one of the primary interfaces between service providers and trans persons, particularly transgender children and youth. Butler asks, what is the price demanded by the diagnosis in terms of the autonomy it constrains and the behavioral and psychological norms it imposes, even as it appears strategically useful to gain access to resources and recognition? The design and structure of GID diagnosis creates, she argues, a paradoxical situation in which "it is possible to say, necessary to say, that the diagnosis leads the way to the alleviation of suffering, and it is possible, necessary, to say that the diagnosis intensifies the very suffering that requires alleviation."

In "Reinscribing Normality? The Law and Politics of Transgender Marriage," Robson highlights the assimilationist tendencies of transgender marriage litigation. The discourse concerning transgender marriage, Robson argues, "too often serves to recapitulate and reinscribe the most traditional visions of marriage and heterosexuality." Marriage is not simply a private emotional union but a state-sponsored mechanism for the distribution or denial of economic resources. In short, Robson asks the thought-provoking question, how "normal" do we want to be and who bears the costs of that normalcy?

Many of the scholars—independent or institutionally located—who contributed to this collection are also, often primarily, advocates for trans people. By foregrounding the political concerns and efforts of trans people, we hope this collection helps shift the center of gravity for intellectual work about transgender people. There is a substantial body of literature in the law, social sciences, and humanities in which trans people appear; however, in much of this work, we tend to be used as exciting examples of the subversion or reification of gender, the undiscovered edges of legal discourse, or some hot new cultural underground. That we are persons with a complex or unacknowledged relationship to state and civil society is often forgotten. This collection strives to be an act of intellectual production that does *not* situate trans people as a means to an end or an intellectual curiosity but considers the well-being of trans people as an end in itself.

These essays bring trans people's activism into view, articulate the specific civil rights challenges we face, and offer a range of concrete perspectives and strategies. While the essays in this collection do not address every type of discrimination faced by transgender people, we hope they provide a real sense of the many types of activism propelling the transgender rights movement. This collection also reflects the current state of the transgender movement and of civil rights activism generally. The essays here generally express a liberalism and a humanism that prize individualism, freedom, and autonomy. Almost certainly, this is not a sufficient political agenda. For the moment, it is a necessary one.

Foundations and Futures

If we return to foundational questions, perhaps the most important one to ask is, simply, "why rights?" For some, the rolling back of the gains of the traditional civil rights movement and the critique of identity-based movements as insufficiently inclusive and incapable of addressing nonidentitarian concerns such as class and poverty lead to a belief that activists and theorists must find a better focus of political practice. Nonetheless, rights discourse remains the commonsense of politics in the United States. The idea of rights provides a familiar, and thus quietly powerful, lexicon through which to challenge injustice. This is particularly the case when violence and exclusion are clearly targeted at particular *kinds* of persons.

What needs to change? Protections on paper are, of course, inadequate. The legal recognition of trans people is meaningful only when it is part of a larger cultural transformation. For example, although Minnesota has included trans people in its nondiscrimination law since 1993, that state's highest court ruled in 2001 that Julie Goins had not been discriminated against when her employer told her she could not use the women's bathroom. The judges in that decision understood quite clearly that the law prohibited discrimination on the basis of "having or being perceived as having a self-image or identity not traditionally associated with one's biological maleness or femaleness." Nonetheless, it seemed nonsensical to them that Goins should have access to women-only space. The success of rights-based arguments depends on creating a culture in which trans people are not just a curiosity or a perversion of nature. At the same time, struggles organized around civil rights are also a form of cultural work. For example, including transgender people in hate crime laws does not create change by enhancing penalties but by educating legislators, the media, the police, and the courts about the violence faced by trans people and by asking the public at large to side with the victims rather than the perpetrators of hate.

Why *transgender* rights? Feminism already has established the ethical and legal basis for gender equality. The idea of gender equality includes transgender people, and so it may seem redundant to argue for the specific inclusion of transgender persons in nondiscrimination legislation. Logically, transgender people already should be covered by existing gender nondiscrimination laws; discrimination on the basis of gender nonconformity is, by its very nature, gender discrimination. In practice, however, courts, civil society, and the mass media typically have failed to apply the principle of gender equality to transgender people. One reason for this broad failure of logic and imagination is that trans people have been seen as examples of sexual "deviants," in the same way that homosexuals have been cast as gender inverts. As a consequence, the transgender movement, as Shannon Price Minter notes in this collection, has continued to be affiliated more strongly with the LGB movement than with the feminist movements that began in the 1960s and 1970s, despite significant conflicts. In the legal arena, the transgender rights movement has striven to expand the inclusivity of the term *gender* beyond its current cultural and legal boundaries; similarly, our political goals also have the potential to close the significant gaps created by the institutional separation between LGB and women's rights advocacy.

The transgender movement is a highly accelerated and fragile reality. In thirty years, trans people have moved from meeting in secret to lobbying Congress, from being arrested for cross-dressing to mobilizing public protests against transphobic violence. We are optimistic that the goals articulated in this book will be achieved. But in reaching our goals, transgender people will not disappear as a constituency or identity. Instead, transgender political work will take on different forms and become reoriented toward other projects and goals. Achieving equality will not be an end for trans people, but the start of a dramatic widening of the cultural and social imagination. What such a new world will look like, and what the transgender generations who live in it will make of their world, remains as yet unwritten.

Notes

1. Dreger complicates this definition: "In fact, because of ever-more discoveries of sexual variation and ever-more developments in sexual politics, medical and lay definitions of 'male' and 'female' have changed repeatedly and continue to change" (Alice Domurat Dreger, "A History of Intersex: From the Age of Gonads to the Age of Consent," in *Intersex in the Age of Ethics,* ed. Alice Domurat Dreger [Hagerstown, MD: University Publishing Group, 1999], 5–6).

2. *Ulane v. Eastern Airlines,* 742 F.2d 1081 (7th Cir. 1984), *cert. denied,* 471 U.S. 1017 (1985).

3. Cheryl Chase, "Hermaphrodites with Attitude," *GLQ* 4, no. 2 (1998): 189–211.

4. Stephen Whittle, "*Goodwin & I v. United Kingdom:* What Does It Mean?" http://www.pfc.org.uk/legal/gimeans.htm. See also the Gender Recognition Act information page, http://www.gra-info.org.uk/.

PART I. LAW

1. Gender Pluralisms under the Transgender Umbrella

Paisley Currah

A lawyer argues in a legal brief that an employee who was not allowed to use the women's bathroom experienced discrimination on the basis of her "transgender status."[1] News stories refer to the historic size (seven) of the "transgender delegation" at the 2004 Democratic National Convention.[2] An attorney explains that his client, a Louisiana truck driver fired when his employer discovered he liked to cross-dress periodically, is "transgender."[3] A newspaper headline announces a "victory for Boston's transgender population" after the city council adds gender identity and expression to a non-discrimination law.[4] A veteran of the Stonewall Riots, Sylvia Rivera, tells members of a New York City Council committee that they should add a broad definition of gender to the city's human rights law because "we lose people like [hate crime victim] Amanda Milan and many, many other trans-gendered women through the streets of New York. . . . We must pass this bill. We have suffered long enough."[5] Who is the "we" invoked by "transgender"? What, precisely, is "transgender"? Why have gender-different people, communities, and practices become subsumed under it, especially in the context of arguments for equal rights in the United States?

The meaning of *transgender* has shifted since it was first coined. Virginia Prince, often recognized as the person who brought *transgenderist* into wide usage, explained its origin to Leslie Feinberg this way: "There had to be some name for people like myself who trans the gender barrier—meaning somebody who lives full time in the gender opposite to their anatomy. I have not transed the sex barrier."[6] For Prince, the term was meant to distinguish

3

people who live full-time as women from both occasional cross-dressers and from transsexual people.[7] From signifying a subject position between cross-dresser and transsexual, the meaning of *transgender* expanded radically in the early 1990s to include them, along with other cross-gender practices and identities. In contrast to the diagnostic category of *transsexual,* which Sandy Stone describes as an attempt by the "body police" to homogenize "a vast heteroglossic account of difference,"[8] *transgender* is a grassroots term in both of its usages. Crafted to resist the imposition of labels created by the psychiatric establishment to define and contain cross-gender identities and behaviors, it is a "term of empowerment rather than disempowerment," writes Gordene O. MacKenzie.[9] "Transgender," according to the longtime activist and legal scholar Phyllis Frye, is "a political term created to fill the need for self-definition by the transgender community."[10] Jamison Green describes the adoption of the term as "an attempt to get beyond identity politics by invoking a term so broad and inclusive as to make room for multiple identities and expressions, and still refer to the specific oppressions that transpeople faced."[11]

It has now become almost axiomatic to define transgender in its current usage as an "umbrella" term. The "transgender umbrella" is usually defined both in broad analytic strokes and in reference to particular constituencies and practices. For example, in an influential 1994 essay that might be said to mark the emergence of "transgender studies," Susan Stryker describes "transgender" as

> an umbrella term that refers to all identities or practices that cross over, cut across, move between, or otherwise queer socially constructed sex/gender boundaries. The term includes, but is not limited to, transsexuality, heterosexual transvestism, gay drag, butch lesbianism, and such non-European identities as the Native American berdache or the Indian Hijra.[12]

That same year, the San Francisco Human Rights Commission produced a report, "Investigation into Discrimination against Transgendered People," written by Green, that also defined "all persons whose perceived gender and anatomic sex may conflict with the gender expression" as subsets of the "umbrella term transgender."[13] The legal theorist and activist Stephen Whittle, the historian Joanne Meyerowitz, and the semiotician Viviane Namaste similarly use the metaphor of an umbrella to explain how "transgender" has come to represent subsets of very different sorts of gender nonconforming people.[14] The phrase *transgender umbrella* also appears in a number of advocacy guides produced by LGBT and other groups to describe the constituencies for whom they advocate.[15]

Beneath the so-called transgender umbrella, however, roil some substantial differences. The incredible variation in the kinds of identities and communities and practices contained under "transgender" could be described, as MacKenzie suggests, as a "gender galaxy," since it includes not only the specific identities and practices described in the definitions above but endlessly proliferating subsets of very specific and historically located ways of crossing gender norms.[16] Many have pointed to the risks in consolidating so much under one category. As Namaste asks, "What does it mean to group the very different identities of FTM transsexuals and heterosexual male cross-dressers? How does this term function to define a specifically *transgendered* social movement? What kinds of issues are overlooked within such a perspective? What important differences within this category are being excluded? Are some bodies invisible within this debate?"[17] Patrick Califia writes in 1997 that "there is a strong possibility that the transgendered movement will be embroiled in identity issues like lesbian feminism in the seventies and eighties."[18] Riki Wilchins predicts that a "transgender rights movement... unable to interrogate the fact of its own existence, will merely end up cementing the idea of a binary sex which I am presumed to somehow transgress or merely traverse."[19] David Valentine has suggested that the use of "transgender" to describe people who do not use it to describe themselves "produces a representational colonization of those lives."[20] Even more significant, perhaps, is that among those in the umbrella's shadow one finds intense debates about gender—about its origin in social or biological forces, for example—and about politics: whether the gender binary should be expanded or only resisted, for example.[21]

Given the extraordinary diversity of cross-gender practices, identities, and beliefs about gender within gender nonconforming communities in the United States, the clear emergence of the "transgender umbrella" as a central, unifying framework is remarkable.[22] Why is *transgender* used so consistently in advocacy contexts, from the media to the courts to the legislative arena, and why has it gained the traction that it now indisputably enjoys? What are the effects of framing so many kinds of gender difference as "transgender" in some way? Is the very shiftiness and fluidity and messiness of the term, its very capaciousness—what Teresa de Lauretis has described as "meaningful only as a sign" bearing "no reference to anything but its own discursive nature"[23]—a strategic and pragmatic point of reference or an erasure of the very different ways gender crossing is lived and experienced? Conversely, does the use of the label—even one coined to include a myriad of practices and identities—inadvertently create the impression that "transgender" can be domesticated, contained in a relatively fixed social location, and thus risk reproducing the exclusions created by a politics of identity? And what are the consequences of *not* invoking this relatively recent identity politics category in advocacy for those who trouble gender norms?

It's not possible in one chapter to address all of these questions with the sustained legal, historical, and political analysis they warrant. I will, however, explore some aspects of how the dynamic between the transgender umbrella and what falls in its shadow plays out in the transgender rights movement in the United States. The effects of using identity-based language differ in the two political arenas that are the subject of this chapter: courts and legis-latures. In the first section, I examine two cases involving students who chal-lenged rules prohibiting them from wearing clothing not typically associated with their birth sex. One student was described as "transgender" by her advo-cates; the other was not. Next, I place the transgender rights movement within the larger context of other movements for civil rights. In the concluding sec-tion, I turn to the legislative work of the movement and examine efforts to amend nondiscrimination laws. In the area of nondiscrimination legislation, I suggest that there is a real and important distinction between the identity-based rhetoric of the transgender rights movement and the actual goals of many trans activists: while largely organizing under the minoritizing rubric of "transgender," the legislative achievements thus far have, for the most part, explicitly expanded the legal meaning of gender to place gender noncon-forming identities and practices on a continuum of gender, rather than create a new category of a protected class.

I write this chapter from the perspective of a scholar and a transgender rights advocate. Although the work is (somewhat) different, I draw no distinctions between my insights as a researcher and my insights as an activist. Also, as an essay examining strategic deployments of identity politics within the trans-gender rights movement, there is no doubt that the analysis here is unavoidably bound up with a liberal rights-based framework. Ultimately, I am in agree-ment with the Marx of "On the Jewish Question": that the chief function of classical liberal individualist ideology in general and of the rights discourse in particular is to make class invisible by locating economic inequality largely outside the "commonsense" boundaries of political life. In dozens of jurisdic-tions in the United States, transgender people can make a claim of discrimi-nation if they were denied a place to live because of their gender identity or expression, but not because of their poverty. Class is not a legal category; gross economic inequality is not "actionable" under the law. But taking the legal structures as we find them, not as they ought to be, transgender rights advocates have pursued reformist goals, seeking state recognition of the self-identified gender identity of trans people and working to end the use of gender norms as a criterion in distributing rights and resources, including jobs, housing, heath care, and the limited social services that do exist.

Litigating Gender: Identity and Expression

Like many seventh-grade girls, "Pat Doe" (a pseudonym) wanted to express her femininity by wearing skirts, makeup, padded bras with tight shirts, and high-heeled shoes to school. At South Junior High in Brockton, Massachusetts, however, Doe's gender presentation was a problem. As a male-bodied girl, the way she expressed her femininity upset school administrators. After a time, when she showed up at school wearing clothing and accessories traditionally associated with girls, the school principal would send her home to change. He justified his disciplinary actions by citing the school's dress code, which prohibited "clothing which could be disruptive or distractive to the educational process or which could affect the safety of the students." By the beginning of her second semester, in the spring of 1999, the principal made Doe check in at his office every morning so he could personally approve her clothing choices. He allowed Doe to wear some feminine attire, but forbade skirts, dresses, or padded bras. Other girls in the school, of course, were allowed to wear those kinds of clothes. Doe often failed the principal's test and was sent home to change. Sometimes she returned to school wearing clothes understood by her peers and teachers as "traditionally male"; sometimes she stayed home, too upset to return. By the time she reached the eighth grade, Doe had pretty much stopped attending school altogether. She had been, her advocates later argued in legal pleadings, "constructively expelled."

When Nikki Youngblood, a seventeen-year-old high school senior in Hillsborough County, Florida, showed up for her senior yearbook portrait in 2001 wearing a shirt and tie, she was told by the photographer that she could not have her picture taken unless she complied with the school's yearbook dress-code policy, which required all girls to wear a revealing, velvetlike, scoop-neck drape for their portraits. In contrast, boys were required to wear a white shirt, tie, and dark jacket.[24] Forced to choose between dressing in girls' clothing or having no picture in the yearbook, Youngblood chose the latter. When the yearbook was published, there was no picture of Youngblood in it. She had been cleansed from her school's official history—even her name did not appear. "It's like I never went to Robinson," Youngblood told a reporter.[25]

That schools are central to reproducing hegemonic cultural norms is made clear by the courts in the many decisions supporting gender-based dress codes in schools. As a federal judge explained in a 1987 case upholding the constitutionality of banning boys from wearing earrings, schools have "the responsibility to teach not only English and History, but the role of young men and women in our democratic society." The expectation for students, the judge added, is "to learn the rules which govern their behavior not only in school but in society."[26] And "rules" reflecting sexual and gender norms are rigidly policed in schools—in a different case, a fourteen-year-old in New York City was suspended in 2003 for wearing a T-shirt with the slogan "Barbie is a lesbian."[27] Public school cases are also especially interesting sites for analysis because constitutional claims, including free speech claims, can be made against them as state actors.

The contrasting legal outcomes in the *Doe* and *Youngblood* cases may tell us something about the way challenges brought by gender nonconforming people become intelligible—or remain incomprehensible—to the courts. While both cases involved plaintiffs who wanted to wear clothes not traditionally associated with their birth sex, Doe's legal challenge to the school policy was successful; Youngblood's was not. Youngblood's gender identity as female was consistent with social expectations for her birth sex, while her masculine gender expression was not. Conversely, while Doe's preferred gender expression conformed to conventions for those whose gender identity is female, it flew in the face of social expectations for those designated male at birth. So while the legal claims put forth by their advocates were substantially the same, the plaintiffs were differently situated in relation to gender nonconformity.

Doe's counsel, Jennifer Levi of Gay and Lesbian Advocates and Defenders, presented several legal claims to a Massachusetts state court—that the school had violated Massachusetts law prohibiting discrimination on the basis of disability, that it had violated her right to freedom of expression, and that it had discriminated against her on the basis of sex. All three claims were explicitly framed in reference to Doe's gender identity and her status as a transgender person. In the first motion submitted by her advocates, she is described as having "a condition known as gender identity disorder" (GID). They explained that "GID is alternately referred to as transgenderism and people with GID are often called transgender," that "the characteristic that defines transgenderism is gender role or identity," and that "transgender people experience a separation between their gender identity and their anatomical sex."

Doe's wearing of "clothing that expresses her female gender identity," they argued, is "consistent with the course of care for her condition." Because her GID "is the basis of her need and desire to dress and appear as she does," the school had discriminated against her because of her disability. On the free expression claim, Doe's attorneys contended, Doe's expressive rights were "not an expression of politics or belief—undeniably important expressions as well—but an expression of the core identity of how she sees herself as a person." Finally, on the sex discrimination claim, they argued that there was no compelling interest for the school principal "to prohibit a transgender student who was ascribed the sex of male at birth from wearing clothing that would be unobjectionable if worn by a girl." Again, this claim was reinforced with the GID diagnosis, which showed, they argued, "that it is medically necessary for her to express her female gender identity."[28]

The court found Doe's arguments to be largely persuasive. The first judge to hear the case, Linda Giles, ruled that forcing her to wear boy's clothes was tantamount to "constructively expelling" her from school and that two of her three central legal claims—that she had been the victim of sex discrimination and that her conduct constituted "expressive speech" that had been unconstitutionally suppressed by the school—were likely to succeed. Giles issued a preliminary injunction barring the school from preventing Doe from wearing girls' clothes. On the sex discrimination claim, the school had argued that girls wearing "distracting items" of men's clothing would be similarly disciplined. The court rejected that argument, finding that this was not the correct way to frame the issue. Since Doe identifies with the female gender, the judge wrote, "the right question is whether a female student would be disciplined for wearing" girls' clothes. If the answer is no, the court reasoned, Doe is being discriminated against on the basis of her sex, which is biologically male.[29] On the free expression claim, the court initially decided that the school's conduct had indeed been an attempt to suppress Doe's speech, but in later proceedings the free expression claim was dropped—it was unclear whether the Massachusetts free expression case law applied to intermediate schools, and her attorneys believed, rightly as it turned out, that it was not necessary to make this particular legal claim.

Judge Giles found Doe's disability claim unconvincing. The Americans with Disabilities Act explicitly excludes "transvestism, transsexualism, and gender identity disorders not resulting from physical impairments."[30] While the Massachusetts disability rights law has no such explicit exclusion, the judge was reluctant to interpret the ADA's state counterpart as including GID. But a different judge, ruling on another motion in the case a few months later, decided that Doe's disability claim did have merit. He, too, found Doe had been constructively expelled, because the school had set conditions that were impossible for her to satisfy. In explaining his reasoning, he made two very telling analogies:

> A student who is five feet tall may be deemed . . . constructively expelled if the
> school administrators forbade her from returning until she became six feet tall. . . .

So too would a severely diabetic student be deemed constructively expelled if she were forbidden from taking insulin during the school day, because the student could not satisfy that condition without endangering her physical health.[31]

These comparisons show how compelling the court found Doe's GID: coming to school in clothes traditionally associated with boys, the court found, would "endanger her psychiatric health."[32]

Youngblood's attorneys, Karen Doering and Shannon Minter of the National Center for Lesbian Rights, made similar legal claims in federal court. Robinson High School, they argued, had discriminated against Youngblood because of her sex and had violated her rights to free expression. (There was no claim of discrimination on the basis of disability.) In describing Youngblood's gender nonconformity, her attorneys focused on its consistency over time. Her refusal to wear the costume mandated for girls, they argued, would be "emotionally damaging" because, from a "very young age, Nicole has not conformed to gender stereotypes about how girls are supposed to look and behave."[33] Later, in an appeal to a federal appellate court, the unchanging aspect of her identity was underscored even more:

From an early age, Nikki . . . has preferred boyish clothing and has had a masculine demeanor. Nikki was a tomboy in grade school and continues to be a masculine or, as some might term it, "mannish" woman. This aspect of Nikki's identity is very deepseated, longlasting, and natural to her. It is part of who she is.[34]

Overall, however, Youngblood's advocates were not able to describe her long history of gender nonconformity as a medical condition or even as an identity, as Doe's attorneys had done, respectively, with their reliance on Doe's GID diagnosis and her "transgender status." Ultimately, the most Youngblood's advocates could do was describe her aversion to feminine clothing as "deepseated" and "longlasting."

The sex discrimination claim, then, focused on the harm caused by gender stereotyping in general. The "archaic" frilly drape to be worn in the portrait, they argued, furthered the "invidious and debilitating stereotype that girls are or should be delicate, submissive, and passive." (Recall that Doe's attorneys had framed her sex discrimination claim with reference to Doe's "medically necessary need.") On the free speech claim, Youngblood's advocates argued that her refusal to wear the drape met both parts of the test required by the jurisprudence: first, Youngblood's desire to wear a shirt and tie in her photo intended to send a particularized message; and second, that there was a reasonable likelihood that her message would be understood by others. Her message? That "women do not have to conform to gender stereo-types."[35] (In contrast, the message of Doe's free expression claim was described by her advocates as an expression of her "core identity.")

Ruling on the school board's motion to dismiss the case, the federal district court judge in Youngblood's case, Susan Bucklew, found "no constitu-tionally protected right for a female to wear a shirt and tie for senior por-traits." On the free expression claim, the judge relied on *Karr v. Schmidt,* an often-cited 1970 decision from the Fifth Circuit that held a school regula-tion mandating short hair for boys was constitutional. Judge Bucklew found that gender-based regulations for senior portraits required "even less justification than a school requiring hair to be cut, which affects students 24-hours a day, seven days a week, nine months a year."[36] On the charge of sex discrimina-tion, Youngblood had argued that, in contrast to the business attire worn by boys, the drape is so revealing and "ultra-feminine" that it reflects invidious gender stereotyping. Inferring from this that Youngblood's objection would be remedied "if the school district changed the required senior portrait attire to be something still feminine yet less 'archaic' and 'stereotypical,'" the judge identified what she saw as a contradiction in Youngblood's "double faceted" argument: "However, Plaintiff argues that she should be allowed to dress in male attire for senior portraits because she has not worn a dress, skirt, or other traditionally feminine clothing since she was in first or second grade." It seems the judge found Youngblood's arguments confusing. Was the prob-lem with gender stereotyping in general—a problem that affects all the girls equally and that could be remedied with more modern and less demeaning yet still feminine clothing for the portrait? Or did the problem lie in Young-blood's personal aversion to wearing *any* piece of clothing coded as tradition-ally feminine?

From the perspective of a transgender rights advocate, of course, the real trouble lies in the judge's binary approach. Simply put, Youngblood's arguments do not cancel each other out: to argue that requiring all girls to wear a frilly drape constitutes gender stereotyping does not annul the more fundamental claim that it is also sex discrimination to force the "mannish" Youngblood in particular to wear it simply because she is a girl. Moreover, what also appears to have made Youngblood's argument unintelligible to Judge Bucklew was her conflation of "female" with "femininity." Quoting the Webster dictionary definition of "feminine" as "female" and "characteristic of or peculiar to women," the judge's ruling depended on and reproduced the same commonsense notions about gender that undergirded the judge's rea-soning in *Doe v. Yunits:* Pat Doe and Nikki Youngblood are both girls, and girls do and should wear girls' clothes. *Doe v. Yunits* was a legal victory because the judge—an out lesbian whom the school board actually tried to have recused for "bias" because of her sexual orientation—affirmed Doe's gender identity. *Youngblood v. School Board of Hillsborough County* was a legal defeat because the judge in this case found the gender expression claim unfathomable. Although the judge in Doe's case described her clothing choices as "conduct," to Judge Giles that conduct was inexorably tied to Doe's need to express her "female gender identity through dress."[37] The judge in Youngblood's case, however, saw her rejection of girls' clothing as mere whimsy ("Plaintiff wanted to wear a white shirt, tie and jacket instead of the drape"), precisely because her desire to wear masculine clothes was not tied to her status as female. In narrating gender nonconformity to the courts, then, it may be that in some circumstances accounts of discrimination more closely connected to affirmations of identity make more sense to the courts than claims based on the less culturally moored and more amorphous concept of gender expression.

In summing up these cases, three points need to be made clear. First, both cases actually resulted in victories for the gender rights movement. While the courts' rulings differed, both cases were ultimately resolved in out-of-court settlements. Doe's litigation ended when the school board settled and allowed her to wear "girls'" clothes to school. And in 2004 the Hillsborough County school board settled and agreed to stop requiring girls to wear drapes for their senior portraits. Both cases also received substantial regional publicity. While some of the news coverage was sensationalist and negative, in the long run it heightened public awareness of the existence of gender nonconforming youth, expanding the social imaginary about different gender possibilities.

Second, with these readings I am not critiquing either of the ways the girls' gender nonconformity was narrated in legal pleadings. Doe's gender identity *is* female, and, while in an ideal world it would not be necessary to produce a diagnosis of GID to make the judge recognize this, it is not wrong to argue that, because she is a girl, she should be able to wear girls' clothes. No one challenges students whose birth sex and gender identity conform to social expectations when they wear clothes associated with their gender; no one requires them to provide an affidavit from a medical expert confirming their gender identity. To find fault with the use of Doe's identity-based argument would be to fail to acknowledge the enormous privilege with which nontransgender people are already endowed. In addition, although some transgender advocates reject the use of disability rights laws in transgender rights litigation because those types of claims purportedly rely on the pathologization of gender nonconformity, that aversion at best indicates a lack of understanding of the disability rights movement and its radical claims (as Jennifer

Levi and Ben Stein point out in another chapter in this volume) and at worst reflects and reproduces the stigma associated with people with disabilities. Finally, suggesting that gender identity rights claims like Doe's might be more intelligible to the courts—and thus more successful—than gender expression claims like Youngblood's is not to argue that cases focusing on transgender identity necessarily undermine cases based on gender expression or fail to bring about social change. Rather, it is simply to note that, despite academic desires to deconstruct and move away from notions of essentialism in legal discourse, identity-based claims remain more juridically intelligible in the way they link identities to bodies, and so often produce better results.

While these cases are interesting because they involve comparable circumstances and legal claims, Youngblood's and Doe's challenges to public school regulation of gender are only two cases out of hundreds in which courts have been the arbiters of gender norms. My reading of these cases does not touch on some of the particular issues raised in other types of transgender rights claims—employment discrimination, the designation of a person's legal sex for marriage and identity documents, access to appropriate sex-segregated facilities, to name a few. The point of looking at them together is not to suggest that the pattern observed in these two cases applies to every decision in cases involving gender nonconformity. As I've pointed out elsewhere, this body of law is riddled with contradictions; the notion that there is some hidden analytic key that, when discovered, will reveal the law's underlying logic assumes an ideological coherence that is just not there.[38] But the different legal outcomes for Doe and Youngblood might tell us something about how identity-based claims can have more traction than conduct-based claims in the courts. They might also suggest why, in cases that could be articulated either way, transgender rights advocates often rely on more seemingly fixed categories such as transgender or gender identity than on concepts apparently less anchored to identity categories, such as gender expression.

Transgender Rights as Civil Rights

An analysis of the work that identity is asked to do in the transgender rights movement should be placed within the larger context of the civil rights tradition in the United States.[39] Thus I offer a truncated history, a caricature perhaps, to describe its influence on the way transgender rights claims are shaped. Since the seventeenth century, slavery in the United States was organized around racial categories, and the legal construction of those categories was naturalized as rooted in biological differences.[40] By the time the civil rights movement's argument that individuals should be not treated differently before the law because of their race started seeping into the popular and legal "common sense," race was well established in the social imaginary, and legally constructed as well, as a presocial, prepolitical, prelegal category—in short, as an immutable characteristic or trait. Moreover, when many of the central arguments and rhetoric of the movement for racial equality were appropriated by other movements for political equality, the idea that claims for equality were best expressed as identity based was also imported into the enunciation of other rights-based movements of the later twentieth century, including the women's and gay rights movements. As Steven Epstein, writing of the development of the gay rights movement in the 1970s, suggests, "To be gay, then, became something like being Italian, or black, or Jewish."[41] One scholar goes so far as to argue that the success or failure of politics of identity will be determined by the ability of a group seeking equal rights to make the "black analogy."[42]

Thus making rights claims on behalf of an identity rather than on behalf of particular practices became an essential part of the civil rights tradition in the United States. By the end of the twentieth century, this particular legacy of the civil rights movement had so come to dominate the public thinking about equality that it became almost unimaginable to base equality claims on anything other than "who one is." With the exception of arguments for religious freedom, grounding an appeal to equality based on "what one does" eventually fell outside the bounds of intelligible rights discourse. Notions of individual agency, of choice, and even of free expression effectively became the constitutive other of civil rights discourse. (I discuss the idea of basing transgender rights claims on the free speech clause of the First Amendment below.) This development, characterized as the conduct/identity distinction, has been the subject of many legal and theoretical analyses of the gay rights movement.[43]

Because of the power of this legacy to sway minds—public opinion polls tell us that the public is much more receptive to the idea of gay rights if homosexuality is understood as ascribed rather than chosen[44]—mainstream gay, lesbian, and bisexual rights advocates consistently argue that "sexual orientation" is not a choice. "Sexual preference" fell out of favor among gay rights advocates because it suggests that homosexuals choose to be attracted to individuals of the same sex. Gay rights advocates describe their constituency as a "people" instead of what might more accurately be described as a series of historically specific and culturally distinct communities who share *some* social practices. They also relentlessly compare the oppression of LGB people to that of people of color and the movement for LGB equality to that of the civil rights movement. Drawing a parallel between the abstract categories of race and sexual orientation reinforces the notion that sexualities are not constituted through racial formations and vice versa; drawing a parallel between the very different histories of racism and homophobia erases the ways that legal and social structures work together and against the people who live at those intersections—queer people of color. For example, in 1995 the leader of the largest gay rights group in the United States used this loaded rhetoric to make the "black analogy": "150 years after the fact, the Southern Baptist Convention—the same institution that has now condemned gays—repented for defending slavery and condoning racism. I believe and we believe at the Human Rights Campaign . . . that someday they will repent their homophobia. Not soon, but we are a patient people."[45] Conversely, opponents of gay rights repeatedly frame homosexuality as a matter of choice. For example, U.S. Senator Orrin Hatch argued against the inclusion of sexual orientation in a hate crimes bill with this (some might suggest infelicitous) contrast: "People of color can't do anything about their color."[46]

Perhaps significantly, the racial analogy has also been raised in struggles for transgender rights, but more often by those opposing such rights. In 2001, for example, the Campaign for California Families took out a full-page news-paper advertisement to argue against proposed legislation (which eventually passed) to amend the definition of "gender" in California's employment dis-crimination statute to include transgender people:

> The State should not promote the transsexual agenda upon society. Little girls should not be influenced in any way to think they are boys, nor little boys influenced to think they are girls. This bill makes the State approve of transsexuality and sets up an unnatural standard for adults and children. . . . This bill makes transsexuality a full blown civil right. This is an insult to people of color and other racial minori-ties who have fought for equal opportunity through civil rights based on unchange-able characteristics. . . . [It] is an attack on nature. People are born with 46 chromo-somes, XX for females, XY for males. You are either born male or female, and there are no in-betweens. This bill would promote an unnatural and radical sexual agenda that erodes nature and attacks the sensibilities of families.[47]

Of course, there *are* "in-betweens": intersexed individuals. Furthermore, the Campaign for California Families suggests that transsexuality is so abominable that prohibiting discrimination against transgender people would debase the long and proud history of the civil rights movement. (The right wing has only recently discovered the term *transgender:* for a long time, right-wing texts described those who fall under the "transgender umbrella" as transves-tites, "she-males," or transsexuals.)

Notably, it's not transgender rights advocates who are making the race analogy, it's the Campaign for California Families. But the right wing's use of the comparison, combined with the by-now customary reference to "unchangeable characteristics," shows how race, the racial analogy, identity-based claims, and assertions of immutability have been fused together in the "commonsense" logics of rights discourse. Although transgender rights advocates certainly do often argue that gender identity is deep-seated and unchangeable, they rarely compare the oppression of transgender people to the oppression of African Americans, or gender identity to race, to make gender nonconforming identities and practices intelligible to the courts and to the public. At one time, the ubiquity of the analogy in gay rights rhetoric led me to hypothesize that this might also be true of transgender rights arguments as well, and so I set off to find examples of the racial analogy in arguments for transgender rights. But an initial review of the legal pleadings in a number of cases and the rhetoric produced by trans advocates in pursuit of nondiscrimination laws indicates that it's rarely invoked.[48]

Nonetheless, the litigation strategies of transgender rights advocates are very much informed by the legacies of the civil rights movement, as are the strategies of those who oppose transgender rights, especially in the emphasis on immutability. It's no surprise that the argument revolves around whether sex and gender are mutable. The conservative columnist John Silber, then chancellor of Boston University, wrote in an op-ed about Pat Doe's case that one of the more "troubling aspects of this case" was the idea "that sex is a matter of choice."[49] By framing the *Doe* decision as creating the right to choose one's sex, Silber invokes a central tenet of the civil rights decision—that rights claims are legitimate only if the identity in question is based on an immutable characteristic—as he attempts to make the *Doe* decision seem outlandish. Even as conservatives have over time accepted the gradual expansion of sex discrimination laws to include discrimination based on gender stereotyping,[50] the notion that sex itself is mutable offends conservative sensibilities. For example, a columnist for a popular conservative magazine argued against a transgender rights law by saying, "expectations and notions of gender may evolve, but gender itself is permanent. Sorry."[51]

The Vatican's official position on the meaning of gender that emerged out of debates during the United Nations Fourth World Conference on Women in Beijing in 1995 is similar. In a written statement submitted as part of the final conference report, the head of the Vatican delegation to the conference, the U.S. political theorist Mary Ann Glendon, wrote, "The term 'gender' is understood by the Holy See as grounded in biological sexual identity, male or female. . . . The Holy See thus excludes dubious interpretations based on world views which assert that sexual identity can be adapted indefinitely to suit new and different purposes."[52] Significantly, however, the Vatican statement distanced itself from a purer biological essentialism: "[The Holy See] also disassociates itself from the biological determinist notion that all roles and relations between the two sexes are fixed in a single, static pattern."[53] This position was not taken in reference to transgender issues—the debate centered on the agenda put forward by women's rights organizations—but the Vatican did make its position on transgender issues very clear in 2003 when the Vatican committee issued rules stating that the Church will not recognize the new gender of Catholics who undergo sex reassignment treatment.[54]

For the social conservatives—as well as for judges in Kansas, Ohio, Texas, and Florida, to name just a few jurisdictions with negative case law— one's sex at birth is one's legal sex for life; gender should exist in a predictable relation to birth sex even as the social norms for gender expand; and those who cross those boundaries should not be protected from discrimination or have any legal recognition of their gender. For example, a Texas appellate court invalidated the marriage of a transsexual woman with this rationale:

> The deeper philosophical (and now legal) question is: can a physician change the gender of a person with a scalpel, drugs and counseling, or is a person's gender immutably fixed by our Creator at birth? . . . There are some things we cannot will into being. They just are. We hold, as a matter of law, that Christie Lee Littleton is a male. As a male, Christie cannot be married to another male.[55]

The odd, through-the-looking-glass aspect of these decisions is both fascinating in its willful ignorance of the lives and experiences of trans people and horrifying in its effects. The very existence of "gender different" people drops out of these normative claims about the meaning of sex and gender. A panel of judges in Florida can rule that the transgender man sitting before them, Michael Kantaras—who has lived exclusively as a man for nearly twenty years and who is fully accepted as a man in every aspect of his life, including by his two children, who have grown up knowing him as their father—is legally female under Florida family and marriage law. Even as the mere fact of the debates about definitions of gender and sex exposes the ultimate futility of attempting to ground gender and sex on anything other than legal rules and political battles about what it ought to be, in some very material senses those battles are all that matter in the present moment. People like Kantaras lose custody of their children, face the brutal effects of being housed with the wrong population in prison, are forced out of middle school, and in a myriad of other ways become strangers to the law. ("Sorry.")

In framing arguments against sentiments such as Silber's, however, in their advocacy in the courts, transgender rights advocates tend not to dismiss the idea of immutability simply to locate the immutable characteristic elsewhere. The relation between sex and gender is reversed: biological sex characteristics are cast as aspects of genders, and largely mutable ones at that. It is gender identity and often even expressions of gender identity, however, that are described as unchangeable, set from an early age. For example, in a New Jersey case challenging the dismissal of a physician after she came out as a transsexual woman in her workplace, her advocates explained "Gender Dysphoria" as "cognitive realization that one was born in the 'wrong' body."[56] In a civil lawsuit against a Nebraska sheriff whose egregious treatment of rape victim Brandon Teena resulted in his rapists' murdering him, advocates explained that "being transgender is not a lifestyle choice; it is a condition or syndrome in which one's identification or desire to live as a member of the other sex is deep-seated, unavoidable, and overwhelming."[57] In another case involving a transgender youth in New York City's foster care system who was disciplined for wearing girls' clothes, advocates argued that their client, "Jean Doe," was "born biologically male but, for as long as she can remember, has considered herself to be female."[58] In these cases, transgender rights advocates stay within the bounds of the logic of civil rights discourse by emphasizing immutability, but, significantly, they reverse the traditional idea that gender is an expression of sexed bodies and instead identify gender identity as the presocial fixed category.

But why not construct gender as a choice in legal arguments? After all, the very first sentence in the International Bill of Gender Rights announces that "all human beings have the right to define their own gender identity regardless of chromosomal sex, genitalia, assigned birth sex, or initial gender role."[59] In work on sexual orientation and the law, many queer legal scholars have focused on the liberatory potential of the free speech clause of the First Amendment.[60] What about using the First Amendment's free speech clause as the basis of rights claims against the state, such as Doe's and Youngblood's, and conceptualizing gender nonconformity as an expressive activity worthy of constitutional protection?

The central case creating the right to expressive conduct in the school context is the 1969 case of *Tinker v. Des Moines Ind. Comm. School District.*[61] In that case, students wore black bands to protest the war in Vietnam, a symbolic act that was promptly banned by the school board to avoid what it feared would be a "disturbance" caused by the armbands among the student population. The Supreme Court, however, found that the wearing of the armbands was so symbolic that it was akin to "pure speech" and that the state was wrong to censure it.[62] *Tinker* has been read by lower federal courts as a defense of speech and expression that is clearly understood as "political."

Significantly, the distinction between expressive activity that falls within the protection of the First Amendment and that which does not is explicitly drawn with reference to dress codes and grooming standards. In *Tinker*, Justice Abe Fortas limns the types of expressive speech to be afforded the protections by describing the kinds of expression that fall outside the bounds of the First Amendment: "The problem posed by the present case does not relate to regulation of the length of skirts or the type of clothing, to hair style, or deportment."[63] Not surprisingly, this particular quote is often cited in lower courts' rulings in cases challenging the regulation of clothing, grooming, and deportment regulations. Not only is wearing antiwar black armbands cast by the Supreme Court as political, that expressive activity is defined as political, symbolic speech precisely by casting grooming and hair length as *not* political, *not* symbolic, *not* "directly and sharply implicat[ing] basic constitutional values"[64]—as, in short, what is constitutively outside political speech. In the school contexts, this area of the law is not restricted to gender-based challenges: there have been challenges to grooming codes claiming that they are implicitly racially coded as well. In one case, a student disciplined for violating a school code prohibiting "sagging pants" argued that by wearing those clothes he had intended to send a particular message—an expression of his link with his black identity. He lost.[65]

A sharp contradiction emerges in the distinction drawn between expressive activity that is protected as symbolic enough to be worthy of First Amendment protection and expressive activity that does not rise to the level of communication significant enough to be protected from censure. On the one hand, the expressive activity, for example, of male-bodied people who want to wear earrings or their hair long and teenagers who want to wear baggy pants and other styles associated with cultural styles like hip-hop get cast as implicitly insignificant—"nebulous," as it was put by a federal circuit court[66]— expressions of "individuality"[67] because they are not sufficiently imbued with a particular (and implicitly political) message. On the other hand, however, the very existence of the regulations and the courts' justifications of them attest to the intensely political significance of wearing clothing and grooming oneself in ways that trouble schools' role of reproducing good citizens by applying "the rules which govern their behavior not only in school but in society."[68]

Of course, coding male-bodied people with long hair or earrings or students wearing very baggy pants as potentially disruptive, as "clashing" with the rights of others, is possible only because of the symbolic power of those practices to subvert hegemonic racialized and gendered norms. Such behavior is targeted precisely because it is the role of the school to reproduce a gender normative, heteronormative, and white-race normative culture.[69] So black students with baggy pants and boys with long hair are simultaneously constructed as political breaches in the supposed social consensus around gender and race-based norms that must be eliminated *and* their free expression claims as so unimportant that their messages do not rise to the level of political speech. Why else, for example, would a male student's desire to have long hair be construed by a judge both as unimportant and as "a clash with the similarly asserted liberties of several thousand others"?[70] Some of the most political expressive activity is not recognized as political precisely because it is has been so effectively naturalized out of sight as inherently not political.

The content of particular expressions and sets of ideas has long been censured in U.S. legal history. The moment when an idea is perhaps the most oppositional to hegemonic social and political arrangements is precisely the moment when it is least likely to be accorded the status of "political" by the courts and receive the protections given to political activity. I am not suggesting that arguments based on free expression should not be made by transgender rights advocates, just that their adjudication in the courts will largely depend on the cultural commonsense notions that distinguish legitimate rights claims from those deemed outlandish.[71] Perhaps gender nonconforming practices will be recognized as expressive activity worthy of constitutional protection at some moment in the future; we will arrive at that moment, in part, by working to change the commonsense truths about gender and by making those claims in as many ways and in as many venues as possible.

Legislating Gender Pluralism

Municipal and state legislatures are among those venues. The absence of legislative definitions of gender or sex in most nondiscrimination laws arrogated the task of defining those terms to the courts. Cases involving people who have brought sex-based discrimination claims after they were fired or denied services because of their transsexuality have their apotheosis in the 1984 case of *Ulane v. Eastern Airlines*. In *Ulane*, as in the many cases citing it as precedent, judges found that transgender people are not protected by laws prohibiting sex discrimination. Karen Ulane, a pilot, was fired by Eastern Airlines after she underwent sex reassignment. After years of litigation, the Supreme Court let stand a court of appeals decision that held,

> Ulane is entitled to any personal belief about her sexual identity she desires. After the surgery, hormones, appearance changes, and a new Illinois birth certificate and FAA pilot's certificate, it may be that society, as the trial judge found, considers Ulane to be female. But even if one believes that a woman can be so easily created from what remains of a man, that does not decide this case. . . . It is clear

from the evidence that if Eastern did discriminate against Ulane, it was not because she is female, but because Ulane is a transsexual—a biological male who
takes female hormones, cross-dresses, and has surgically altered parts of her body
to make it appear to be female.[72]

This dismissive language is typical of that used in many other cases in which
judges denied protection to transgender litigants on the grounds that they were
neither men nor women, but rather something other or in-between.[73] In the
past few years, a growing number of courts have rejected these older decisions and have held that transgender people *are* protected by laws prohibiting
sex or disability discrimination; for the moment, however, these negative decisions continue to be the governing precedents in most jurisdictions in this
country.[74]

Because of the judiciary's long practice of refusing to recognize that
discrimination against transgender people is a type of gender discrimination,
advocates turned to the legislative arena for redress. By adding or amending
definitions of sex, gender, or even sexual orientation, or by adding a new category, usually "gender identity," legislation can make it clear to the courts that
nondiscrimination laws should and do include gender nonconforming people.
Since the first such law was passed in Minneapolis, Minnesota, in 1975, others
have been enacted in dozens of local jurisdictions and in eight states—California, Hawai'i, Illinois, Maine, Minnesota, New Mexico, Rhode Island, and
Washington.[75] In 2006, 30 percent of the U.S. population lived in jurisdictions that have passed "transgender rights" legislation, although many of the
municipal laws have little legal effect.[76] At the federal level, after years of
resistance, all national LGBT groups now support including gender identity
and expression in the main federal gay rights vehicle, the Employment Non-
Discrimination Act. This includes the Human Rights Campaign, the largest
and most influential such group, which formally changed its federal legislative
policy to be fully inclusive of transgender people in 2004.

While in much of the litigation discussed above "transgender" figures
strongly as a category of identity, its deployment in activism focused on legislative change is much more nuanced and limited. *Transgender* certainly
operates as a central organizing term. It appears in many, though not all, of
the names of groups activists have formed; it shows up in news accounts,
often accompanied by references to "gender identity or expression"; it sometimes is heard in testimony as a way to introduce a variety of cross-gender
behaviors and identities. But it rarely finds its way into the legislation itself.
Gunner Scott, an activist from the Massachusetts Transgender Political
Coalition who lobbied the Boston City Council to add "gender identity or

expression" to the city's nondiscrimination law, told the *Boston Herald*, "This is the first step in awareness that there is a transgender community, that transgender people should be treated with the same respect and dignity as everyone else."[77] Later, in an interview describing his activist work, Scott explains that he referred to "gender identity and expression" along with "transgender" in his advocacy because "we try to make it a broader issue instead of specifically [limited to] transgender and transsexual people."[78]

According to the Massachusetts activist Jody Marksamer, "transgender" is an "important organizing tool because . . . a lot of people can hear that word and say 'I fit there and this group is representing my interests because LGBT isn't doing it at all."[79] Yet he does not refer to "transgender" in his testimony before the Boston City Council. Instead, Marksamer refers repeatedly to "gender identity and expression." Donna Cartwright, who has worked to pass legislation in New York, New Jersey, and at the federal level, talks about "transgender people" in her lobbying visits to legislators: "I think that legislators, like other people, like to think in or define social categories. That is, 'who is this about?'"[80] Similarly, Lori Buckwalter, a longtime activist in Oregon who has also advocated successfully for transgender rights legislation, chooses to emphasize people over practices in her advocacy. She explains that, "With identity rights I think people generally would, if you polled them . . . say, 'it's not right to discriminate against who you are.'" In Buckwalter's experience, "when trans rights become perceived as rights of expression, now all of a sudden they're [seen as] qualified rights" that "can be subject to negotiation."[81]

My research on activists fighting for this legislation suggests that there is a commonly held view that while it might be pragmatic to deploy "transgender" in many advocacy contexts, the legal instantiation of a new identity category—transgender—is not the ultimate goal of the activists who deploy it. Beth Plotner describes the people who would benefit from her activism this way: "Generally I'm fighting for the gender variant community, which includes mostly the transgender community. But also anybody who would be perceived as stepping outside society's boundary lines of gender in a strict bi-gender society of male and female. And as most informed people know, gender is a very wide spectrum in how people choose to express it."[82] Because activists invoke the vernacular of identity politics to draw attention to their (our) cause—legislators appear to respond better to the needs of constituents than to social practices they can't so easily imagine attached to voters—some assume that the focus on identity is mirrored in the legislation itself. For example, Riki Wilchins suggests that, because so many of the activists involved in advocating for this legislation are themselves "transsexual" (it's not clear how she knows how the thousands of activists across the United States identify themselves), the legislation itself "focus[es] solely on transsexuality and gender identity" and "disregard[s] gender *expression*."[83]

An examination of the actual statutes, however, shows that the language of identity politics has not been imported into the actual laws activists are fighting for and that gender expression is almost always included in these laws. In the vast majority of jurisdictions, "transgender" has not been added to the list of human rights categories. Instead, most statutory changes have defined sex, gender, or sexual orientation broadly, or added a new category of "gender identity."[84] For example, the law passed in Boston in 2003 defined "gender identity or expression" as

> a person's actual or perceived gender, as well as a person's gender identity, gender-related self-image, gender-related appearance, or gender-related expression whether or not that gender identity, gender-related self-image, gender-related appearance, or gender-related expression is different from that traditionally associated with a person's sex at birth.[85]

That definition is similar to the language in other jurisdictions with "transgender rights" laws on the books. The emerging standard in these statutes is to include broad language that attempts to describe the prohibited discrimination in conceptual terms—the first part of the definition of the transgender umbrella—rather than any mention of specific identity categories and practices underneath it. For example, activists in Minnesota—the first state to pass such a law in 1993—decided to avoid mention in the law of any specific terms that might lose or change their meanings over time and instead to use less potentially time-bound words that reflect more general concepts. According to Diana Slyter, "We had considered doing a laundry list, but the house legislative counsel recommended that we go instead with a list of behaviors."[86] As Brett Beemyn explained at a 1996 public hearing on the Iowa City ordinance, "I can foresee a future where somebody who is not transsexual or does not define himself as a transvestite faces discrimination and doesn't have protection because they're not officially included in the ordinance wording."[87]

In these statutes, the language used is often so broad that it effectively eliminates, for the purposes of nondiscrimination law, any legally prescribed relationship between biological sex, gender identity, and gender expression—a normatively structured series of relations that governs everyone, not just self-identified transgender people. Within the arena governed by the judiciary, transgender rights advocates situate transgender identities firmly within the cultural logics of gender as part of a strategy of gradually expanding the courts' interpretation of gender as a legal category. Within the legislative arena, however, these definitions of sex, gender, or gender identity are more likely to free gender from its naturalized and depoliticized foundations. As Peter LaBarbera, author of a right-wing "exposé" of the transgender rights movement, suggests, "Today's 'trans' revolutionaries—led by men who cross-dress or 'live' as 'women'—promote a worldview in which 'gender' and male/female norms are no longer objectively defined by the sex organs a person was born with, but are subjective and socially constructed."[88]

Conclusion

Even as activists work to unmoor legal gender from the confines of the sex gender system and its attendant assumptions—that sex is binary and biologically transparent, that gender maps easily and predictably onto sex—they (we) have framed their arguments in terms intelligible to those outside the "gender community" by strategically deploying the language of identity. As a movement, however, the ultimate goal of transgender rights does not seem to be to contain gender nonconforming identities and practices within slightly expanded yet still-normative gender constructions and arrangements. Indeed, in other legal and policy contexts, many of these same activists are working to "dis-establish" gender from the state by ending the state's authority to police the relation between one's legal sex assigned at birth, one's gender identity, and one's gender expression; by attempting to stop the state's use of "sex" as a marker of identity on identification documents; and by ending the state's reliance on sex as a legal category to distribute resources—through bans on same-sex marriage, for example.

The transgender rights movement might be described as an identity politics movement that seeks the dissolution of the very category under which it is organized. The precarious relationship between the "transgender umbrella" and what falls under it described at the beginning of this chapter is strategic and provisional and meant to bring us to a different historical moment: a moment when the often intense disagreements and differences about gender that roil beneath the umbrella need not be contained within a neat and circumscribed (and minoritizing) category, when there will be no pressing urgency to obfuscate the lived experiences of a series of very different identities and practices and networks and communities and cultures. Those working under the trans umbrella are seeking a world in which we have the luxury of disagreeing about gender without worrying about which narrative is more compelling to those who have the power to deny access to social services, to take away children, or to dismiss discrimination claims out of hand.

Notes

This chapter was produced with the support of the Wayne F. Placek Award of the American Psychology Foundation and a PSC-CUNY grant from the Research Foundation of the City University of New York. I am indebted to my Brooklyn College student research assistants, Jasmine Joseph-Perez and Lisa Shannon, for their work transcribing interviews; to Franklin Romeo for his work in collecting the legal briefs and decisions; and to Tomasz Busiuk, Megan Davidson, Sonia Katyal, Jennifer Levi, Shannon Price Minter, Tara Montgomery, María Gómez, Lisa Moore, and Jeanne Theoharis for their comments on drafts of this chapter.

1. Brief of Amici Curiae National Center for Lesbian Rights at 9, *Goins v. West Publishing Company*, 635 N.W.2d 717 (Minn. 2001).

2. Ethan Jacobs, "Trans Community Makes Inroads into Democratic Party," *Bay Windows*, July 29, 2004.

3. Plaintiff's motion for summary judgment at 2, *Oiler v. Winn Dixie*, 89 Fair Empl. Prac. Cas. (BNA) 1832 (E.D. LA, September 16, 2002).

4. Libby Alder, "A Victory for Boston's Transgender Community," *Boston Globe*, December 21, 2002.

5. Transcript of the Minutes of the Committee on General Welfare, New York City Council, May 4, 2001, 149.

6. Leslie Feinberg, *Transgender Warriors* (Boston: Beacon, 1996), x.

7. As Dallas Denny points out in another essay in this volume, Prince's model presented transgender as a heterosexual phenomenon, and her organizations tended to exclude those who were not heterosexual.

8. Sandy Stone, "The Empire Strikes Back: A Posttranssexual Manifesto," in *Bodyguards*, ed. Julia Epstein and Kristina Straub (New York: Routledge, 1991), 293.

9. Gordene O. MacKenzie, *Transgender Nation* (Bowling Green, OH: Bowling Green State University Popular Press, 1994), 2.

10. Phyllis Randolph Frye, "Facing Discrimination, Organizing for Freedom: The Transgender Community," in *Creating Change: Sexuality, Public Policy, and Civil Rights*, ed. John D'Emilio, William B. Turner, and Urvashi Vaid (New York: St. Martin's, 2000), 460.

11. Jamison Green, *Becoming a Visible Man* (Nashville, TN: Vanderbilt University Press, 2004), 81.

12. Susan Stryker, "My Words to Victor Frankenstein above the Village of Chamounix: Performing Gender," *GLQ* 1, no. 3 (1994): 251n2. See also Stryker, "The Transgender Issue: An Introduction," *GLQ* 4, no. 2 (1998): 149.

13. Jamison Green, "Investigation into Discrimination against Transgendered People," Human Rights Commission, City and County of San Francisco, September 1994.

14. Stephen Whittle, *The Transgender Debate* (Reading, MA: South Street, 2000), 16; Joanne Meyerowitz, *How Sex Changed: A History of Transsexuality in the United States* (Cambridge, MA: Harvard University Press, 2002), 10; Viviane Namaste, *Invisible Lives: The Erasure of Transsexual and Transgendered People* (Chicago: University of Chicago Press, 2000), 1. Others who define *transgender* as an umbrella term include

MacKenzie, *Transgender Nation*, 56; Andrew N. Sharpe, *Transgender Jurisprudence: Dysphoric Bodies of Law* (London: Cavendish, 2002), 1; Henry Rubin, *Self-Made Men: Identity and Embodiment among Transsexual Men* (Nashville, TN: University of Vanderbilt Press, 2003), 19. Similarly, Judith Halberstam suggests that "'transgender' can be used as a marker for all kinds of people who challenge (deliberately or accidentally) gender normativity" ("Telling Tales: Brandon Teena, Billy Tipton, and Transgender Biography," in *Passing: Identity and Interpretation in Sexuality, Race, and Religion,* ed. Maria Caria Sánchez and Linda Schlossberg [New York: New York University Press, 2001], 21). Jason Cromwell describes "transgender" as an "encompassing term" (*Transmen and FTMs: Identities, Bodies, Genders, and Sexualities* [Urbana: University of Illinois Press, 1999], 22–23).

15. See, for example, Jamison Green, introduction to *Transgender Equality: A Handbook for Activists and Policymakers,* by Paisley Currah and Shannon Minter (New York: Policy Institute of the National Gay and Lesbian Task Force, 2000), 7; Lisa Mottet and John M. Ohle, *Transitioning Our Shelters* (New York: National Gay and Lesbian Task Force Policy Institute and National Coalition for the Homeless, 2003); "One Umbrella, Many People," Gay, Lesbian, and Straight Education Network, 2003, http://www.glsen.org/cgibin/iowa/educator/library/record/1292.html.

16. Gordene O. MacKenzie, "50 Billion Galaxies of Gender," in *Reclaiming Genders,* ed. Kate More and Stephen Whittle (London: Cassell, 1999), 216. See also Dylan Vade, "Expanding Gender and Expanding the Law: Toward a Social and Legal Conceptualization of Gender That Is More Inclusive of Transgender People," *Michigan Journal of Gender and the Law* 11 (2005).

17. Namaste, *Invisible Lives,* 60–61.

18. Pat Califia, *Sex Changes: The Politics of Transgenderism* (San Francisco: Cleis, 1997), 273. See also K. L. Broad, "Transgender Collective Identity (De)Constructions," *International Journal of Sexuality and Gender Studies* 7, no. 4 (2002): 241–64; Josh Gamson, "Must Identity Movements Self-Deconstruct? A Queer Dilemma," in *Social Perspectives in Lesbian and Gay Studies,* ed. P. M. Nardi and B. E. Schneider (New York: Routledge, 1995), 589–604.

19. Riki Wilchins, *Read My Lips: Sexual Subversion and the End of Gender* (Ithaca, NY: Firebrand Books, 1997), 67.

20. David Valentine, "'The Calculus of Pain': Violence, Anthropological Ethics, and the Category Transgender," *Ethnos* 68, no. 1 (2003): 45.

21. Dean Spade, "Resisting Medicine, Re/modeling Gender," *Berkeley Women's Law Journal* 18 (2003): 16–26.

22. It's important to note that one national organization, GenderPAC, generally avoids reference to "transgender people" as a group and frames its advocacy as working to end violence and discrimination caused by gender stereotypes. See the GenderPAC mission statement, http://www.gpac.org/gpac/.

23. Teresa de Lauretis, "Gender Symptoms, or, Peeing Like a Man," *Social Semiotics* 9, no. 2 (1999): 261.

24. *Complaint for Damages and Demand for Jury Trial, Nicole Youngblood, by and through her next friend, Sonya Youngblood, v. School District of Hillsborough County, Florida,* U.S. District Court, Middle District of Florida, Tampa Division, June 2002, 2.

25. Marilyn Brown, "Gay Teen Sues over Year Book Photo," *Tampa Tribune*, June 20, 2002.

26. *Olesen v. Board of Education*, 676 F. Supp. 820 (U.S. Northern District of Illinois, Eastern Division, 1987).

27. Mick Meenan, "Gutsy Teen Lesbian, Pride of Queens," *Gay City News*, June 27, 2003, 4.

28. Motion for Preliminary Injunction and Incorporated Memorandum of Law, *Doe v. Yunits* at 4, 10, 9 (MA Sup. Ct., September 26, 2000).

29. Memorandum of Decision and Order on Plaintiff's Motion for Preliminary Injunction, *Doe v. Yunits* at 16, 11 (MA Sup. Ct., October 11, 2000).

30. 42. U.S.C. 12211(b) (2000).

31. Memorandum of Decision and Order on Defendants' Partial Motion to Dismiss and Plaintiff's Motion for Leave to Amend, *Doe v. Yunits*, 15 Mass. L. Rep. 278 (MA Sup. Ct., February 26, 2001). In another case involving a transgender girl in a state foster care system who had been disciplined for wearing girls' clothes, a New York judge also found the claim of disability discrimination compelling. See *Doe v. New York City Administration of Children's Services* (N.Y. Sup. Court, January 9, 2003).

32. Ibid.

33. Complaint for Damages and Demand for Jury Trial, *Youngblood v. School Board of Hillsborough County* at 2 (June 2002).

34. Plaintiff's Appeal of a Final Order of the District Court for the Middle District of Florida, *Youngblood v. School Board of Hillsborough County* at 2, 3 (May 2003).

35. Plaintiff's Opposition to Defendants McCarthy and Fyfe's Motion to Dismiss, Request for Oral Argument, and Memorandum of Law, *Youngblood v. School Board of Hillsborough County* at 6, 11 (July 25, 2003).

36. *Youngblood v. School Board of Hillsborough County*, No. 8:02-cv-1089-T-24MAP at 6 (Middle District, Florida, September 24, 2002).

37. Memorandum of Decision and Order on Plaintiff's Motion for Preliminary Injunction, *Doe v. Yunits* at 8 (MA Sup. Ct., October 11, 2000).

38. Paisley Currah, "The Transgender Rights Imaginary," *Georgetown Journal of Gender and the Law* 4 (2003): 712.

39. Paisley Currah, "Searching for Immutability: Homosexuality, Race, and Rights Discourse," in *A Simple Matter of Justice*, ed. Angelia R. Wilson (London: Cassell, 1995), 51–90.

40. Ian F. Haney Lopez, *White by Law: The Legal Construction of Race* (New York: New York University Press, 1996).

41. Steven Epstein, "Gay Politics, Ethnic Identity: The Limits of Social Constructionism," *Socialist Review* 17 (May–August 1987): 12.

42. John D. Skrentny, *The Minority Rights Revolution* (Cambridge, MA: Harvard University Press, 2002), 12.

43. See, for example, Janet Halley, "'Like Race' Arguments," in *What's Left of Theory?*, ed. Judith Butler, John Guillory, and Kendall Thomas (New York: Routledge, 2000), 40–74; David A. J. Richards, *Identity and the Case for Gay Rights: Race, Gender, Religion as Analogies* (Chicago: University of Chicago Press, 1999); Judith Butler,

Excitable Speech: A Politics of the Performative (New York: Routledge, 1997); Lisa Duggan, "Queering the State," *Social Text*, no. 39 (1994): 1–14.

44. Patrick J. Egan and Kenneth Sherrill, "Neither an In-Law nor an Outlaw Be: Trends in Americans' Attitudes toward Gay People," *Public Opinion Pros* (February 2005), http://www.publicopinionpros.com; Gregory M. Herek, "Gender Gaps in Public Opinion about Lesbians and Gay Men," *Public Opinion Quarterly* 66, no. 1 (2002): 40–66; Raymond A. Smith and Donald P. Haider-Markel, *Gay and Lesbian Americans and Political Participation* (Denver: ABC-CLIO, 2002).

45. Elizabeth Birch, speech at the Human Rights Campaign's Second Annual Dinner, Washington, DC, September 19, 1998 (excerpted in *HRC Quarterly* [fall 1998]: 14).

46. "Hatch Resents Charge of Intolerance," Associated Press, August 13, 1999.

47. Campaign for California Families, "Oppose AB 1649: The Intolerant Transsexual Agenda," http://www.savecalifornia.com/legislative/press_releases/ab1649-july-4-01-analysis.htm (accessed August 14, 2001); http://www.savecalifornia.com/newspaper_ads/pdf/Horton-Washington.pdf.

48. This is part of an ongoing research project, "Judging Gender: Narrating Transgender Identity in the Courts," that examines the way transgender rights advocates describe gender nonconformity in the courts in a wide range of cases involving gender nonconforming litigants in the United States. My point about the race analogy is not to suggest the analogy is never raised. For example, Cole Thaler, an activist from the Massachusetts Transgender Political Coalition, explained in an interview that when he first started lobbying to include gender identity and expression in a municipal law in Boston, he would explain that everyone has a gender identity, not just transgender people, just like everyone has a race. "And then I would see, kind of, this flicker of 'Oh God, this is some race analogy' in the eyes of the people I was talking to and I realized that it was probably going down a road I didn't want to go down. So I would stick to things . . . and I would say religion. Just like everyone has a religion. Some people are discriminated against because of their religion, others aren't" (Cole Thaler, interview with Paisley Currah, Kansas City, MO, November 2002).

49. John Silber, "Court Ruling Does No Favor for 'Pat Doe,'" *Boston Herald,* October 17, 2000.

50. Even Justice Antonin Scalia recognizes this, pointing out that "the word 'gender' has acquired the new and useful connotation of cultural or attitudinal characteristics (as opposed to physical characteristics) distinctive to the sexes. That is to say, gender is to sex as feminine is to female and masculine to male" (*J.E.B. v. Alabama Ex Rel. T.B.*, 511 U.S. 127 [1994]).

51. Jonathan Goldberg, "Transgender Bender," *National Review Online,* updated June 11, 1999, http://www.nationalreview.com/goldberg/goldberg.html (accessed June 14, 1999).

52. Significantly, however, the Vatican statement moved away from a pure biological essentialism that sees no distinction between sex and gender: "[The Holy See] also disassociates itself from the biological determinist notion that all roles and relations between the two sexes are fixed in a single, static pattern" (United Nations, "Reservations and Interpretative Statements on the Beijing Declaration and Platform

for Action, Report of the Fourth World Conference on Women," Beijing, September 4–15, 1995, gopher://gopher.undp.org:70/00/unconfs/women/off/a--20.en).

53. The Vatican took exception to a statement prepared by the UN Commission on the Status of Women in advance of the conference, which posited that "in many countries, the differences between women's and men's achievements and activities are still not recognized as the consequences of socially constructed gender roles rather than immutable biological differences" (Commission on the Status of Women, "Proposals for Consideration in the Preparation of a Draft Declaration for the Fourth World Conference on Women," May 24, 1995, para. 28, gopher://gopher.undp.org:70/00/unconfs/women/off/al--1.en).

54. *Catholic News Service,* January 16, 2003.

55. *Littleton v. Prange,* 9 S.W.3d 222, 224, 231 (Tex. App. 1999).

56. Plaintiff's brief to the Superior Court of New Jersey, Appellate Division, *Enriquez v. West Jersey Health Systems* at 17.

57. Brief of Amici Curiae Harry Benjamin International Gender Identity Association, *Brandon v. Richardson,* 624 N.W.2d 604 at 4 (Neb. 2001).

58. Memorandum of Law in Support of Petitioner's Motion for Preliminary Injunction, *Doe v. New York City Administration of Children's Services* (May 2003).

59. See International Bill of Gender Rights, http://www.transgenderlegal.com/ibgr.htm; and appendix to this book.

60. See, for example, Janet Halley, "Misreading Sodomy: A Critique of the Classification of 'Homosexuals' in Federal Equal Protection Law," in *Bodyguards: The Cultural Politics of Ambiguity,* ed. Julia Epstein and Kristina Straub (New York: Routledge, 1991); Nan Hunter, "Expressive Identity: Recuperating Dissent for Equality," *Harvard Civil Rights–Civil Liberties Law Review* 35 (2000): 1.

61. 393 U.S. 503 (1969).

62. Ibid. at 508.

63. *Tinker v. Des Moines Independent Community School District,* 393 U.S. 503, 507, 508 (1969).

64. *Epperson v. Arkansas,* 393 U.S. 97 (1968).

65. *Bivens v. Albuquerque Public Schools,* 899 F.Supp. 556 (District of New Mexico, 1995) (school regulation banning the wearing of saggy pants does not abridge students' rights to freedom of speech, expression, and association).

66. Ibid.

67. For descriptions of the expressive activity of students as mere expressions of individuality, see, for example, *Freeman v. Board of Education of Hobbs Municipal School District,* 448 F.2d 258, 260 (10th Cir. 1971) (regulation of male hair styles in state public schools is not protected under the First Amendment because, "at most, it is symbolic speech indicative of expressions of individuality rather than a contribution to the storehouse of ideas"); *Brick v. Board of Ed., School Dist. No. 1,* 305 F.Supp. 1316, 1320 (D. Colo. 1969) ("In the present case plaintiff has acknowledged that his hair style does not symbolize any political, religious, sociological or moral point of view; stating that the length of his hair was an expression of his individuality. Such symbolic expressions of individuality are not within the First Amendment"); *Karr v. Schmidt,* 460 F.2d 609, 614 (5th Cir. 1972) ("the right to style one's

hair as one pleases in the public schools does not inherit the protection of the First Amendment").

68. *Olesen v. Board of Education,* 676 F.Supp. 820 (U.S. Northern District of Illinois, Eastern Division, 1987).

69. Robin D. G. Kelley, *Race Rebels: Culture, Politics, and the Black Working Class* (New York: Free Press, 1994), 205.

70. *King v. Saddleback Junior College,* 445 F.2d 932, 938 (9th Cir. 1971).

71. In this sense, the courts are reflecting the same a priori boundaries of "the political" set by some contemporary liberal thinkers. For example, John Rawls's suggestion that the domain of public reason be limited to what appears "reasonable" and to exclude reasoning that seems "outrageous" simply reinforces popular notions of "reasonableness," which of course often lag far behind the outer boundaries of human thought and action (*Political Liberalism* [New York: Columbia University Press, 1993], 212–54).

72. *Ulane v. Eastern Airlines,* 742 F.2d 1081 (7th Cir. 1984), *cert. denied,* 471 U.S. 1017 (1985).

73. Susan Etta Keller, "Operations of Legal Rhetoric: Examining Transsexual and Judicial Identity," *Harvard Civil Rights–Civil Liberties Law Review* 34 (1999): 329, 375–79.

74. See Shannon Price Minter, "Representing Transsexual Clients: Selected Legal Issues" (San Francisco: National Center for Lesbian Rights), http://www.nclrights.org/publications/tgclients.htm (accessed May 12, 2005).

75. See "Non-Discrimination Laws That Include Gender Identity and Expression," Transgender Law and Policy Institute, http://www.transgenderlaw.org/ndlaws/index.htm.

76. Lisa Mottet, "Populations of Jurisdictions with Explicit Transgender-Inclusive Anti-Discrimination Laws," National Gay and Lesbian Task Force, February 2006, http://www.thetaskforce.org/downloads/trans/PopulationsJurisdictionsVertica/Feb06.pdf (accessed March 18, 2006).

77. Ellen J. Silberman, "Mayor Set to Approve Transgender Protection," *Boston Herald,* October 24, 2002.

78. Gunner Scott, interview with Paisley Currah, November 2002.

79. Jody Marksamer, interview with Paisley Currah, November 2002.

80. Donna Cartwright, interview with Paisley Currah, March 20, 2003.

81. Lori Buckwalter, telephone interview with Paisley Currah, March 15, 2003.

82. Beth Plotner, interview with Paisley Currah, Kansas City, MO, November 2002.

83. Riki Wilchins, "Freedom of Expression," *The Advocate,* September 2, 2003.

84. Generally, the statutory language that activists refer to as "transgender-inclusive" has been added to nondiscrimination laws under definitions of sex or gender, sexual orientation, or gender identity. For a discussion of the reasoning by activists' choices about which category to use, see Paisley Currah and Shannon Price Minter, "Unprincipled Exclusions: The Struggle for Legislative and Judicial Protections for Transgendered People," *College of William and Mary Journal of Women and the Law* 7, no. 1 (2000): 37–66.

85. City of Boston Code, chap. 12, sec. 12.9–2.

86. Diana Slyter, telephone interview with Paisley Currah, March 7, 2000.

87. Brett Beemyn, testimony at Iowa City Council meeting, September 26, 1995.

88. Peter LaBarbera, "Gender Games: Homosexual Groups Get behind the 'Transgender' Revolution," Americans for Truth Reports, June 11, 2001, http://www.ntac.org/news/01/06/17web2.html.

2. The Ties That (Don't) Bind: Transgender Family Law and the Unmaking of Families

Taylor Flynn

What if you were declared a "legal stranger" to your child and were prohibited from ever seeing her again? What if you were told that your marriage never existed, your name is not your own, or your sex is not what you know it to be? These are the lived experiences of many transgender people who walk into civil or family court every day. The underlying legal claim might involve traditional family law actions such as marriage, divorce, and custody, or such seemingly disparate claims as an inheritance dispute or a petition to amend one's birth certificate. In all of these intimate aspects of our lives, trans women and men face the possibility of a systematic obliteration of their personal identity, a legal shredding of self.

Consider Michael Kantaras's situation, one confronting many transgender parents. When Michael and his wife separated after nearly ten years of marriage, he faced a shock. In what should have been an ordinary custody dispute, Michael's wife argued that he had no legal rights to their children. Linda Kantaras based her claim on her husband's transsexualism. Although born anatomically female, Michael had identified from a young age as male. Long before he met Linda, Michael spent several years undergoing a sex reassignment protocol, which for him included a mental health diagnosis to ensure that hormone replacement therapy and reconstructive surgeries were appropriate.

Although she acknowledged that Michael had shared this history with her, and despite medical opinion to the contrary, Linda claimed that Michael was female. She then invoked the fact that Michael was not biologically related to their two children (their son, to whom Linda had given birth shortly before their marriage, was adopted by Michael; their daughter was conceived via alternative insemination using Michael's brother as the donor). Relying on case law holding that nonbiological gay or lesbian parents are legal strangers to their children, Linda argued, in essence, that theirs was a lesbian relationship,[1] and the Florida Court of Appeal agreed.[2] The ramifications of this argument are vast. By ruling that Michael was legally female, the Florida court, in one fell swoop, invalidated Michael's marriage, left open the possibility that Michael's legal rights to his children could be voided in the future, and (in his home state and most others) prohibited Michael from marrying again.

This chapter examines the contradictory and largely oppressive jurisprudence of transgender family law. We live in a highly gendered society where sex distinctions have significant legal consequences, particularly within the realm of the family—these distinctions affect issues including whom you can marry, whether you can inherit your spouse's estate, or whether you provide an "appropriate" role model for your children. Transgender family law decisions reflect society's almost fetishistic attitude toward trans individuals, evident in the courts' reductionist tendency to replace substantive analysis (whether Michael is a good parent) with a relentless focus on sexual anatomy (whether Michael has a penis).

This tendency not only is damaging and discriminatory but also results in incoherent legal approaches to one of the most intimate and defining aspects of our lives—gender identity, or our sense of ourselves as male or female. Different jurisdictions, for instance, can and have come to different conclusions about how to determine legal sex: most take the essentialist approach that sex is immutable and fixed at birth, while a small minority recognizes the complexities of sex and looks to a person's gender identity as the primary determinant of legal sex. Because each jurisdiction is free to define sex as it chooses, a trans person's sex can, in effect, change as she crosses state borders.[3] Despite the contingency of legal sex, jurisdictions nevertheless continue to view it as the sine qua non for many family law issues—the crucial thing the law needs to determine the validity of such major life events as marriage and parenthood.

In addition to this state-to-state incoherence, judicial decisions are replete with internal inconsistencies. Judges who ringingly proclaim that one's sex cannot be "changed," and whose opinions insist on maintaining strict, binary gender boundaries, in the same breath acknowledge the fluidity and complexities of sexual development and gender identity.[4] The explicit social meanings of a particular decision often clash with those that are implicit. Courts whose approaches are the most socially conservative and prudish frequently issue opinions that can fairly be described as sex obsessed (whether with genitalia or sexual activity) to the point of prurience.[5] Yet another paradox arises when the law's rigid view of sex collides with its privileging of heterosexuality. When the ban on same-sex marriage meets the insistence that legal sex may not be changed, the result is as fitting as it is ironic: in these jurisdictions, transgender gay and lesbian couples *can* legally marry. Assume a transsexual woman lives in a state where birth anatomy (here, a penis) forever defines legal sex. As a legal male, she is free to marry another woman, even though she, her partner, and society at large view them as lesbian. While it may be gratifying that the law of gender dichotomies, along with its concomitant heterosexual imperative, requires adherents to choose between denying marriage rights to gay *or* transgender individuals (rather than both), the quandary such jurisdictions find themselves in demonstrates the folly of the law's attempt to reify sex as an inflexible category, one on which the right to marry turns. In this chapter, I critique the predominant approach taken by courts in determining legal sex and suggest possible directions I believe the law should take. The determination of legal sex should be considered within the context of our constitutional values—values that reflect a deep suspicion of governmental intrusion on individual rights. As a normative matter, this framework of autonomy-preserving guarantees (including the rights to privacy, freedom of expression, and bodily integrity) creates constitutional space for an as-of-yet-unarticulated right, the right to self-determination of sexual identity. While I leave elaboration of this right to another day (e.g., What is its scope? Can you have multiple or fluctuating identities?) and acknowledge that the current state of jurisprudence all but forecloses its development, I nonetheless believe that its articulation is important. Such an approach would attempt not only to reclaim a rights-protecting view of the Constitution but also envisions a world free of our current investment in policing a boundary between (or among) the sexes.

In addition to this aspirational vision, I urge an approach already taken by a handful of courts—relying on gender identity as the defining basis for determining legal sex. This approach respects an individual's autonomy and does so without the need to invoke constitutional rights: it simply reflects the current understanding of sex. An individual's sex includes physical characteristics (such as external and internal reproductive anatomy, chromosomes, hormones, and secondary-sex characteristics) and a person's gender identity. Typically, these line up, making the shorthand use of one's birth genitalia to identify sex unproblematic. Particularly for transsexual and intersexed persons, gender identity and the physical characteristics of sex in some way(s) conflict. When there is a conflict, a person's gender identity is the determinative component;

treatment, if any is desired, consists of assisting the individual's transition to her identified sex, with or without surgeries or other medical intervention.[6]

Reliance on gender identity to determine legal sex is straightforward. It would obviate the need for an individualized, complex inquiry for each person. Instead, recognition of gender identity would provide the law with a consistent, relatively simple approach that accords with (although does not necessarily require) medically accepted standards.[7] Moreover, for transsexual individuals, it avoids the problematic requirement, enunciated by some courts, that a person undergo surgical intervention before her identified sex will be legally recognized—procedures that for some individuals are not only unnecessary but may cause permanent physical damage. The first part of this chapter, which discusses the "sexing" of trans people by the state, is most relevant to persons whose gender identity is in conflict with their anatomical birth sex, typically transsexual (or, in some instances, intersexed) individuals. The second part, which concerns issues of child custody and visitation, is relevant to all transgender persons: whether the parent is an effeminate man, tranny boi, drag queen or king, or transsexual, a gender nonconforming parent faces a host of risks and biases when a court is attempting to determine what form of parent-child relationship, if any, that person is permitted to maintain.

The Power to Define Legal Sex

A small number of courts have recognized that gender identity plays a central role in determining sex. As early as 1976, a New Jersey court upheld the marriage of a transsexual woman (known to us only as "J. T.") by ruling that she is legally female.[8] The court relied on the predominant view within the medical establishment that, among the many components involved in determining sex, chief among them is gender identity. When birth anatomy and gender identity conflict, the court stated, the role of anatomy is merely "secondary."[9] In a more recent decision, the Australia Family Court similarly upheld the validity of a marriage between Jennifer and her husband, Kevin, a trans man.[10] The Australian court cited expert testimony that "brain . . . or mental sex . . . [is thought to] explain the persistence of a gender identity in the face of . . . external influences."[11] Based on its conclusion that Kevin "is and always has been psychologically male," the court ruled that Kevin likewise is legally male.[12]

In J. T.'s and Kevin's cases, as in most successful trans litigation, medical and psychological evidence has been pivotal. Courts need to be educated that our everyday view of sex (e.g., that "vagina = girl") is unduly narrow—that while these correspondences may hold true for much of the population, this view fails to encompass the complex interplay of components that make up sex. The need for expert evidence presents significant obstacles, however. Most important, presenting sex from a medico–mental health model risks pathologizing the lives and experiences of transgender individuals. In addition, many trans litigants may find it impossible to access the tools of medical and legal privilege necessary to bring suit. The cost of retaining a lawyer, much less hiring one or more experts, may well be prohibitive. This is particularly true for those trans persons who are multiply marginalized, including many trans persons of color, as well as those who are immigrants, sex workers, poor, or homeless.

While a person's gender identity should be the focus of a court's determination of legal sex, courts also have looked to other legal contexts that may suggest recognition of a person's identified sex. This would include much of the documentation that makes up our official interactions with governmental entities. Does J. T.'s driver's license state that she is female? Did Kevin legally change his name? Depending on the jurisdiction, one of the most useful forms of legal recognition is state statutory law permitting amendment of birth certificates. Although some courts reject the argument that a state's issuance of an amended birth certificate reflects the state's recognition of an individual's posttransition sex,[13] at least one court has done so. In *Vecchione v. Vecchione*, a California court upheld the marriage of Joshua, a trans man, to his wife, Kristie.[14] The court placed great weight on a state statute permitting an individual to change the sex designation on one's birth certificate: this law, the court ruled, represented a legislative judgment that "California recognizes the post-operative gender of a transgendered person."[15]

While the number of cases such as *Vecchione* is slowly growing, more common among jurisdictions is the view that, as one court put it, sex is "immutably fixed by our Creator at birth."[16] These courts adopt a rigid and simplistic view: trans individuals are legally the sex assigned to them at birth, period. Before analyzing these cases, it is helpful to discuss the likely consequences of such a ruling. A trans woman, for instance, who is declared to be legally male may not be able to change identifying documentation (such as a birth certificate, driver's license, or passport) to reflect her identified sex, an outcome that exposes her to potential discrimination, harassment, and violence in the countless transactions that make up our daily lives. What should be a simple task of purchasing an item with a credit card (where identification may be required) can become a nightmare: a trans person risks humiliation, refusal to be served, and possible harm by onlookers who—now aware of her gender variance because of the reaction of the store clerk—may follow her out of the store. Her marriage may be invalidated; a speeding ticket or an international vacation may put her at risk. She may be denied a loan, refused service at a bank, or land the job of her dreams only to be fired as soon as she presents identifying documentation on her first day.

Being "Sexed" by the State

In adhering to the view of sex as genitalia-at-birth, the majority of courts simultaneously "de-sex" and hypersexualize trans men and women. Given the centrality of sex and gender in our lives, both are dehumanizing moves. In the recent decision *Matter of the Estate of Gardiner,* the Supreme Court of Kansas essentially ruled that trans persons do not have a "real" sex at all. In invalidating her marriage, the court framed the issue before it as whether Kansas's marriage statute applied to J'Noel Gardiner, a trans woman.[17] The court concluded that the law, which restricts marriage to persons of the "opposite sex," did not apply. The court stated in no uncertain terms that, in our common parlance, trans persons are neither "male" nor "female," nor even truly sexed: "The words 'sex,' 'male,' and 'female' in everyday understanding *do not encompass transsexuals.*"[18] "The plain, ordinary meaning of 'persons of the opposite sex,'" the court continued, "contemplates a biological man and a biological woman and not [transsexuals]."[19]

According to the state of Kansas, then, any time a statute refers to "men," "women," or persons of either "sex," trans people would be exempted unless otherwise specified. If we were to take this notion seriously, a trans person could claim exemption from many of our laws: "I didn't have to obey that criminal law, your Honor, or pay my taxes—those laws apply to 'men' and 'women,' but the legislature said nothing about transsexuals." Clearly, though, we are not meant to take the court's reasoning at face value: this desexing of trans people will not be enforced unless it has (undoubtedly discriminatory) social meaning. Here it serves a dual purpose: protecting the "purity" of marriage from trans heterosexuals while reinforcing the ban against same-sex marriage for lesbians, bisexuals, and gay men.

In determining legal sex, courts typically use an approach that I call a "body-parts" checklist: the court meticulously scrutinizes a litigant's sexual anatomy and compares its various features to a presumed norm. This hypersexualization of trans women and men occurs in favorable as well as unfavorable decisions. In upholding the validity of J. T.'s marriage, for example, the court engaged in a detailed, clinical discussion of J. T.'s genitalia, concluding that "her vagina had a 'good cosmetic appearance' and was 'the same as a normal female vagina after a hysterectomy.'"[20] For the court, it was important not only that J. T.'s genitals look "normal" but also that she is capable of participating in penile-vaginal sex. It may surprise some people to learn that lack of vaginal penetration remains grounds for annulling a marriage in some states.[21] J. T. escaped annulment of her marriage based in part on the court's conclusion that she has "a vagina and labia which [are] 'adequate for sexual intercourse' and could function as any female vagina, that is, for 'traditional penile/vaginal intercourse.'"[22] While the court includes a discussion of J. T.'s life experience with (relative) sensitivity, its exaltation of male penetration of women has the effect of reducing J. T. to little more than a receptacle for intercourse and her marriage to little more than the missionary position.

The converse is equally true for transgender men. Michael Kantaras's three-week custody trial was devoted almost entirely to a single issue: whether Michael has a penis deemed sufficient for penetration. His wife's attorney barraged Michael with questions—whether he could urinate standing up, whether he used a dildo, whether he could have (in her words) "normal sex." She asked what sexual positions he used and feigned disbelief when Michael stated that he and his wife had enjoyed a fulfilling sexual relationship. Michael's answers—which included intimate statements such as, "Sometimes [we had sex] in the missionary position with me on top, sometimes she was on top," and "the size of my penis may have been small, but there was penetration"— were broadcast with sensationalist enthusiasm on *Court TV* and were enshrined on the program's Web site.[23]

As Michael's case suggests, although family law disputes generally involve some invasion into one's home life, trans individuals must undergo an almost unimaginable host of intrusive inquiries about their bodies, medical history, and sex lives. A litigant can object to such requests on the grounds of privacy and relevancy, but if the court overrules an objection, she has little choice but to answer the questions. In theory, a litigant may appeal the trial court's ruling before providing the information, but because this may take years, most litigants—particularly those with custody at stake—simply do their best to respond. Trans women and men thus must participate in a system that robs them of dignity and privacy to protect the most precious and personal aspects of their lives.

The *Kantaras* court, in essence, was asking Michael whether he was "man enough" to be a father to his children. In addition to the intrusive and demeaning nature of this inquiry, the court's body-parts approach means that virtually identical cases may be resolved in dramatically different ways. Joshua Vecchione's situation is almost indistinguishable from Michael's: both men completed their reassignment protocol prior to marriage, married women who were fully informed of their gender status, and had children via alternative insemination—in fact, each used his brother as the sperm donor. Both men underwent hormone therapy, reconstructive chest surgery, reproductive surgery, and received documentation stating that, medically, he is male. The only difference is that Joshua underwent the surgical construction of a phallus (known as a "phalloplasty"), whereas Michael did not. Michael's decision is the more common choice among trans men for a number of reasons. Phalloplasty is not only deemed unnecessary by medical experts but is a procedure that many experts affirmatively counsel against. This surgery presents significant risks, including permanent loss of orgasmic capability, severe scarring, and irreversible damage to the urethra. Moreover—in addition to the exorbitant cost (typically not covered by health insurance) that may exceed one hundred thousand dollars—medical technology has not advanced to the stage where the procedure results in a functioning penis.

Consistent with a body-parts rationale, the contrast between the outcomes in Joshua's and Michael's cases is stark. Joshua is legally male, his marriage (and any future marriage) is valid, important legal documentation demonstrates that he is male, and he may seek custody of his daughter. Michael's life, in comparison, has been torn apart—his marriage and his maleness invalidated, any future marriage prohibited, and the rights to his children uncertain. Such an approach makes one's sex turn on how much money a trans individual has (is it enough to pay for surgery?), that person's view of whether surgery is appropriate for himself or herself, and the current state of medical knowledge. Furthermore, because the medical establishment can surgically construct fully functioning vaginas but presently cannot do so for penises, the body-parts rationale results in far more trans women receiving legal recognition of their identified sex than trans men. The possibility of such incongruous and discriminatory results suggests (at a minimum) that making legal sex turn on the existence or extent of surgery is a flawed undertaking. Reliance on gender identity, in contrast, would produce a legal regime that is far more consistent and just.

"Erasing" Marriages

Recall J'Noel Gardiner: the Kansas Supreme Court invalidated her marriage on the ground that she is legally male; using the same rationale, the Texas Court of Appeals recently invalidated the marriage of Christie Littleton.[24] When a court invalidates a marriage, this has a very different meaning legally and symbolically (although, as explained below, not necessarily in effect) from a declaration of divorce. In granting a divorce, the law declares the marriage to be over. In contrast, when a court invalidates a marriage, the law engages in the legal fiction that the marriage never existed. You could have been married for decades, have children and grandchildren—suddenly, that marriage has been officially erased.

As a result of the *Littleton* and *Gardiner* rulings, Christie and J'Noel cannot, in the vast majority of states, marry again.[25] More precisely, they are left with the same empty right to marry as most gay men and lesbians: Christie and J'Noel can marry someone of the "opposite" sex; as legal males, this means they can marry only women. Massachusetts's landmark ruling, *Goodridge v. Dept. of Public Health,* which ruled the state's ban on same-sex marriage unconstitutional, undoubtedly will benefit some transgender individuals.[26] Because same-sex marriages are legal in Massachusetts, a trans person who marries and later divorces in that state does not have to worry that her marriage may be annulled as an invalid same-sex union. Because Massachusetts is the only state in which sex is an irrelevant criterion for marriage, however, when the laws of another state arguably apply, the marriage's validity is open to challenge.

What if the couple marries in another state, moves to Massachusetts and divorces there: could the non-trans spouse invalidate the marriage? Although there is a strong argument that Massachusetts should apply its own law to its residents and recognize the marriage, the Massachusetts courts have not yet addressed this issue. If the couple marries in Massachusetts and subsequently moves to and divorces in another state, many of those jurisdictions are likely to invalidate the marriage.[27] Nor is recognition of the marriage from the federal government forthcoming.[28] In short, until the U.S. Supreme Court or the remaining forty-nine states declare the same-sex marriage ban unconstitutional—or until gender identity determines legal sex in all states—marriages of transgender men and women will continue to be in jeopardy.

As mentioned earlier, what is a tragic loss for heterosexual trans people like J'Noel and Christie is in some ways a gain for gay and lesbian trans couples. In a rare example where two "wrongs" actually *do* make a "right," when the ban against same-sex marriage is combined with the ruling that a trans individual cannot legally change her birth sex, the result is that gay trans people can legally marry their same-sex partners. Not long after the ruling in *Littleton,* for instance, the Texas papers ran numerous stories of same-sex couples, one of whom is transgender, who had decided to legally marry; similar marriages have been reported in other states as well as abroad.[29]

What are the effects of an annulment or invalidation of marriage? Courts often use the terms synonymously: they are largely indistinguishable in effect (both result in a marriage's legal "erasure"), and any difference rests primarily in annulment's historical roots. A holdover from centuries-old ecclesiastical law, annulment frequently is permitted on a number of archaic grounds. One essentially reduces marriage to a couple's reproductive capacity, providing that a marriage can be annulled on the basis of infertility. A second, often referred to as "physical incapacity" or "lack of consummation," is based on lack of penile-vaginal intercourse. As was evident in J. T.'s situation, this ground tends to differ from a "fertility" inquiry: the court focuses, without regard to reproduction, on the husband's ability to penetrate his wife's vagina. The last principal ground for annulment is fraud—the claim that trans individuals have defrauded their spouses as to their "real" sex. Joshua Vecchione's situation demonstrates the vulnerability of trans spouses to a fraud claim: courts typically will hear evidence on the claim, which in Joshua's case forced him to endure long and anguishing trial proceedings before the fraud claim was ultimately rejected.

Under early American law, annulment had dire consequences. Rather than make property and custody determinations as it would in a divorce, a court would attempt to return the parties to their "original position." Needless to say, this approach resulted in gross inequities along gender lines: a court would "return" property to the "owner" (inevitably the husband), while children typically were "returned" to the mother (who was not entitled to support on the theory that no marriage had occurred). In an attempt to avoid such devastating and unjust results, modern legal doctrine generally provides that—for purposes of determining property division, support, and custody—annulment should be treated like divorce.[30] This is significant for nonbiological trans parents whose marriages have been voided: both parents, regardless of biological ties, would have an equal claim to custody. "But," you may ask, "weren't the trials of Michael and Joshua premised on the notion that they would lose all rights to their children?" Unfortunately, this appears to have been the working assumption of opposing counsel in those cases, if not of the courts. This incorrect premise may stem in part from lack of practical experience: while couples continue to seek religious annulments from their churches, the issue of legal annulment rarely comes before the courts. Because this is an infrequently litigated area, education is crucial to ensure that trans parents and their lawyers are aware that in most jurisdictions, annulment changes nothing with regard to a parent's right to seek custody or visitation.

Transgender Parents, Their Children, and the Law

The law traditionally has recognized three (and only three) types of parent-child ties as bases for legal parenthood—those established through biology, adoption, or marriage. The legal arguments about whether a transgender parent may retain a relationship with her child after divorce or annulment may differ depending on the form of the legal tie. Thus, although the depth and intensity of a parent's bond in no way depend on a person's route to parenthood, this section considers each in turn.

The Unmaking of Parents

When biological parents divorce, the law presumes that each parent will receive either custody or visitation. Significant restrictions on visitation are rare: typically, they are issued only in cases of physical, emotional, or sexual abuse, and often not even then.[31] These principles appear to fly out the window when a parent is transgender. Not only is custody rarely granted, but visitation may be stringently restricted or terminated entirely. In a fairly recent case, a transsexual woman who was the children's biological father had transitioned postdivorce; she had not been permitted to see her children for nearly two years.[32] The trial court had prohibited physical contact with the children for one year and had ordered that she "not cohabit with other transsexuals" (one of her roommates was transsexual) or "sleep with another female" (she identifies as lesbian).[33] On appeal, the court rejected her argument that the order violated her right to privacy, citing the need to protect the children's "moral development."[34] The appellate court upheld the order and went one step further by extending the prohibition on physical contact for an indefinite period.[35]

Some decisions are even more draconian. These courts have done the unthinkable, terminating parental rights (either legally or in effect). One appellate court terminated visitation rights, asking, "Was [the parent's] sex change simply an indulgence of some fantasy?"[36] In what was surely an empty gesture, this court stated that it was not foreclosing visitation permanently, heaping that razor-thin possibility with qualifications: "*If and when* by growth and maturity of the children *and proper evidence* presented . . . and with a *thorough investigation* by the trial court *with expert investigation and advice* there *may* be a time when the trial court can order visitation . . . *with a continuing plan protecting* the best interests of the . . . children."[37] In Nevada, that state's highest court upheld the termination of parental rights for Suzanne Daly, a trans woman who was the child's biological father.[38] The Nevada Supreme Court accepted the conclusion below that, by bringing her anatomy into congruence with her gender identity, Suzanne had shown herself to be "a selfish person whose own needs, desires and wishes were paramount."[39] The court concluded with perhaps its most offensive assertion of all—that Suzanne, and not the court, had terminated her parental rights: "It can be said that Suzanne, in a very real sense, has terminated her own parental rights as a father. It was strictly [Suzanne's] choice to discard...fatherhood and assume the role of a female."[40]

Thankfully, a few courts have refused to engage in such gender hysteria. Nearly thirty years ago, the Colorado Court of Appeals refused to modify Mark Randall's custody of his children.[41] Custody originally had been granted to Mark, the children's biological mother, prior to his gender transition. After Mark's transition, the trial court ruled that custody should be transferred to the children's biological father. The lower court refused to take the children's preference into account—they wanted to stay with Mark—concluding that their preference indicated that they were "mentally disturbed."[42] The court of appeals rejected the assumption that a desire to remain with a transgender parent meant that the children were mentally ill, stating that "the interviews with the four girls indicate no abnormality whatsoever, but only a sincere desire to remain with [Mark], on lucid, logical bases."[43] Colorado law, the appellate court continued, provides that in determining a child's best interests, "the court shall not consider conduct of a proposed custodian that does not affect his relationship with the child."[44] The court concluded that Mark's gender transition was exactly that, rendering it irrelevant to the custody determination.

When a child has been adopted, the legal rights and obligations of the parents are generally indistinguishable from those of biological parents. Typically, there is only one way in which a completed adoption can be "undone," and it is quite difficult to effectuate: the birth parent must prove that she was subject to fraud, coercion, or undue influence in agreeing to the adoption.[45] Fraud is the basis most likely to be used against trans parents; Linda Kantaras's claim may be the first documented example of its usage regarding adoption. Interestingly, Linda's claim is not that *she* was defrauded when she agreed to allow Michael to adopt her son: Linda acknowledged that she was aware that Michael is a trans man. Instead, her claim appeared to be that there was fraud on the state. The state of Florida, where the Kantaras family lives, bars gay men and lesbians from adopting children.[46] Presumably, Linda's multistepped, rather strained argument is that (1) Michael is legally female; (2) because of his relationship with Linda, he is lesbian; (3) this violates Florida's ban; and (4) the state should annul the adoption, ten years later. Even the state of Florida—renowned for its antiqueer agenda spearheaded by Anita Bryant in the 1970s[47]—may be unwilling to stretch that far.[48] The mere fact of the adoption challenge, however, suggests that for transgender parents a finalized adoption may not be a secure one.

A person also can become a legal parent through marriage. There are typically two routes to parenthood via marriage, and both usually apply to fathers. First, some states privilege marriage by providing that a child born during the marriage is the legal child of the married couple, even in the face of a paternity claim from another man demonstrating that he is the child's biological father.[49] In such a jurisdiction, if Linda Kantaras had given birth to her son one month later (i.e., after the couple's marriage), Michael automatically would have become the boy's legal father. The second means is pursuant to a state's rules on alternative insemination (AI). Alternative insemination may be an appealing route to parenthood for trans men and women who have undergone reproductive surgery and thus are infertile. In many jurisdictions, if a married woman seeks AI at a fertility clinic in compliance with statutory requirements, her husband is the child's legal father.[50]

Michael and Linda conceived their second child through AI: Linda argued that their marriage was invalid and that, as a result, the statute's provision (that the husband is the child's legal father) was inapplicable. The ideal way for this argument to be defeated is for the court to uphold the validity of the marriage. The trans spouse then is a legal parent under either rationale—because the child was born during the marriage or because the AI requirements were met. Even if the marriage is held invalid, it may be possible for a trans parent to prevail on the latter ground. Some AI statutes lack a marriage requirement, and even when the statute expressly refers to a "married" woman, some jurisdictions have held that it applies to unmarried women as well.[51]

One of the few courts to directly address this issue, however, recently rejected the state's AI statute as an independent basis for legal parenthood for a transgender father. Sterling Simmons argued that despite the court's invalidation of his marriage, he was the legal father of his daughter pursuant to Illinois's AI law.[52] Sterling pointed to the statute's language, which specifically provides that a man is the legal father of the child "even though the marriage is or could be declared invalid."[53] Like most AI statutes, though, the Illinois law is written with the most common AI situation in mind: it establishes legal parenthood to "a man" whose female partner undergoes insemination. Rather than look to the statute's underlying purpose of ensuring that both intended parents, rather than the sperm donor, are the child's legal parents, the *Simmons* court held the law inapplicable on the ground that Sterling "is not a man within the meaning of the statute"[54]—a rationale that also may preclude parentage claims by women whose female partners undergo AI.

Even if a trans parent succeeds in defeating marriage or AI claims, the battle is only partially complete. The parent is now in the same position as a trans biological parent—subject to a grueling inquiry as to whether she should receive custody or visitation, or whether her parental rights should be terminated altogether.

Any Other Recourse?

When a court rules that a transgender parent is not a legal parent, all parental ties may be cut and the parent may have no right even to visit or contact her child. While a transgender parent would face significant barriers,[55] it may be possible to convince a court to permit continued contact with the child, despite a ruling that the trans parent is not a legal parent. In fact, the Florida Court of Appeal in *Kantaras* left open the possibility that Michael might retain his ability to seek visitation. Although it invalidated Michael's marriage on the ground that he is legally female, the court specifically stated that its ruling "does not take into consideration the best interests of the children involved in this case."[56] The remand is double-edged, however: the court of appeal's rather ominous instruction that the lower court "determin[e] ... the legal status of the children" may portend a complete severing of Michael's parental rights, including visitation.[57]

If the lower court decides to grant custody or visitation rights to Michael, it could do so by utilizing its equitable powers; these powers are based on the notion that "equity" may step in when application of the legal rules results in injustice. There are two doctrines a transgender parent may be able to invoke: that of estoppel (applied in a family law context in numerous jurisdictions) and functional parenthood (likely applicable only in two jurisdictions). The doctrine of estoppel prohibits one party in a lawsuit from taking an action to the detriment of another, or benefiting from her inconsistent actions, when she has engaged in conduct at odds with her legal claim. In many jurisdictions, for instance, courts have refused to terminate a man's child support payments despite his recent discovery that he is not the child's biological father.[58] Because the man had created an established parent-child relationship, the courts reason that he was estopped from shirking his parental obligations—even though he is not the child's legal parent. On remand, Michael Kantaras may be able to assert an estoppel claim on the ground that he has developed enduring parent-child bonds with his children—bonds created and encouraged in part by his former spouse.

A significant obstacle to an estoppel argument is that the published opinions generally involve the payment of child support, with no claim to custody or visitation. The *Simmons* court distinguished prior cases on precisely this ground: the court asserted that while estoppel may be the basis for a claim of financial support and what it called "parental responsibility," it could not serve as the basis for a claim of legal parenthood.[59]

Some courts have used the doctrine of functional parenthood, also known as "de facto" parenthood,[60] to grant varying degrees of continuing contact with a child to persons who have established a parentlike relationship with the child; its most common use has been to grant grandparents visitation rights. While some jurisdictions have rejected applicability of the doctrine in a gay or transgender parenting context,[61] most jurisdictions have yet to address the issue. In contrast, the highest courts in Massachusetts and New Jersey have applied the doctrine to nonbiological lesbian parents who had not adopted their partner's child.[62] Upon each couple's separation, the biological parent claimed that the nonbiological parent had no legal rights to their child. Pointing out that the doctrine applies to any person who meets the criteria, both courts examined the quality and depth of the nonbiological parent's relationship with the child to determine whether she should be extended parenting rights. The courts looked to a similar, carefully crafted set of standards for determining functional parenthood, including whether the nonbiological parent resided with the child, acted as a parent with the consent and encouragement of the legal parent, and shared care-taking responsibilities.[63] As with estoppel claims, the rights of a functional parent vary: in jurisdictions that have applied the doctrine largely to grandparents, only visitation typically is permitted; Massachusetts and New Jersey, in contrast, appear to extend full parenting rights to the functional parent.[64]

Conclusion

At the core of the law's power over trans women and men is its ability to pronounce individuals legally female or male, regardless of their gender identity or expression. The majority of courts disregard abundant evidence demonstrating that gender identity is the paramount consideration in determining sex—testimony from experts, any physical transition to one's identified sex, and an individual's negotiations through the world as male or female. You can be a husband, a father, and even have male-pattern baldness, yet a court can declare, nonetheless, that you are female. When a court subordinates these realities to the orthodoxy of "sex-as-genitalia," it enforces a social and legal paradigm in which trans women and men have no place.

Transgender women and men find themselves caught in the law's fevered anxiety over families, gender, and children. Undoubtedly, our personal experiences of each run deep. Perhaps this explains why family law is the area in which sex distinctions and gender-role stereotyping appear to be the most intractable—based on their own experiences, judges may believe that they "know" what sex is, just as they "know" what is best for children. In addition to the enormous individual losses suffered by trans women and men who come before these courts, the resulting sex-system is incoherent and contrary to our conceptions of individual autonomy. Can the law make something as central to our notion of selfhood as our sex depend on the vagaries of where we reside? On an individual's desire for, or ability to afford, surgery? On the current state of medical knowledge?

Fortunately, not all is bleak. A small (but hopefully growing) body of law is developing in which gender identity has been recognized as the central component in determining legal sex. The effects of such rulings ripple outward, protecting marriages from claims of invalidity and extending some measure of protection to the legal tie between a trans parent and her child. More important than these individual legal gains, however, is activism. Like members of other civil rights movements before them, trans women and men are educating the public about their lives and the discrimination they face—in the hopes of moving the law along with them as they go.

Notes

The asterisks that appear with page numbers in these notes refer to screen page numbers from a database.

1. Interestingly, Linda attempted to distance herself from the stigma of homosexuality by suggesting that despite this proclaimed lesbian relationship, she was not lesbian. See http://www.courttv.com/trials/kantaras/020502_ctv.html (discussing Linda's claim that she had resisted Michael's sexual advances throughout their marriage).

2. See *Kantaras v. Kantaras*, 884 So.2d 155 (Fla. Cir. Ct. 2004) (invalidating parties' marriage on ground that transgender father is legally female), *review denied*, No. SC04–1953, 2005 Fla. LEXIS 373 (Fla. February 23, 2005). In an impressive initial victory, the trial court had ruled that Michael was legally male and gave him custody of the couple's children. For a copy of the more than eight-hundred-page decision, see http://www.courttv.com/archive/trials/kantaras/docs/opinion.pdf. While the trial court's opinion was an important success, the considerable length of the opinion, as well as its focus on a large volume of specialized medical testimony, suggests that a more clear and straightforward approach (one that is also medically supported) would be to determine legal sex based on an individual's gender identity. See generally the first part, below.

3. Although it is unclear whether one state must give full faith and credit to another state's determination of legal sex, it is clear that two people in identical circumstances can be of different legal sexes depending on the jurisdiction where they reside.

4. As discussed in the first part, most courts take the position, contrary to the view generally accepted within the medical and psychological communities, that a person's sex is fixed at birth and hence cannot be changed. There is, however, an important way in which a transgender person's sex does not change. Because gender identity is established at a very young age and is the primary determinant of an individual's

sex, a person with female anatomy who has identified as male since childhood is, and always has been, in the deepest and most significant of ways, male. At least one court has articulated this distinction. See note 13.

5. See the discussion in "'Sexed' by the State," below. Justice Harry Blackmun made a similar observation with respect to homosexuality in his dissent in *Bowers v. Hardwick,* 478 U.S. 186, 200 (1986) (Blackmun, J., dissenting) (majority's opinion exhibited an "almost obsessive focus on homosexual activity"), overruled by *Lawrence v. Texas,* 530 U.S. 558 (2003).

6. See, generally, Collier M. Cole, Lee E. Emory, Ted Huang, and Walter J. Meyer III, "Treatment of Gender Dysphoria (Transsexualism)," *Texas Medicine* 90, no. 5 (May 1994); Harry Benjamin International Gender Dysphoria Association, *The Harry Benjamin International Gender Dysphoria Association's Standards of Care for Gender Identity Disorders,* 6th ed., February 2001, http://www.hbigda.org/soc.cfm.

7. While an extensive analysis of the difficulties posed by reliance on a medical model of sex is beyond the scope of this article, some ramifications of the law's emphasis on surgical and hormonal intervention are discussed below in the first part.

8. *M.T. v. J.T.,* 355 A.2d 204 (N.J. Sup. Ct. 1976).

9. Ibid., 205.

10. See *In the Matter of the Estate of Marshall G. Gardiner,* 42 P.3d 120, 131–32 (Kan. 2002) (discussing *In re Kevin,* Family Court of Australia, at Sydney, 2001).

11. Ibid., 132.

12. Ibid.

13. See, for example, *Simmons v. Simmons,* Nos. 1–03–2284 and 1–03–2348, 2005 Ill. App. LEXIS127 (App. Ct. Ill. February 16, 2005).

14. *Vecchione v. Vecchione,* CA Civ. No. 95D003769 (Orange County, filed April 23, 1996).

15. *Minute Order* (November 26, 1997), Vecchione (on file with author). It is unfortunate that this opinion, like many of the favorable decisions, appears to limit its ruling to persons who have undergone at least some surgical intervention.

16. *Littleton v. Prange,* 9 S.W.3d 223, 224 (Tex. App. 1999), *cert. denied,* 2000 U.S. LEXIS 5855 (U.S. October 2, 2000).

17. *Gardiner,* 42 P.3d at 136–37.

18. Ibid., 135.

19. Ibid.

20. *M.T. v. J.T.,* 355 A.2d at 206.

21. See, for example, Cal. Fam. Code 2210(f) (Deering's 2001) (marriage can be voided if spouse is "physically incapable of entering into the marriage state"). While there is a strong argument that annulment on this ground is unconstitutional, to my knowledge there have been no modern challenges to such statutes.

22. *M.T. v. J.T.,* 355 A.2d at 206.

23. For one such discussion on the Web site, see http://www.courttv.com/trials/kantaras/013102_ctv.html.

24. *Littleton,* 9 S.W.3d at 231.

25. Assuming they meet state residency requirements, Christie and J'Noel would be able to marry in one of the few jurisdictions that recognize a person's posttransition sex; if they were to move to Massachusetts, which permits marriage regardless of the

sex of the parties involved, they could also marry. Although an unsettled question, if they were to marry in one of these jurisdictions without becoming residents, it is unlikely that the jurisdictions in which they reside would recognize their out-of-state marriages. See notes 26–30 and accompanying text.

26. *Goodridge v. Dept. of Public Health,* 440 Mass. 309, 798 N.E.2d 941 (2003). The Supreme Judicial Court rested its decision on the Massachusetts, rather than federal, constitution.

27. While subject to constitutional challenges on a number of grounds, forty states (as of April 2005) have adopted so-called mini-DOMA laws, modeled after the federal Defense of Marriage Act (DOMA); these statutes prohibit same-sex marriage in the enacting state and deny recognition to same-sex marriages from other states. See, for example, www.thetaskforce.org/downloads/marriagemap.pdf. As of the same date, eighteen states (many of which also have enacted mini-DOMA laws) have passed state constitutional amendments barring same-sex marriage (ibid.).

28. In 1996 the federal government passed what has become known as the Defense of Marriage Act, Pub. L. No. 104–199. The statute, arguably in violation of several Constitutional provisions, denies federal recognition to same-sex marriages and purports to permit states to likewise deny recognition.

29. See, for example, Adolfo Pesquera, "Lesbian Couple Get License to Wed," *San Antonio Express-News* (Texas), September 7, 2000; "Oregon Couple Adds Twist to Love Story," *Morning News Tribune* (Oregon), December 14, 1996; Chris Beam, "For Better or for Worse?" *OUT* (England and Ohio), May 2000.

30. See, for example, 63 A.L.R.2d 1008 (West 2002) (custody, child support), 52 Am Jur. 2d *Marriage* 85 (West 2001) (property).

31. See, for example, *V.C. v. M.J.B.,* 748 A.2d 539, 554–55 (NJ 1999) (denial of visitation rights is an "extraordinary proscription" invoked only where physical or emotional harm is present).

32. *J.L.S. v. D.K.S.,* 943 S.W.2d 766 (Mo. App. 1997).

33. Ibid., 769.

34. Ibid., 775.

35. Ibid.

36. *Cisek v. Cisek,* 1982 Ohio App. LEXIS 13335, *4 (Oh. App. July 20, 1982).

37. Ibid., *5 (emphasis added).

38. *Daly v. Daly,* 715 P.2d 56 (Nev. S. Ct. 1986).

39. Ibid., 71.

40. Ibid.

41. *Christian v. Randall,* 516 P.2d 132 (Colo. App. 1973).

42. Ibid., 133.

43. Ibid.

44. Ibid., 132.

45. 2 Am. Jur. 2d *Adoption* § 101 (West 2001).

46. See, for example, *Lofton v. Kearney,* 358 F.3d 804 (11th Cir. 2004) (upholding ban on adoption by gay or lesbian parents against constitutional challenge), *cert. denied,* 125 S. Ct. 869 (2005).

47. See, generally, Barry D. Adam, *The Rise of a Gay and Lesbian Movement,* rev. ed. (New York: Macmillan Reference, 1995), 102–8.

48. The Florida Court of Appeal left open the question of whether the adoption was valid; it remanded the case for a determination of Michael's legal relationship to the children (*Kantaras v. Kantaras,* 884 So.2d. at 161).

49. See, for example, *Michael H. v. Gerald D.,* 491 U.S. 110 (1989).

50. See, for example, Cal. Fam. Code § 7613 (2001) (providing that a husband is the legal father of a child conceived by alternative insemination when the requirements of statute are met).

51. *Buzzanca v. Buzzanca,* 72 Cal. Rptr. 2d 280, 285 (Ct. App. 1998).

52. *Simmons,* Case Nos. 1–03–2284 and 1–03–2348, at *13–18.

53. Ibid., *17.

54. Ibid., *18.

55. A principal limitation in applying these doctrines is a claim by the nontransgender parent that her constitutionally protected parenting rights have been violated because the child's contact with a nonlegal parent is being enforced over the legal parent's objection. See, for example, *Troxel v. Granville,* 530 U.S. 57 (2000) (striking down, as violative of a parent's due process rights, a state visitation statute permitting any person to petition for visitation with a child at any time). Moreover, application of these doctrines is left to the discretion of the individual judge, which—given the bias against transgender parents—makes their use less likely.

56. *Kantaras v. Kantaras,* 884 So.2d. at 161.

57. Ibid.

58. See, for example, *Brinkley v. King,* 549 Pa. 241, 701 A.2d 176 (1997) (upholding doctrine of paternity by estoppel).

59. *Simmons,* Case Nos. 1–03–2284 and 1–03–2348, at *19–20.

60. In addition, courts have used the terms "psychological" or "emotional" parent, as well as the term "parenthood in fact."

61. *Simmons,* Case Nos. 1–03–2284 and 1–03–2348 at *20–22 (drawing on prior case law concerning lesbian nonbiological parent to reject applicability of de facto parenthood doctrine to nonbiological transgender father).

62. *E.N.O. v. L.M.M.,* 711 N.E.2d 886 (MA 1999); *V.C. v M.J.B.,* 748 A.2d 539 (NJ 1999).

63. *V.C.,* 748 A.2d at 551 (quoting *E.N.O.,* 711 N.E.2d at 891) (emphasis added).

64. Ibid., 554 (noting that the functional parent stands "in parity with the legal parent").

3. The Roads Less Traveled: The Problem with Binary Sex Categories

Julie A. Greenberg

For decades, the medical and psychological communities have attempted to resolve the issue of how a person's sex should be determined for medical purposes. Until the last decade, however, many legal institutions have been blind to the need to define these terms for legal purposes. Often, the law has operated under the assumption that the terms *male* and *female* are fixed and unambiguous, despite medical literature to the contrary.

Recent studies indicate that approximately 2 percent of the world's population may be intersex and have either ambiguous or noncongruent sex features.[1] Thus, the manner in which the law defines the terms *male* and *female* will have a profound effect on millions of people.

Whether an individual is classified as a male or a female has increased significance now that Congress has passed the Defense of Marriage Act (DOMA) and the majority of states have adopted equivalent state legislation. Defining these terms will become even more critical if the United States adopts a constitutional amendment limiting marriage to one man and one woman. DOMA, its state equivalents, and the proposed constitutional amendment are intended to prohibit marriages between individuals of the "same sex." These legislative enactments, however, fail to define the terms *male* and *female,* so that determining who is now legally permitted to marry is unclear.

A variety of factors could contribute to determining whether an individual should be considered male or female for legal purposes. These factors include chromosomal sex, gonadal sex, external morphologic sex, internal morphologic sex, hormonal patterns, phenotype, assigned sex, and self-identified sex.[2] For most individuals, these factors are all congruent. For the millions of individuals with incongruent or ambiguous sex features, however, legal institutions must establish which factor(s) will determine a person's legal sex.

This chapter explores how the law has defined and should define the terms *male* and *female* in the context of marriage.[3] It starts with a comparative analysis of how these terms have been used in varying disciplines and by Western society and other cultures and provides insight into the various legal approaches that could be adopted. It continues with a detailed description of the medical conditions involving ambiguous sexual features that affect millions of people and demonstrates why these terms must be defined carefully. It then provides a summary of the marriage cases in which the courts have grappled with how to define these terms. It concludes with a proposal that legal sex reflect scientific developments that emphasize the importance of self-identification. Such an approach will benefit the people most affected by these laws and is consistent with principles of justice and other legal values.

Sex across Cultures

"Sex" is commonly used to refer to a person's status as a man or woman based on biological factors. Although sex reflects a person's biology, as opposed to gender, which is generally considered to be socially constructed, the biological aspect of the body that determines a person's sex has not been legally or medically resolved.

Traditionally, a person's legal sex is established by the sex that the birth attendant places on the birth certificate. Thus, for infants born with unambiguous external genitalia, the external genitalia typically control the sex determination. If the genitalia appear ambiguous, sex is assigned, in part, based on sex-role stereotypes. The presence of an "adequate" penis in an XY infant leads to the label *male,* while the absence of an "adequate" penis leads to the label *female.*[4] A genetic (XY) male with an "inadequate" penis (one that physicians believe will be incapable of penetrating a female's vagina when the child reaches adulthood) is "turned into" a female even if it means destroying his reproductive capacity. A genetic (XX) female who may be capable of reproducing, however, is generally assigned the female sex to preserve her reproductive capability, regardless of the appearance of her external genitalia. If her phallus is considered to be too large to meet the guidelines for a typical clitoris, it is surgically reduced, even if it means that her capacity for satisfactory sex may be reduced or destroyed.[5] In other words, men are defined based on their ability to penetrate females, and females are defined based on their ability to procreate. Sex, therefore, can be viewed as a social construct rather than a biological fact.

In the presence of ambiguous genitalia, medical professionals generally suggest that surgery be performed to "fix" the genitalia so that they conform to the medically established norm. The sex that matches the surgically created genitalia is then assigned on the birth record.[6] Because a person's birth certificate will often be used to obtain other legal documents, an individual's legal sex is generally established based on the appearance of the person's external genitalia.

Implicit in legislation using the term *sex* is the assumption that only two biological sexes exist and that all people fit neatly into one of these two categories. In other words, despite medical and anthropological studies to the contrary, the law presumes a binary sex model. For the most part, the law ignores the millions of people who are intersex. Although the American legal system clings to a binary sex and gender paradigm, anthropologists who have studied other societies have found cultures that reject binary sex and gender systems. These societies formally recognize that more than two sexes exist.[7]

For instance, in several villages in the Dominican Republic, a significant number of children who are chromosomally XY and who develop embryonic testes have external female genitalia at birth and therefore are raised as girls.[8] At puberty, their testes descend, their voices deepen, and their clitorises transform into penises.[9] Anthropologists have reported that the villagers have special terms for these individuals. They are called *guevodoche* (balls at twelve) or *machihembra* (male female).[10] An intersex condition of the same biological origin exists among several people in Papua, New Guinea. The term used to describe these children is *kwolu-aatmwol* (hermaphrodite), which signifies that at puberty the children will turn more into men than women. These children are treated as a third sex.[11]

Many Native American cultures recognize a third gender. These individuals are called two-spirit (formerly known as berdache) and enjoy a special status in their societies. They function as neither male nor female.[12] This third sex/gender status is also recognized in India, where intersex or transgender people are called *hijras*. *Hijras* are considered neither male nor female, but contain elements of both.[13] A third sex was also recognized in some ancient cultures. The Greek myths tell the story of Hermaphroditus, who became half-male and half-female when his body fused with the body of a nymph who fell in love with him.

Some religious texts also recognize the existence of intersex persons. For instance, the Talmud and the Tosefta, the Jewish texts that set forth rules governing relationships and behavior among Jews, contain detailed rules relating to the legal rights and responsibilities of intersex persons. These texts use the terms *androgynos* and *hermaphrodite* and define them both as "an animal or individual having both male and female characteristics and organs." Various views exist in the Jewish texts as to whether a hermaphrodite is of uncertain sex (either male or female), is of mixed sex (part male and part female), or is sui generis (neither male nor female). These texts regulate hermaphrodites' behavior in a variety of areas; depending on the circumstances, hermaphrodites may be treated as male, female, both, or neither.[14]

Other religious texts have also recognized the existence of intersex persons and have established marital rules applying to them. According to one religious tract, a hermaphrodite can contract marriage with a man or a woman depending on which sexual characteristics dominate. Hermaphrodites coming "closer to the male sex than the female that have the signs of virility, a beard and so forth, should be understood to be able to contract marriage with a woman."[15]

It also appears that early English law recognized three classifications of humans. According to Henry de Bracton's *On the Laws and Customs of England*, "Mankind may also be classified in another way: male, female, or hermaphrodite." Although the law recognized three classifications of humans, it did not recognize three classifications of laws governing human behavior. For legal purposes, "[a] hermaphrodite [wa]s classed with male or female according to the predominance of the sexual organs."[16] In the sixteenth century, Lord Coke, the renowned jurist, writing about the laws of succession in England, declared, "Every heire is either a male, or female, or an hermaphrodite, that is both male and female. And an hermaphrodite (which is also called Androgynus) shall be heire, either as male or female, according to that kind of the sexe which doth prevaile."[17]

These historical, religious, and cross-cultural examples illustrate that rules governing intersex persons have existed throughout history in various cultures and religions. Although the United States and other modern societies utilize a binary sex paradigm in which intersex persons are classified as either male or female for legal purposes, other societies have recognized a multisex or multigender model.

Understanding the Biological Determinants of Sex

The current legal approach to sex determination does not reflect the modern scientific understanding of sexual development. Medical experts recognize that many factors contribute to the determination of an individual's sex. According to medical professionals, the typical criteria of sex include genetic or chromosomal sex, gonadal sex, internal morphologic sex, genitalia, hormonal sex, phenotypic sex, assigned sex/gender of rearing, and self-identified sex.[18]

For most people, these factors are all congruent, and a person's status as a male or female is uncontroversial. For intersex persons, some of these factors may be incongruent, or an ambiguity within a factor may exist.

> The assumption is that there are two separate roads, one leading from XY chromosomes at conception to manhood, the other from XX chromosomes at conception to womanhood. The fact is that there are not two roads, but one road with a number of forks that turn in the male or female direction. Most of us turn in the same direction at each fork.[19]

The bodies of the millions of intersex people have taken a combination of male and female forks and have followed the road less traveled. These individuals have noncongruent sexual attributes. For these individuals, the law must determine which of the sexual factors will determine their sex and whether any one factor should be dispositive for all legal purposes.

Because the law often looks to the scientific community for guidance in determining how an individual's sex should be legally established, the complex nature of sexual differentiation must be understood. All human embryos are sexually undifferentiated during the first seven weeks after conception. At seven weeks, the embryonic reproductive system consists of a pair of gonads that can grow into either ovaries (female) or testes (male). The genital ridge that exists at this point can develop either into a clitoris and labia (female) or a penis and a scrotum (male). Two primordial duct systems also exist at this stage. The female ducts are called Mullerian ducts and develop into the uterus, fallopian tubes, and the upper part of the vagina if the fetus follows a female path. The male ducts are called Wolffian ducts and are the precursors of the seminal vesicles, vas deferens, and epididymis.[20]

At eight weeks, the fetus typically begins to follow one sex path. If the fetus has one X and one Y chromosome (46XY), it will start down the male path. At eight weeks, a "master switch" on the Y chromosome, called the testis-determining factor, signals the embryonic gonads to form into testes. The testes begin to produce male hormones. These male hormones prompt the gonads and genitalia to develop male features. Additionally, the testes produce a substance called Mullerian inhibiting factor, which causes the female Mullerian ducts to atrophy and be absorbed by the body, so that a female reproductive system is not created.[21]

Because the typical female fetus is 46XX and does not have a Y chromosome, the master switch that leads to the development of male organs is not turned on. The fetus continues on what is considered the default path, and in the thirteenth week the gonads start to transform into ovaries. Because no

testes exist to produce male hormones, the remainder of the sex system develops along a female path. During this time, the Wolffian (male) ducts shrivel
up. In other words, unless the body is triggered by hormonal production to
follow the male path, the fetus will normally develop as a female. Therefore,
although chromosomes generally control the hormones that are produced, it
is actually the hormones that directly affect sexual development.[22]

To summarize, if the typical path is followed, males and females will
have the following sexual features:

	Males	*Females*
Genetic/chromosomal sex	XY	XX
Gonadal sex (reproductive sex glands)	testes	ovaries
External morphologic sex	penis and scrotum	clitoris and labia
Internal morphologic sex	seminal vesicles, prostate	vagina, uterus, and fallopian tubes
Hormonal sex	primarily androgens	primarily estrogens
Phenotypic sex (secondary sex characteristics)	facial and chest hair	breasts
Assigned sex/gender of rearing	male	female
Self-identified sex	male	female

Two circumstances may lead to an intersex condition: (1) one or more
features may differ from the typical criteria for that factor; or (2) one or more
factors may be incongruent with the other factors.

Ambiguity within a Factor

Chromosomal ambiguity. Certain individuals have chromosomes that differ
from the typical pattern of either XY or XX. Doctors have discovered people
with a variety of combinations, including XXX, XXY, XXXY, XYY, XYYY,
XYYYY, and XO.[23]

Gonadal ambiguity. Some intersex persons do not have typical ovaries
or testes. Instead, they have "streak" gonads that do not appear to function as
either ovaries or testes. Others have ovotestes, a combination of both male
and female gonads. Still others have one ovary and one testis.[24]

External morphologic sex. Some individuals' external genitalia are neither
clearly male nor clearly female. In addition, some women have clitoral hyper-

trophy, a clitoris larger than the typical clitoris, that may more closely resemble a penis, and is sometimes accompanied by an internal vagina.[25]

Internal morphologic sex. Some individuals have incomplete internal sex organs or a complete absence of an internal sex organ. In addition, some individuals are born with a combination of male and female internal organs.[26]

Hormonal sex. The male hormones are referred to as androgens. The female hormones are estrogen and progesterone. Although they are referred to as male and female hormones, all human sex hormones are shared by men and women. Typically, men and women have hormones of each type, but the levels of production and reception of each hormone are highly variable among all individuals. Different medical disorders further influence levels of hormone production and reception.[27]

Phenotypic sex. Individuals may have various combinations of incongruent phenotypic characteristics. In other words, an individual may have characteristics typically associated with a male (heavy facial hair) and characteristics typically associated with a female (developed breasts).[28]

Assigned sex/gender of rearing. Although it occurs rarely, some parents have raised their child as a gender other than the sex assigned by the medical attendant at birth. In addition, in some circumstances, doctors have recommended that a child be raised as the sex different from the one assigned at birth.[29]

Self-identified sex. Self-identified sex refers to how individuals would identify themselves. Some individuals do not consider themselves to be either male or female; they identify themselves as a third sex.

Ambiguity among Factors

Some individuals have an incongruence among the factors because of a sexual differentiation disorder. In other words, some factors may be clearly male, some may be clearly female, and others may be a mixture of the two. Incongruity among factors can result from a number of disorders and circumstances, including chromosomal sex disorders, gonadal sex disorders, internal organ anomalies, external organ anomalies, hormonal disorders, gender identity disorders, and surgical creation of an intersex condition.

Chromosomal sex disorders: Klinefelter syndrome and Turner syndrome. Klinefelter syndrome, which affects approximately one in five hundred to one thousand "males," is a condition in which a mostly phenotypic male does not fall neatly into the XY chromosome complement. Such individuals will typically have two or more X chromosomes. The testes, and often the penis, are smaller than in unaffected XY males.[30]

Typically, a diagnosis is not made before puberty, because no easily identifiable sign exists prior to the onset of puberty. The swelling of the breasts (gynecomastia) that occurs in adolescence is typically the first sign of the existence of this intersex condition. Most individuals report a male psychosexual orientation. Many take supplemental testosterone, which further results in a male phenotype (e.g., facial hair).[31]

Disorders of chromosomal sex also appear in phenotypic females. Turner syndrome affects approximately one in five thousand newborn females. Individuals typically will have an XO chromosomal pattern, not falling neatly into the XX, XY binary system, and bilateral "streak" gonads (unformed and nonfunctioning gonads), instead of clearly defined ovaries or testes. The absence of complete ovaries or testes in utero means that the fetus has little exposure to either female or male hormones. In the absence of male hormones, the fetus will follow the female path.[32]

Individuals with Turner syndrome are typically shorter than XX females. They have female-appearing genitalia, but little breast development in the absence of exogenous estrogen administration. Because women with Turner syndrome have a uterus, with proper hormonal treatment they are able to menstruate and carry a child to term. The egg must be donated by another woman because women with Turner syndrome lack ovaries and eggs.[33]

Gonadal sex disorders: Swyer syndrome. Pure gonadal dysgenesis is a condition sometimes referred to as Swyer syndrome. This syndrome is similar to Turner syndrome in that individuals with this syndrome will have only streak gonads. In contrast to Turner syndrome, in which a chromosome is missing (XO), individuals with Swyer syndrome have XY (male) chromosomes. Although Swyer syndrome individuals have a Y chromosome, the chromosome may be missing the sex-determining segment. Without this segment, the embryo cannot develop testes, and, as a result, the masculinizing hormones are also missing. In the absence of the masculinizing hormones, the fetus will take the "default" female path and will develop a uterus, but will not have any ovaries.[34]

Typically, this condition is not apparent at birth, and the child will be raised as a girl. The syndrome is generally diagnosed at puberty when the absence of menstruation and breast enlargement causes suspicion. Individuals with Swyer syndrome are able to carry a child to term in the same way that individuals with Turner syndrome can carry a child to term.[35]

Internal organ anomalies—persistent Mullerian duct syndrome. Individuals with this syndrome have internal organs that are typical of males as well as females. These individuals have a male chromosomal pattern and therefore develop testes that secrete androgen, but for some reason fail to secrete anti-

Mullerian hormones. The androgens cause the fetus to follow the male path and develop the external appearance and internal organs of a male. Fallopian tubes and a uterus are also formed, however, because the anti-Mullerian hormones are not acting to inhibit this development. This condition is generally not diagnosed at birth. Individuals with this syndrome are reared as males and typically self-identify as males.[36]

External organ anomalies: Hermaphroditism. Individuals who have ambiguous external genitalia (neither clearly male nor female) are commonly referred to as hermaphrodites. Hermaphrodites are often classified into three categories: true hermaphrodites, male pseudohermaphrodites, and female pseudohermaphrodites. A "true hermaphrodite" has some ovarian and some testicular tissue. So-called true hermaphrodites have either one ovary and one testis, two ovotestes (a combination of an ovary and testis in a single gonad), or some combination thereof (e.g., one ovotestes and one ovary). The exact incidence of true hermaphroditic conditions is unknown, but is rarer than many of the other intersex conditions. A male pseudohermaphrodite has testes and no ovaries and some aspect of female genitalia. A female pseudohermaphrodite has ovaries and no testes and some aspect of male genitalia.[37]

A variety of disorders can lead to hermaphroditic conditions, which are named according to their etiologies (e.g., partial androgen insensitivity syndrome [PAIS] or congenital adrenal hyperplasia [CAH]) unless the etiology of the condition remains unknown.

Hormonal disorders: Androgen insensitivity syndrome, 5-alpha-reductase deficiency, congenital adrenal hyperplasia, progestin-induced virilization. Androgen insensitivity syndrome (AIS) affects approximately one out of every twenty thousand genetic males. AIS can be either complete (CAIS) or partial (PAIS). Individuals with AIS are born with XY chromosomes and normally functioning testes, which would otherwise suggest a normal male fetus. Individuals with CAIS, however, have a receptor defect and are unable to process the androgens produced by the testes.[38]

Because the body cannot process the androgens, the fetus will follow the default path of female development. External female genitalia will form. No internal reproductive organs will form because the Mullerian inhibiting factor produced by the testes will inhibit the growth of the uterus and fallopian tubes. The vagina will be shorter than in the typical woman (or may only be a dimple) and will end blindly because there are no female internal reproductive organs with which to connect.[39]

Unlike people with several other intersex conditions, individuals with CAIS typically are identified as "normal" females at birth, because externally they are indistinguishable from XX females. The disorder is sometimes diagnosed in infancy because of inguinal hernias that contain the testes. Often, however, CAIS is not diagnosed until after the onset of puberty as a result of a failure to menstruate. At puberty, breasts will form because of the estrogen produced by the testes. Until puberty, many CAIS women have no reason to suspect that they are not XX females.[40]

In PAIS, an XY individual with testes will be partially receptive to androgens. Unlike individuals with CAIS, individuals with PAIS may fall anywhere along a spectrum from an almost completely male external appearance and male self-identity to a completely female external appearance and female identity. The degree to which the individual has male features depends on the degree to which the receptors can process the male hormones the testes produce.[41]

The external phenotype of PAIS individuals will initially be determined by the degree of androgen reception in the body. Thus, a PAIS individual may have a phallus resembling either a clitoris or a penis, the labia may be fused, and during adolescence breast development may occur because of the conversion of testosterone produced by the gonads to estradiol, an estrogen compound.[42]

5-alpha-reductase deficiency is similar to the androgen resistance syndromes. Individuals have XY chromosomes and testes, but appear phenotypically female at birth. This condition results from the body's failure to convert testosterone to dihydrotestosterone, the more powerful form of androgen responsible for the development of male external genitalia. Despite a female appearance during childhood, by the onset of puberty, the body will masculinize. The testes descend, the voice deepens, muscle mass substantially increases, and a "functional" penis capable of ejaculating develops from what was thought to be the clitoris. The prostate, however, remains small, and beard growth is scanty. Although the individual is often raised as a girl, at puberty psychosexual orientation typically becomes male. In other words, virilization will occur at puberty in the absence of medical intervention.[43]

Individuals with CAH have XX chromosomes, ovaries, and other female internal structures, but they have a more masculinized external appearance or demeanor because of an abundance of androgen production in utero. CAH occurs in approximately one out of five to fifteen thousand births. Both the chromosomes and gonads of CAH individuals are indistinguishable from unaffected females. The genitals, however, may be ambiguous and may more closely resemble male genitalia.[44]

Some CAH individuals have been identified as males at birth and are reared as boys, despite the presence of XX chromosomes and ovaries. In other cases, the masculinization that occurred during prenatal life is interrupted at birth, and the child is surgically and hormonally treated and reared as a girl. These girls often have characteristics that are popularly stereotyped as masculine.[45]

Progestin-induced virilization (PIV) is similar to CAH. PIV is caused by exposure of an XX infant in utero to progestin that has been taken by the mother during pregnancy. Like individuals with CAH, PIV women will frequently have clitoral hypertrophy.[46]

Gender identity disorder. Some individuals may be seemingly harmonious in all of the first six factors (chromosomes, gonads, external and internal morphology, hormones, and phenotype), but do not identify themselves with the sex associated with these factors. These individuals are often labeled *transsexuals* or persons with gender dysphoria or gender identity disorder (GID). Science has yet to definitely isolate a biological common denominator that causes these individuals to feel transgendered. A recent study, however, has determined that a section of the brain area essential for sexual behavior is larger in men than in women and that the brain structures of genetic males who self-identify as transsexuals are more similar to female than male brain structures.[47] Some transsex individuals choose to undergo hormonal treatment and/or surgery, so that their bodies comport with their sexual identity, while other transsex persons do not choose to undergo such treatment.

Transsexualism is not necessarily related to sexual orientation. Some transsex persons identify themselves as gays or lesbians while others identify themselves as heterosexuals. In other words, a male-to-female transsex person who has undergone surgery to acquire female genitalia may still prefer to have sex with another female, and a female-to-male transsex person may still prefer to have sex with another male.

Surgical creation of an intersex condition. In addition to cases in which intersex individuals may be assigned a sex that does not comport with their own sexual identity, some persons have had their sexual features altered either purposefully or accidentally. For example, some individuals have had their penises removed or reduced at a young age because they were mistakenly identified as females, and the penis was considered an oversized clitoris that required reduction. In addition, some cases of an accident that destroyed a boy's penis have been reported. Although these cases are rare, they illustrate the complex nature of sexual identity formation.[48]

The most famous surgical alteration case involves a male whose penis was accidentally destroyed when he was eight months old and undergoing a circumcision. The doctors recommended that his genitals be reconstructed to appear female and that he be raised as a girl even though all other sexual factors were congruent and were male. The doctors also recommended that his "history" as a male be hidden from him.[49]

This surgical alteration case made headlines in 1973 when the doctors involved in the surgical alteration reported that the child and the parents had successfully adapted to the sex/gender alteration. Thus, texts in sociology, psychology, and women's studies were rewritten to argue that "this dramatic case . . . provides strong support . . . that conventional patterns of masculine and feminine behavior can be altered. It also casts doubt on the theory that major sex differences, psychological as well as anatomical, are immutably set by the genes at conception."[50]

For more than twenty years, the scientific literature continued to report that the surgical alteration was successful and the child's sexual identity was female. This case made headlines again in 1997 when Milton Diamond and Keith Sigmundson reported in the *Archives of Pediatrics and Adolescent Medicine* that the boy who was turned into a girl was now living as a man.[51]

According to the Diamond and Sigmundson report, David had always thought of himself as different from other girls. As a child, he preferred "boy" toys and preferred to mimic his father's rather than his mother's behavior. He also preferred to urinate in a standing position although he had no penis. Because of the cognitive dissonance, David (who was called Brenda during his life as a girl) often had thoughts of suicide.

At twelve, Brenda was put on an estrogen regimen. She rebelled against the regimen and often refused to take the medication. At fourteen, Brenda confessed to a doctor that she had suspected that she was a boy since second grade. At that point, the doctors agreed with Brenda that she should be remasculinized.

At age fourteen, Brenda became David and returned to living as a male. David received male hormone shots and a mastectomy. He underwent surgery to reconstruct a phallus at ages fifteen and sixteen. David was eventually accepted as a boy by his peers. He married and helped raise his wife's children. Sadly, David committed suicide in 2004 after his identical twin brother also committed suicide.

David was not born an intersex person. He became an intersex person when doctors removed his penis, constructed external female genitalia and administered female hormones. Despite this intervention, David always felt that he was not a female.

The significance of this and other similar reports is that they exemplify the difficulties law and medicine must confront in defining sex. At birth, David's sex factors were congruent and were male. After the original intervention, he was turned into an intersex person with male chromosomes and ambiguous genitalia, but he was treated by society as if he were female. Once he decided to live as a male, he had his body remasculinized to the extent possible, and society and legal institutions recognized him as a male.

The reports about David and other intersex persons, whose self-identities do not conform to their assigned genders, have forced the medical and psychiatric communities to question their long-held beliefs about sexual identity formation. Just as current scientific studies have caused the scientific communities to question their beliefs about gender identity formation, the legal community needs to more carefully question its assumptions about the legal definitions of the terms *male* and *female*.

Legal Definitions of Male and Female

Although scholars in law and other disciplines are beginning to recognize the complex and nonbinary nature of sexual categories, some legal institutions have been slow to acknowledge these developments. Traditional jurisprudence requires that individuals be classified into discrete and often binary categories, even though such categories do not reflect reality. Legal scholars have criticized this traditional binary system for its failure to adequately protect individuals in a society in which people do not fall neatly into two opposite classifications. The inadequacies of a bijurisprudence system have been exposed in a variety of areas including race, sexual orientation, and disability law. In addition, legal scholars have begun to criticize the bisexual/bigender system that limits the sex and gender categories to only male and female.

Just as some scholars in the multiracial discourse are calling for a rejection of binary categories that measure race by rules like the one-drop rule, but minimize the more important factor of racial self-identification, legal scholars and institutions must determine whether sexual categories should be limited to the two traditional classifications of male and female or whether sex categorization should be expanded to include intersexuality as a sex category. Even if traditional notions of justice require the rejection of multisexual categories in favor of a binary system, how the categories male and female are defined must be reexamined. Legal institutions must explore whether the law should continue to rely on traditional sex criteria such as chromosomes, genitalia, and gonads to define a person's legal sex or whether these factors should be subordinated to self-identified sex.

The remainder of this chapter analyzes the sex determination issue that has been litigated the most frequently: how a person's legal sex is determined for purposes of marriage. Courts first began to struggle with this issue in the

1970s, when only a handful of cases were litigated.[52] During the past decade, the number of lawsuits determining the legal sex of a transsex person has increased dramatically in the United States and other countries.[53] Thus far, no clear consensus has been reached about how the law will determine a person's legal sex for purposes of marriage.

Most states have adopted marriage statutes that limit marriage to one man and one woman, or two people of the opposite sex.[54] Even in states in which no legislation exists, most courts assume that a valid marriage requires a union of one man and one woman.[55] Originally, this presumption was based on the courts' belief that the "marriage relationship exists for the purpose of begetting offspring" or that heterosexual intercourse is an essential element on which the family is built.[56] Given the number of legal marriages between people who cannot procreate or do not intend to procreate, the current intent of these statutes appears to be to ensure that the state does not sanction gay and lesbian marriages.

Although a majority of states have adopted statutes that either define a marriage as a union between a male and a female or prohibit marriages between individuals of the same sex, none of these statutes define or attempt to define how to determine a person's legal sex. The Defense of Marriage Act also defines marriage at the federal level as a "legal union between one man and one woman as husband and wife, and the word spouse refers only to a person of the opposite sex who is a husband or a wife."[57] When Congress adopted DOMA, however, it also failed to define these terms.

Because legislators have failed to define the terms *male* and *female* or *man* and *woman,* courts in the United States and other countries have been forced to define these terms when two people who are arguably of the same sex seek a marriage license or when someone seeks to void a marriage based on the legislative prohibition against same-sex marriages. In these cases, the courts have split sharply over how to define the terms. Most of the older cases and some of the more recent cases have relied solely on biological criteria at birth and have ignored self-identified sex and medical or surgical intervention. Some courts, however, have given more weight to scientific advances about gender identity formation and the importance of an individual's self-identified sex.

Since 1970, when a court was first asked to determine the legal sex of a transsex person for purposes of marriage, until the turn of the century, almost every court that addressed this issue determined that transsex persons could not marry in the gender role that comported with their self-identified sex. Courts in Australia,[58] Canada,[59] England,[60] South Africa,[61] Singapore,[62] New

York,[63] Ohio,[64] and Texas[65] ruled that transsex persons could marry only in the gender role that they had been assigned at birth. In addition, the European Court of Human Rights consistently held that countries that refused to allow transsex persons to marry in their self-identified gender roles did not violate the Convention for the Protection of Human Rights and Fundamental Freedoms.[66] During this same time, only three jurisdictions—New Zealand,[67] New Jersey,[68] and California[69]—declared that transsex persons could marry in their self-identified gender role.

The earlier cases that ruled that transsex persons are legally the sex assigned to them at birth did so based on a number of questionable grounds. Some relied on a combination of biological sex indicators, including chromosomes, gonads, and genitalia.[70] In these cases, the courts relied on the status of the sex indicators at birth and did not consider any medical intervention or surgical alteration that had occurred. Other courts focused on the transsex person's inability to beget offspring as a proper justification for finding the marriage invalid.[71] Finally, some courts decided that surgical intervention is only capable of creating "artificial" sex attributes that courts do not have to recognize.[72]

On the other hand, the earlier cases that ruled that transsex persons could marry in their self-identified sex roles focused more on psychological and social sex aspects, rather than the biological sex attributes present at birth. These courts rejected the rulings that heavily relied on chromosomes, genitalia, and gonads and instead emphasized the overriding importance of social and psychological factors.[73]

Beginning in the mid-1990s, a number of occurrences led to an increase in appellate courts rendering opinions on this topic. First, transsex and intersex activists formed organizations that provided information about these issues and increased public awareness of the topic. Second, the issues at stake in the more recent cases have increased. The earlier sex determination cases were brought primarily to determine whether the parties should be granted an annulment or a divorce. Recent court rulings have had the potential to affect a person's right to be a legal parent[74] or the ability to obtain large sums of money.[75] The increased stakes involved have resulted in more trial court opinions being appealed. Finally, the scientific research on sexual identity formation has called into question some long-held assumptions about the roots of sexual identity formation.[76]

Although many courts have started to rely on scientific studies and focus on the importance of psychological sex, a number of courts still define sex solely in terms of chromosomes or some combination of chromosomes, gonads, and genitalia. During the past decade, courts in Texas,[77] Kansas,[78] Florida,[79] Ohio,[80] and England[81] have rejected self-identity as a proper determinant of a transsex person's legal sex. On the other hand, during this same time, courts in California,[82] Maryland,[83] Australia,[84] New Zealand,[85] and the European Court of Human Rights[86] have adopted a more humane approach and have ruled that self-identified sex should be a critical determinant of legal sex.

Courts That Reject Self-Identification as a Proper Indicator of Legal Sex

The recent cases that have rejected self-identified sex in favor of biological factors have not provided an extensive analysis of the literature available on sex determination. For example, the Texas Court of Appeals relied on religious rhetoric and ruled that when God created Christie Littleton, a male-to-female transsexual, God created a man that neither the law nor the medical community could turn into a woman. Therefore, the court ruled that as a matter of law, Christie was a male. Although the court recognized that its decision raised profound philosophical, metaphysical, and policy concerns, it did not address these concerns, but instead ruled that because Christie had been born with a "male body," she was legally still a male.[87]

Three years later, when the Kansas Supreme Court was asked to determine whether a male-to-female transsexual could be declared a legal wife, the court ruled as a matter of law that transgender persons remain the sex that they were assigned at birth. Although the Kansas Supreme Court had extensive scientific evidence before it that had convinced the Kansas Court of Appeals to adopt a multifactor test, the Kansas Supreme Court reversed the court of appeals and instead chose to use *Webster's New Twentieth Century Dictionary*'s definitions of male and female. According to the dictionary and the court, *male* is defined as "designating or of the sex that fertilizes the ovum and begets offspring: opposed to female." *Female* is defined as "designating or of the sex that produces ova and bears offspring: opposed to male."[88] Courts in Florida[89] and Ohio[90] have followed the Kansas approach and also have relied on the dictionary to determine legal sex. Therefore the implication in Kansas, Florida, and Ohio is that people incapable of begetting or bearing offspring are neither males nor females.

Courts That Accept Self-Identification as a Proper Indicator of Legal Sex

In contrast to the few courts that have relied on one or only a few biological sex indicators, most of the courts that have considered this issue during the past decade have adopted a multifactor and interdisciplinary approach to determining legal sex. Most courts, including trial courts in California[91] and Florida,[92] the court of appeals in Kansas,[93] the court of appeals of Maryland,[94] the family courts in Australia[95] and New Zealand,[96] and the European Court of Human Rights[97] have rejected the older narrow approach. Instead, these courts have reviewed medical and psychological evidence and have considered the long-term legal and societal effects of their rulings.

Many of these courts have also emphasized the importance of considering medical and scientific advances, rather than relying on historical, dictionary, or religious definitions of male and female. For example, the court of appeals of Kansas emphasized that sex should be determined by considering genetic sex, gonadal sex, internal morphologic sex, external morphologic sex, hormonal sex, phenotypic sex, assigned sex and gender of rearing, and sexual identity.[98] Courts that base their determinations on medical and scientific evidence that proves that sex is multifactored typically find that legal sex should comport with self-identified sex.

The time at which the sex determination is made will also be critical. The cases that reject medical and surgical alterations typically rule that sex is determined at birth and cannot be changed, unless a mistake occurred when the sex was recorded on the birth certificate.[99] On the other hand, most courts have held that a person's legal sex for purposes of marriage should be determined at the time the marriage license is issued, rather than at the time of birth.[100] For transsex persons who have undergone surgical and hormonal treatment, the time frame that the court uses will be critical. If sex features at birth are dispositive, transsex individuals will be treated as the sex that does not comport with their self-identities. If, instead, sexual features at the time of the marriage control sex determination, their legal sex will comport with their self-identities because after surgical and hormonal intervention, the only biological sex indicator that would be opposite to their self-identities would be their chromosomes.

Finally, and more important, these courts have considered the effects of their rulings on transgender persons and society. Not only have a number of courts ruled that transsex persons can marry in their self-identified sex roles, but the European Court of Human Rights has ruled that a nation that denies transsex persons this right violates the European Convention on Human Rights. In 2002 the European Court of Human Rights refused to follow a series of rulings in which it had upheld a country's sex determination that was based solely on biological criteria. Instead, it reversed itself and ruled that member states that refuse to allow postoperative transsex persons to change their official documents to indicate their postoperative sex violate articles 8 and 12, which protect the right to privacy and the fundamental right to marry.[101]

Conclusion

Transgender individuals do not fit conveniently into binary systems; they cannot easily be categorized as either males or females. Many legal institutions have imposed their need to maintain clear distinctions between the sexes on persons who do not fit neatly into distinct groups.

Until recently, the medical community also recommended that intersex persons be surgically and/or hormonally altered at an early age so that they have the physical appearance of only one sex. This recommendation is based on the questionable assumption that obviously intersex individuals would be so scorned by society that they would suffer severe humiliation and psychological trauma. This assumption ignores a substantial body of case histories, compiled primarily between 1930 and 1960, before surgical intervention became the norm, that describe well-adjusted intersex persons. Early surgical intervention to alter intersex persons so that they appear to be clearly male or female is currently being seriously questioned by some intersex individuals and by some medical experts.

Surgical alteration of intersex persons is also based on the assumption that sexual identity can be manipulated easily. Recent medical studies now suggest that sexual identity cannot necessarily be medically controlled via surgery and hormones. How sexual identity is established is as yet unclear.

The medical community is learning that sex and gender cannot easily be defined by biological factors alone. Just as the medical system's binary sex categories that de-emphasize self-identity are now being questioned by medical authorities, legal institutions must also examine how the law should define sex. Legal authorities must determine whether a binary legal system that traditionally categorizes people according to their chromosomes or the appearance of their genitalia at birth is appropriate.

If legal institutions choose to regulate behavior based on a person's sex, they must clearly define their terms. If they insist on clinging to a binary system, they must find a way to define male and female so that the rights and obligations of intersex persons are clearly delineated.

Society, the medical community, and the law must acknowledge the existence of intersexuality. Currently, intersexuality is often viewed as a shameful secret to be hidden and borne in silent suffering. "To share such a secret is to invite ridicule and rejection; to keep such a secret condemns one to a life of loneliness and isolation."[102] The law, by clinging to a binary system that blindly ignores the existence of intersex persons and the importance of self-identity, reinforces the perception that intersexuality is unacceptable. It also ignores the reality of intersexuality. The law should not continue to force intersex persons further into the deepest recesses of their closets by failing to acknowledge their existences and their self-identities.

Notes

For a more detailed discussion of the issues discussed in this chapter, see Julie A. Greenberg, "Defining Male and Female: Intersexuality and the Collision between Law and Biology," *Arizona Law Review* 41 (1999): 266. This chapter summarizes and provides an update of the issues first discussed in the Arizona article.

1. A recent survey of the medical literature from the last half of the twentieth century estimates that the number of people who deviate from the sexually dimorphic norm may be as high as 2 percent of live births. See Melanie Blackless, Anthony Charuvastra, Amanda Derryck, Anne Fausto-Sterling, Karl Lauzanne, and Ellen Lee, "How Sexually Dimorphic Are We?" *American Journal of Human Biology* 12 (2000): 151.

2. John Money, *Sex Errors of the Body and Related Syndromes: A Guide to Counseling Children, Adolescents, and Their Families*, 2nd ed. (Baltimore, MD: Brooks, 1994).

3. This chapter focuses on the marital implications of sex determination because of the 1,049 federal rights linked to marital status and the recent judicial and legislative developments on same-sex marriage. For a detailed discussion of the other legal implications of sex determination, including sex indicators on official documents, employment discrimination, equal protection violations, the ability to participate in athletic competitions as a female, the obligation to serve in the military, and liability under some criminal statutes, see Julie A. Greenberg, "Defining Male and Female: Intersexuality and the Collision between Law and Biology," *Arizona Law Review* 41 (1999): 266, 274. For a thorough analysis of the constitutional implications of these rulings, see Julie A. Greenberg and Marybeth Herald, "You Can't Take It with You: Constitutional Consequences of Interstate Gender-Identity Rulings," *Washington Law Review* 80 (2005): 819.

4. Alice Domurat Dreger, "'Ambiguous Sex'—or Ambivalent Medicine? Ethical Issues in the Treatment of Intersexuality," *Hastings Center Report* 28 (1998): 24, 27–28.

5. Ibid.

6. Ibid.

7. For a comprehensive anthropological and historical perspective, see Gilbert Herdt, ed., *Third Sex, Third Gender: Beyond Sexual Dimorphism in Culture and History* (New York: Zone, 1996).

8. Julianne Imperato-McGinley et al., "Steroid 5-Alpha-Reductase Deficiency in Man: An Inherited Form of Male Pseudohermaphroditism," *Science*, December 27, 1974, 1213.

9. Ibid.

10. Ibid.

11. Gilbert Herdt, "Mistaken Sex: Culture, Biology, and the Third Sex in New Guinea," in Herdt, *Third Sex, Third Gender*, 420.

12. Francisco Valdes, "Queers, Sissies, Dykes, and Tomboys: Deconstructing the Conflation of Sex, Gender, and Sexual Orientation in Euro-American Law and Society," *California Law Review* 83 (1995): 1, 102.

13. Serena Nanda, "The Hijras of India: Cultural and Individualized Third Gender Role," in *The Many Faces of Homosexuality: Anthropological Approaches to Homosexual Behavior*, ed. Evelyn Blackwood (New York: Harrington Park, 1986), 35.

14. Rabbi Alfred Cohen, "Tumtum and Androgynous," *Journal of Halacha and Contemporary Society* (1999), http://www.daat.ac.il/daat/english/journal/cohen-1htm.

15. Henry A. Finlay, "Sexual Identity and the Law of Nullity," *Australian Law Journal* 54 (1981): 115, 120n51.

16. Henry de Bracton, *On the Laws and Customs of England*, trans. Samuel E. Thorne, vol. 2 (Cambridge, MA: Harvard University Press, 1968), 31.

17. E. Coke, *The First Part of the Institutes on the Laws of England*, vol. 1, Institutes 8.a (1st American ed. 1812; 16th European ed. 1812).

18. Money, *Sex Errors of the Body and Related Syndromes*, 4.

19. John Money and Patricia Tucker, *Sexual Signatures: On Being a Man or a Woman* (Boston: Little, Brown, 1975), 6.

20. Robert Pool, *Eve's Rib: Searching for the Biological Roots of Sex Differences* (New York: Crown, 1994), 67.

21. Money, *Sex Errors of the Body and Related Syndromes*, 25.

22. Pool, *Eve's Rib*, 68.

23. Ibid., 70–71.

24. Anne Fausto-Sterling, "The Five Sexes: Why Male and Female Are Not Enough," *Sciences*, March–April 1993, 20–21.

25. Money, *Sex Errors of the Body and Related Syndromes*, 49–57.

26. Ibid., 31–33.

27. Ibid.

28. Ibid.

29. Jenni Millbank, "When Is a Girl a Boy? RE A (a child)," *Australian Journal of Family Law* 9 (1995): 173; Fayek Ghabrial and Saa M. Girgis, "Reorientation of Sex: Report of Two Cases," *International Journal of Fertility* 7 (1962): 249, 252; Bernardo Ochoa, "Trauma of the External Genitalia in Children: Amputation of the Penis and Emasculation," *Journal of Urology* 160 (1998): 1116; Milton Diamond and H. Keith Sigmundson, "Sex Reassignment at Birth: A Long Term Review and Clinical Implications," *Archives of Pediatrics and Adolescent Medicine* 151 (1997): 298.

30. Money, *Sex Errors of the Body and Related Syndromes*, 13.

31. Ibid.

32. Ibid., 14–15.

33. Ibid.

34. Ibid., 22.

35. Ibid.

36. Ibid., 31.

37. Ibid., 31–33.

38. Pool, *Eve's Rib*, 68–69.

39. Money, *Sex Errors of the Body and Related Syndromes*, 29.

40. Ibid.

41. Garry L. Warne, *Complete Androgen Insensitivity Syndrome* (Victoria, Australia: Royal Children's Hospital, 1997), 7.

42. Ibid.

43. Money, *Sex Errors of the Body and Related Syndromes,* 44–45; Imperato-McGinley et al., "Steroid 5 Alpha-Reductase Deficiency," 1213.

44. Money, *Sex Errors of the Body and Related Syndromes,* 172.

45. Ibid.

46. Ibid.

47. Frank Kruijver, Jiang-Ning Zhou, Chris Pool, Michel Hofman, Louis Gooren, and Dick Swaab, "Male to Female Transsexual Individuals Have Female Neuron Numbers in the Central Subdivision of the Bed Nucleus of the Stria Terminalis," *Journal of Clinical Endocrinology and Metabolism* 85 (2000): 2034.

48. See, for example, Ochoa, "Trauma of the External Genitalia in Children," 1116; Diamond and Sigmundson, "Sex Reassignment at Birth," 298.

49. Diamond and Sigmundson, "Sex Reassignment at Birth," 299.

50. Ibid., 303 (quoting *Time,* January 8, 1973).

51. Ibid., 298–304.

52. See, for example, *Corbett v. Corbett,* [1970] 2 All E.R. 33; *M.T. v. J.T.,* 355 A.2d 204 (N.J. 1976); *B. v. B.* 355 N.Y.S.2d 712 (N.Y. Sup. Ct. 1974); *Anonymous v. Anonymous,* 325 N.Y.S.2d 499 (N.Y. Sup. Ct. 1971); *In Re Ladrach,* 513 N.E.2d 828 (Ohio Prob. Ct. 1987); *In Marriage of C. and D. (Falsely called C.)* (1979) 35 F.L.R. 340; *W. v. W.,* [1976] 2 SALR 308.

53. See, for example, *Attorney General v. Otahuhu Family Court,* [1991] NZLR 603; *Lim Ying v. Hiok Kian Ming Eric,* [1991] SLR Lexis 184; *Littleton v. Prange,* 9 S.W. 3d 223 (Tex. App. 1999); *In re Estate of Gardiner* 22 P.3d 1086 (Kan. Ct. App. 2001) *aff'd in part, rev'd in part,* 42 P.3d 120 (Kan. 2002); *Kantaras v. Kantaras,* 884 So.2d 155 (Fla. Dist. Ct. App. 2004); *In re Heilig,* 816 A.2d 68 (Md. 2003); *Bellinger v. Bellinger,* [2002] UKHL 21; *I. v. The United Kingdom* [Eur. Ct. of H.R. 2002]; *Goodwin v. The United Kingdom* [Eur. Ct. of H.R. 2002]; *Attorney General v. Kevin,* (2003) 172 F.L.R 300; *In re Nash,* 2003 WL 23097095 (Ohio Ct. App. December 31, 2003); *Vecchione v. Vecchione* Civ. No. 96D003769, reported in *L.A. Daily Journal,* November 26, 1997.

54. For a discussion of these statutes, see Greenberg, "Defining Male and Female," 297–98.

55. See Greenberg, "Defining Male and Female," 298–99. The only state supreme court in the United States to mandate same-sex marriage is Massachusetts. See *Goodridge v. Department of Public Health,* 798 N.E.2d 941 (Mass. 2003).

56. *Corbett v. Corbett; B. v. B.*

57. *Defense of Marriage Act,* Pub. L. No. 104–199, 110 Stat. 2419 (1996).

58. *In Marriage of C. and D. (Falsely called C.).*

59. *M v. M,* 42 R.F.L. (2d) 55 (1984).

60. *Corbett v. Corbett.*

61. *W. v. W.*

62. *Lim Ying v. Hiok Kian Ming Eric.*

63. *B. v. B.; Anonymous v. Anonymous.*

64. *In Re Ladrach.*

65. *Littleton v. Prange.*

66. *The Cossey Case* [Eur. Ct. of H.R. 1991] 2 FLR 492; *The Rees Case* [Eur. Ct. of H.R. 1987] 2 FLR 111.

67. *Attorney General v. Otahuhu Family Court.*

68. *M.T. v. J.T.*

69. *Vecchione v. Vecchione.*

70. *Corbett v. Corbett.*

71. See, for example, *B. v. B.*

72. See, for example, *Corbett v. Corbett.*

73. See, for example, *M.T. v. J.T.; Attorney General v. Otahuhu Family Court.*

74. See, for example, *Kantaras v. Kantaras; In re Marriage of Simmons,* 825 N.E.2d 303 (Ill. App. Ct. 2005).

75. See, for example, *Littleton v. Prange; In re Estate of Gardiner* 22 P.3d 1086 (Kan. Ct. App. 2001) *aff'd in part, rev'd in part,* 42 P.3d 120 (Kan. 2002).

76. See, for example, William Reiner and John Gearhart, "Discordant Sexual Identity in Some Genetic Males with Cloacal Extrophy Assigned to Female Sex at Birth," *New England Journal of Medicine* 350 (2004): 333.

77. *Littleton v. Prange.*

78. *In re Estate of Gardiner,* 42 P.3d 120 (Kan. 2002).

79. *Kantaras v. Kantaras.*

80. *In re Nash,* 2003 WL 23097095 (Ohio Ct. App. December 31, 2003).

81. *Bellinger v. Bellinger.* This decision was reversed by the Gender Recognition Act, 2004, c. 7 (Eng.).

82. *Vecchione v. Vecchione.*

83. *In re Heilig.*

84. *Attorney General v. Kevin.*

85. *Attorney General v. Otahuhu Family Court.*

86. *I. v. The United Kingdom; Goodwin v. The United Kingdom.*

87. *Littleton v. Prange.*

88. *In re Estate of Gardiner,* 42 P.3d 120, 135 (Kan. 2002).

89. *Kantaras v. Kantaras.*

90. *In re Nash.*

91. *Vecchione v. Vecchione.*

92. *Kantaras v. Kantaras,* Case No. 98–5375CA (Circuit Court of the Sixth Judicial Circuit, Paseo County, FL, February 19, 2003) *rev'd* 884 So.2d 155 (Fla. Dist. Ct. App. 2004).

93. *In re Estate of Gardiner,* 22 P.3d 1086 (Kan. Ct. App 2001) *aff'd in part, rev'd in part,* 42 P.3d 120 (Kan. 2002).

94. *In re Heilig.*

95. *Attorney General v. Kevin.*

96. *Attorney General v. Otahuhu Family Court.*

97. *I. v. The United Kingdom; Goodwin v. The United Kingdom.*

98. *In re Estate of Gardiner,* 22 P.3d 1086 (Kan. Ct. App. 2001) *aff'd in part, rev'd in part,* 42 P.3d 120 (Kan. 2002).

99. See, for example, *Littleton v. Prange.*

100. See, for example, *Attorney General v. Otahuhu Family Court; In re Estate of Gardiner,* 22 P.3d 1086 (Kan. Ct. App. 2001) *aff'd in part, rev'd in part,* 42 P.3d 120 (Kan. 2002); *In re Heilig; I. v. The United Kingdom; Goodwin v. The United Kingdom; Attorney General v. Kevin.*

101. *I. v. The United Kingdom; Goodwin v. The United Kingdom.*

102. Money, *Sex Errors of the Body and Related Syndromes,* x.

4. Pursuing Protection for Transgender People through Disability Laws

Jennifer L. Levi and Bennett H. Klein

Courts or administrative agencies in at least seven states have found that transgender people are protected under state civil rights laws that prohibit discrimination on the basis of disability.[1] Despite that fact, many people both within and outside the transgender community are profoundly uncomfortable about relying on disability laws to secure legal protections for transgender people. Indeed, on one occasion, an official at an administrative agency conveyed to the authors of this chapter that while the agency agreed that transgender persons logically should be protected under the disability law the agency was charged with administering, the agency was reluctant to issue such an opinion for fear of offending members of the community. What is the basis of these objections and the concern of offending the community? Should these objections and concerns be a reason not to pursue laws that otherwise might be a source of protections for transgender people in employment, public accommodations, credit, and housing?

Some transgender people (and allies) worry that using the legal category of disability to secure legal protections for transgender people will perpetuate social myths and stereotypes that transgender people are sick, abnormal, or inferior. This concern stems largely from the stigma still associated with the term *disability*, which in its colloquial sense is all too often misunderstood to mean physical infirmity, debilitation, or inability to work. What this concern fails to recognize, however, is that disability antidiscrimination laws do not use the term *disability* in its colloquial or popular sense. The notion that these laws prohibit discrimination only against individuals who have debilitating impairments reflects a fundamental misunderstanding of contemporary disability civil rights laws. Today, such laws prohibit discrimination against individuals with a wide range of health conditions who are fully capable of working and participating in society. The barriers to equal opportunity that such individuals face are found not in physical incapacity or inferiority but in the prejudice, hostility, and misunderstanding of others about their health conditions. Disability antidiscrimination laws cover both those who experience some limitations because of a health condition, as well as those who experience discrimination solely because of ignorance, stereotypes, and misperceptions about their health conditions. Rather than discard an important source of legal protections, the transgender community must work with others both inside and outside the disability community to eliminate the stigma associated with disability and to ensure that state courts properly understand and apply disability antidiscrimination laws.

In this chapter, we first explain the concept of "disability" in civil rights laws in order to address objections from both inside and outside the transgender community. We then examine how this concept applies to the range of people who comprise the transgender community. Finally, we present the legal argument that transgender persons who experience discrimination in employment, housing, public accommodations, and other areas fit neatly within the definition of "disability" used in modern civil rights laws.

The Controversy and the Usual Objections

Our proposal, we acknowledge, is controversial. Therefore, we begin by responding to some objections. In addition to objections based on stigma associated with disability law (discussed further below), the two most common objections to pursuing disability protections stem from concerns about class and the social construction of gender.

The first objection usually takes the following form: by pursuing disability law as an avenue for protecting transgender people, many (perhaps most) transgender people facing discrimination will not be covered because they cannot afford to access the medical system either to formally be diagnosed with some condition (like gender identity disorder) or to purchase hormones or surgeries. Responding to this objection is easy. One need not have obtained a medical diagnosis to demonstrate that one has a disability. More fundamentally, one need not demonstrate that one is receiving medical care or treatment in order to claim discrimination on the basis of disability.

An alternate way to see the fallacy of this objection is to consider it in the context of any other health condition. One would not object to a person with cancer bringing a claim of disability discrimination because the individual could not afford medical treatment for his or her cancer. Similarly, one would not object to a pregnant woman bringing a claim of pregnancy discrimination simply because she could not afford prenatal care. In the same way, a transgender person can bring a disability claim regardless of whether the person can afford any medical treatment for being transgender. The ability to afford treatment simply is not a prerequisite for claiming disability discrimination. In fact, to object to using disability claims from a class-based analysis is to turn that analysis on its head. The result of that position is to deny poor people with health conditions protection from discrimination that is otherwise extended to persons of means, an untenable position from any progressive perspective.

The second objection comes from a crude postmodern perspective that all gender is socially constructed, in a very reductive sense, and that there is nothing essential about gender identity. Proving or disproving this basic point is beyond the scope of this chapter. However, this objection, taken to its logical conclusion, posits that transsexualism does not exist. In other words, persons arguing from this perspective believe that if people could fully embrace their masculinity (from the FTM perspective) or femininity (from the MTF perspective) despite the social construction of biologically female traits as feminine or biologically male traits as masculine, then no one would ever need to take hormones or have surgery to fully express their gender identities. According to this view, transgender persons should rely exclusively on sex discrimination laws for legal protection. This argument is dangerously dismissive of transsexual people and fails to accord with their lived experiences and understandings of their own identities. In its naive representation of hormonal and surgical alteration of the body as inherently "unnatural," it is reminiscent of the equally naive representation of homosexuality as inherently "unnatural" in older progressive arguments that in an ideal word, where men and women were truly equal, there would be no need for same-sex relationships.

In any case, however, any underlying disagreements about the cause or meaning of transsexualism need not be resolved in order to pursue disability protection. Both disability and gender-based claims can be pursued when a transgender person experiences discrimination that is rooted in both. No one would argue (we hope) that a Jewish person with Gaucher's disease should not pursue both disability and religion-based claims simply because there is nothing essential about religion or because not all Jewish persons have Gaucher's disease. Using disability discrimination law does not create identity characteristics; avoiding identity-based discrimination claims does nothing further to question them.

Finally, at the outset, we acknowledge the limitation of pursuing disability protections under federal law. Unlike many state disability laws, both the federal Americans with Disabilities Act (ADA) and the federal Rehabilitation Act expressly exclude any protection for persons discriminated against because of "transvestism," "transsexualism," or "gender identity disorders not resulting from physical impairments."[2] While these exclusions close the door to federal disability protections for transgender people, they do not preclude seeking protection under most state disability laws. Moreover, even apart from the exclusion of transgender persons, many federal courts have generally given an unreasonably narrow interpretation to the definition of disability in federal antidiscrimination laws, undermining the original congressional purpose of such laws to eradicate discrimination against people with a wide range of health conditions. Today, state law provides the most fertile grounds to realize the true goals of disability antidiscrimination laws—including for transgender persons.

Despite our advocacy of the pursuit of disability cases, we also recognize its limitations. At the heart of the federal exclusion of transgender people from the ADA lies bias, bigotry, and misunderstanding of transgender people. We acknowledge that some courts will share those attitudes and may, as a result, judicially craft exemptions where none exist. Indeed, some have already done so. However, a risk of exclusion is not a basis for avoiding potential protection against discrimination for the community.

The Concept of "Disability" in Civil Rights Laws

Some background on the differing social conceptions of "disability" is critical to understanding the principled basis for including transgender persons within current disability antidiscrimination laws. Throughout much of Western history, people with disabilities have been viewed as inferior and subjected to segregation and inequality.[3] While Western religions once regarded impairment as a reflection of "inner spiritual inferiority," a medical model predominated during the late nineteenth and most of the twentieth century.[4] That model viewed disability as an infirmity of the individual to be responded to with treatment and pity.[5] According to the model, an individual's problem lies in his or her impairment; accordingly, the social response was to provide aid and assistance through medical intervention to "cure" the person's condition or rehabilitation programs to help a person approximate standards of "normalcy."[6] The medical model perpetuated the stigma and social prejudice associated with disability because, as one commentator noted, "it treats the individual as deficient and inherently inferior because she falls below an arbitrary physiological standard that delineates social acceptance and that can only be 'normalized' and incorporated into society through a medical cure."[7]

Until the 1970s virtually all state and federal legislative policy on disabilities was based on the medical model, focusing on either vocational rehabilitation to help individuals "overcome" their disabilities or, if that could not be achieved, benefits entitlement programs.[8] The definition of disability in these laws was narrow and based on the common perception that disability interfered with work. For example, the Vocational Rehabilitation Act of 1920 authorized services to people who "by reason of physical defect or infirmity" may be incapacitated from work. Similarly, Title XVI of the Social Security Act, enacted in 1972, provides financial assistance to people unable to work because of a physical or mental impairment.[9] Given this long-standing perception of "disability" as a personal infirmity, it is not surprising that a new and fundamentally different understanding of "disability," only recently embodied in federal and state antidiscrimination laws, has not yet replaced the medical model in much of our popular consciousness.[10]

In the 1950s and 1960s the disability rights movement emerged and articulated a fundamentally different understanding of the limitations experienced by individuals with a physical or mental health condition. Disability rights advocates began to understand that the barriers to full equality faced by persons with a wide range of health conditions were caused not so much by physical attributes as by the prejudice and attitudinal barriers they experienced.[11]

In a now-classic 1963 book, *Stigma: Notes on the Management of Spoiled Identity,* Erving Goffman radically reframed the concept of stigma and the stigmatization of people with disabilities. Rather than locating the pathology in individuals and seeing *their* rehabilitations as a problem for society to solve, Goffman reversed the logic, locating the problem in the social norms that construct people with mental or physical impairments as outsiders to a society made up of presumably able-bodied persons. As the disability studies scholar Lennard J. Davis points out, Goffman's reworking of the concept of disability as a sociological problem rather than an emotional issue spurred the disability rights movement to reject the medical rehabilitative model of impairment in favor of a vision of social justice that called for radical transformations of the economic, legal, and physical architectures that create barriers for people with impairments.[12] So, instead of reproducing ableist thinking by fearing the association of transgender rights with disability rights, transgender advocates would be well served to understand the thinking behind disability rights.

The new civil rights model builds on the work of Goffman and others by recognizing the existence of physical and mental differences, but not viewing limitations on full participation in society as either natural or an inevitable result of biological or physiological characteristics.[13] Instead, under the more modern view, the "disadvantaged status of persons with disabilities is [viewed as] the product of a hostile (or at least inhospitable) social environment, not simply the product of bodily defects."[14] As one commentator noted, a new concept of disability "must acknowledge the existence of functional impairments, but it must also focus on ways society can reasonably adapt to a wider range of mental and physical differences than the handicapped-or-normal dichotomy has permitted."[15] For example, if 75 percent of the population were in a wheelchair, buildings would be constructed differently; in particular, stairs would not be the norm. Similarly, if most people had Tourette's syndrome, people would not react with fear to random utterances incorporated within language or assume that a person with such a speaking style had a problem.

This distinction between disability and impairment became crucial to the politics of the disability rights movement and to the emerging field of disability studies. As Davis points out, "Disability scholars make the distinction between impairment and disability. An impairment involves the loss or diminution of sight, hearing, mobility, mental ability, and so on. But an impairment only becomes a disability when the ambient society creates environments with barriers. . . . For example, a person using a wheelchair is only disabled if there are no ramps."[16]

This new understanding that social barriers, not individual inferiority, caused the disadvantaged status of individuals with disabilities led to the first antidiscrimination statutes in the 1970s. The year 1973 marked a fundamental transformation in federal disability policy. When Congress reauthorized federal vocational and other programs in the Federal Rehabilitation Act of 1973 (FRA), it included for the first time a prohibition against discrimination on the basis of handicap by recipients of federal funds.[17] Recognizing that FRA's definition of handicap was too narrow and focused on limitations to meet the statute's new civil rights goals, Congress the very next year amended the definition of "handicapped individual" applicable to the nondiscrimination provisions. That amendment defined an individual with a handicap as "any person (A) who has a physical or mental impairment which substantially limits one or more of such person's major life activities, (B) has a record of such impairment, or (C) is regarded as having such an impairment."[18]

The first prong of the amended definition contained broad language flexible enough to reach a wide range of impairments for individuals with health conditions that are not so debilitating as to preclude working, but who nevertheless experience discrimination. Congress included the second and third prongs to address discrimination arising from stereotypes and ignorance about physical and mental impairments. Since 1974 most states have incorporated this definition of disability into their own antidiscrimination statutes. In addition, in 1990, Congress passed the Americans with Disabilities Act (ADA), a law that broadened antidiscrimination provisions to cover private employers and public accommodations, and incorporated into that statute the FRA's definition of disability.

Disability Civil Rights Laws as Applied to Transgender People

The term *transgender* is intended to cover a broad range of experiences, including transsexual people who undergo medical care and treatment to transition from their assigned sex at birth to the sex that is consistent with their gender identities, people who undergo no medical treatment but also take steps to conform their gender expressions to meet their gender identities, as well as people who take no such steps but are gender nonconforming in some way. The three-pronged definition of disability in the federal models specifying the class protected from discrimination is broad and flexible enough to encompass many different visions of transgender identity. Because the disability nondiscrimination laws are intended to protect people from discrimination both because they have a physical or mental health condition or because they experience discrimination based on the perception that they do, most transgender people who face discrimination because of being transgender may bring a claim.

For example, consider the transsexual person who experiences intense discomfort with the misalignment of his or her anatomy and gender identity and takes steps to align them. Most such individuals, who seek to fix or "cure" what they experience as a medical condition, will be covered by the first prong of the definition of disability. For this category of people, the underlying condition, whether characterized as "gender dysphoria," "gender identity disorder," an endocrinological condition, or something different, should meet the test of being a "physical or mental impairment." While helpful to explain the condition to a court, no such diagnosis need actually have been obtained to state a claim even under the first prong.

One objection against bringing a disability claim on behalf of a transsexual person who has pursued medical care and treatment to transition from one sex to another is rooted in disagreement over the origins of the transgender condition and, more specifically, rejection of a mental health diagnosis. The diagnosis of "gender identity disorder" (GID) or "gender dysphoria" as defined in the *Diagnostics and Statistical Manual of Mental Disorders* (DSM-IV) is admittedly a politically controversial one, and many members of the transgender community object to placing the diagnosis under the rubric of "mental disorder." The pursuit of antidiscrimination claims by individuals who meet the first prong of the definition of disability, however, does not require resolving this disagreement over the etiology of the transgender condition as an "impairment." There need not even have been an associated DSM-IV diagnosis for an individual to be covered by law. In other words, it is enough that the impairment simply be acknowledged to be a health condition in order for an individual to come within the definition. It need not be the condition referred to by the diagnosis of GID in the DSM-IV.

Recent studies suggest that being transgender has a physiological, not a psychological, etiology. These studies may support the conclusion that being transgender is just one variation in the broad range of human physical experiences. Under this view, the origin of transsexualism is a physical, not a mental, health condition. Since most disability laws include both physical and mental health conditions, the disagreement over whether to classify transsexualism as a physical or mental health condition need not be resolved in order for transgender people to pursue disability claims. Even people who object to the mental health diagnosis may pursue claims, since they may root them in the impairment being a physical one. As a practical consideration, given the broad medical consensus that transsexualism is a legitimate medical condition for some people requiring medical care and treatment, defining it as a diagnosable condition is important for many purposes, including as a gateway to the care and treatment required. Defining it as a diagnosable condition is not, however, essential to the pursuit of a disability claim.

At the same time that some disability laws cover those individuals who view their transsexualism as a medical condition requiring treatment, the definition of the protected class also covers transgender people, whether they identify as transsexual or not, if they feel discomfort with the misalignment of anatomy and gender identity. This should be true regardless of whether they associate the discomfort with something internally generated or something caused purely by cultural prejudices rooted in gender stereotypes. These individuals can pursue claims under the "regarded as" prong of the definition of disability. After all, a primary purpose of modern disability antidiscrimination laws is to recognize the social roots of discrimination regardless of what impact a health condition actually has on one's life. Thus modern disability laws are sufficiently expansive to be compatible with both a medical and a social model of transgender identity.

Despite the clear, intended coverage of the law, many transgender people object to pursuing disability discrimination cases because of the stigma associated with disability. Stigma is not a principled reason to avoid using the law for protection. The answer to this objection is to address the stigma, not to enhance it by avoiding the law. Encouraging people to work toward eradicating the stigma associated with disability may, however, require a better understanding of the origin of this objection as it relates to transgender people. One origin is in a perceived distinction between other categories (such as sex, race, or religion) included in federal employment antidiscrimination law and the category of disability. One perception often voiced is that disability is unlike the other categories in that being disabled would be unappealing regardless of the existence or absence of widespread bias and prejudice. In other words, goes the argument, the only reason to choose or prefer to be one race over another is because of the lack of cultural prejudice against some particular majority race. For example, in most Middle Eastern countries, one would choose to be of Middle Eastern descent; in most Asian countries, one would choose to be of Asian descent, and so on. But no one would choose to be a person with a disability even if there were some way to remove the cultural biases against people who do not meet certain physical and mental health norms.

There are several responses to this distinction. First, pressed to any degree, the artificial conclusion (about preferencing any race but not preferencing disability in any circumstances) seems tenuous at best. The premise that, for example, cultural bias can be removed to the extent the hypothetical requires is unimaginable in light of the pervasiveness and ubiquitousness of cultural norms. In other words, the ability to walk becomes preferable over other forms of motion (such as wheeling in a chair) as long as architectural norms assume the ability to walk. It is nearly impossible to conceive of a world that does not presume the able-bodiedness of its inhabitants, which makes the question of whether one would choose to have a "disability" absent the cultural bias and prejudice associated with it unanswerable. There may, of course, be limits to this not-so-veiled suggestion that if the cultural barriers to participation were removed, there would be no distinction between the preference for race versus the lack of preference for disability. It is hard to imagine that one would choose to be mobile only by a wheelchair, given the "natural" limitations it could impose—running on the beach, for example. Of course, even that limitation may be answerable by focusing on the limits of walking. Consider, for example, the benefits of a wheelchair for speed and energy conservation on most smooth surfaces.

In light of the irresolvability of the general hypothetical, the more relevant question is whether one would "choose" to be transgender absent cultural prejudices. Properly situating disability law and understanding the modern laws' perspectives reveal that it does not really matter. Disability laws are intended to cover both persons whose lives are impacted "naturally" by their physical or mental health conditions as well as those whose lives are impacted by the social consequences of their having a condition (including just the perception of their having a condition). Accordingly, resolving society's view of the transgender condition (much less an individual's view) makes no difference as to the applicability of existing law.

Moreover, existing law should cover both those transgender persons who avail themselves of medical interventions and those who do not. Using the most crass distinctions, compare a person who identifies as transsexual with one who identifies as nontranssexual transgender. For this thought experiment, assume that the transsexual person feels an intense discomfort with the misalignment of his or her anatomy and gender identity and takes steps to align them. Assume that the nontranssexual transgender person feels similar discomfort but identifies with a thread of the transgender movement that rejects a medical or rehabilitative model and embraces a model that associates the discomfort solely with cultural prejudices. Either way, the disability law provides an avenue for appropriately pursuing protections. As explained above, for coverage under the law one need only demonstrate that he or she either has an impairment or is regarded as having such an impairment. The history of the adoption of disability nondiscrimination laws incorporates both the medical rehabilitative model of transgender identity and a model that posits that only cultural biases are at the root of discriminatory treatment. Therefore an objection to pursuing protection through disability law rooted in whether it is preferable to be transgender is merely a distraction (even if an interesting one) without a legal difference.

The Legal Framework for Using Disability Laws to Prohibit Discrimination against Transgender Persons

When properly understood, modern antidiscrimination laws transform the colloquial understanding of disability. While significant stigma and misunderstanding still exist, the response by transgender persons who experience discrimination should be to challenge those misconceptions by building a strong legal case that argues for a meaningful understanding of disability antidiscrimination laws. In this section, we discuss the legal arguments available to transgender persons for bringing successful discrimination claims.

A critical point is that transgender persons must bring claims under state rather than federal disability antidiscrimination laws. When Congress passed the ADA in 1990, it excluded from the definition of disability "transsexualism" and "gender identity disorders not resulting from physical impairments."[19] At the same time, Congress similarly amended the definition of disability in the FRA that had first been passed in 1974 with no such exclusion.

Although the inclusion even within federal law of gender identity disorders resulting from physical impairments offers some hope for protection as the physical etiology of gender identity disorder is more thoroughly researched and understood, transgender people for the most part must turn to state disability discrimination laws for coverage.

Importantly, many state laws use the same language to define disability as in federal law but contain no exclusion of transsexualism or gender identity disorders. Indeed, Congress must have believed that the general language-defining disability could include transgender persons; otherwise, it would have had no reason to explicitly exclude transgender persons from the ADA and FRA. Moreover, prior to the adoption of the explicit exclusion in the ADA and FRA, federal courts determined transsexualism to be covered by the ADA's precursor, the FRA. Therefore those interpretations of the definition of disability, absent any transgender exclusion, are precedent for state laws that modeled their definitions of disability on federal law.

To prevail under disability antidiscrimination laws, the biggest challenge is to prove inclusion within the protected class. Having accomplished that, a plaintiff must prove that discrimination occurred on the basis of disability. The language of state and federal disability antidiscrimination laws provides three ways to come within the protected class: the individual (1) has a physical or mental impairment that substantially limits a major life activity; (2) has a record of such an impairment; or (3) is "regarded as" having such an impairment. While some federal courts have inappropriately given a narrow interpretation to the meaning of the ADA and FRA, utilizing state law provides an important opportunity to realize the true purpose of disability antidiscrimination laws.

The language of many state disability laws mirrors their federal analogues but without the explicit mention of transgender people. Therefore an examination of the congressional intent of the FRA and ADA provides important arguments for the broad implementation of state disability laws. While some federal courts have given a narrowing construction to aspects of the ADA and FRA, many state courts and administrative agencies have given their own laws a broader interpretation.

Impairment That Substantially Limits a Major Life Activity

Following guidelines of federal agencies implementing the ADA and FRA, many state laws define "impairment" as *any* physiological disorder affecting a body system, or a mental or psychological disorder.[20] Gender dysphoria, gender identity disorder, or transsexualism is a mental and physical disorder characterized by a strong and persistent desire to be a member of another sex coupled with a continued discomfort with one's biological sex.[21] Adults with gender dysphoria intensely desire to adopt both the social role and physical characteristics of another sex.[22] There is also evidence of physical differences in the brains of men compared with the brains of male-to-female transsexual people.[23] One study also points to distinctions in the central nervous system between transsexuals and nontranssexuals.[24] Either a mental health approach or a physical etiological approach works to meet the requirement to show that a person has an impairment.

The first prong of the definition of disability does not cover all persons who can demonstrate an impairment. The impairment must also substantially limit a major life activity. The United States Supreme Court has recognized that this language is "broad" and encompasses more than "traditional handicaps."[25] Like its ADA analogue, the first prong of state disability definitions typically reflects the legislatures' rejections of a narrow, technical definition in favor of a broad, flexible concept designed to facilitate the statutory goal of eradicating discrimination against people with a wide range of health conditions. The language is broad and inclusive as well because, unlike the definition of disability in benefits laws like the Social Security Act, falling within the statutory class is of no relevance unless there is discrimination because of the health condition at issue.

Similarly, because the statute has the purpose of enabling people with disabilities to work despite the prejudices of others, the "substantial limitation" requirement is also broadly construed. Under this language, health conditions need not preclude participation in the "major life activities." The statutory language rejects a requirement that an individual absolutely cannot or chooses not to engage in a particular life activity. Rather, an impairment substantially limits a major life activity if it is restricted or made more complex as compared with persons without the impairment.[26]

Caring for one's self is a major life activity under disability antidiscrimination laws. The need for regular, ongoing health care should be considered a significant aspect of caring for one's self. Many transgender people require regular, ongoing, and lifelong self-administered medical management. This treatment may include ongoing psychotherapy and counseling sessions, periodic hormone treatment, long-term electrolysis sessions, periodic outpatient body-contouring procedures, and other medically necessary procedures to effectuate and maintain the transition from one sex to another. Without these procedures, transgender people would suffer serious, adverse effects from their conditions even though, with the treatment, they are otherwise happy and well-adjusted. Some transgender people may need ongoing medical care, including daily or weekly hormone therapy. Hormones help regulate a host of bodily functions, including, but not limited to, mood, eating, sleeping, sexual desire, and body temperature. Men and women have different types and levels of hormones. To treat or respond to one's transgender condition, a transgender person may require a combination of hormones to create the proper hormone levels to maintain the outward representation of the desired gender. Additionally, hormone therapy can have side effects that further limit or complicate a transgender person's ability to care for himself or herself. These side effects can include physical discomfort and may increase a transgender person's risk for certain other diseases or conditions. But the key piece of the analysis of the impairment's effect is that, without the ongoing medical management, the individual's physical and psychological health would be significantly affected.

Examples from other health conditions suggest that being transgender can substantially limit the major life activity of caring for oneself, including with respect to health care. For example, one court found that a plaintiff with HIV was substantially limited in the ability to care for himself because of his need for continued medical care.[27] Similarly, another court found that the plaintiff was substantially limited in his ability to care for himself in part because of his daily medication.[28]

One need not be subject to a daily medication regime, however, to be considered substantially limited in the ability to care for one's health. The key is that the need for regular health care for the rest of one's life on an ongoing basis, regardless of intensity or frequency, as a result of having the impairment, is sufficiently substantially limiting of the major life activity of caring for oneself. For example, if a doctor prescribes an antidepressant infrequently, for example, once every other week, to treat someone for depression, that regular, ongoing medical regime would be a substantial limitation on that person's major life activity of caring for himself or herself despite the infrequent and arguably insignificant nature of the treatment.

Reproduction and intimate sexual activity are also major life activities as defined in disability antidiscrimination laws.[29] Some transgender people have genital surgery to complete their transitions. Although not a necessary requirement for everyone, it is a requirement for some. To the extent one's transgender condition requires an individual to make different choices about sexual activities and reproduction, it may substantially limit, as a legal matter, one's ability to engage in sexual relations or procreation.

One federal court of appeals found that a plaintiff's medication-induced impotence substantially limited his ability to engage in sexual relations.[30] In that case, the court relied on both Supreme Court precedent and decisions from other courts of appeals to conclude that sexual relations are a major life activity.[31] "Sexuality is important in how 'we define ourselves and how we are perceived by others' and is a fundamental part of how we bond in intimate relationships."[32] Therefore an alteration in one's approach to sexual intimacy caused by treatment for a health condition satisfies the legal requirement of limitation of a major life activity.

It is important to acknowledge that pursuing protections under disability law may not protect all transgender people. This is not a reason, however, to forgo pursuing critical nondiscrimination protections for those transgender people who can meet the definition of disability. Rather, it is simply a truism of a limitation of disability antidiscrimination laws generally. Some impairments—such as blindness—always limit substantially a major life activity. Other impairments—such as allergies or arthritis—have a wider range of consequences, requiring persons with those impairments to make an individualized showing of substantial limitation. Indeed, case law under all federal and state disability antidiscrimination laws is replete with examples of people with the very same conditions, such as cancer, heart disease, or back problems, some of whom can and some of whom cannot make out an individualized showing that they are substantially limited in major life activity. While disability advocates maintain that many people are unfairly excluded from coverage because of an improperly narrow interpretation of disability, the reality that some transgender people may not fit within the statute is hardly unique.

Record of a Past Impairment

The second way a transgender person can fall within the coverage of disability antidiscrimination laws is if an impairment substantially limited a person's major life activity in the past but does not presently. Such a person is covered because he or she has a "record of" a substantially limiting impairment. A person treated for cancer five years ago may be entitled to protection from disability discrimination, despite being currently cancer-free.[33] Similarly, a transgender person may have been substantially limited in one or more major life activities. While those limitations may no longer exist, a transgender person will still be protected from disability discrimination because of his or her past condition and medical intervention. No current limitation on a major life activity is required. Therefore being transgender is a disability when a person has a medical history of the disorder that substantially limited the major life activity of caring for himself or herself or engaging in sexual relations.

"Regarded as" Having a Disability

Finally, a transgendered person may be "regarded as" having a substantially limiting impairment. This prong of the definition of "disability" is a clear example of how the federal courts have misinterpreted Congress's intent in passing the ADA, significantly reducing its effectiveness in protecting people from discrimination. These misinterpretations, however, do not justify abandoning pursuit of that original intent in state courts. When understood in terms of its congressional purpose, however, the "regarded as" prong remains a strong basis to create protections under state disability antidiscrimination laws.

Congress added the "regarded as" prong to the FRA's definition of "handicap" in 1974 to address discrimination because of stereotypical attitudes and ignorance about impairments.[34] In its foundational ruling on the meaning of the "regarded as" prong, the U.S. Supreme Court declared that "the basic purpose of [the FRA]... is to ensure that handicapped individuals are not denied jobs or other benefits because of the prejudiced attitudes or ignorance of others."[35] The Court specifically observed that the inclusion of "cosmetic disfigurement" (which is not at all to suggest that any treatments for transsexualism are cosmetic) in the regulation's definition of "impairment" supported the conclusion that the statute covers limitations caused by stereotypical attitudes about an impairment.[36] "Such an impairment might not diminish a person's physical or mental capabilities, but could nevertheless substantially limit that person's ability to work as a result of the negative reactions of others to the impairment."[37]

Similarly, the regulatory definition of handicap (the predisability language) under the FRA provides that a person is "regarded as" having an impairment if he or she

(A) has a physical or mental impairment that does not substantially limit major life activities but that is treated by the [covered entity] as constituting such a limitation;

(B) has a physical or mental impairment that substantially limits major life activities *only as a result of the attitudes of others* toward such impairment; or

(C) [does not have an impairment] but is treated by the [covered entity] as having such impairment.[38]

Subsection (B) is intended to cover stigmatized impairments that create reactions based on fear and ignorance.

The legislative history of the ADA also expressly adopts the above-discussed Supreme Court analysis of the "regarded as" test as well as the preexisting FRA regulatory definition of "regarded as."[39] A person is protected under the "regarded as" prong if he or she is excluded from any "basic life activity, or is otherwise discriminated against, because of a covered entity's negative attitudes towards that person's impairment."[40] The legislative history reflects that the "regarded as" prong is "particularly important" for persons with "stigmatic" conditions, such as a person with severe burns who is denied work because of the employer's discomfort with the applicant's appearance.[41] This history makes clear that the "regarded as" prong is intended to prohibit discrimination against persons with impairments that invoke fear and discomfort in others.[42]

Being transgender is a quintessentially stigmatic condition that has engendered fear and discomfort in others wholly separate and apart from the effect that being transgender has on any one person's life. Transgender people are often substantially limited not as any inherent result of the condition but as a result of the negative attitudes of others. A transgender person may be subjected to discrimination or ostracism by family, friends, and neighbors. In the employment context, transgender employees have been shunned by employers, coworkers, and customers. Pursuing coverage under the "regarded as" prong focuses the lens of discrimination on the reactions of others, not on the degree to which being transgender either has or does not have any limiting effect on a person's life.

The irrational fears attached to transgender people are analogous to the type of stigma and stereotypes associated with HIV. Indeed, numerous courts have found that people with HIV are "regarded as" disabled and covered by disability discrimination laws because of the deeply rooted social stigma associated with that condition.[43] A transgender individual is similarly protected from irrational discrimination based on an adverse reaction to his or her condition.

Conclusion

State disability laws have significant potential for protecting transgender people from discrimination. While some have raised serious reservations about pursuing protections for transgender people under these laws, most of those reservations stem from a lack of information or misinformation about both the history and the scope of the laws as well the modern disability movement. Transgender activists and supporters would do well to learn from the disability movement, rather than to adopt and perpetuate social myths and stigmas about disabilities. This chapter has focused on providing some of the relevant history, taking seriously the objections and formulating the legal analysis to make the case for transgender inclusion under disability law. At least in many states, the law and the courts are ready for us. Time will tell if our community is ready for the courts.

Notes

The asterisks that appear with page numbers in these notes refer to screen page numbers from a database.

1. *Smith v. City of Jacksonville Corr. Inst.*, 1991 WL 833882 (Fla. Div. Admin. Hrgs. 1991) (holding that an individual with gender dysphoria is within the disability coverage of the Florida Human Rights Act, as well as the portions of the Act prohibiting discrimination based on perceived disability); *Evans v. Hamburger Hamlet & Forncrook*, 1996 WL 941676 (Chi. Com. Hum. Rel. 1996) (denying defendant's motion to dismiss disability claim brought by transsexual plaintiff); *Lie v. Sky Publ'g Corp.*, 15 Mass. L. Rptr. 412, 2002 WL 31492397 (Mass. Super. 2002) (holding that transsexual plaintiff had established a prima facie case of discrimination based on sex and disability under state law prohibiting employment discrimination); *Doe v. Brockton Sch. Comm.*, 2000 WL 33342399 (Mass. App. Ct.), *aff'g sub nom, Doe v. Yunits*, 2001 WL 664947 (Mass. Super. 2000) (holding that a transgender student had stated a viable disability discrimination claim); *Jette v. Honey Farms Mini Market*, 2001 WL 1602799 (Mass. Comm'n Against Discrimination 2001) (holding that transsexual people are protected by state law prohibitions against sex and disability discrimination); *Jane Doe v. Electro-Craft Corp.*, No. 87-B-132 (N.H. Sup. Ct. 1988) (holding that transsexualism is a disability within the meaning of the state employment discrimination statute); *Enriquez v. W. Jersey Health Sys.*, 342 N.J. Super. 501, 777 A.2d 365 (N.J. Super.), *cert. denied*, 170 N.J. 211, 785 A.2d 439 (N.J. 2001) (concluding that transsexual people are protected by state law prohibitions against sex and disability discrimination); *Jean Doe v. Bell*, 754 N.Y.S.2d 846 (N.Y. Sup. Ct. 2003) (holding that transsexual foster youth protected by state law prohibiting discrimination on the basis of disability in housing); *Doe v. Boeing Co.*, 846 P.2d 531, 536 (Wash. 1993) (holding that gender dysphoria "is a medically cognizable condition with a prescribed course of treatment," but that the plaintiff [a male-to-female transsexual] had failed to prove that she was discriminated against because of her transsexualism).

2. Footnote to 42 U.S.C. § 12211(b)(c).

3. Jonathan C. Drimmer, "Cripples, Overcomers, and Civil Rights: Tracing the Evolution of Federal Legislation and Social Policy for People with Disabilities," *UCLA Law Review* 40 (1993): 1341–1410; Wendy E. Parmet, "Plain Meaning and Mitigating Measures: Judicial Interpretations of the Meaning of Disability," *Berkeley Journal of Employment and Labor Law* 21 (2000): 56–57.

4. Drimmer, "Cripples, Overcomers, and Civil Rights," 1346, 1347; Parmet, "Plain Meaning and Mitigating Measures," 56.

5. Drimmer, "Cripples, Overcomers, and Civil Rights," 1347–55; Parmet, "Plain Meaning and Mitigating Measures," 56.

6. Mary Crossley, "The Disability Kaleidoscope," *Notre Dame Law Review* 74 (1999): 651–54.

7. Drimmer, "Cripples, Overcomers, and Civil Rights," 1348.

8. For a survey of state and federal legislation, see Drimmer, "Cripples, Overcomers, and Civil Rights," 1361–75. See also Crossley, "Disability Kaleidoscope," 628–30.

9. See 42 U.S.C. Sec. 423 (d)(2)(A) (claimant must be unable "to engage in any other kind of substantial work which exists in the national economy").

10. Crossley, "Disability Kaleidoscope," 653.

11. Parmet, "Plain Meaning and Mitigating Measures," 56–57.

12. Lennard J. Davis, *Bending over Backwards: Disability, Dismodernism, and Other Difficult Positions* (New York: New York University Press, 2002), 136. See also Erving Goffman, *Stigma: Notes on the Management of a Spoiled Identity* (New York: Prentice Hall, 1963). This book became a founding text of the new interdisciplinary field of disability studies. Other important publications in the field include Lennard J. Davis, *Enforcing Normalcy: Disability, Deafness, and the Body* (London: Verso, 1995); Simi Linton, *Claiming Disability: Knowledge and Identity* (New York: New York University Press, 1998); Paul K. Longmore and Lauri Umanski, eds., *The New Disability History* (New York: New York University Press, 2001); Lennard J. Davis, ed., *The Disability Studies Reader* (New York: Routledge, 1997); Doris Zames Fleisher and Frieda Zames, *The Disability Rights Movement* (Philadelphia: Temple University Press, 2001).

13. Drimmer, "Cripples, Overcomers, and Civil Rights," 1357.

14. Crossley, "Disability Kaleidoscope," 654.

15. Robert L. Burdorf Jr. and Christopher G. Bell, "Eliminating Discrimination against Physically and Mentally Handicapped Persons: A Statutory Blueprint," *Mental and Physical Disability Law Reporter* 8 (1984): 64.

16. Davis, *Bending over Backwards*, 41.

17. See Pub. L. No. 93–112, Sec. 504, 87 Stat. 355, 394 (1973), codified at 29 U.S.C. Sec. 794(a).

18. See Pub. L. No. 93–516, Sec. 111, 88 Stat. 1617, 1619 (1974), codified at 29 U.S.C. Sec. 706(8)(B)(1988 ed.).

19. 42 U.S.C. § 12211(b)(1).

20. See, for example, Secretary of the Commonwealth of Massachusetts, *Commonwealth of Massachusetts Commission against Discrimination Guidelines: Employment Discrimination on the Basis of Handicap — Chapter 151B* (1998), 2, emphasis added (hereafter cited as *Guidelines*).

21. See *Diagnostic and Statistical Manual of Mental Disorders*, 4th ed. (1994). See also *Smith v. Rasmussen*, 57 F.Supp.2d 736, 741 (N.D. Iowa 1999) (describing the general diagnostic features of gender dysphoria).

22. Ibid.

23. See Dr. Ludovicus Gooren's expert witness statement in *Northwest Lancashire Health Authority v. A, D & G* (on file with Gay and Lesbian Advocates and Defenders). See also J.-N. Zhou, M. A. Hofman, L. J. Gooren, and D. F. Swaab, "A Sex Difference in the Human Brain and Its Relations to Transsexuality," *International Journal of Transgenderism* 1 (1997), at http://www.symposion.com/ijt/ijtc0106.htm (describing that an area of the brain that may be involved in human sexual or reproductive functions, normally larger for men than for women, was female-sized in male-to-female transsexuals).

24. See Richard Green, "Reflections on 'Transsexualism and Sex Reassignment,' 1969–1999," presidential address, XVI Harry Benjamin International Gender Dysphoria Association Symposium, August 17–21, 1999, in *International Journal of Transgenderism* 4 (January–March 2000): 1, P7, "Mysteries of the origins ... ," at http://www.symposion.com/ijt/greenpresidental/green00.htm.

25. *School Board of Nassau County v. Arline*, 480 U.S. 273, 280 n.5 (1987).

26. See, for example, 28 C.F.R. Part 36, App. B § 36.104 (a person is substantially limit[ed] in any activity if, "in comparison to most people," he or she is "restricted as to the conditions, manner or duration under which it can be performed").

27. See *Hernández v. Prudential Ins. Co. of Am.*, 977 F.Supp. 1160 (M.D. Fla. 1997) (deciding claims brought under the ADA and the Florida Civil Human Rights Act).

28. See *United States v. Happy Time Day Care Ctr.*, 6 F.Supp.2d 1073 (W.D. Wisc. 1998) (deciding claim brought under the ADA).

29. *McAlindin v. County of San Diego*, 2000 WL 29658, *5–6 (January 18, 2000) (plaintiff was taking medication for anxiety, panic, and somatoform disorders). See also *Bragdon v. Abbott*, 524 U.S. 624, 641 (1998) (endorsing Department of Justice legal opinion that sexual relations is a major life activity).

30. *McAlindin v. County of San Diego*, 2000 WL 29658, *5–6.

31. Ibid., *5.

32. Ibid. (citation omitted). See also 524 U.S. at 641.

33. See *Guidelines*, 2.

34. See 88 Stat. 1617, 1619 (1974); S. Rep. No. 1297, 93rd Cong., 1st sess. 16, 37–38, 50 (1974), reprinted in 1974 U.S.C.C.A.N. 6373, 6388–91, 6413–14.

35. *School Board of Nassau County v. Arline*, 480 U.S. 273, 284 (1974).

36. Ibid., 283 n.10.

37. Ibid., 283.

38. 45 C.F.R. Section 84.3(j)(2)(iv), emphasis added.

39. See H. Rep. No. 485, Part 2, 101st Cong., 2d sess. 31, 53, reprinted in 1990 U.S.C.C.A.N. 303 (hereafter referred to as "H. Rep. –2"); H. Rep. No. 485, Part 3, 101st Cong., 2d sess. 25, 30, reprinted in 1990 U.S.C.C.A.N. 445 (hereafter referred to as "H. Rep. –3"); S. Rep. No. 116, 101st Cong., 1st sess. 8, 3–24 (1989) (hereafter referred to as "S. Rep.").

40. H. Rep. –2, 53.

41. H. Rep. –3, 30–31; S. Rep., 24.

42. The regulations under the ADA adopt the same definition of "regarded as" as the committee reports and FRA regulations, including when the impairment substantially limits a major life activity only as a result of others' attitudes toward the impairment. See 29 C.F.R. Section 1630.2(1); 28 C.F.R. Section 36.104(4).

43. See, for example, *Severino v. North Fort Myers Fire Control Dist.* 935 F.2d 1179, 1182 n.4 (11th Cir. 1991) (finding that an HIV-positive firefighter was "regarded as" handicapped and noting that the "contagiousness of the disease brings AIDS within the definition of handicap"); *Support Ministries v. Village of Waterford*, 808 F. Supp. 120, 132 (N.D.N.Y. 1992) ("individuals with asymptomatic HIV were substantially limited in major life activities due to the prejudice and apprehension which AIDS engenders on a social level").

5. The Evolution of Employment Discrimination Protections for Transgender People

Kylar W. Broadus

Employment discrimination is a pressing issue for transgender people. In a recent survey, the Transgender Law Center found that nearly one of every two respondents had experienced gender identity discrimination on the job.[1] A 1999 study by the San Francisco Department of Public Health reached a similar result, finding that 46 percent of transgender people reported workplace discrimination.[2] The circumstances under which transgender people encounter discrimination at work are varied. Many transgender people are fired when they transition on the job. A transgender candidate may not be hired because the gender reflected in the person's documents or work history may differ from the person's current gender. A transgender employee may be terminated if an employer or coworker becomes aware of the person's transgender status. Finally, many transgender people have lost jobs because of prejudice and irrational fears about bathroom access. Just as was true for many other marginalized groups in the past, some employers and coworkers do not wish to share a bathroom with a transgender person.[3]

While workplace discrimination against transgender people is common, transgender people increasingly are receiving support and assistance during their on-job transition. Lynn Conway, a transsexual woman who is a famed pioneer of microelectronic chip design, has a Web site devoted to transgender persons who have transitioned successfully on the job with the support of their employers.[4] Similarly, according to the Human Rights Campaign, more than two hundred employers have adopted nondiscrimination policies that protect transgender workers.[5] Documenting these success stories is important, both as a source of hope for other transgender people and as evidence that, with a little support and guidance, employers can behave in a nondiscriminatory manner toward their transgender employees.[6] Nonetheless, the brutal reality is that many transgender people still will face unemployment or severe underemployment solely because they are transgender. That is particularly (although certainly not exclusively) true in the South, where negative attitudes toward transgender people tend to be more pronounced and where the absence of legal protections is often particularly stark.

As an African American FTM (female-to-male transsexual) who lost my career after transitioning on the job at a private company in Missouri, I have experienced this reality firsthand. Like many other transsexual people, I repressed my transgender identity and struggled to live in my birth sex for many years. For me, that meant trying to live as a masculine-appearing black woman. Despite the challenges I faced in that identity, I was able to build a successful career as a claims adjustor for State Farm Insurance, where I worked for eight years, from 1989 to 1997. During that time, I was promoted on several occasions and eventually worked as a claims specialist—not a glamorous job, but one that I enjoyed and at which I excelled.

In 1995, at the age of thirty-two, I came out to my employer as transsexual. As part of my medically supervised transition, I began to dress and live as a man, including at my job. From that point forward, I faced a constant barrage of criticism about my appearance, dress, demeanor, and performance. While my superiors could tolerate a somewhat masculine-appearing black woman, they were not prepared to deal with my transition to being a black man. With growing despair, I watched my professional connections, support, and goodwill evaporate, along with my prospects for remaining employed. Before fully accepting that reality, however, I tried everything possible to save the career I had worked so many years to build, including filing a lawsuit alleging sex discrimination against State Farm in federal court.[7] Like the vast majority of other transsexual plaintiffs in that era, I lost.

Had I brought my case today, it is possible, though far from certain, that the outcome would have been different. In the past few years, transgender plaintiffs have been successful in sex discrimination cases in a growing number of jurisdictions and courts. The following is an overview of how the legal landscape for transgender plaintiffs alleging workplace sex discrimination has begun to change.

The first reported cases in which transsexual plaintiffs sought protection under sex discrimination statutes date to 1975. In that year, two different federal district courts in California and New Jersey held that Title VII, a federal law prohibiting sex discrimination in employment, does not protect transsexual employees. In *Voyles v. Ralph K. Davies Medical Center,* a hemo-dialysis technician was fired shortly after she informed her supervisor that she was transsexual and intended to undergo sex reassignment from male to female.[8] The employee filed a lawsuit under Title VII, alleging that the hospital had discriminated against her on the basis of sex. The court dismissed her case, holding that Congress had enacted Title VII to protect women, not transsexuals, and that nothing in the legislative history of Title VII indicated any congressional intent "to embrace 'transsexual' discrimination, or any permutation or combination thereof."[9]

Similarly, in *Grossman v. Bernards Township Bd. of Educ.,*[10] a teacher who was fired after she underwent sex reassignment surgery filed a lawsuit alleging that the school had violated Title VII. Like the court in *Voyles,* the court dismissed her case, concluding that she was fired "not because of her status as a female, but rather because of her change in sex from the male to the female gender."[11] Also as in *Voyles,* the court noted "the absence of any legislative history indicating a congressional intent to include transsexuals within the language of Title VII," concluding that the term "sex" must be given "its plain meaning."[12]

In the decades following *Voyles* and *Grossman,* most courts adopted the reasoning in those early decisions. With few exceptions, courts dismissed claims by transgender people on the grounds that (1) sex discrimination laws were not intended to protect transgender people; and (2) the "plain" or "traditional" meaning of the term *sex* refers only to a person's biological identity as male or female, not to change of sex. In case after case, courts simply recited these arguments formulaically, with little analysis or genuine consideration of whether or how sex discrimination statutes should be applied to transgender people.[13]

Over time, however, these two rationales have become increasingly anachronistic and difficult to reconcile with the increasingly expansive interpretation of sex discrimination laws in cases involving nontransgender plaintiffs. In 1989, for example, the U.S. Supreme Court expressly rejected the notion that the term *sex* in Title VII refers only to a person's biological status as male or female, holding that it also includes stereotypical assumptions and preconceptions about how men and women are supposed to behave, dress, and appear.[14] Ann Hopkins, the plaintiff in the case, was denied a partnership in an accounting firm, in part because her demeanor, appearance, and personality were deemed insufficiently "feminine."[15] To improve her chances for partnership, Hopkins was told that she should "walk more femininely, talk more femininely, dress more femininely, wear make-up, have her hair styled, and wear jewelry."[16] The Supreme Court rejected the employer's argument that Title VII should be applied to prohibit only discrimination against women for being women or against men for being men, as opposed to prohibiting employers from enforcing stereotypical assumptions based on gender. "As for the legal relevance of sex stereotyping, we are beyond the day when an employer could evaluate employees by assuming or insisting that they matched the stereotype associated with their group, for '[i]n forbidding employers to discriminate against individuals because of their sex, Congress intended to strike at the entire spectrum of disparate treatment of men and women resulting from sex stereotypes.'"[17]

After *Price Waterhouse*, courts increasingly have been hard-pressed to explain why the reasoning in that decision would not apply equally to a transgender person. Logically, if Title VII prohibits an employer from discriminating against an employee because of her allegedly "unfeminine" personality or appearance, then must it not also prohibit an employer from discriminating against a transsexual person, either for retaining some characteristics of his or her birth sex or for assuming a masculine or feminine identity? In either case, the employer has discriminated on the basis of sex by "assuming or insisting that employees match the stereotypes associated with their group."[18] In my own case, for instance, I cited *Price Waterhouse* to argue that State Farm had violated Title VII by treating me adversely because, after beginning my transition, I did not conform to their expectations about how a "woman" should appear. Unfortunately, the court simply held that "in *Price Waterhouse*, the plaintiff was not a transsexual."[19] More recently, however, as explained further below, some courts have begun to take the impact of *Price Waterhouse* on cases involving transgender persons much more seriously.

In another important case decided in 1996, the U.S. Supreme Court also expressly rejected the notion that Title VII must be applied narrowly to prohibit only forms of discrimination expressly contemplated by Congress. In *Oncale v. Sundowner Offshore Oil Services, Inc.*,[20] a male employee sued his former employee under Title VII, alleging that he was subjected to physical sexual attacks by his male coworkers. The Fifth Circuit held that Title VII does not prohibit same-sex harassment because that is too far afield from what Congress intended when it enacted the statute. In a unanimous decision authored by Justice Antonin Scalia, the Supreme Court reversed. The Court acknowledged that when Congress enacted Title VII, it was not specifically concerned about same-sex harassment. The Court noted, however, that "statutory prohibitions often go beyond the principal evil to cover reasonably comparable evils, and it is ultimately the provisions of our laws rather than the principal concerns of our legislators by which we are governed."[21] In principle, the same reasoning should apply to discrimination against transgender employees. Regardless of whether Congress was specifically concerned about transgender people when it enacted Title VII, discrimination on this basis is a "reasonably comparable evil" and one that falls squarely within the statute's language and purpose.

In light of *Price Waterhouse* and *Oncale,* some courts have begun to recognize that the question of whether Title VII and similar state laws protect transsexual people must be reexamined. In 2000, in *Rosa v. Park W. Bank & Trust Co.,*[22] the First Circuit held that a male plaintiff dressed in "traditionally feminine attire" could seek redress under *Price Waterhouse* for discrimination based on the perception that his "attire did not accord with his male gender."[23] Also in 2000, the Ninth Circuit relied on *Price Waterhouse* and *Oncale* in concluding that transgender people must be protected under federal sex discrimination laws.[24] The plaintiff in the case, Crystal Schwenk, was a transgender prisoner who sued under the Gender Motivated Violence Act after being assaulted by a guard. On appeal, the guard argued that sex discrimination laws do not protect transgender people, citing the many previous cases holding that the term *sex* in Title VII refers only to a person's biological identity as male or female.[25] The Ninth Circuit rejected the guard's argument, stating: "The initial judicial approach taken in [older] cases . . . has been overruled by the logic and language of *Price Waterhouse.* In *Price Waterhouse,* . . . the Supreme Court held that Title VII barred not just discrimination based on the fact that Hopkins was a woman, but also discrimination based on the fact that she failed 'to act like a woman'—that is, to conform to socially-constructed gender expectations."[26] The court concluded that Schwenk had stated a viable sex discrimination claim. "The evidence offered by Schwenk tends to show that [the guard's] actions were motivated, at least in part, by Schwenk's gender—in this case, by her assumption of a feminine rather than a typically masculine appearance or demeanor."[27]

Most recently, in a case decided in 2004, the Sixth Circuit held that Title VII protected a transsexual police officer who was fired for being insufficiently "masculine," after more than twenty years of service on the force.[28] In the past, as described above, most courts dismissed such claims out-of-hand, despite the precedent of *Price Waterhouse,* based on the notion that simply by definition, a transgender person is not entitled to protection. In *Smith,* the court rejected this categorical exclusion of transgender people as unprincipled, holding: "Sex stereotyping based on a person's gender non-conforming behavior is impermissible discrimination, irrespective of the cause of that behavior; a label, such as 'transsexual,' is not fatal to a sex discrimination claim where the victim has suffered discrimination because of his or her gender non-conformity."[29]

In addition to these groundbreaking federal precedents, state courts also have become more receptive to sex discrimination claims brought by transgender plaintiffs under state sex discrimination laws. In New Jersey, for example, an appellate court held that transgender people are protected under a New Jersey law prohibiting sex discrimination in employment.[30] After discussing several prior decisions that rejected sex discrimination claims by transgender plaintiffs, the court explained: "We disagree with the rationale of these decisions. A person who is discriminated against because he changes his gender from male to female is being discriminated against because he or she is a member of a very small minority whose condition remains incomprehensible to most individuals. The view of sex discrimination reflected in these decisions is too constricted."[31] Holding that "sex" is "broader than anatomical sex" and "comprises more than a person's genitalia at birth," the court concluded that the New Jersey statute protected the plaintiff "from gender stereotyping and discrimination for transforming herself from a man to a woman."[32]

Similarly, in 2000 the Connecticut Human Rights Commission held that transsexual people are protected under a Connecticut law prohibiting sex discrimination in employment. The commission noted that, "following the lead of the U.S. Supreme Court in *Price Waterhouse v. Hopkins,* 490 U.S. 228 (1989), more and more courts have ruled that having specific expectations that a person will manifest certain behavior based upon his or her gender is not only conceptually outmoded sexual stereotyping, but also an unlawful form of sex discrimination."[33] Other states with positive administrative or court decisions on this issue include Massachusetts and New York.[34] The European Court of Justice and courts in other countries also have reached similar results.[35]

These recent positive decisions may be the harbinger of a new trend. As we enter the twenty-first century, it is possible that federal and state courts generally will be more receptive to transgender plaintiffs and more willing to construe sex discrimination statutes to include them. From a purely legal perspective, it is perhaps too soon to tell, and we would do well to remember that a single negative U.S. Supreme Court decision on this issue could bring these recent positive developments to a screeching halt, at least in the federal courts. From a broader perspective, however, there can be no doubt that this judicial shift is an indicator of a much broader and more important change than any mere evolution in legal doctrine. Despite much recent right-wing rhetoric about "judicial activism," courts generally are much more prone to follow changes in the larger society than to create them. For those of us (myself included) who are activists as well as lawyers, it is clear that decisions such as those in *Rosa, Schwenk,* and *Smith* reflect a cultural change that has been decades in the making. Rather than seeing transgender people as lurid oddities, both the public and the courts have begun to view transgender people as a legitimate minority and to see us as human beings who are entitled to equal dignity and equal protection under the law.

As a former litigant in a transgender discrimination case, I am keenly aware of the law's tremendous power to reflect and shape larger societal messages of acceptance or rejection. When I lost my case, I was devastated not only by the loss of my job and my career but, even more profoundly, by the terrible message that loss conveyed—that as a transgender person, I was not worthy of legal protection or recognition. For many years, progressive scholars and activists have cautioned against placing too much emphasis on the law and on the discourse of "rights" in particular, based on well-founded concerns that doing so can channel our political energies too narrowly and render us too fixated on the chimerical goal of achieving normalcy and approval from the state. At the same time, other progressive voices—and particularly those of people of color—have cautioned against jettisoning the notion of rights altogether. In the words of Patricia Williams:

> For the historically disempowered, the conferring of rights is symbolic of all the denied aspects of humanity: rights imply a respect which places one within the referential range of self and others, which elevates one's status from human body to social being. For blacks, then the attainment of rights signifies the due, the respectful behavior, the collective responsibility properly owed by a society to one of its own.[36]

This point is equally applicable to transgender people. Rights both empower transgender people to contest discrimination and allow us to envision ourselves, and to be seen by others, as fully human. As lawyers and litigants continue to struggle to win individual cases and to set precedents that will benefit the community as a whole, we must not lose sight of this fundamental dimension of legal advocacy.

Notes

The asterisks that appear with page numbers in these notes refer to screen page numbers from a database.

1. Chris Daley and Shannon Minter, *Trans Realities: A Legal Needs Assessment of San Francisco's Transgender Communities* (San Francisco: Transgender Law Center, 2003).

2. K. Clements-Nolle, W. Wilkinson, K. Kitano, and R. Marx, "HIV Prevention and Health Service Needs of the Transgender Community in San Francisco," in *Transgender and HIV: Risks, Prevention, and Care,* ed. W. Bockting and S. Kirk (New York: Hayworth, 2001), 69–89.

3. In the only reported court decision to consider the issue, a federal court rejected the argument that sharing a bathroom with a transgender coworker violates any right

to privacy or constitutes sexual harassment. See *Cruzan v. Special Sch. Dist. #1*, 294 F.3d 981 (8th Cir. 2002) (holding that a female teacher who objected to sharing a restroom with a transsexual woman had failed to state a viable privacy, sex discrimination, or religious discrimination claim).

4. See http://ai.eecs.umich.edu/people/conway/conway.html.

5. See Human Rights Campaign, Employers with Non-Discrimination Policies That Include Gender Identity, http://www.hrc.org.

6. For sample nondiscrimination policies and information on the best practices of employers who wish to support their transgender employees, see the Center for Gender Sanity, http://www.gendersanity.com/index.shtml.

7. *Broadus v. State Farm Ins. Co.*, 2000 WL 1585257 (W.D. Mo. 2000).

8. *Voyles v. Ralph K. Davies Medical Center*, 403 F. Supp. 456 (N.D. Cal. 1975).

9. Ibid. at 456.

10. 1975 U.S. Dist. LEXIS 16261 (September 10, 1975).

11. Ibid. at *9.

12. Ibid. at *9.

13. For an overview of these decisions, see Paisley Currah and Shannon Minter, "Unprincipled Exclusions: The Struggle to Achieve Judicial and Legislative Equality for Transgender People," *William and Mary Journal of Women and the Law* 7 (2000): 37.

14. *Price Waterhouse v. Hopkins*, 490 U.S. 228 (1989).

15. Ibid. at 234–35.

16. Ibid. at 235.

17. Ibid. at 251 (internal citations omitted).

18. *Price Waterhouse*, 490 U.S. at 251.

19. *Broadus v. State Farm Insurance Co.*, at *11. See also, for example, *Sweet v. Mulberry Lutheran Home*, 2003 U.S. Dist. LEXIS 11373, 2003 WL 21525058 (S.D. Ind. 2003) (holding that transsexual people continue to be excluded from Title VII after *Price Waterhouse*).

20. 523 U.S. 75 (1998).

21. Ibid. at 79.

22. 214 F.3d 213, 214–16 (1st Cir. 2000).

23. Ibid. at 215.

24. *Schwenk v. Hartford*, 204 F.3d 1187 (9th Cir. 2000).

25. Ibid. at 1201.

26. Ibid. at 1201–02.

27. Ibid. at 1202.

28. *Smith v. City of Salem*, 378 F.3d 566 (6th Cir. 2004).

29. Ibid. at 575. See also *Sturchio v. Ridge*, 2004 U.S. Lexis 27345 (E.D. Wash. December 20, 2004) (holding that a transsexual woman could bring a sex discrimination claim under Title VII).

30. *Enriquez v. West Jersey Health Systems*, 777 A.2d 365 (N.J. Super. Ct. App. Div. 2001).

31. Ibid. at 372.

32. Ibid. at 373.

33. *Declaratory Ruling on behalf of John/Jane Doe* (Conn. Human Rights Comm'n 2000).

34. *Lie v. Sky Publishing Corp.*, 15 Mass. L. Rptr. 412, 2002 WL 31492397 (Mass. Super. 2002) (holding that a transgender plaintiff had stated a claim of sex discrimination where she alleged "that the defendant's conduct was based on stereotyped notions of 'appropriate' male and female behavior in the same manner as the conduct of the defendant in *Price Waterhouse*"); *Maffei v. Kolaeton Industry, Inc.*, 626 N.Y.S.2d 391 (N.Y. Sup. Ct. 1995) (holding that "an employer who harasses an employee because the person, as a result of surgery and hormone treatments, is now of a different sex has violated [the] prohibition against discrimination based on sex").

35. *See P v. S and Cornwall Co. Council*, 1996 ECR I-2159 (holding that where a person suffers discrimination on the ground that "he or she intends to undergo, or has undergone gender reassignment, he or she is treated unfavourably by comparison with persons of the sex to which he or she was deemed to belong before undergoing gender reassignment"). See also *Plaintiff v. Maison des Jeunes and C.T. and A.T.*, File No. 500–53–00078–970, District of Montreal Human Rights Tribunal July 2, 1998) ("it is not clear how discrimination based on transsexualism or on the process of transsexualism could ultimately be anything other than sex-based").

36. Patricia Williams, "Alchemical Notes: Reconstructing Ideals from Deconstructed Rights," *Harvard Civil Rights–Civil Liberties Law Review* 22 (1987): 401, 416.

6. Deciding Fate or Protecting a Developing Autonomy? Intersex Children and the Colombian Constitutional Court

Morgan Holmes

In 1999 the Constitutional Court in Bogotá decided a case pivotal to contemporary debates on the care of minors, sexual autonomy, and the medicalization of intersexuality.[1] The court's determination suggests that intersexed minors may constitute a minority group entitled to special protection against prejudice and its potential consequences. The ruling also suggests that where parental attitudes show prejudice against the intersexed child, then the court cannot support parental consent to "normalising" surgical intervention.

This introduction to the case provides a critical framework through which one can better apprehend both the promise and the limitations of the court's decision. Because of the influence of the Intersex Society of North America (ISNA) amicus brief presented to the court, and because the joint press releases of the ISNA and the International Lesbian and Gay Association (ILGA) sought to encourage domestic politicians to take notice of legal alterations in the standard protection of parental power over their intersexed children,[2] the decision has central political utility for domestic application. The decision, of course, requires serious attention because of its apparent progressive impulses. It ought not, however, be left uncritically assessed, for it also contains more conservative elements in its concluding recommendations. This chapter explores the limitations of the ruling's declared progressive intent and draws attention to the decision's more conservative turns.

In the following, I critically examine key considerations central to the Colombian decision. Specifically, I address recent historical changes in popular awareness of intersex, shifting cultural norms that influenced the court's approach, how progressive rhetoric can serve conservative impulses, and limitations that inhere in specific aspects of the ruling. I conclude by suggesting that we need to rethink the traditional primacy of parental rights to privacy against the obligation of parents to protect the developing autonomy of their children; that is, as an obligation of noninterference.

Intersex Moves into Popular Consciousness

In the early 1990s when groups like the ISNA were forming, there was almost no public awareness of intersexuality. By the winter of 1996–97, largely because of the efforts of a few "grassroots" organizations as well as academic and popular reports, intersexuality had been brought into popular consciousness. Intersexuality has shifted in the past decade from being a concept that few audiences outside medical circles would recognize without first invoking either classical mythology or Herculine Barbin, and even then its salience would have been limited to undergraduate discussions on "the sex/gender question." Intersex is now a reasonably well-considered concern in academic work in a wide range of disciplines and is a fashionable topic for various popular-culture venues.[3] In short, "hermaphrodites" have stepped out of and beyond pubescent male jokes about "chicks with dicks" and "he-shes," although it would be going too far to say that this new popular awareness was based on an adequate understanding of the various and shifting complexities of sex and gender.

Questions posed by my students indicate a substantial concern for "authenticity" in sexual identity. Thus, at the end of one undergraduate lecture, a young man asked me whether I thought he ought to have his fiancée's chromosomes tested to find out if she was *really* a woman. Obviously, he had not clearly understood the point of my lecture: that intersexuality was not an obvious medical problem, though it does trouble taken-for-granted ideas about the distinct and oppositional "nature" of male and female sex categories. One can hardly blame him as a novice for his naïveté; high school students still learn in biology classes that "hermaphroditism" is a reproductive peculiarity of some animal species (like worms) and in humans is a pathology of fetal development that has either been disrupted or run afoul of a presumed master plan. Existing critical research on intersex shows that the latter model of developmental biology remains the one most often reiterated to parents of intersex neonates.[4]

Prior to 1993 with the publication of Anne Fausto-Sterling's article "The Five Sexes" and the founding of the ISNA,[5] there was little opportunity to alter popular awareness of intersexuality. At that time, the decision of Colombia's Constitutional Court to protect the "developing autonomy" of a minor would have been unthinkable. Two significant perceptual/political changes had to occur before the Colombian decision could be formed. The changes took place in the chronological order that I mention them here. First, at a general level, courts and international NGOs such as UNICEF had to recognize that children were not the property of their parents but individual beings holding distinct rights of their own. Second, largely through the work of critical academic scrutiny, the medicalized and stigmatized status of intersexuals had to shift. Critical perspectives had to develop an alternate, popular, and sympathetic awareness of the treatment to which intersexed persons are subject. This took place in the context of broader shifts in rights lobbying such as the LGBT movement(s), which Sharon Preves notes "acknowledge(s) the importance of the agency individuals have in constructing not only their own identities but also in responding to and negotiating social expectations of who they ought to be."[6] Preves's brief point is an appreciation of the centrality of agency and autonomy as indispensable mechanisms for challenging and overcoming the negative stigma traditionally attached to difference. Furthermore, they are practical and compelling focal points for legal advances because of their entrenchment as constitutionally guaranteed rights in many Western countries.

Throughout the mid- to late 1990s, intersex activists launched an appeal to persuade popular, academic, and medical audiences that there was no compelling reason to deny the rights of agency and autonomy to intersexed children. The first popular media feature, an article by Donna Alvarado, appeared in the *San Jose Mercury News* supplement, *West Magazine,* in 1994; it would be followed by other features in magazines as diverse as *Time, Newsweek,* and *Out.* As the 1990s came to a close, various cable programs in Canada, Europe, and the United States, with syndicated versions broadcast around the globe, would devote significant time to the controversy over the "standard of care" for intersexed children.

By the time media attention turned to the intersex movement, the medical establishment, as represented by its governing bodies such as the American and Canadian Medical Associations, had become aware of the need to provide not only the provisions for consent but the conditions for the exercise of *informed consent.* Thus the legal provision to protect autonomy was already in place to support the rights discourse of intersex groups. In a contiguous dialogue, intersexed persons and the movement in general both urged the implementation of these provisions. In 1996, for example, a handful of ISNA members and their supporters converged on the American Academy of Pediatrics meetings in Boston to draw attention to the fact that the AAP's own ethical guidelines were compromised in treatment standards applied to intersexuality. In 1995 the AAP committee on bioethics determined that "unless the patient has diminished decision-making capacity or must undergo legally authorized 'involuntary' treatment,"[7] then patients have a legal and ethical right to make their own decisions. The committee even acknowledged that proxy consent is deeply problematic because health-care providers "have legal and ethical duties to their child patients to render competent medical care based on what the patient needs, not what someone else expresses."[8] At the 1996 demonstration, ISNA pointed out to the AAP that in carrying out cosmetic surgeries on intersexed children because of parental wishes to have "normal" children, surgeons were contravening the AAP's own guidelines.

At that demonstration, Max Beck and I went as officially appointed spokespersons of the ISNA to try to garner support from surgeons and nurses working with infants and children they had diagnosed as intersexed. We went to deliver information on long-term outcomes and to challenge their still-prevailing opinion that cosmetic surgery to "fix" intersexed genitals was the best course of action and to challenge their data on "nerve-sparing" techniques for clitorectomy and other highly invasive procedures such as the construction of neovaginas on infants who were to be assigned a female sex but who had no vagina. We were met, officially, with hostility and were escorted out of the conference by security guards who saw us as a potential danger. Various supporters of the ISNA's intervention, including members of the Massachusetts-based Middlesex Group and Riki Wilchins from Transsexual Menace, joined us outside the convention center where we spent several hours debating and discussing with medical professionals. The clinicians who stopped to talk with us were at least curious enough about, if not sympathetic to, our cause to engage with us rather than writing us off as unusually hostile former patients. A surgeon from the southern United States explained to me that he saw some wisdom in what we were saying but was unsure of what to do about "Southern families" who were not inclined to see sex as infinitely variable but as a simple matter of binary opposition in which there are only two choices: male and female.

Within a year of that demonstration, however, there would come a handful of articles questioning the status quo surgical interference with intersexed infants and children. Those publications were soon followed by the media frenzy over the story of David Reimer, perhaps still better known as the "John/Joan" case. John Money, a psychoendocrinologist at Johns Hopkins, famously distorted and knowingly concealed information about the case in order to use it as the benchmark to show that assigning intersexed persons as females was in almost all cases the best course of action, regardless of how invasive surgery and medical management would have to be to enforce that assignment.[9] The media attention to the failure of Reimer's female assignment was terribly embarrassing to the medical establishment, and increasing media sympathy for the intersex movement and its activists pushed the AAP to make a gesture of reparation.

The AAP formed the North American Task Force on Intersexuality (NATFI) to examine the concerns that ISNA members raised, but its relevance and efficacy for day-to-day practice remain hazy. It is unclear precisely how the NATFI impacts current day-to-day practice in the United States or in Canada,[10] where many pediatric specialists are members of AAP and work according to AAP guidelines even though Canada has its own umbrella organization in the Canadian Medical Association. For example, an acquaintance in the second year of medical school in Ontario recently remarked that when intersexuality is diagnosed, the course of action is clear: you simply "fix it." Clearly, contemporary teaching practices continue to advocate officially outmoded standards and practices.

Against a cultural backdrop of upheaval and persistent confusion/fascination over intersexuality, and with medical experts prevailing on the court to support the mother's appeal to be allowed to consent for surgery in the case, it is remarkable that the decision enforces the principle that parents do not have the right to alter their children to suit their own desires or manage their own anxieties. On this point the court argues that the UN convention on the rights of the child "orders the States to adopt the necessary measures to protect children from all forms of discrimination . . . when under the custody of the parents, legal guardians or another person in charge of their care."[11] The premise on which the UN convention is founded presumes that human beings have a right to autonomy and dignity of their persons, including bodily integrity. Over 191 countries, including Colombia, have ratified the UNICEF convention,[12] but the Colombian Constitutional Court is unique among them in its apparent commitment to upholding those principles. Other countries have shared views, at least in principle, but the medical treatment of intersexed children continues to contradict those values and guidelines.

The Canadian Law of Consent to Treatment drafted in 1990, for example, "assumes that all patients—including children—are legally competent to give authorization for treatment."[13] The law makes the point that if minors are capable of demonstrating an ability to discern risks and benefits in any proposed intervention, then they should be treated as a mature person, regardless of chronological age.[14] This recognition is an important one because the ability to consent is premised on an awareness of risks and benefits and also presupposes that one has the right to withhold consent.

For intersexed persons, legal developments in tort, battery, and consent law are of more than just coincidental importance to the effective ability to form a salient political movement. What various intersex groups have had to point out is that fairly recent alterations to consent law, including the recognition that consent could be validly given only if it were properly informed and free of coercion, were recognitions not being applied equally to their own treatment(s). Intersexed persons were thus denied an enfranchisement to which they were entitled: the right not only to consent but to refuse. In addition, intersexuality had to become enough a part of the common, popular lexicon that parents would not be hearing about it for the first time in delivery room "emergency" situations. Intersex groups argue that such "emergency scenarios" are actually the creation of standard medical practice and render the principle of consent impossible to fulfill. A valid consent is possible only when intersex conditions are understood in neutral terms and not viewed as cause for alarm.

As it stands now in Canada and the United States, all medical interventions require that the criteria for the provision of valid consent be fulfilled; to do otherwise is to render the consent meaningless, and the medical procedure is then a form of battery or assault. Where consent is possible, there is a legal obligation to protect its exercise. The following section provides some cultural context for the climate changes of consent and perception as they relate to intersexuality.

"A Period of Normative and Cultural Transition": Ambivalence in Legal Thought

It is not possible to appreciate fully the contemporary general discussion of how best to manage intersexuality if one approaches it solely as a discrete, biomedical fact to be identified and rectified. Rather, the instantiation of diagnosis and the implementation of proposed treatments are caught up in other questions about medical authority, "proper" parenting, and anxieties in general over social norms related to sexuality and gender.

The court ruling under examination here notes the shifts in sociocultural norms related to intersexuality and observes that such shifts must be accounted for: "The Constitutional Court of Colombia understands that our present day society is undergoing a period of normative and cultural transition in relation to the theme of hermaphrodism."[15] Against the background of popular but vague understanding, biological determinism, and cultural transition, the Colombian court demonstrates a unique consciousness of the need to protect the potential for a person not only to consent but also to refuse any proposed intervention. In so doing the court moves toward actively effecting the legal conditions to uphold the UN declaration in the Convention on the Rights of the Child, that

1. States Parties shall assure to the child who is capable of forming his or her own views the right to express those views freely in all matters affecting the child, the views of the child being given due weight in accordance with the age and maturity of the child.
2. For this purpose, the child shall in particular be provided the opportunity to be heard in any judicial and administrative proceedings affecting the child, either directly, or through a representative or an appropriate body, in a manner consistent with the procedural rules of national law.[16]

As the translator for the Colombian rulings pointed out in the course of her work, the convention's declaration means that for legal purposes each child is a "developing autonomy" and not the property of the parents. This does not mean that children are independent of their parents, but that in certain circumstances, children must be emancipated from the parents. This is especially the case if, as in the ruling under consideration, the parent or guardian is suspected of holding prejudicial attitudes about the child or is perhaps not capable of understanding the choices available. It is worth explaining here precisely what characterizes "the theme of hermaphroditism" as one in transition.[17] A transition presumes an original point of departure and at least a provisional destination, but the history of hermaphroditism is not quite so linear in its fluctuations. Rather, it seems that for as long as there have been persons of "ambiguous sex," there has been ambivalent discourse about how to best manage such embodied difference. The court is by no means alone in recognizing that intersexuality is a politicized nodal point in shifting sexual norms.

The Dangers of Juridical Management

When the Colombian decision was rendered in 1999, Michel Foucault's introduction to the Herculine Barbin case of the 1860s in France had long been established as *the* benchmark text on the potential threat to social-sexual norms that an inappropriate management of intersexuality might cause.[18] In addressing the Barbin case, Margaret McLaren deftly summarizes the concern and the transformation of the management of intersexuality in medieval France:

> In the middle ages, hermaphrodites were considered to have two sexes, and at the time of baptism the father or godfather decided which sex the child would be raised as; then at adulthood, the hermaphrodite was able to decide whether to continue on with this sex designation or switch to the other. This decision was to take place before marriage, and once the decision was made it could not be changed without penalties and social sanctions.[19]

Barbin's memoirs demonstrate that the political climate in France had changed significantly by the mid-nineteenth century, precluding any decision making on the part of the intersexed person. Barbin's memoir of her early years indicates that she was content to live as she was: as an exceptional female. The courts, however, perceived her courting of a female lover as an indication that she had, in fact, refused her female sex assignment and had taken on a male one or, perhaps, that she had been male all along and that only a medical error had caused the female assignment in infancy. The court took upon itself as one of its due juridical powers to *realize* Barbin's "true sex" through a juridical redesignation of her sex to male. Furthermore, the court and religious officials involved in the case effectively punished Barbin for transgressing the limits of femaleness by removing her from the convent and from all contact with her lover. Barbin was thus made to bear the price of exceeding the symbolic limits of her culture's sex categories.

The current picture for intersexuals is that they are made to pay the price a priori through medical intervention intended to ward off what is presumed to be "only a matter of time" if one is allowed to grow up with an ambiguous body: namely, that one will make ambiguous choices that exceed contemporary sexual taxonomy. Published shortly prior to the delivery of the Colombian court decision, Alice Dreger's book *Hermaphrodites and the Medical Invention of Sex* demonstrates the complicated manner in which "hermaphrodites" have been made to bear the burden of symbolic and political shifts in the structural and political importance of this thing that we call "sex." These concerns have long sat at a nexus point where law and medicine converge. Dreger points out that the symbolic and political relevance of chastity is central to the manner in which Barbin was treated and that, more generally, a concern that "accidental homosexuality" not be allowed to flourish because of cases of "mistaken sex" has motivated both the juridical and medical management of intersexuality.[20]

More recently, Judith Butler's critical assessment of the battle waged between social constructionists and biological determinists upon the body of David Reimer notes that the war over gender/sexuality and those who live in its interstices is significant because the stakes center on the foundational questions of human existence:

> When we ask what the conditions of intelligibility are by which the human emerges, by which the human is recognized, by which some subject becomes the subject of human love, we are asking about conditions of intelligibility composed of norms, of practices, that have become presuppositional, without which we cannot think the human at all.[21]

Put most simply, intersexed bodies challenge social presuppositions about a life course that will move in only one of two possible trajectories, either toward adult maleness or toward adult femaleness, and all that those two end points entail: heterosexual marriage and the creation of social, if not biological, family units.

For Marianne Valverde, the heterosexism of everyday assumption appears quite clearly in the cliché that "opposites attract."[22] The essentialist notion that sexual pairing through *opposition* is the only appropriate mode has enormous practical and ideological consequences. Medical debates such as those at the heart of the Colombian Constitutional Court decision do not take place in a vacuum but in a cultural context that still presumes, at least in some locations, that marriage requires defense against those who would tear at its moral center by asking that persons of the same sex be able to marry.[23] Such assumptions follow from the common and powerful cultural belief that there are only two sexes and that they are, naturally, opposite. Amy Potts, for example, in her critique of the enormously popular books by John Gray on Venusians and Martians, points out that his entire thesis for all the work rests on the (highly marketable) presupposition that "Martians and Venusians [are] from different planets and are supposed to be different."[24] Similarly, Valverde argues in her book *Sex, Power, and Pleasure* that there is a tendency to assume that all erotic attraction and activity "depend in an essential way on *difference* and specifically *genital difference*."[25]

The Difference between Intention and Discourse in a Progressive Court

Heteronormative behavior and attitudinal stances develop out of and re-create existing kinship systems and symbolic relationships. For the Colombian court to recognize that the social norms that aid in this organization of subjects are visibly in contestation, and not to retrench against that uncertainty in its ruling, is no small feat. Instead of worrying about the future of marriage and heterosexuality, the court focuses its attention on the future well-being of the child and on the value of protecting such abstract concepts as autonomy and citizenship. More central to the court's decision than the future of marriage is a need to determine whether in protecting the minor's potential autonomy the court then undermines the autonomy of families. Based on the material put before them, including an amicus brief from the ISNA, reports from clinicians who favor standard surgical responses, and reports from those who question them, the magistrates ultimately decide that in this specific case the child has already attained sufficient self-awareness to warrant protection from the court that exceeds any protections it might choose to amplify for families.

Although this court ruling is a benchmark for its position that the autonomy and physical integrity of the intersexed person must be considered central and protected rights because of the minority status of the intersexed person, this is by no means the first significant entry of intersexed persons into the purview of the courts, as I have already indicated. Herculine Barbin's sex reassignment was a juridical rather than a medico-surgical matter, although medical arguments buttressed the court's decision, and, as Dreger demonstrates, sex assignment in cases of apparent ambiguity was a power of the courts rather than a power of medicine in seventeenth- to nineteenth-century France. That is to say, medicine might have been called on to advise the courts, but the final word resided with legal rather than medical powers; medicine could advise, but only the courts could pronounce and enact a sex assignment.

What distinguishes the case at hand is that the court does not ultimately pronounce a sex for the child, for it is no longer being called on to do this; rather, it is being called on to address the question of whether the child is entitled to decide for itself what course, if any, of medical treatment to pursue. In this sense, the courts recognize the power of medicine to *pronounce* first the status of intersexuality, and then to *enact* a sex assignment. What the court sees as critical is that the enactment not interfere with the child's autonomy, and this point is cause for great consternation of the ruling magistrates. In sections 88 and 89 of the ruling, the court notes that one is not born with autonomy. Noting that autonomy develops over time, the court observes that the child on whose case they are commenting has clearly reached an age at which children have an independently formed, fairly coherent "cognitive map of the different gender roles."[26] The court thus argues that part of the rationale of its decision rests on the child having entered into Piaget's "operational" stage of development, "which implies the development of intelligence and a consciousness of what occurs in . . . [its] surroundings."[27]

It is precisely the court's focus on the already developed autonomy of the child that makes me hesitate to share ISNA's enthusiastic endorsement of the court's recognition that "intersexed people constitute a minority entitled to protection by the state against discrimination."[28] Among those whom the court consulted for input in its decision was the ISNA, which supplied the courts with an amicus brief. The court noted in its decision that it had relied heavily on the amicus. In its press release on the Colombian court decisions, the ISNA noted that

> the decision dramatically limits the ability of doctors in Colombia to perform early genital surgery on intersexed infants. The court has established new rules restricting parents' authority to authorize genital surgery on their intersexed children, with the goal of forcing parents to put the child's best interest ahead of their own fears and concerns about genital ambiguity.[29]

Although the court's decision is indeed groundbreaking, law is notoriously slow to make change and is known to be well behind social change in general. ISNA's press release is perhaps somewhat too optimistic. I have no intention of minimizing the importance of the decision or of ISNA's monumental influence in helping move the courts forward; my own work was included in the amicus, after all. There are, however, a number of critical issues arising in the decision that require further discussion.

Without a doubt, this is a remarkable recognition on which those interested in civil rights discourses and practical strategies will want to focus. However, the court's decision is not made independently from the information it demands of the medical community, and its decision does not supersede the authority of medicine to define what counts as a sexual anomaly. Rather, the decision suggests that it is merely the relatively advanced age of the child that prevents surgeons from imposing what would otherwise be a workable and useful solution. Although much is made of the need to protect the child's autonomy in this case, the decision rests on a notion that the child in question *already* has some self-awareness. As the court understands it, the child has already progressed through various sociopsychological cognitive stages required to have a self-concept that includes a vision of its own body. The court, then, is not ruling precisely that any intersexed child be allowed to achieve this state but is merely recognizing that because of circumstances, in this case it is a fait accompli. The court is not advocating a future in which intersexed children be allowed to achieve the same state, but merely that if they do, and if they also have parents who are presumed to be poorly equipped to make meaningful choices and decisions about their children's treatment, then the children should be permitted access to conditions that will protect their autonomies. The decision does not undermine the authority of medical knowledge or of practitioners to explain to parents and families what the proper course of action should be when an intersexed child *is born.* In its worst potential implications and uses, the court's decision may simply amplify the need to expedite procedures, making sure they take place in the neonatal period before the infant has acquired any self-awareness at all.

To read this decision only for its best features neglects the authority that it still invests in medical professionals. The authority of doctors is not inconsequential in Euro-American cultures, and Jay Katz proposes that the authority of the doctor as "knower" constitutes a powerful relationship of *faith* between patients and their medical practitioners. It is a faith that he claims practitioners are convinced would be undercut by admitting the uncertainties inherent in any course of treatment or procedure:

> Learning to live more comfortably with uncertainty...has been impeded by other strongly held, although largely unexamined professional beliefs: that patients are unable to tolerate awareness of uncertainty, and that faith in professionals and their prescriptions makes a significant contribution to the treatment of disease. In the light of these and other problems it is not surprising that doctors are most reluctant to share authority with patients and instead insist that patients follow doctors' orders.[30]

Limits of the Decision

Why is there so much interest in the sex/gender question and the necessity to deny the legitimacy of an uncertain outcome? As the court decision suggests, sexuality forms the underpinning of family organization, and for anyone who has done any work on social structures, it is apparent that all societies require a coherent system for classifying and regulating kinship relations. Intersexuality, like transsexuality and transgender, challenges the common perception that such relations are natural and obvious. The court then has quite a time determining how to protect the family's sanctity, as well as the individual's autonomy, and this difficulty severely limits the scope and power of the court's decision. This section of the introduction to the case examines what some of those limitations are and how they could undermine the best intentions of the ruling and uphold some suspect medical practices and perceptions.

There is an odd requirement in the decision, which states in section 89, "This team would then decide when the minor has had sufficient autonomy to make an informed consent if she chooses to undergo the surgeries and hormonal treatments."[31] To understand better the nuances of the distinction between obtaining consent and obtaining an *informed* consent, I wish to pause to consider a case in Canada that set the distinction out quite clearly, mandating a new approach to obtaining a valid consent. *Reibl v. Hughes* was decided at the federal level of the Supreme Court and determined that it simply was not enough to obtain a patient's consent to interfere with his or her body.[32] The court found that one must, rather, obtain consent based on the delivery of a rational and objective discussion of risks and benefits with a patient.

Reibl v. Hughes demonstrates that determining just what constitutes a "reasonable and objective" awareness and appreciation of the risks and benefits of any proposed procedure is uncertain if the assessment falls to the medical establishment to make on its own, according to its own standards. The problem of who gets to determine the criteria of reasonable and objective decision making has made the guarantee of a free and informed consent extremely controversial in Canadian medical circles and in the relevant legal realm of tort and battery law. The problem, argues the medical realm, is that it is impossible to know at what point the patient has acquired sufficient education *and* understanding to weigh the risks and benefits of the situation. The medical establishment argues that only they, as trained experts, are able to make such a determination. The *Reibl v. Hughes* case determined, however, that the medical establishment could not have sufficient awareness of any individual's particular circumstances (in Reibl's case, pension and employment situations) and how they might legitimately influence a decision. The case, decided in 1983, forever altered at least the principles according to which medical experts had to adhere in order to obtain consent; indeed, the ruling made clear that it was no longer sufficient to obtain consent but that permission to interfere with the body had to be given with knowledge adequate to the patient's needs in order to determine whether such interference was truly the most appropriate course of action.

In short, the case determined that the events leading up to a catastrophic stroke that left Mr. Reibl paralyzed could have been avoided had the primary care provider, Mr. Hughes, provided enough information to Reibl to determine for himself whether he ought to have surgery on his carotid artery to prevent a possible stroke. The medical information Reibl had received suggested to him that he had a 100 percent chance of having a stroke without the surgery. The court determined that, in fact, Reibl's physician had failed to reveal the medically known, significant risk that the surgery could cause a stroke. Furthermore, Reibl's risk of a stroke occurring in the remaining five-year period that Reibl had to obtain a full pension from his trade job was lower than the surgical risk. The court determined that *all* patients were entitled to weigh their own needs and circumstances against the potential and probable risks of any procedure and that a "rational" decision had to be determined by balancing both the personal and clinical profile. The court's decision was that Hughes had failed to inform his patient properly and in so doing had failed to obtain a valid consent, failed to provide a minimally adequate level of care, and had thus committed a battery against Reibl. The ruling mandated that, ever after, one would have to allow a patient to weigh for himself or herself the risks and benefits of a proposed procedure and that all patients were entitled to all the information necessary to make that assessment.

Some difficulties remain, however, and they interfere with implementing the ruling, especially where there is an enormous age, articulation, and power discrepancy between physicians/surgeons and patients. A conceptual and practical mess for consent law in Canada remains because the tension between "expert knowledge" and personal awareness remains powerful and unresolved—especially where the treatment of minors and the elderly are concerned. This trouble is not unique to Canada but shows up also in general discussions by American ethicists such as those at the Hastings Center, and by the general membership of the American Society for Bioethics and Humanities, with many discussions focusing on the problems of obtaining valid consent from the elderly and the young.

Pitting Expert Scrutiny against Autonomy in Sections 88 and 89

The elderly and the young are especially vulnerable to inspections, such as the provision in section 89 of the Colombian decision. Inspections by "expert teams" determine whether the minor or the elderly patient with a potential cognitive impairment is capable of understanding what is taking place.[33] The risk is always that any position that disagrees with the medical determination will be deemed "wrong." Buttressing themselves against charges of paternalism, medical experts are inclined to argue that they serve the requirement of beneficence by refusing to allow patients' lack of awareness to negatively influence their future health. Protection of autonomy is thus superseded by the requirement of beneficence, and the Colombian court ruling falls short of providing a clear protection of the right of the intersexed person to disagree with medical experts about the most appropriate course to follow.

In section 88 the court proposes that autonomy exists when the child has developed a self-concept, but does not attempt to make any specific ruling about when such autonomy could be said to exist:

> An obvious question arises, at what age can we presume the psychological changes have occurred that invalidate the paternal surrogate consent to treat the genital ambiguity of minor XX? There is no clear answer to this question, because different people develop at different rates.... Obviously, it is not this Entity's duty to decide on these debates.[34]

The court's statement thus creates yet another requirement that the intersexed child be subject to scrutiny beyond that of typical children, to assess the child's state of development. The intentions are good, but have their own pitfalls. The court would have done well to draw out the fact that a surrogate consent may be valid only insofar as the surrogate or proxy representative is actually representing the wishes of the person on whose behalf they are providing consent. In other cases of proxy consent, such as in appointments of power of attorney to consent to medical care or to make medical decisions on behalf of one who has lost the capacity to do so, the principle that must be adhered to is that the surrogate is making decisions congruent to those the individual himself or herself would make if possible. The court fails to adequately note then that the treatment of children often seems to neglect the usual requirement of concordance. In so doing the court also fails to adequately protect the developing autonomy not only of the child whose case was being deliberated but also of other children whose parents might consent to invasive procedures that the child would not choose once having obtained maturity. This failure belies the court's covert legal concern to protect parental rights more than children's rights, a concern more explicitly expressed elsewhere in the decision.

Still Protecting Parents' Rights over Children's Rights

For example, section 84 indicates that early surgery, without ever informing the child of its completion, remains a valid and necessary means of managing intersexuality. The court acknowledges and thereby implicitly endorses current protocols for the treatment of intersexuality, stating that "the urgency of this surgery has disappeared, because the present protocol justifies early surgeries so that the child can develop a gender identity that coincides with his/her genitalia."[35] The statement agrees that in the neonatal period there *is* an urgency to perform surgery, and, clearly, this would be preferable to the court rather than allowing a child to get to a point where he or she would be aware of his or her own embodied difference, having integrated that awareness into a self-concept. The decision rendered here then applies only to those children whose "ambiguity" is either discovered or is to be remedied after the period of infancy, somewhere prior to the development of language. The ruling, then, is not as focused on the protection of the potential autonomy of the child as it might be. Rather, its focus is only to protect what it presumes to be an already developed autonomy. In all other cases, the privacy of the family and the constitutional protection of "pluralism" supersede the protection of the infant, a position rendered clearly in section 78 where the court writes that "in the majority of cases, it is the right of the parents to decide to authorize early surgeries designed to reshape the genitalia of their children."[36]

Not All Families Are Equal

In addition to maintaining the protection of the family before the autonomy of the child, section 77 requires us to be aware that poor parents are more likely to be subject to the enactment of the provisions of this ruling than the wealthy Colombian families who access private medical care delivered outside the purview of social services. This is a unique result of socialized medicine that provides medical care to all citizens, but which is delivered in a two-tiered system wherein the divisions between the wealthy and the poor are especially marked. That the poorest families will be the most likely to have their capacities to understand medical information and to give consent called into question is troubling; it will not serve the families especially well and may exacerbate already existing abuses of power by medical and social welfare workers against the families. In countries like the United States and Canada, where similar two-tier models are developing or are already in place, families using public health care could be similarly vulnerable.

The above limitation also impacts negatively on the court's recognition of intersexuals as a minority group. For the court, there is no a priori or prima facie duty to recognize intersexuals as a minority group with constitutional protections. The requirement exists only insofar as any individual with intersexed characteristics has already achieved a sense of self-concept and embodied subjectivity. In all other cases, the intersexed infant is just an infant, and the family's interests supersede the child's interests. In other words, the only escape route from surgical management is to "slip through the cracks" in infancy; the ruling does not actually recognize intersexuality as an integral feature of one's being.

The ISNA's public statements solidly endorse the court's recognition of intersexed persons as persons with a minority status and neglect the more-subtle maneuvering of the court on this point. In short, the court has not recognized intersexed persons as a minority group but has asserted that some intersexed persons, given some conditions, would constitute a minority group. This limitation, however, is only an explicit problem of the ruling. Outside the text, the court fails to provide an even more important recognition. It is not over the value of intersexuality or of the degree of autonomy that a child has already developed; rather, it is the need to recognize the intrinsic value of a human being and of every human being's right to bodily integrity. To protect infants and children from surgeries that may be unnecessary, that pose significant risk, and to which, by virtue of age, the child cannot properly consent, the court has merely to recognize that these children, like all children, have a right to bodily integrity. This right does not rest on something as idiosyncratic as a diagnosis resulting in an assigned status as intersexed. Nor does this right rest on the adult's ability to claim status as an intersexual, a member of an identity group that borrows heavily from the identity politics of other adult movements, including the civil rights movement as it is broadly defined, and more specifically from queer and feminist identity-based movements. The child's right to safety and to protection of its developing autonomy falls closely in line with a general Western ideology that claims that each of us has the right to self-actualization. Whatever the limits of that particular ideology, at least protecting children in ways consistent with it would not perpetuate the legal perception and social treatment of children as a subclass but rather as developing subjects.

The Parental Obligation of Noninterference

Readers may object that my position threatens the privacy and sanctity of the family that the ruling tries so hard to negotiate, but I would argue that, in fact, it does not. When a family welcomes a new member through birth or adoption, it is expected that the family will love, nurture, and protect that child, regardless of whether it is the sex they had hoped for, is as smart as they had hoped for, or has the physical characteristics they desired. In short, we cannot send our children back for a surgical "makeover" because they have brown eyes when we had hoped for green, because they are paler or darker skinned than we had hoped, and so forth. Here I begin to tread into areas that we have yet to settle in bioethics and in law, such as the use of growth hormone for children of short stature, the use of drugs to treat the controversial "problems" of ADD and ADHD, and the pursuit of gene therapy to obliterate a host of differences. It is impossible to settle those questions here, but it is worth asking why so many conditions are medicalized and why we seek to "normalize" them when we might just as easily seek to value them.

The rights to protection of autonomy or of developing autonomy do not depend on minority status, and the court is misguided in using the minority status argument to secure its ruling. The rights of the intersexed child are not different from any person's right to autonomy and protection from interference, and following the UNICEF declaration that children are not somehow less human and therefore not subject to those protections is all that the court needs to do. That the ruling goes beyond this and hedges its bets indicates that the court is not actually as interested in protecting children's autonomy as it first appears. We will have to wait longer yet for such a legal will to develop and ruling to occur.

Notes

1. Decision SU-337/99, T-131547 (1999).

2. Intersex Society of North America and the International Lesbian and Gay Association, "Colombia High Court Restricts Intersex Genital Mutilation: First High Court to Address Human Rights Violation," October 26, 1999, http://www.ilga.info/Information/Legal_survey/americas/supporting%20files/colombia_high_court_restricts_in.htm.

3. For example, in Canada the Discovery Channel's program *The Sex Files* regularly broadcasts an episode focused on intersexuality, and the CBC's French-language program *Zone Libre* profiled intersexuality in the spring of 2001. In the United States, popular medical dramas such as *ER* and *Chicago Hope* have both had intersexed patients roll through their wards, and intersexuality has been the talk of daytime television on programs such as *Montel* and *Jerry Springer*. Not all these representations and attention are of equal quality or value, but that is not the point here; rather, I am merely demonstrating the movement of intersexuality into popular consciousness. In academic circles, Judith Butler, Suzanne Kessler, Anne Fausto-Sterling, and Alice Dreger, to name only a few representative theorists cited below, have addressed the ethical and cultural concerns that are apparent in the standard medical approaches to intersexuality and to the burgeoning intersex movement. Finally, in the literary world of fiction, Jeffrey Eugenides' novel *Middlesex* (Toronto: Knopf Canada, 2002), a modern story of a "true hermaphrodite," won a Pulitzer Prize.

4. See, for example, Alice Dreger, ed., *Intersex in the Age of Ethics* (Hagerstown, MD: University Publishing Group, 1999); Morgan Holmes, "Rethinking the Meaning and Management of Intersexuality," *Sexualities* 5, no. 2 (2002): 159–79; Suzanne Kessler, *Lessons from the Intersexed* (New Brunswick, NJ: Rutgers University Press, 1998); and Sharon Preves, *Intersex and Identity: The Contested Self* (New Brunswick, NJ: Rutgers University Press, 2003).

5. Anne Fausto-Sterling, "The Five Sexes," *The Sciences*, March–April 1993, 20–25.

6. Preves, *Intersex and Identity*, 89.

7. Committee on Bioethics, American Academy of Pediatrics, "Informed Consent, Parental Permission, and Assent in Pediatric Practice," *Pediatrics* 95, no. 2 (1995): 314–17.

8. Ibid.

9. See John Money and Anke Ehrhardt, *Man and Woman, Boy and Girl: The Differentiation and Dimorphism of Gender Identity from Conception to Maturity* (Baltimore, MD: Johns Hopkins University Press, 1972). The distortions were first pointed out by Milton Diamond, "Sexual Identity: Monozygotic Twins Reared in Discordant Sex Roles and a BBC Follow-up," *Archives of Sexual Behavior* 11 (1982): 181–85. More recently, see Milton Diamond and Keith Sigmundsen, "Sex Reassignment at Birth: A Long Term Review and Clinical Implications," *Archives of Pediatrics and Adolescent Medicine* 150 (1997): 298–304.

10. Anecdotal reports from persons who had some affiliation with NATFI suggest that the task force was ineffectual and has become de facto nonexistent.

11. Decision Su-337/99, sec. 68.

12. Canada is among the 190 signatories to the convention; the United States is not.

13. Lorne Elkin Rozovsky and F. A. Rozovsky, *The Canadian Law of Consent to Treatment* (Scarborough, ON: Butterworths Canada, 1990), 3.

14. Ibid., 5.

15. Decision Su-337/99, Final Note.

16. UNICEF, *United Nations Declaration on the Rights of the Child* (1990), http://www.unicef.org/crc/fulltext.htm.

17. Decision Su-337/99, Final Note.

18. Michel Foucault, introduction to *Herculine Barbin: Being the Recently Discovered Memoirs of a Nineteenth Century Hermaphrodite,* trans. Richard McDougall (New York: Pantheon, 1980), vii–xvii.

19. Margaret A. McLaren, *Feminism, Foucault, and Embodied Subjectivity,* SUNY Series in Contemporary Continental Philosophy (Albany: State University of New York Press, 2002), 129–30, emphasis added.

20. Alice Domurat Dreger, *Hermaphrodites and the Medical Invention of Sex* (Boston, MA: Harvard University Press, 1998), 76.

21. Judith Butler, "Doing Justice to Someone: Sex Reassignment and Allegories of Transsexuality," *GLQ* 7, no. 4 (2001): 621.

22. Marianne Valverde, *Sex, Power, and Pleasure* (Toronto: Women's Press, 1985), 58.

23. In June 2003 the Ontario Supreme Court ruled that same-sex partners had a constitutional right to marry and that refusing to grant marriage licenses to persons of the same sex was a discriminatory practice. At the time of writing the present chapter the federal government claims to be in the process of making a decision about whether to appeal that decision to the Supreme Court of Canada. The federal government's reasons for appealing might not indicate opposition to the ruling but, rather, a desire to have the highest court possible ruling in favor of the Ontario court decision so that the country would have one clear law applying to all provinces. Otherwise, provinces may decide individually to appeal. However, it appears that there is no particular will for any of the provinces to challenge the ruling, and so the federal government may decide to leave things as they are. The implications of this turn of events for the treatment of intersexed persons is not clear because surgeons do not treat intersexuality with the express purpose of negating the possibility of "accidental homosexuality"; rather, they operate according to an ideology of normalcy that assumes that in a liberal framework even a homosexual union requires that the genitals of each partner be recognizable as the same. This biological reductionism and determinism is blinkered to its own internal contradictions.

24. Amy Potts, "The Science/Fiction of Sex," *Sexualities* 1, no. 2 (1998): 154.

25. Valverde, *Sex, Power, and Pleasure,* 55.

26. Decision Su-337/99, sec. 88.

27. Ibid.

28. See www.isna.org/colombia/background.html.

29. Ibid.

30. Jay Katz, *The Silent World of Doctor and Patient* (Baltimore, MD: Johns Hopkins University Press, 1984), xvii.

31. Decision Su-337/99, sec. 89.

32. *Reibl v. Hughes,* Dominion Law Reports vol. 114 (3d).

33. For example, youth is de facto a cognitive impairment, while Alzheimer's is an acquired impairment.

34. Decision Su-337/99, sec. 88.

35. Ibid., sec. 84.

36. Ibid., sec. 78.

7. The Rights of Intersexed Infants and Children: Decision of the Colombian Constitutional Court, Bogotá, Colombia, 12 May 1999 (SU-337/99)

Translated by Nohemy Solórzano-Thompson

Editor's Note

In 1999 the Colombian Constitutional Court affirmed the importance of protecting bodily autonomy and informed consent for an intersexed minor over a parent's desire that she undergo potentially "risky surgeries or treatments that do not produce health benefits." It was not a decision that the court arrived at easily. The following selections, taken from the later portions of the court's lengthy decision, make visible the key ethical and legal principles that they sought to balance, including the rights individuals have over their bodies, the necessity and limitations of informed consent, the protection of minors, the privacy of families, and the rights of parents. The UN Convention on the Rights of the Child plays a significant role for the court, but its voice is not unequivocal. These selections also make visible the debates and arguments about medical practices, developmental psychology, and social norms that the court sought to incorporate into its decision making.

Throughout its decision, the court implicitly asks, what rights, protections, and freedoms should prevail in the relationships among children, parents, and the state? As Morgan Holmes observes in her chapter, the decision, while a victory for intersexed children, does not offer an unconditional set of protections. Instead, the court offers a complex balance of rights and protections; the rights of intersexed children, while strengthened, remain enmeshed within the rights and powers of families, parents, medical professionals, and the state.

The following translation was commissioned for this volume. The anonymity of the minor and her family is maintained by the court throughout its decision and is reflected in the text. The complete decision, in Spanish, can be found on the Web site of the Intersex Society of North America (http://www.isna.org/node/166).

Richard M. Juang

SU-337/99

Legal consequences of the previous analysis, the illegitimacy of surrogate consent in the case of the minor XX

68—The classification of these treatments as invasive and risky procedures has legal consequences on the legitimacy of surrogate consent by the minor's parents. Actually, as it was stated in the 12th legal fundament of this court decision, the necessity of informed consent is more important in the case of invasive and risky procedures, because this consent is the only way to protect a patient's dignity. This special requirement is in perfect accordance with the Constitution because, as the Court has often stated, children are not the property of their parents, since they possess their own individuality and dignity, and constitute a developing autonomy. The rights of the parents over their children are based only on their abilities to protect the rights of the minor, so that the minor can develop as an autonomous person. Article 18 of the Convention on the Rights of the Child, approved and ratified in Colombia, states that "parents or, as the case may be, legal guardians, have the primary responsibility for the upbringing and development of the child," but that "the best interests of the child will be their basic concern." Thus parents cannot force their children to undergo risky surgeries or treatments that do not produce health benefits, as this type of decision affects a minor's best interest.

69—A conclusion emerges from the previous analysis: the mother of the minor XX cannot authorize operations or hormonal treatments that attempt to reshape the appearance of her daughter's genitalia, because in this case, these types of procedures are not urgent, and, in fact, there exists evidence that they are risky and very invasive. At this time, these procedures would be contrary to the principles of beneficence and autonomy, thus the mother's surrogate consent is not constitutionally allowable.

70—Taking this into account, the previous conclusion could be objected to on the grounds that there is no proof that these procedures are dangerous and unnecessary in all cases. However, this objection, which is based on fact, does not contradict that this is an invasive treatment; in fact, it has been proven that these procedures have caused grave and irreversible harm to the patient, while their usefulness remains in doubt, thus the protection of the minor's best interest is necessary.

The limits of the previous solution and the privacy of homes

71—This Court believes that the previous argumentation is very convincing, because it is the duty of the authorities to protect the rights of children, which are above those of others (Constitutional Article 44). Thus a risky, invasive, and seemingly not urgent treatment of the minor XX cannot be allowed, even if the mother authorizes it. However, it could be argued that the prohibition of a parent's surrogate consent gravely contradicts other constitutional principles; hence it is not clear what the Court's decision should be, which once again shows the complexity of this matter. In effect, this Entity believes that this type of decision (i) profoundly invades the privacy of homes and also (ii) could condemn a hermaphrodite girl and her mother to be the unwilling leaders of a movement to change the way society sees genital ambiguity. This Entity will now analyze these two objections.

72—The analysis of the scientific debate about the early treatment of hermaphrodite minors shows that these procedures are not proven to be necessary or useful. However, it has not been proven that these medical interventions are harmful in all cases, or that a person with genital ambiguity cannot develop satisfactorily without undergoing an operation. This situation has produced two opposite conclusions. The advocates of these types of procedures tend to argue that it is legitimate that these operations continue with a parent's consent, as long as it is not proven that in the majority of the cases these procedures fail and cause harm; on the contrary, the critics of these procedures argue that these interventions should be suspended until there is a systematic evaluation and analysis of long-term risks and benefits. This proves that, as an analyst of this situation states, "these disagreements arise partly from two empirically exclusive points of view," making it impossible to determine with exactness which perspective is correct.

73—Thus, in this specific case, this Entity should recognize that because of this uncertainty, all harmful medical procedures should be avoided (the principle of *primun non nocere* or "First, do not harm"), especially when this affects minors who cannot give consent. This conclusion is in principle legitimate, although risky, because it is questionable that a parent would subject his/her child to these dangers.

However, this conclusion could be considered problematic because the absence of treatment could also imply a danger to the health of the minor, and it is not possible to have medical studies that will ascertain the benefits and risks of this type of therapy before a potential harm because of lack of medical care can occur. In effect, to prohibit a parent's authorization of this treatment, until it is adequately proven, could deprive the child of a beneficial therapy.

Thus let us suppose that an infant has a grave cancer and that there is a new treatment for it, but its benefits are not guaranteed; furthermore, let us presume that some important scientists question the theoretical basis of this type of therapy, which is known to be physically aggressive on patients, to the point that, in some cases, it is proven that it accelerates death. However, other scientists believe that this treatment works against this type of cancer, which so far does not have a satisfactory treatment. In this case, should the parents be forbidden to authorize a treatment that has not been proven to work in adults? While the treatment is tested, it is possible that the child might die. In these types of situations, isn't it more reasonable to permit the parents to make a medical decision, after weighing the risks and eventual benefits of this medical intervention?

74—Then, mutatis mutandi ("when what must be changed has been changed"), the medical status of genital ambiguity is similar to the previous example. The actual treatments have caused harm, and there is no convincing evidence that they are necessary or beneficial; however, it is not clear if they are entirely useless or harmful in the majority of cases. In effect, as one of the Colombian experts suggests, waiting to perform the surgery until the minor can consent causes problems because of the fact that our environment still has a culture of intolerance on matters of sexual diversity. It is possible then that a person with ambiguous genitalia will have to confront a hostile social (and even home) environment; which can severely affect his/her psychological development. Furthermore, because of the lack of specialized psychotherapists, it is not certain if the minor and his/her parents could receive the adequate attention, which plays an important part in the success of alternative treatments. Similarly, the lack of networks of intersexuals, who could aid the parents and the minor, also limits the development of these alternative protocols.

Finally, but no less important, the decision to prohibit, in this case absolutely, early surgery and hormonal treatments could potentially not be understood by the mother of the minor, who could think that the Constitutional Judge has forced her daughter to retain some physical problems that could be medically corrected. This perception is understandable, since in our society, many interpersonal relationships are grounded in the existence of only two biologically defined genders. As it has been suggested earlier, the parents of a hermaphrodite experience a difficult situation because their child is "defective." This difficult situation could produce resentment if the parents believe that this "abnormality" could be corrected, but a judicial decision blocks the performance of the pertinent medical interventions. This reaction could have two grave effects: on the one hand, the desperation could drive the parents to search for clandestine and unsafe means to "normalize" their child by unspecialized personnel. Like the case Meyer Bahlbrug discussed, about a girl who had to be hospitalized because her father tried to tear off her unusual clitoris with his own hands. These situations are obviously extreme and should be sanctioned, but they show the other risk, which is not so unusual: the prohibition of these surgeries could deprive children of their parents' love, because [the parents] believe a judicial decision left them with defective children. Several studies have shown that minors with defects (such as deafness or paralysis) or with unusual physical characteristics (such as hermaphrodites) above all need the support, love, and understanding of their parents in order to develop well psychologically and socially. In these cases, parental support enhances the self-esteem of the minor, which augments his/her ability to confront potential social stigmatizations. Thus, in their study on persons born with micropenises (see Legal Fundament Number 46 above), Reilly and Woodhouse conclude that parental attitude is perhaps the most decisive factor in the fate of these people. If the parents are better informed and more tolerant, then the children are "more confident and better adapted"; but if the parents emphasize the "abnormality" of their children or refuse to discuss their problems with them, the parents provoked shyness and anxiety in their children. Several advocates of these types of surgeries agree in this point. The psychoendocrinologist David Sandberg states that in his clinical experience, "a strong factor in determining how an intersexual child will behave throughout life depends on the capacity of the parents to accept the child and understand what has happened in a form that does not hurt the upbringing of the child." This specialist also states that the parents' attitude is independent of surgery, but in his experience, "many parents do not accept a child whose genitalia have not been corrected surgically." It is true that early surgery is not absolutely necessary, however, as the pediatrician Justine Schoberg says, "surgeries appease parents and doctors, but psychological support also appeases people and is not irreversible." However, the absolute prohibition of these medical interventions could alter the affection parents have toward their children.

75—The argument above shows that if the Court prohibits the treatment of this hermaphrodite minor, it could eventually cause irreversible damage, since the decision could force the girl and her family to lead, in the following months and years, a type of social experiment, since these people will have to create environments that are tolerant of her physical difference, without knowing what the results of this process will be on the personal development of the minor. In these circumstances, the Court's decision to declare a moratorium on the surgery until the girl can consent could hinder the girl along with her mother, since they will be forced to lead difficult social transformations in order to create new tolerant environments. The prohibition of this medical intervention means then that they will be forced to undergo a social experiment, whose effects on the minor (whose essential interests the Court must protect) would be unknown.

In these circumstances, not knowing the full extent of the harm and given the little urgency of the surgery, prudence should guide the judicial decision; and it would seem that the mother should evaluate the risks and make the best decision on behalf of her daughter, without the intervention of the judges, since the decision belongs to the sphere of the privacy of homes.

76—The previous reasoning leads to the last objection to a Constitutional prohibition against performing any early surgery on this minor; the objection is the following, through any decision, the judges would interfere severely in the autonomy and privacy of homes, because the treatment of the minor would be defined by a Court order and not by her mother. The family is not only the nucleus of society (Constitutional Articles 5 and 42), it is also one of the essential spaces where pluralism develops, which is a relevant Constitutional principle (Constitutional Articles 7, 8, and 70). Thus the respect for the privacy of homes is upheld as a right under the autonomy of adults, and undoubtedly fulfills this function. Through this protection of the intimacy of homes, pluralism is also encouraged, thus preventing that all peoples be educated in the same way, since it is the primary responsibility of the parents to raise their children. Families play a fundamental role in the socialization of children. In this manner, the different points of view of the parents allow the children of different homes to develop diverse cultural perspectives; a state-controlled system, on the other hand, would create a heavily uniform culture. Thus cultural diversity is a valued element that enriches society and should be promoted, as the Constitution ensures (Constitutional Articles 7 and 8); thus it is necessary to protect a family's right to educate their children, because allowing the parents to do so is a manner of preserving pluralism.

This protection of the parents' dominant role in the education of their children is clear in the discussions of this subject. Thus the Constitution explicitly states that the parents have the right to choose their children's education (Constitutional Article 68). At the same time Article 3.2 of the Convention on the Rights of the Child endorses the State's right to ensure the protection, care, and well-being of children, taking into account the rights and duties of their parents, guardians, or other people responsible under the law. Similarly, Article 5 asserts that the States will respect the responsibilities, rights, and duties of the parents (or, when appropriate, those of the extended family or community according to local custom), the guardians or other people legally responsible for the upbringing of the child, according to the evolution of the child's faculties, to provide direction and orientation so that the child can exercise his/her legal rights. Article 7 states that a child has the right to know his/her parents and to be taken care of by them as much as possible. And finally, Article 14–2 of this treaty establishes that the States will also respect the rights and duties of the parents, and when appropriate, that of the legal guardians, to guide the child to exercise his/her rights in a manner appropriate to the evolution of his/her faculties.

Thus the Constitution and human rights agreements give the parents the essential responsibility to raise their children, not only because it is considered that the parents are those who can best understand and satisfy the needs of the minors but also because it is a way to protect diverse lifestyles and cultural perspectives. Other societies have adopted other forms of raising children, for example, allowing the State to educate and satisfy the needs of the minors, but this state-centered strategy has a homogenizing effect on culture, while a decentralized state is one of the building blocks of and contributors to pluralism in our society, and hence deserves special state protection.

77—The intimacy of homes is not absolute, since the State also has the obligation to protect the rights of children, who are one of the weakest members in a family. Thus the Constitution establishes that not only the family but also the State and society "have the obligation to assist and protect the child in order to guarantee their harmonious and complete development and the full exercise of their rights" (Constitutional Article 44) and all forms of intrafamilial violence will be prosecuted (Constitutional Articles 42 and 44). Similarly, the Convention on the Rights of the Child adds that the superior interest of the minors could justify the suspension of the rights of parents and guardians. Hence Article 19 orders the States to adopt the necessary measures to protect children from all forms of discrimination, physical or mental abuse, neglect, exploitation, including sexual abuse, when under the custody of the parents, legal guardians, or another person in charge of their care. According to Article 20, in the event of abuse or in the event that the child's superior interest dictates this course of action, the affected child will be removed temporarily or permanently from the family environment and will be granted protection and special assistance from the State. However, the parents and family of a child are granted the right to raise their children, and this type of state intervention is exceptional, and is only carried out in situations where the child's well-being is threatened.

78—Family privacy and its important effects on the development of pluralism affect the judges' ability to exclude parents from making certain medical decisions for their children. In effect, as it can be witnessed in this decision, there is also pluralism among the medical community, since there are several methods to treat suffering, and hence the States should avoid the prevention of the parents' rights to choose their children's treatment. Legal interference in this area should be minimized because of its possible negative effects on the protection of the intimacy of homes and medical pluralism. An obvious question follows this argument: what is the threshold that would allow a legal intervention in this area? Or, as several authors have phrased it, where does a parent's authority cease so that an "external savior" can intervene?

It is not easy to answer this question, which is derived from the tension that exists between the guardian's right to choose on behalf of the minor and the State's duty to ensure the child's best interest. The Court believes that to face this difficult medical subject it is necessary to take into account the following: (i) the necessity and urgency of the treatment, (ii) its impact and risks, (iii) the age and maturity of the minor. However, the prima facie parental right to educate their children, as well as the importance of family intimacy in the development of pluralism, even in the medical field, allows us to make a concluding remark in difficult cases, which are equivalent to *in dubio pro familia* ("when it doubt, advocate in favor of the family"): if the judge doubts which decision to take, then he should rule in favor of the preservation of the privacy of homes, and thus minimize the State's interference with the parents in making these decisions on behalf of their children. Thus, in this case, because it is not proven exclusively that these types of treatments on intersexual minors are always dangerous and unnecessary, the doubt should be resolved in favor of the privacy of the home. It needs to be stated that there is a medical pluralism in dealing with genital ambiguity, and thus, in the majority of cases, it is the right of the parents to decide to authorize early surgeries designed to reshape the genitalia of their children.

The limits of parental consent and the medical privacy of families

79—In all, it could be argued that the above conclusion is not valid because the prima facie right of the parents to make medical decisions on behalf of their children is based on two basic assumptions: (i) that parents are those who best understand and protect the interest of minors, and (ii) that within certain limits, the families can develop pluralistic perspectives when dealing with health problems. However, there is strong evidence that parents rarely develop these pluralistic options on their own and, in fact, many times experience difficulties when trying to understand the interests of children with genital ambiguity. In fact, the subject of hermaphroditism has not been discussed openly in our society, thus forcing the parents of intersexual children to go through an incomprehensible trauma when their child is born. In these circumstances, it is foreseeable that a parent's decision be based on [the parent's] own fears and prejudices and not on the interests of the child. In many ways, the parents are part of a majority whose gender has been biologically defined and hence see hermaphrodites as strange beings that hopefully can be "normalized" as quickly as possible. The children then are in danger of being discriminated against by their own parents.

80—In this case of hermaphroditism, there are objective difficulties that prevent the mother from understanding and defending the interests of her child, especially because her daughter, apparently because of her age, has greater self-awareness of her body and individuality. Hence it would appear that the family would be unable to develop any alternative forms of treatment, not only because the medical establishment proposes early surgeries as the only alternative but also because this option alleviates the fears of the parents by allowing them to believe that their child has been normalized thanks to the surgery. At this point, the Court points out that one of the Constitutional judges' fundamental duties is to protect minorities. The Court then should assume the tutelage of the minor, which is a valid action because in the case of gender ambiguity, the judges legitimately can interfere in the privacy of homes in order to protect the superior interests of a child that should have a greater autonomy in a decision concerning her sexuality. Through this Court decision, then it could be stated that early surgeries and hormonal treatments should be delayed until the minor herself can make an informed consent, given that the parental decision could not be based on the child's best interests.

The problem of surrogate consent in the case of the girl NN, the parents' tutelage, and special state protection for the minor

81—The preceding analysis leaves us at another dead end: the Court cannot prohibit access to the surgery, because it would invade family privacy and could condemn the girl to an uncertain social experiment; but it is also not adequate that the mother decide for the child, because her decision might not be based on the child's best interest, given that the child should have more of a say in her future. Hence a question arises: is there a way to reconcile the protection of family privacy with the special protection that a hermaphrodite minor deserves against discrimination (Constitutional Article 13), including discrimination from her own parents? The Court believes that an equilibrium must be achieved through a careful study of each case; and in this case, the Court believes that it should favor the informed consent of the minor, with the mother's guidance, while it is necessary to establish some guidelines so that the mother understands the present medical debate, deliberates, and makes a decision based on her daughter's best interests.

82—In effect, if guidelines were established to guarantee that the parents understand the complexity of intersexuality, as well as the risks of the present treatments, then there would be no need for legal interference in the family's privacy because the interests of the children would be better protected. Obviously, this information should be conveyed to the mother in an easy-to-understand language, according to her educational level, and interdisciplinary teams should ensure that the information has been understood properly. This means that during this complex and difficult process, the mother should have access to information and to the necessary psychological support that would allow her to understand and overcome the emotional impact that the present situation of her daughter could have on her.

83—In this decision, the Court has already stated that the surrogate consent of the mother to remodel the genitalia of NN leads to two objections: on the one hand, the general criticisms to this type of treatment; and on the other hand, the fact that NN is not a small infant, she is in fact over eight years of age, which eliminates the urgency of this type of surgery, even according to the dominant medical practice, and hence it represents a greater invasion of her autonomy. This Entity, in order to resolve the present case, examined *in extenso* ("extensively") the legal consequences presented by the critics of the present treatment of intersexual minors, and concluded that the girl can enjoy the special support of her mother, who should have an "informed, qualified and persistent consent"; in other words, she should be sufficiently capable of supporting the minor's decision. In addition, the girl should have access to the special support the State offers to people with genital ambiguity.

84—This Entity believes that if one takes into account that the minor already has a cognitive, social, and emotional development that allows her to have a clear awareness of her body and gives her a defined gender identity, then parental surrogate consent loses Constitutional legitimacy, and surgeries and hormonal treatments to remodel her genitalia should wait until the patient can authorize them. The Court reached this decision because of three reasons.

On the one hand, the urgency of this surgery has disappeared, because the present protocol justifies early surgeries so that the child can develop a gender identity that coincides with his/her genitalia; but in this case, what is the urgency if there is no life-threatening danger? It is not clear then. Furthermore, if the girl already has a solid gender identity, what contribution to her psychological development can these risky interventions have? This is not evident, especially because the child already has developed cognitively and emotionally to the point of having an awareness of her own body and of what happens to it, and hence the minor would be completely aware of a surgical modification of her genitalia and thus the operation would fail in its purpose of assigning her a gender identity.

The demand for tutelage and some of the statements of the experts have stated that, in the present case, there is no evident urgency, but that these surgeries should be performed before puberty; however, in the judgment of this Entity, they have not presented a substantial argument that supports that thesis. Although it is possible that the girl will be victim to jokes and marginalization because of her unusual genitalia, it is not reasonable to assume that the surgery can prevent the psychological impact of the genital ambiguity because the minor would be perfectly aware of the fact that her genitalia were different and hence surgically altered. Similarly, when people reach puberty, they develop sexual curiosity, and according to psychoanalysis, this leads to an awareness of the fact that their genitalia are different from those of the majority of people. Hence this is the moment in which a person can be most affected by their genital ambiguity, especially if hormonal changes provoke modifications in the body that could be associated with the opposite gender of the one assigned, as could be the case of minor NN. However, this situation does not legitimate the mother's surrogate consent on behalf of an older child; instead, it leads us to the opposite conclusion: the reasonable thing to do is to allow the minor, after she experiences changes during puberty, to define her gender identity with the adequate psychological support and then decide if she wishes to expose herself to the risks of the surgeries and hormonal treatments that would reconstruct her genitalia.

85—Second, if the minor has an awareness of her body, then a surgery whose purpose is not clearly defined (and according to the present protocol, this should be performed to prevent a possible ambiguity when forming gender identity), it is possible that the infant would perceive the surgery as an aggression, abuse, or punishment, which could have serious or devastating psychological effects, as related in included testimonies of people who have undergone these surgeries as older children. In effect, these changes in the body, when they are not properly explained, can profoundly affect the minor's identity, as this Entity proved in another case where it analyzed an intervention that was barely invasive and reversible, like a haircut, which could cause a psychological trauma in a four-year-old girl. The testimony of the expert consulted in that case is relevant to this case, since she stated:

> The conception of self is first corporal. *It is important for the minor to observe his/her body and that of the parents during the first life stages. If we understand that a child's basic identity is corporal, if we interpret that he/she must construct his/her individuality through that, then we understand the child's difficulties when dealing with changes in his/her body.* Change always brings forth ambivalent feelings. Even desired changes can produce anxiety or angst intermingled with cheerful feelings. Regardless of the change, be it a change of home, of relationship, or in a person's appearance, *the changes are better assimilated if the child is prepared beforehand to receive them, and even better if they are not drastic. Small children can experience minimal changes with a disproportionate magnitude,* depending on their unconscious fantasies, the way in which the parents handle the situation, and the surrounding environment. (emphasis added)

86—Finally, if the minor is older, then she has gained a degree of autonomy that deserves a greater Constitutional protection, and hence the legitimacy of the paternal surrogate consent is reduced considerably. In effect, as it has been pointed out earlier in this decision, the more personal autonomy, the more legal protection there is for the free development of personality (Constitutional Article 16), in accordance with the Convention on the Rights of the Child, which states that a "child who is capable of forming his or her own views [has] the right to express those views freely in all matters affecting the child, the views of the child being given due weight in accordance with the age and maturity of the child."

87—According to this, the Court concludes that because in this case the hermaphrodite girl has already passed the critical threshold of gender identification and has a clear awareness of her body, the paternal surrogate consent is not legitimate and thus cannot approve an operation given that the risks are great, there are no clear benefits to the performance of this operation before the patient can authorize it, and the minor already possesses a degree of autonomy that should be consulted when important decisions affecting her are taken. In this situation, the principles of beneficence and autonomy dictate that in this case the surgeries be postponed, because the rule that privileges the intimacy of homes does not operate in the case of minor XX, because the Constitutional judge is not overruling the family on medical decisions, and instead is privileging the minor's autonomy within the home, which should be taken into account. Hence the Court decides that in these situations, the surgeries and hormonal treatments should be postponed until the minor can authorize them.

88—An obvious question arises, at what age can we presume the psychological changes have occurred that invalidate the paternal surrogate consent to treat the genital ambiguity of minor XX? There is no clear answer to this question, because different people develop at different rates, and there exist different points of view within the various psychology schools about how humans evolve from birth to maturity. Obviously, it is not this Entity's duty to decide on these debates.

However, it is important to point out that several evolutionary psychology studies and the various psychology schools do agree that within the first five years a minor has developed not only a defined gender identity but also an awareness of his/her body and possesses sufficient autonomy to manifest different gender roles and express his/her feelings. Thus, to quote but a few of the more important studies, from a Freudian psychological perspective, at this age, the child has completed the phallic stage (where he/she shows a particular interest in exploring genitalia and in understanding the difference between the genders) and the child now undergoes the oedipal stage, where he/she defines his/her gender identity. Similarly, according to Kohlberg, children at ages three and four develop a cognitive map of the different gender roles and begin behaving according to those roles.

Finally, from a cognitive point of view, according to Piaget's studies, between two and five years, infants complete the preoperational stage and begin to focus on concrete operational thought, which implies the development of intelligence and a consciousness of what occurs in their surroundings, because the minors, according to the terminology of this author, can decenter thought, focus on the actions and not only on the states, and mentally invert the operations.

89—Hence the Court concludes that because there is no clear risk that affects the life of the minor if the operation is not performed, it is not possible to allow the mother to authorize the medical intervention and hormonal treatments on behalf of the daughter, who is over eight years old. Thus these interventions can be authorized only by the informed consent of NN, and hence the tutelage should not be conceded, because the mother's request to allow the treatments will not be honored. However, the Constitutional judge needs to take the necessary measures to protect the fundamental rights of the minor. Hence the Court will protect the right to develop a gender identity, the free development of personality, and the equality of the petitioner NN (Constitutional Articles 1, 5, 13, and 16) and will order the competent authorities to take the necessary measures so that the girl and her mother receive the necessary psychotherapist and interdisciplinary support so that they can adequately understand their situation. Similarly, an interdisciplinary team should be formed with medical professionals, a psychotherapist, and a social worker that should attend to the minor NN and her mother during this whole process. This team would then decide when the minor has the sufficient autonomy to make an informed consent if she chooses to undergo the surgeries and hormonal treatments.

90—A question arises from the previous analysis, at what age is the girl expected to make a decision on these medical interventions and hormonal treatments? There is no clear answer to this question, and even those who defend alternative treatments acknowledge that this is a difficult problem. Hence, in each case, it is the duty of the interdisciplinary teams to make the necessary tests to evaluate if a person has sufficient autonomy to make an informed consent. The Court considers that some normative elements are clear and should guide the actions of these teams. Hence, first of all, it should not be necessary to wait until the minor reaches the age of majority, because as it has been stated in this Court decision, the legal capacity of a person is not the same as their autonomy to make medical decisions, and thus a minor who has not reached legal capacity can competently make a medical decision. Some health professionals believe that children of eight or nine years of age have sufficient autonomy to authorize certain treatments. Second, the Court believes that in this case the minor should authorize the medical intervention because it is invasive, risky, and irreversible, and hence, according to the guidelines stated in this decision, her consent needs to be qualified. The Court believes then that if the minor authorizes a medical intervention, these interdisciplinary teams should not only provide psychological support but also develop a method to ensure that the patient's authorization is informed and genuine. Thus, in some cases, it is possible that at the onset of puberty, even if the minor has sufficient autonomy to authorize a medical intervention, the interdisciplinary team can decide that it is necessary to delay the operation because the minor does not understand the risks and benefits of the intervention.

Similarly, it is possible that according to the medical protocols, the interdisciplinary teams choose to authorize the treatment in stages, so that hormones with reversible effects are administered first, and only after a while can irreversible interventions, such as surgery, be allowed. Hence, to quote a specialist on the matter, Professor William Reiner, "In the end, only children themselves can identify who and what they are. It is our duty as clinicians and researchers to listen and learn."

The Decision

91—According to the preceding arguments, the Court has taken the following decisions. First of all, this Entity has decided to guard the privacy of the petitioner and her mother by sealing this file and protecting their names, although the scientific tests that inform this decision can be consulted in the Court's see. Second, the Court will not honor the mother's request, because it is the minor who should decide on her gender identity. Third, the Court will protect the minor's right to freely develop her personality and equality, and hence will order the formation of an interdisciplinary team that will tend to her case and offer the minor and her mother the psychological and social support necessary to fully understand the situation they are confronting. The Court believes that the medical services should be provided by the ISS (Institute for Social Security), where the minor is affiliated, but this Entity believes that because of their child protection services, the ICBF (Colombian Institute for Family Well-Being) should coordinate, in this case and in similar cases, the interdisciplinary team composed of medical professionals, a psychotherapist, and a social worker that will accompany the minor NN and her mother throughout this process. It is the duty of this team to establish when the minor has sufficient autonomy to make an informed choice to authorize surgeries and hormonal treatments, if she chooses to undergo them.

Final Note

The Constitutional Court understands that within the present-day cultural frameworks, the birth of a child with genital ambiguity creates difficulties for the family and the minor. The Court is perfectly aware of the suffering that these types of situations produce and thus allies itself with the minor and her mother. Similarly, this Entity understands that not only does intersexuality produce moral, legal, and social problems, but it also is an evolving theme both from a social and ethical perspective and from a scientific point of view. Thus, as the European Human Rights Tribunal decided in a similar case dealing with transsexuality, the Constitutional Court of Colombia understands that our present-day society is undergoing a period of normative and cultural transition in relation to the theme of hermaphroditism. Thus, in the near future, it will be necessary and inevitable to make some changes to regulate, whenever possible, the challenges that intersexual states cause in our society. This has important consequences on the scope of this decision, as well as on the responsibility of the different state organisms and on the Colombian society regarding this subject. Thus this Entity considers that the guidelines established in this decision are the ones that best preserve at this time fundamental Constitutional rights and values. In addition, the Court recognizes that in the present case, the decision and investigation had to be limited to this case; however, the Court reiterates that the 1991 Constitution attempts to construct a society where all forms of diversity are not subject to violence and marginalization but instead are recognized as a source of invaluable social wealth. Differences and similarities are both protected under the Constitution, which hopes to give people access to all available opportunities. Intersexual states hence expand our tolerance and challenge us to accept differences. Public authorities, the medical community, and the citizens need to open social spaces for these people, who have been silenced until now. Hence, paraphrasing the words of Professor William Reiner, previously quoted, it is our duty to listen to these people, to learn to live with them and to learn from them.

III. Decision

In lieu of the aforementioned, the Constitutional Court of the Republic of Colombia, in name of the people and through Constitutional mandate, issues the following,

Resolution

First: To protect the right of privacy of the minor NN and her mother, their names will be protected and this file is sealed, and can only be consulted by those interested in accordance to the guidelines stated in the 2nd Legal Fundament of this decision. The General Clerk of the Constitutional Court and the XX Court Clerk who first decided this case need to guarantee this exclusion.

Second: To protect the public access to these proceedings, the Constitutional Court's Secretariat, in collaboration with the office of the deciding magistrate, will make copies of the most relevant scientific data, as long as these do not allow the identification of the petitioner. These documents will be kept in an archive that will be accessible in the Constitutional Court's see to those who are interested in the subject.

Third: To confirm the decision made by family court judge XX, who was responsible for this case, who denied the mother's petition to be granted tutelage.

Fourth: To protect the right to develop a gender identity, the free development of personality and the equality of the petitioner NN (Constitutional Articles 1, 5, 13, and 16). According to the terms stated in the 91st Legal Fundament of this decision, an interdisciplinary team should be formed to consult on her case and bring the necessary psychological support for the minor and the mother. Medical services should be granted by the ISS, and the ICBF should be responsible for the coordination of the interdisciplinary team, composed of medical professionals, a psychotherapist, and a social worker who will accompany the minor NN and her mother throughout this process. It is the duty of this team to establish when the minor has sufficient autonomy to make an informed consent to authorize surgeries and hormonal treatments, if she chooses to undergo them.

Fifth: To notify of this decision the National Academy of Medicine, the Colombian Society of Urology, and the officially recognized medical organizations of the Defense of the People and the Colombian Institute for Family Well-Being, and the Ministry of Health.

Sixth: Through the General Secretariat, IT IS ORDERED that in reference to the communications specified in Article 36 of the 1991 decree number 2591, the XX Court will personally notify the mother of the petitioner NN of this court decision, with the adequate prudence to protect the intimacy and privacy of the home.

> Copy, notify, communicate, obey, and insert it in the Constitutional Court's Gazette
>
> Eduardo Cifuentes Muñoz, President
>
> Antonio Barrera Carbonell, Magistrate
> Alfredo Beltran Sierra, Magistrate
> Carlos Gaviria Díaz, Magistrate
> José Gregorio Hernández Galindo, Magistrate
> Martha V. Sáchica de Moncaleano, Magistrate
> Alejandro Martínez Caballero, Magistrate
> Fabio Morón Díaz, Magistrate
> Vladmiro Naranjo Mesa, Magistrate
>
> Pablo Enrique Leal Ruiz, General Secretary

PART II. HISTORY

8. Do Transsexuals Dream of Gay Rights? Getting Real about Transgender Inclusion

Shannon Price Minter

"Is this testing whether I'm an android,"
Rachel asked tartly, "or whether I'm homosexual?"
The gauges did not register.

—**Phillip K. Dick,** *Do Androids Dream of Electric Sheep?*

The questions "what is homosexuality" and "who is
homosexual" are profound questions, the answers to
which have a history and an ever-evolving politics. If
discussion of racial, sexual, and economic-class
stratification can posit "real" answers to similar
questions, . . . nothing of the kind is possible in arguments
about sexual orientation. The definitional ground of study
constantly reasserts itself as a source of uncertainty.

—**Janet Halley,** "Intersections: Sexuality, Cultural Traditions, and the Law"

We can't even get it clear among ourselves what
we're talking about when we use the words
"homosexual" and "gay."

—**Bruce Bawer,** "Confusions Reigns"

Should the gay rights movement expand its borders to include transgender people?[1] In the past few years, gay organizations have been obliged to confront this question in multiplying contexts.[2] Should transsexual women be permitted to attend lesbian events?[3] Should gay legal organizations represent transgender clients?[4] Should proposed legislation to protect gay people from discrimination be drafted to protect transgender people as well?[5] Should gay advocacy groups broaden their missions to include transgender issues?[6] More generally, does it make sense to group gay and transgender people together for the purposes of social, political, and legal advocacy? In almost every case in which a dispute over transgender issues has emerged, those on different sides of these questions have approached each other with different (in some instances wildly different) assumptions about what is at stake. Lesbian and gay leaders who oppose transgender inclusion tend to assume that transgender people are outsiders with no intrinsic connection or claim to gay rights. Those who hold this view may acknowledge that transgender people suffer discrimination and deserve legal protections, but they do not consider transgender people to be part of the gay community.[7] From this perspective, lumping transgender issues with gay issues is like mixing apples with oranges: it is a category mistake that can lead to nothing but confusion and a loss of focus and effectiveness for all concerned.[8]

In contrast, many transgender people consider the gay community to be their only viable social and political home.[9] In part, this is because a sizable percentage of transgender people also identify as lesbian, gay, or bisexual.[10] More fundamentally, it is because homophobia and transphobia are tightly intertwined, and because antigay bias so often takes the form of violence and discrimination against those who are seen as transgressing gender norms. Gender nonconforming people consistently have been among the most visible and vulnerable members of gay communities—among the most likely to be beaten, raped, and killed; among the most likely to be criminalized and labeled deviant; among the most likely to end up in psychiatric hospitals and prisons; among the most likely to be denied housing, employment, and medical care; among the most likely to be rejected and harassed as young people; and among the most likely to be separated from their own children. Perhaps because of these vulnerabilities, transgender people were also, as it turned out, the most likely to fight back at Stonewall—that "moment of explosive rage in which a few transvestites and young gay men of color reshaped gay life forever."[11]

From this perspective, the question that calls for an explanation is not whether transgender people can justify their claims to gay rights, but rather how did a movement launched by bull daggers, drag queens, and transsexuals in 1969 end up viewing transgender people as outsiders less than thirty years later? How did transgender people become separated at the birth of gay liberation? These are not meant to be rhetorical questions. Why do many lesbian and gay leaders view transgender issues as unrelated to gay rights? What histories have we lost or failed to map in arriving at a place where transgender inclusion in the gay movement seems like a self-evident necessity to many gay people and completely illogical to many others? Why have transgender people emerged as a visible, self-identified constituency at this particular point in queer history? How is the controversy over transgender inclusion related to earlier, but still unresolved, controversies over the place of lesbians, bisexuals, people of color, working-class people, and others who have been marginalized within the mainstream gay movement? Finally, what would meaningful inclusion of transgender issues entail? Would it entail a drastic reformulation of gay politics and gay identity, as those on both sides of the question have tended to assume? Or is this assumption a symptom of the overly polarized manner in which the debate has been framed?

Despite the complexity of these questions, addressing them is important if we hope to avoid a reprise of the vitriolic intracommunity battles that periodically have derailed the lesbian and gay movement in recent years.[12] John D'Emilio has emphasized the dangers of treating each new controversy within the gay movement as an unprecedented crisis, with no connection to the debates or struggles of the past. "The dilemmas we face today are not new. Yet, because we have not done a very good job of keeping alive our history of political resistance, we often seem to act as if we were inventing the alphabet of movement building."[13] This warning seems especially pertinent to the debate over transgender inclusion. Depending on one's perspective, transgender people have been depicted as misguided interlopers who suddenly have wandered into gay politics by mistake,[14] or as the long-awaited vanguard of a radical new politics of gender transgression.[15] In either case, the novelty of transgender issues is greatly overstated.

While some issues raised by transgender people may be new, conflict over the relationship between gay identity and gender nonconformity is not. Changes in the social meaning of gayness have been entangled with changes in the social meaning of gender for at least the past hundred years.[16] Similarly, dissension over the relationship between sexual orientation and gender has been a central feature of gay politics since the homophile movement of the 1950s.[17] The current controversy over transgender inclusion is a direct product of these long-standing struggles and concerns. No matter how startling or novel transgender issues may initially appear, they are rooted in conflicts and tensions that have divided and sometimes polarized the gay movement from the beginning.

In what follows, I examine the current debate over transgender inclusion in this broader historical context, with the goal of moving beyond the short-term, zero-sum, all-or-nothing framework that has dominated prior discussions.

In part 1, I argue that some gay scholars and advocates have appropriated cross-gendered identities as part of "gay" history without acknowledging that these identities might just as plausibly be considered "transgender," and without being willing to acknowledge any affiliation between gay and transgender people in the present. Paradoxically, in other words, gay scholars have claimed transgender people as ancestors, but not as contemporary kin.

Part 2 traces this paradox to the emergence of an expressly nontransgender, or gender-normative, model of gay identity in the twentieth century. Part 2 also examines the class- and race-based divisions that gave rise to this model and that continue to underlie it. Class- and race-based animosities played a central role in forming a gender-normative model of gay identity, and they continue to play a central role in the ongoing devaluation of gendervariant and transgender people in the contemporary gay movement.

Part 3 identifies these divisions as a significant motivating factor in the birth of the contemporary transgender movement. At least in part, the transgender movement has arisen in direct response to the exclusion of crossgendered lesbians and gay men from the mainstream gay movement, as described in part 2, as well as to the recognition of transsexualism as a medical condition and the availability of hormone therapy and sex reassignment surgeries.

Part 4 is a critical examination of attempts on the part of some gay and transgender theorists to outflank gay resistance to transgender inclusion by redefining gay people as a subset of the transgender community. While acknowledging the power and appeal of this approach, I argue that it is more useful as a thought experiment or tool for exposing the limitations of a rigidly gender-normalizing model of gay identity than as the foundation for a radical new approach to gay rights.

Ancestors but No Longer Kin: The Anomalous Position of Transgender People in Contemporary Lesbian and Gay Scholarship and Advocacy

Although the 1969 riots at the Stonewall Inn in New York City have long been recognized as the symbolic birth date of the contemporary gay rights movement, "movements for social change do not spring full blown into existence, like Athena from the head of Zeus."[18] Numerous recent histories have dispelled the myth that the modern gay movement in the United States sprang out of nowhere at Stonewall. These histories have uncovered a wealth of evidence that lesbian and gay people were building communities, organizing, theorizing, and engaging in a variety of everyday forms of survival and resistance from the turn of the twentieth century through the decades prior to Stonewall.[19] It would be a mistake to suppose that the contemporary transgender movement is any more likely to have sprung out of nowhere, or that transgender people do not have a history that is equally varied and complex.[20]

Commenting on the efforts of gay intellectuals who "sought to construct a gay historical tradition" at the turn of the century, George Chauncey has observed:

> One of the ways groups of people constitute themselves as an ethnic, religious, or national community is by constructing a history that provides its members with a shared tradition and collective ancestors.... By constructing historical traditions of their own, gay men defined themselves as a distinct community. By imagining they had collective roots in the past, they asserted a collective identity in the present.[21]

Similarly, one way that contemporary lesbians and gay men have constructed themselves as a community and fostered a sense of social and political legitimacy is by documenting the existence of gay people in the past. These efforts have been especially important in the wake of the U.S. Supreme Court's devastating decision in *Bowers v. Hardwick*, which characterized same-sex acts (and, by extension, lesbians and gay men) as antithetical to the very foundations of Western civilization.[22] Following *Bowers*, opponents of gay civil rights redoubled their efforts to disparage homosexuality as a deviant behavior rather than a minority status and to depict the gay rights movement as a radically new, dangerous, and illegitimate development, with no connection to history or to established legal principles.[23] Gay advocates have responded to these attacks by marshalling historical evidence that lesbians and gay men are a legitimate minority, a "distinct community" with "collective roots in the past . . . [and] a collective identity in the present."[24]

In constructing a usable past, gay scholars have not hesitated to lay claim to a wide range of cross-gender identities and to label these identities as unambiguously "gay" or "lesbian," with little or no acknowledgment that, in many cases, they might just as plausibly or even more plausibly be termed "transgender." To mention one of many possible examples, William Eskridge's scholarship on same-sex marriage and Leslie Feinberg's history of the transgender movement cover much of the same historical ground, but where Eskridge sees same-sex couples, Feinberg sees transgender people.[25] Similarly, Patrick Califia has documented the extreme lengths to which many gay historians and anthropologists have gone to claim cross-gendered identities within Native American cultures as gay while vehemently rejecting any comparison with transgender people.[26] The same disdain for contemporary transgender people is evident in many of the accounts of "passing women" featured in numerous gay histories.[27] With few exceptions, gay historians have claimed these historical figures as lesbian forebears, with little or no room for discussion, ambiguity, or debate as to whether some of these individuals would be described more accurately as transgender.[28]

From a practical perspective, the necessity for gay advocates to draw on the same historical material claimed by transgender people is clear. Gender variance is a deep and recurring theme in gay culture and gay life—from the mollies of eighteenth-century London,[29] to the lesbian and gay artists of the Harlem Renaissance,[30] to contemporary queer performers such as kd lang and RuPaul. Given the predominance of these ostensibly cross-gendered ways of expressing same-sex desire and of being lesbian or gay throughout much of the past, to deny any historical affiliations with transgender people would be to sever contemporary lesbians and gay men from a rich and varied history and to strand gay rights advocates with little in the way of a citable or usable past.

Unfortunately, however, the practical necessity of incorporating cross-gendered identities in constructing a gay past has not often translated into a recognition that transgender people are an important or legitimate part of gay life in the present. Disturbingly, in fact, some lesbians and gay men appear to have taken a page from their own right-wing opponents by characterizing contemporary transgender people as upstarts and newcomers who have appeared on the scene with no roots in the past and no connection to gay history or gay life. Thus, while lesbian and gay scholars have been willing to lay claim to transgender ancestors to refute the argument that contemporary gay people "came out of nowhere," they sometimes have been complicit in launching the same "came out of nowhere" attacks on the newly emerging transgender movement. In the first edition of their casebook on sexuality, gender, and the law, for example, the gay scholars William Eskridge and Nan Hunter discussed transsexualism almost exclusively as a contemporary medical phenomenon and appeared to suggest that transsexual people literally emerged from a Johns Hopkins laboratory in the 1950s.[31] Similarly, in the legislative arena, gay advocates who are reluctant to include transgender people in gay rights legislation often argue that as a "new" group, transgender people must wait their turn and cannot expect to "piggyback" or "ride on the coattails" of the gay movement.[32] From the perspectives of many transgender people, however, these arguments fail to acknowledge that transgender people have been present in gay liberation and gay rights struggles from the beginning. In the words of Riki Wilchins, the executive director of the Gender Public Advocacy Coalition, "It's not even a valid question to ask if [transgender people] should be included, they are and always have been part of the movement." Saying the transgender movement "isn't part of the gay movement is like saying water isn't part of the earth."[33]

From Gender Inversion to Sexual Object Choice: The Class- and Race-Based Origins of Modern Gay Identity

In the United States, the exclusion of transgender people from the mainstream gay movement is rooted in the expressly nontransgender, or gender-normative, model of gay identity that has dominated gay rights advocacy since the transition from the nineteenth-century model of homosexuality as gender inversion to the dominant contemporary model of sexual object choice. In the nineteenth century, most people understood lesbian and gay identity primarily in terms of gender inversion: only masculine lesbians were seen as truly lesbian, and only feminine gay men were seen as truly gay.[34] Today, in contrast, most people take for granted that being lesbian or gay is primarily about same-sex desire: lesbians are assumed to be women who are sexually attracted to other women, and gay men are assumed to be males who are sexually attracted to other males, regardless of their gender presentation.

George Chauncey's history of gay male culture in New York City between 1890 and 1940 offers one particularly illuminating example of how the current tensions between gay and transgender people grew out of this definitional shift.[35] Disputing the misconception that gay people prior to Stonewall were uniformly closeted and invisible, Chauncey documents the previously unknown existence of a "highly visible . . . gay male world" that flourished in working-class African American and immigrant communities in New York City from the turn of the century through the decades prior to World War II.[36] Within these urban communities, lesbians and gay men were a conspicuous and integral part of everyday social life:

> Fairies drank with sailors and other workingmen at waterfront dives and entertained them at Bowery resorts; "noted faggots" mixed with other patrons at Harlem's rent parties and basement cabarets; and lesbians ran speakeasies where Greenwich Village bohemians—straight and queer alike—gathered to read their verse.[37]

The dominant understanding of what it meant to be gay in these settings was not based on same-sex behaviors or desires, as it is today, but on one's gender presentation or gender status.

> The fundamental division of male sexual actors in much turn-of-the-century working class thought . . . was not between "heterosexual" and "homosexual" men, but

between conventionally masculine males, who were regarded as men, and effeminate males, known as fairies or pansies, who were regarded as virtual women, or, more precisely, as members of a "third sex" that combined elements of the male and female.[38]

Chauncey concludes that it was not until after World War II that a "new dichotomous system of classification, based on sexual object choice rather than gender status, superseded the old."[39] He attributes this shift, at least in part, to a white middle-class backlash against the growing visibility of gay culture in working-class immigrant and African American communities.[40] In the decades prior to World War II, visibly gay men were subjected to increasingly brutal repression by police, antivice squads, and other "social purity" forces, under the aegis of solicitation, sodomy, prostitution, cross-dressing, disorderly conduct, and similar statutes.[41] This antigay backlash was part of a much broader middle-class social reform movement, which sought to police working-class culture more generally and, in particular, to combat what middle-class reformers perceived as the degenerate influence of urban immigrant communities, stigmatized as hotbeds of alcoholism, prostitution, homosexuality, and other forms of "un-American" unruliness, disorder, and vice.[42]

Convinced that the survival of the family and the dominance of white culture were at stake, these reformers were determined to impose white middle-class norms about gender and sexuality on immigrant working-class communities.[43] In particular, the reformers sought to counter "the threat . . . posed by men and women who seemed to stand outside the family," including

> the men . . . who gathered without supervision in the "dissipating" atmosphere of the saloons; the women whose rejection of conventional gender and sexual arrangements was emblematized by the prostitute; the youths of the city whose lives seemed to be shaped by the discordant influences of the streets rather than the civilizing influences of the home; and . . . the gay men and lesbians who gathered in the niches of the urban landscape constructed by these groups.[44]

As any visible deviation from middle-class gender norms became a lightning rod for criminal sanctions and police brutality,[45] white middle-class gay men increasingly "blamed anti-gay hostility on the failure of fairies to abide by straight middle-class conventions of decorum in their dress and style."[46] "I don't object to being known as a homosexual," noted one such man in the mid-1930s, "but I detest the obvious, blatant, made-up boys whose public appearance and behavior provoke onerous criticism."[47] Seeking the protection of invisibility, growing numbers of white middle-class gay men rejected the appellation of *fairy* in favor of the term *queer,* in an effort to dissociate their sexual desires for men from any connotation of deviation from an otherwise "normal" masculine identity.[48] Queers "maintained that their desire for men revealed only their 'sexuality' (their 'homosexuality'), a distinct domain of personality independent of gender. Their homosexuality, they argued, revealed nothing abnormal in their gender persona."[49]

In sum, the demise of gender inversion as the dominant model of gay identity was not due to the emergence of a more enlightened understanding of same-sex desire, as many contemporary gay people tend to assume,[50] but rather to the growing "class antagonism" between fairies and queers.[51] In significant part, our modern understanding of homosexuality as based on same-sex desire rather than on gender status was a product of white middle-class gay men's embattled efforts to dissociate themselves from the dangerous visibility of working-class gay culture and to salvage the safety and status to which they felt entitled as a matter of race and class. "As the cultured, distinguished, conservative Jew or Negro loathes and deplores his vulgar, socially unacceptable stereotype, plenty of whom unfortunately are all too visible," explained one of the white middle-class gay men who began to forge this new conception of gay identity in the 1920s and 1930s, "so does their homosexual counterpart resent his caricature in the flaming faggot. . . . The general public [makes no distinction], and the one is penalized and ostracized for the grossness and excesses of the other."[52]

In citing this history, I do not mean to suggest that Chauncey has pinpointed the precise historical moment at which gender inversion gave way, once and for all, to sexual object choice as the dominant model of gay identity.[53] On the contrary, one of the most striking features of Chauncey's account of the tension between "fairies" and "queers" is the remarkable extent to which it resonates with contemporary gay debates.[54] As Urvashi Vaid has rightly remarked, many of the queer men in Chauncey's history sound "a lot like gay conservatives today."[55]

One can recognize the resonance of these "queer" sentiments not only in contemporary gay conservatism but, more generally, in the persistence and centrality of conflict over gender norms throughout recent gay history. In fact, what might now be called "transgender" issues repeatedly have been at the core of shifts and tensions in the meaning of modern gay identity and, in particular, at the center of class- and race-based stratifications within the gay movement. Lillian Faderman, for example, has described how profoundly conflicts over gender norms divided working-class and middle-class lesbians in the 1950s and 1960s.[56] While many working-class lesbians identified as butch or femme[57] and adopted the same highly differentiated masculine and feminine styles characteristic of working-class culture generally,[58] many white middle-class lesbians adopted professional feminine attire[59] and cringed at the sight of butches "with cigarettes rolled in their sleeves" and "their overdressed femmes with too much lipstick and too high heels."[60] The political interests of many working-class lesbians lay in fighting for the right to be visibly lesbian on the streets, at work, and in other public spaces. In contrast, the interests of many white middle-class lesbians lay in the opposite direction. For example, a primary goal of the Daughters of Bilitis, which was founded in 1955 as the first lesbian political organization in the United States, was "advocating [to lesbians] a mode of behavior and dress acceptable to society."[61] Like the white middle-class gay men chronicled by Chauncey, the Daughters of Bilitis sought to distance themselves from "the kids in fly front pants and with butch haircuts and mannish manner [who were] the worst publicity we can get."[62]

Class-based conflicts over gender have continued to be a source of internal conflict in the post-Stonewall era. In the 1970s, for example, many middle-class lesbian-feminists condemned working-class butch and femme lesbians for "imitating" oppressive heterosexual "roles" and perpetuating "stereotypical" images of lesbian identity.[63] As Joan Nestle, Cherríe Moraga, Lyndall MacCowan, Esther Newton, Minnie Bruce Pratt, Biddy Martin, and others have noted, these attacks were "old class putdowns, clothed in new political sanctity."[64]

These class-based conflicts are also apparent in the increasing invisibility of transsexuals, cross-dressers, and drag queens in the decades after Stonewall, as "gay liberation" gave way to "gay rights" and to an emphasis on "dispelling the stereotypes" that lesbians and gay men are all bull dykes and flaming fairies. In an important sense, the mainstream gay rights movement defined itself and emerged as an organized political and legal movement by embracing an explicitly nontransgender, or gender-normative, model of gay identity.[65] Over time, the increasing hegemony of this gender-normative model has resulted in the increasing isolation of gender-variant lesbians and gay men within the mainstream movement, and increasing tensions between gay and transgender people. Eventually, these tensions permitted gender-variant people to emerge as a distinct constituency, or as what is now known as the "transgender" movement.

Where Do Transgender People Come From? The Birth of the Transgender Movement

Lesbian and gay scholars have documented the shift from an older model of homosexuality as gender inversion to the dominant contemporary model of sexual object choice; for the most part, however, they have not acknowledged contemporary transgender people or questioned whether all those fairies and other gender inverts running around in "gay" history were really gay. To the contrary, as described in part 1, many gay historians have appropriated ostensibly cross-gendered figures from the past and labeled those figures as gay while renouncing any affiliation between gay and transgender people in the present. The emergence of a self-identified transgender movement has made it possible for transgender people to reclaim much of this inverted "gay" history as their own. More important, the transgender movement has made it possible to say that transgender is not just a marginalized or anachronistic way to be gay, but a distinct identity.

What has allowed this to happen? What has prompted transgender people to come out of the closet, both as a self-conscious constituency within the gay world and as a relatively autonomous movement at this particular point in time?

There surely is no single explanation or cause, but it seems safe to say that the recognition of transsexualism as a medical phenomenon in the 1950s and the relatively widespread access to hormones and sex reassignment surgeries in the 1960s and 1970s were necessary, if not sufficient, conditions for transgender people to emerge as a self-conscious social and political group.[66] By identifying and labeling transsexual people as a distinct group, the acknowledgment of transsexualism as a medical condition and the availability of hormones and surgeries paved the way for a politicized transgender movement.[67]

As a medical identity, however, transsexualism initially was defined in rigid, heterosexist terms, and access to sex reassignment was conditioned on compliance with overtly homophobic and sexist standards.[68] Until very recently, for example, transsexual people who also are lesbian, gay, or bisexual—that is, male-to-female transsexuals who are sexually attracted to women or female-to-male transsexuals who are sexually attracted to men—were denied access to sex reassignment because they were not seen as "real" transsexuals.[69] Similarly, only transsexual people who conformed to stereotypical gender norms and who were deemed capable of "passing" in their new sex were able to obtain treatment.[70] More generally, the ability of transsexual people to gain access to medical services and to legal recognition and protection has depended on how successfully they could hide their transsexual status and approximate a "normal" heterosexual life, with the result that those who are unable or unwilling to comply with these oppressive standards have had little or no protection at all.

The transgender activist and theorist Ki Namaste has aptly described the oppressiveness of these medical and legal standards:

At gender-identity clinics, transsexuals are encouraged to lie about their transsexual status. They are to define themselves as men or women, not transsexual men and women. Individuals are encouraged to invent personal histories in their chosen genders; female-to-male transsexuals, for example, should speak about their lives as little boys. Furthermore they are to conceive of themselves as heterosexuals, since psychiatry cannot even begin to acknowledge male-to-female transsexual lesbians and female-to-male transsexual gay men. This elision of transsexual specificity has profound political implications.[71]

Politically, this sexist and heterosexist legacy has had a profoundly negative impact on transgender people. The medical model of transsexual identity, with its overriding emphasis on the requirement that transsexual people should "disappear" and blend into mainstream society, has made it difficult for transsexual people to mobilize politically around being transsexual or to create a transsexual movement. As Kate Bornstein has observed, "the dynamic of transsexualism today is the dynamic of an oppressed people faced with no alternative to forced assimilation into a culture that would rather see them dead."[72] Or, in the words of Sandy Stone, "it is difficult to generate a counter-discourse if one is programmed to disappear."[73]

Historically, the recognition of transsexualism as a medical condition has also complicated and in certain respects embittered the relationship between gay and transsexual people. As James Green has noted,

To gain access to medical treatment, transsexual people had to censor their own experiences and beliefs and, in particular, had to renounce any similarity to or affiliation with lesbians and gay men. This coercive dynamic perpetuated many inaccurate stereotypes about trans people, including the widespread misconception (which is unfortunately shared by many GLB people) that transsexual people are homophobic and reactionary and have no political goals other than being accepted as "normal" heterosexuals.[74]

Part of the impetus behind the emergence of the transgender movement is precisely the strongly felt desire to create a less-restrictive social and political space in which it is possible to be openly transsexual, as well as to regain some autonomy and control over the personal meaning of transsexual identity and over access to medical care. This includes recognition of the freedom to be transsexual as a civil and human right, not just as a clinical decision made by medical authorities.[75] This relatively new self-consciousness of transsexualism as having a political, as well as medical, dimension has led many transsexual people to question the old medical directive to "disappear" after transitioning and to reject the clinical definition of transsexuals as categorically separate and distinct from gay people, transvestites, and other gender-benders. Instead, growing numbers of transsexual people are refusing to conceal their personal histories or to consider transsexualism a shameful secret that should be hidden at all costs. They are also recognizing their common political cause with cross-dressers, drag queens, butch and femme lesbians, feminine gay men, intersex people, and other gender-variant people.[76]

In short, the politics of transsexual identity have undergone a fairly radical evolution in an astonishingly short period of time. After being defined as a distinct group, in part, by the sexist and homophobic standards used to regulate access to sex reassignment, transsexual people have burst the boundaries of clinical categories and emerged to play a leading role in mobilizing gender-variant people, both within and outside the gay community, into a self-consciously new transgender movement. They have played a key role in challenging the mainstream gay movement's gender-normalizing model of gay identity and its marginalization of gender-variant lesbians and gay men.[77]

Do Gay People Dream of Transgender Rights?

Not surprisingly, established gay groups have not responded to the sudden emergence of a "transgender" constituency with immediate understanding or acceptance. At least in the first instance, many gay leaders and groups have been inclined to view transgender people as outsiders and to greet the suggestion that transgender people are an integral part of the gay community with astonishment and anger. At its worst, this reaction stems from a visceral and phobic antipathy to transgender people. More commonly, however, I believe this resistance reflects genuine confusion and concern about how to reconcile transgender issues with the modern, nontransgender model of gay identity that has dominated legal and political advocacy on behalf of lesbians and gay men for several decades.

Although usually unspoken, I believe some gay leaders also feel resentment and fear that transgender people will co-opt or derail the hard-won resources and political power that gay people have worked so long to achieve. This fear is most pronounced in the legislative and legal arenas, where gay activists and civil rights litigators feel a responsibility to coordinate a coherent, long-term strategy based on a model of incremental progress toward greater equality and acceptance within the mainstream. From this perspective, the sudden emergence of a transgender constituency demanding inclusion in the gay movement might well appear to be a destabilizing and potentially threatening element.

In response to this resistance and, in particular, in response to the repeated argument that gay and transgender issues are completely unrelated, those in favor of transgender inclusion frequently have sought to justify transgender people's claims to membership in the gay movement by subsuming gay identity under the transgender umbrella. They have argued that lesbians and gay men are discriminated against because same-sex relationships undermine traditional gender roles and gender hierarchy, not because of their sexual behaviors or desires per se. Kate Bornstein, for example, has argued that "when a gay man is bashed on the street, . . . it has little to do with imagining the man [engaging in sexual conduct with another man]. It has a lot to do with seeing that man violate the rules of gender in this culture."[78] Accordingly, she has suggested that "it's the transgendered who need to embrace the lesbians and gays, because it's the transgendered who are in fact the more inclusive category."[79]

Similarly, Gabriel Rotello, a gay man, has argued that "homophobes don't hate us for how we make love. They hate how we make love because it violates our expected gender roles."[80] "When I was 10 and was taunted for throwing the ball 'like a girl,'" he notes, "I don't think those school-yard bullies suspected me of actually sleeping with men."[81] Rotello concludes that "all gay and transgendered people occupy places on a continuum between the two main genders" and that "the root of our difference is not merely how we make love but the larger fact that we exist between the two genders in a variety of ways, some sexual and some not."[82] "This idea," he continues, "has immense implications—because if the ultimate cause of our oppression is gender transgression, then shouldn't it also be the focus of our identities and our movement? Shouldn't we stop being the les-bi-gay-trans-whatever movement, with a new syllable added every few years, and simply become the trans movement?"[83]

As a strategy for gaining entrance where one is not welcome, the argument that all gay people are on a transgender continuum and the characterization of transgender people as the vanguard of a new queer movement is strikingly reminiscent of the analogous strategy used by some lesbian-feminists to argue for lesbian inclusion in the mainstream feminist movement in the 1970s. Initially, Betty Friedan, the founder of the National Organization for Women, and other mainstream feminist leaders refused to recognize lesbianism as a legitimate feminist issue or to include lesbians as a legitimate constituency within the women's movement.[84] Friedan, most notoriously, disparaged lesbians as a "lavender menace" and feared that including lesbians in the feminist movement would fatally undermine its credibility.[85] In response,

lesbian-feminists undertook what one scholar has termed a "stunningly effica-
cious re-visioning . . . of same-sex desire as being at the very definitional center of each gender. . . . Women who loved women were seen as more female . . .
than those whose desire crossed boundaries of gender."[86] This strategy rejected the dominant perception of lesbianism as a deviant sexual practice and
redefined it as the touchstone of radical feminist identity. Instead of a marginalized and unwelcome minority within the feminist movement, lesbians
became "women-identified-women" and argued that all women were on a "lesbian continuum."[87] From this new perspective, lesbianism became "the feminist solution" to male oppression,[88] a political expression of solidarity with
other women, and a symbol of "the rage of all women condensed to the point
of explosion."[89]

This kind of deconstructive reversal can be an effective political strategy,
but it can also be dangerous if used to replace one monolithic and exclusionary version of identity with another. At least in the case of certain versions of
lesbian-feminism, what began as a way to counteract the homophobia of mainstream feminism, and to underscore the connections between lesbians and
other women, turned into an increasingly rigid and essentialist theory that
defined lesbian-feminism solely in opposition to men, with little regard for
the impact of race or class. This led some lesbians to misfocus their anger on
other oppressed groups—heterosexual and bisexual women who "collaborated
with the enemy" by sleeping with men;[90] working-class lesbians who identified
as butch or femme;[91] gay men, who were deemed to be even more "male" and
thus even "more loyal to masculinity and to male supremacy" than other men;[92]
and, above all, transsexual women.

Janice Raymond and Mary Daly, among other lesbian feminist theorists,
demonized transsexual women as the epitome of misogynist attempts to invade
women's space and appropriate women's identity. Describing transsexualism
as equivalent to necrophilia and rape, Raymond and Daly launched a full-scale
political attack on clinics that provided medical services to transsexual people
and played a significant role in the closing of many of those clinics in the late
1970s and early 1980s.[93] Raymond's and Daly's disparaging views of transsexual people were picked up by young feminists, discussed in feminist support
groups and on college campuses, and eventually came to permeate much of
lesbian culture. To this day, the analyses of transsexualism that Raymond and
Daly put forward continue to inform many lesbians' perceptions of transgender
people and particularly of transsexual women.[94]

The damage caused by this essentialist vision of lesbian identity has
not been limited to transsexual women. To the contrary, the idea that lesbians

are "women-identified-women" and other arguments originally developed to defend lesbians against mainstream feminist attacks have been used subsequently to disparage lesbians who do not conform to a largely white, middle-class model of acceptable gender norms.[95] Lesbians who are seen as "too masculine" have had their legitimacy as feminists and their place in lesbian culture called into question,[96] as have those who are seen as "too feminine."[97] Even today, lesbians who strongly identify as butch or femme are likely to be marginalized within middle-class lesbian settings and to be viewed as misguided or "backward." Lillian Faderman, for example, has expressly chastised "working-class lesbians [who] . . . identify as butch or femme in the 1980s with the same deadly seriousness that characterized many women of the 50s."[98]

As these examples of the damage that can be done to real people in the name of identity politics should remind us, making a place for transgender issues in the gay movement need not require the undifferentiated assimilation of all queer people under the rubric of a new gender-based movement. In fact, given how persistently the devaluation of cross-gendered expression has been tied to the devaluation of working-class, African American, and immigrant people within queer history, it seems dangerous to assume that gender is necessarily the only or even the most important frame of reference for understanding transgender issues. Historically, for example, focusing on gender alone—without reference to class, race, or nationality—would provide only a very partial and inadequate account of the antagonism between "fairies" and "queers" in the pre–World War II era, the exclusion of masculine lesbians and drag queens from the homophile movement of the 1950s, or the controversy over butch-femme relationships among lesbians in the 1970s. Gender alone is equally inadequate for understanding transgender issues today, as evidenced, for example, by the growing body of scholarship on the importance of gender-variant and transgender identities in contemporary queer communities of color.[99]

Moreover, while the claim that gay people are a subset of the transgender community is a powerful antidote to antitransgender bias and a powerful lens for illuminating the connections between antigay and antitrans oppression, those who have qualms about this approach also surely are right to insist on the continued importance of sexual orientation as a specific social and political category. They are also right to insist on the need to recognize sexual orientation and gender as at least relatively distinct frames of reference. Homophobia and sexism undoubtedly work hand in hand; few lesbian or gay scholars today would dispute this. But simply conflating them altogether may obscure the particular forms of sexism faced by women,[100] just as it may fail to capture the particular animosity directed at same-sex practices and desires or the specific social and legal vulnerabilities of lesbian, gay, and bisexual people.

More pragmatically, the gay rights movement has worked too hard to gain recognition of gay people as a distinct minority in need of specific civil rights protections to reverse course in midstream and abruptly subsume gay identity under the transgender umbrella. If the controversy over transgender inclusion is framed as a choice between these two mutually exclusive extremes—either excluding transgender people altogether or redefining all gay people as gender nonconforming—then we are bound to adopt a position that is unworkable and that disregards the complexity of real people and real lives.

Fortunately, there is no reason to frame the issue in these polarized terms or to view these as the only choices.[101] Getting real about transgender issues means moving beyond this zero-sum frame. We need not disregard the complexities of our communities or of our individual lives to engage in collective political action.

While arguments that claim to identify the singular cause of antiqueer oppression can be exhilarating and compelling, they are also dangerous and patently untrue.[102] This warning applies equally to analyses focused only on sexual orientation, as well as to analyses that attempt to supplant this narrow model with an equally unidimensional model based on gender. Gender-based arguments underscore the impossibility of drawing any bright line between transgender and gay, and illuminate the connections between sexist and homophobic oppression in powerfully new ways. These analyses do not, however, provide a reliable foundation for launching an affirmative new politics based on subsuming gay people under the transgender umbrella, and they do not eliminate the need for multidimensional analyses that recognize the multiplicity of specific issues and constituencies within queer communities.[103] At the end of the day, there is no single term or frame of analysis—whether it be gay, transgender, or queer—that can eliminate the need for multiple strategies and multiple frames of reference.[104]

The inescapability of this multiplicity militates strongly in favor of fully integrating and incorporating transgender issues within the gay movement. Despite the fears of some gay people, this incorporation need not entail the erasure of gay identity or jeopardize existing legal protections for lesbians and gay men. Although it will require a significant expansion of the gay rights agenda and a significant broadening of vision, this expansion is not an all-or-nothing proposition, any more than broadening the gay rights agenda to include the specific needs and concerns of lesbians or of people with HIV and AIDS has been an all-or-nothing proposition. For example, the gay movement has addressed issues of child custody and parenting despite the fact that, until quite recently, these issues have been far more important to lesbians than to gay men. Similarly, the gay movement has fought to secure health care and nondiscrimination protections for persons with HIV and AIDS, despite the fact that these issues are not directly about sexual orientation per se. In exactly the same way, the gay movement can and should address issues affecting transgender people, regardless of whether these issues affect all gay people or fall under the rubric of sexual orientation in the most narrow sense of the term.

Conclusion: Getting Real about Transgender Inclusion

Do transsexual people dream of gay rights? Ultimately, what both gay and transgender people aspire to is neither "gay rights" nor "transgender rights" but simply human rights. As the U.S. Supreme Court recognized in *Romer v. Evans*,[105] there is nothing "special" about the legal protections gay people seek and nothing ersatz about the damage inflicted by laws that exclude gay people from equal participation in social and political life:

> We find nothing special in the protections Amendment 2 withholds. These are protections taken for granted by most people either because they already have them or do not need them; these are protections against exclusion from an almost limitless number of transactions and endeavors that constitute ordinary civic life in a free society.[106]

Similarly, in *Baker v. State*, the Vermont Supreme Court recognized that extending basic civil rights to gay people is not a radical step but rather, "simply, when all is said and done, a recognition of our common humanity."[107] Most recently, in *Lawrence v. Texas*, the U.S. Supreme Court expressly rejected the notion that gay people may be excluded from fundamental human rights.[108] Reversing its prior decision in *Bowers v. Hardwick*, the Court struck down laws criminalizing same-sex intimacy. More important, the Court resoundingly affirmed the full humanity of gay people and their entitlement to the same liberty guaranteed to others in "choices central to personal dignity and autonomy."[109]

Matt Coles, a leading gay rights strategist and attorney, has commented on the shortsightedness of excluding transgender people from gay rights bills:

> To be sure, there are differences between gay people and transgendered people. . . . But our commonalities far outweigh our differences. Often it is nearly impossible to distinguish between discrimination based on gender identity and sexual orientation, because so much of it turns on ideas of how men and women should act. We

have more to gain by taking on this sort of bias in a way that addresses all of its manifestations than we do by trying to parse out who the target is, and choosing who to protect.[110]

In deciding whether to include transgender people in the gay movement, gay rights advocates would do well to keep this expansive perspective in mind. Historically, clinging to a narrow and exclusive conception of gay identity has not only marginalized transgender and gender-variant gay people, it also has exacerbated divisions based on race and class. To the extent gay and transgender people are capable of learning from our shared queer past, the challenges posed by transgender inclusion offer an opportunity to build a less fractured and more humanistic movement.

Notes

1. Throughout this chapter, I use *transgender* as an umbrella term including transsexuals, transvestites, cross-dressers, drag queens and drag kings, butch and femme lesbians, feminine gay men, intersex people, bigendered people, and others who, in Leslie Feinberg's words, "challenge the boundaries of sex and gender." See Leslie Feinberg, *Transgender Warriors: Making History from Joan of Arc to RuPaul* (Boston: Beacon, 1996), x. For an overview of current debates about terminology within the transgender community, see ibid., ix–xi. I use *gay* when referring to the dominant contemporary model of homosexuality as a discrete status defined exclusively by sexual object choice, with no intrinsic relation to gender, race, or class. I use *queer* to refer to lesbian, gay, bisexual, and transgender people.

2. See, for example, Chryss Cada, "Issue of Transgender Rights Divides Many Gay Activists, Transgender Activists Seek a Greater Voice," *Boston Globe,* April 23, 2000.

3. See, for example, Zachary Nataf, *Lesbians Talk Transgender* (London: Scarlet, 1996), 35–53 (presenting a variety of perspectives on the controversy over whether transsexual women should be included in women-only spaces). See also Feinberg, *Transgender Warriors,* 109–19n4 (critiquing the stereotype that "transsexual women are . . . a Trojan horse trying to infiltrate women's space").

4. For an early and remarkably prescient analysis of this question, see Mary C. Dunlap, "The Constitutional Rights of Sexual Minorities: A Crisis of the Male/Female Dichotomy," *Hastings Law Journal* 30 (1979): 1131. For a more recent exploration of why gay rights groups should advocate on behalf of transgender people, see Taylor Flynn, "Transforming the Debate: Why We Need to Include Transgender Rights in the Struggles for Sex and Sexual Orientation Equality," *Columbia Law Review* 101, no. 2 (2001): 392.

5. See, for example, Paisley Currah and Shannon Minter, *Transgender Equality* (Transgender Law and Policy Institute, 2000), http://www.transgenderlaw.org, arguing that gay groups should include transgender people in legislative initiatives. See also Paisley Currah and Shannon Minter, "Unprincipled Exclusions: The Struggle to Achieve Judicial and Legislative Equality for Transgender People," *William and Mary Journal of Women and the Law* 7, no. 1 (2000): 37, describing the need for legislation to protect transgender people.

6. The National Lesbian and Gay Law Association and the National Gay and Lesbian Task Force were among the first national gay organizations to formally acknowledge their commitments to transgender people. Since then, a number of others have followed suit, including Parents, Families, and Friends of Lesbians and Gays and, most recently, the Human Rights Campaign. For a description of some of the lobbying efforts and political struggles underlying these changes, see Phyllis Randolph Frye, "Facing Discrimination, Organizing for Freedom: The Transgender Community," in *Creating Change: Sexuality, Public Policy, and Civil Rights,* ed. John D'Emilio, William B. Turner, and Urvashi Vaid (New York: St. Martin's, 2000), 451.

7. For an unusually forthright articulation of this perspective, see Bruce Bawer, "Confusion Reigns," *Advocate,* October 18, 1994, 140–41n3 (noting that bisexual and transgender people "deserve all kinds of freedom, but . . . are these people in any reasonable sense gay or gay and lesbian? Are their issues ours? Do they experience discrimination on the basis of sexual orientation? . . . No") (internal quotations omitted).

8. See, for example, Christopher Cain, "'T' time at the Human Rights Campaign," *Southern Voice,* April 11, 2001, expressing concern that including transgender people in gay civil rights advocacy will confuse and dilute the message that "our freedom and civil rights should not be curtailed based upon who we love."

9. See, for example, Stephen Whittle, "Gender Fucking or Fucking Gender?" in *Blending Genders: Social Aspects of Cross-Dressing and Sex-Changing,* ed. Richard Ekins and Dave King (New York: Routledge, 1996), 196, 201–2 (noting that "many transgendered individuals have made their home in . . . the homosexual community" and that "lesbians and gay men have often provided a safe and welcoming space for transgendered people").

10. Although medical authorities initially assumed that all transsexual people are heterosexual, there is growing evidence that many transsexual people are lesbian, gay, or bisexual. See, for example, Ann Bolin, "Transcending and Transgendering: Male-to-Female Transsexuals, Dichotomy and Diversity," in *Third Sex, Third Gender: Beyond Sexual Dimorphism in Culture and History,* ed. Gilbert Herdt (New York: Zone Books, 1993), 447, 460 ("Of my sample, only one person was exclusively heterosexual, three of the six exclusive lesbians were living with women who themselves were not self-identified as lesbian, one bisexual was living with a self-identified lesbian, and two male-to-female transsexuals were living with one another"); Nataf, *Lesbians Talk Transgender,* 32 ("My research showed that of the FTMs that responded 33 percent identified as bisexual, 40 percent as heterosexual, 2 percent as asexual and 25 percent as gay men," citing Stephen Whittle); Martin S. Weinberg et al., *Dual Attraction: Understanding Bisexuality* (Oxford: Oxford University Press, 1994), 59–65 (attempting to account for the higher incidence of homosexuality and bisexuality among transsexual people); Feinberg, *Transgender Warriors,* 92 (noting that the "sexuality of some trans people [cannot] be easily classified"); Shadow Morton, "Perspective," *Anything That Moves* 13 (spring 1997): 14 (describing his experience as a gay FTM and noting that "I've been a gay activist for eighteen of my 35 years—first as a lesbian, later as a gay man").

11. John D'Emilio, "After Stonewall," in *Making Trouble: Essays on Gay History, Politics, and the University* (New York: Routledge, 1992), 234, 240. See also Feinberg,

Transgender Warriors, 97 (noting that visibly trangender people often have borne the brunt of antilesbian and antigay violence and discrimination, and suggesting that "it was no accident that gender outlaws led the Stonewall Rebellion").

12. For a concise account of these internal battles, see D'Emilio, "After Stonewall," 256, 271. See also Urvashi Vaid, *Virtual Equality: The Mainstreaming of Lesbian and Gay Liberation* (New York: Anchor Books, 1995), 274–306, 346–72 (describing conflicts over issues of racial and gender diversity in the gay movement).

13. D'Emilio, "After Stonewall," 235–36.

14. See, for example, Bawer, "Confusion Reigns," 140–41.

15. See, for example, Gabriel Rotello, "Transgendered Like Me," *Advocate*, December 10, 1996 (arguing that "an emerging definition of all gay people as transgendered is the wave of the future").

16. See notes 39–72 and accompanying text.

17. Vaid, *Virtual Equality*, 274–306; D'Emilio, "After Stonewall," 246–71 (describing how profoundly conflicts over gender have shaped the lesbian and gay movement in the post-Stonewall era). For an indication of how vitriolic conflicts between lesbians and gay men can still become, see Stephen H. Miller, "Gay White Males: PC's Unseen Target," in *Beyond Queer: Challenging Gay Left Orthodoxy*, ed. Bruce Bawer (New York: Free Press, 1996), 24–37 (accusing lesbian feminists of mounting a "siege against gay male culture").

18. D'Emilio, "After Stonewall," 235.

19. See, for example, Susan Stryker and Jim Van Buskirk, *Gay by the Bay: A History of Queer Culture in the San Francisco Bay Area* (San Francisco: Chronicle Books, 1997); Elizabeth Lapovsky Kennedy and Madeline Davis, *Boots of Leather, Slippers of Gold: The History of a Lesbian Community* (New York: Routledge, 1993); Allan Berube, *Coming Out under Fire: The History of Gay Men and Women in World War II* (New York: Free Press, 1990); Martin Duberman, Martha Vicinus, and George Chauncey Jr., eds., *Hidden from History: Reclaiming the Gay and Lesbian Past* (New York: New American Library, 1989); Joan Nestle, *A Restricted Country* (Ithaca, NY: Firebrand Books, 1987); Walter L. Williams, *The Spirit and the Flesh: Sexual Diversity in American Indian Culture* (Boston: Beacon, 1986); John D'Emilio, *Sexual Politics, Sexual Communities: The Making of a Homosexual Minority in the United States, 1940–1970* (Chicago: University of Chicago Press, 1983); Jonathan Katz, *Gay/Lesbian Almanac: A New Documentary* (New York: Harper & Row, 1983); Audre Lorde, *Zami: A New Spelling of My Name* (Trumansburg, NY: Crossing, 1982); Lillian Faderman, *Surpassing the Love of Men: Romantic Friendships and Love between Women from the Renaissance to the Present* (New York: Morrow, 1981).

20. See, for example, Feinberg, *Transgender Warriors* (tracing transgender history from Joan of Arc to the present); Vernon and Bonnie Bullough, *Cross Dressing, Sex, and Gender* (Philadelphia: University of Pennsylvania Press, 1993) (documenting the history of cross-dressing); Dallas Denny, "Transgender in the United States," *Siecus Report* 8 (1999): 27 (noting that "many societies have had formal and often honored social roles for transgender men and women").

21. See George Chauncey, *Gay New York: Gender, Urban Culture, and the Making of the Gay Male World, 1890–1940* (New York: Basic Books, 1994), 285–86.

22. *Bowers v. Hardwick,* 478 U.S. 186, 192 (1986) (noting that proscriptions against homosexual conduct have "ancient roots"). See also ibid. at 196–97 ("Condemnation of [homosexual] practices is firmly rooted in Judeo-Christian moral and ethical standards. . . . To hold that the act of homosexual sodomy is somehow protected as a fundamental right would be to cast aside millennia of moral teaching") (Burger, J. concurring). In *Lawrence v. Texas,* 539 U.S. 558 (2003), the Court backtracked from this sweeping historical condemnation, acknowledging that "the historical grounds relied upon in *Bowers* are more complex than the majority opinion and the concurring opinion by Chief Justice Burger indicate. Their historical premises are not without doubt and, at the very least, are overstated" (at 571).

23. See, for example, Hadley Arkes, "Homosexuality and the Law," in *Homosexuality and Public Life,* ed. Christopher Wolfe (Dallas: Spence, 1999), 157 (referring to "the new thing among us, the public controversy over homosexuality" and invoking Bowers for the proposition that homosexuality is contrary to sexual morality); Michael Pakaluk, "Homosexuality and the Common Good," in *Homosexuality and Public Life,* ed. Christopher Wolfe (Dallas: Spence, 1999), 179, 181 (defending laws criminalizing same-sex intimacy on the ground that such laws are "a link with the past"). See also Jane S. Schacter, "The Gay Civil Rights Debate in the States: Decoding the Discourse of Equivalents," *Harvard Civil Rights–Civil Liberties Review* 29 (1994): 283 (describing and analyzing right-wing arguments that gay rights are "special rights").

24. See, for example, Janet E. Halley, "Intersections: Sexuality, Cultural Tradition, and the Law," *Yale Journal of Law and the Humanities* 8 (1996): 97–98 (noting that some gay legal scholars "have picked up a historiographical gauntlet thrown down" by the Court in *Bowers*).

25. See William N. Eskridge Jr., "A History of Same-Sex Marriage," in *From Sexual Liberty to Civilized Commitment: The Case for Same-Sex Marriage* (New York: Free Press, 1996), 15, 27–30, 37–39 (discussing "the berdache [i.e., two-spirit] tradition" and marriages involving "women passing as men" as examples of same-sex relationships). See also Feinberg, *Transgender Warriors,* 21–29, 83–89 (discussing two-spirit people and female-bodied people who lived their lives as men as examples of transgender people).

26. Patrick Califia, *Sex Changes: The Politics of Transgenderism* (San Francisco: Cleis, 1997).

27. "Passing women" refers to women who wore male clothing and otherwise lived their public lives as men. See, for example, Jonathan Ned Katz, *Gay American History: Lesbians and Gay Men in the U.S.A.* (New York: Meridian, 1992), 209–79 (describing passing women from 1782 to 1920).

28. See, for example, Katz, *Gay American History,* 252 (summarily rejecting the suggestion that Edward Prime Stevenson, born Anna Mattersteig, might have been transsexual). See also Nan Alamilla Boyd, "Bodies in Motion: Lesbian and Transsexual Histories," in *A Queer World: The Center for Lesbian and Gay Studies Reader,* ed. Martin Duberman (New York: New York University Press, 1997), 134, 137–42 (discussing scholarly battles over how to identify passing women and noting that "lesbian and transgender communities construct a usable past around the recuperation of many of the same historical figures").

29. See, for example, Randolph Trumbach, "The Birth of the Queen: Sodomy and the Emergence of Gender Equality in Modern Culture, 1660–1750," in Duberman, Vicinis, and Chauncey, *Hidden from History,* 129 (describing the emergence of a subculture of feminine gay men known as "mollies" in eighteenth-century London).

30. See Eric Garber, "A Spectacle in Color: The Lesbian and Gay Subculture of Jazz Age Harlem," in Duberman, Vicinis, and Chauncey, *Hidden from History,* 318–31 (describing the strong association between cross-gender behavior and homosexuality among lesbian and gay artists and performers in the Harlem Renaissance).

31. William N. Eskridge Jr. and Nan D. Hunter, *Sexuality, Gender, and the Law: Teacher's Manual* (Westbury, NY: Foundation, 1997), 42 ("Reconstructive surgery such as that pioneered at Johns Hopkins has literally created a class of persons . . . transsexuals are a medical creation in a more literal way than homosexuals or transvestites are").

32. See, for example, Cada, "Issue of Transgender Rights" ("I have a problem with the transgendered movement riding on the coattails of the gay-rights movement when the two actually have very little in common. . . . We try to be politically correct and include everybody, and as a result lose our focus as a movement. And, as much as I hate to say it, there is a freak factor with transgendered individuals that sets us back as a movement," quoting Lyn Raymond, a lesbian activist in Colorado).

33. Cada, "Issue of Transgender Rights."

34. See, for example, Kennedy and Davis, *Boots of Leather,* 323–26.

35. See Chauncey, *Gay New York.*

36. Ibid., 1.

37. Ibid., 355.

38. Ibid., 48. "Men's identities and reputations simply did not depend on a sexuality defined by the anatomical sex of their sexual partners. Just as the abnormality of the fairy depended on his violation of gender conventions, rather than his homosexual practices alone, the normality of other men depended on their conformity to those conventions rather than on an eschewal of homosexual practices which those conventions did not require" (97).

39. See Chauncey, *Gay New York,* 21. Chauncey's primary conclusion is that "the hetero-homosexual binarism, the sexual regime now hegemonic in American culture, is a stunningly recent creation. Particularly in working class culture, homosexual behavior per se became the primary basis for the labeling and self-identification of men as queer only around the middle of the twentieth century; before then, most men were so labeled only if they displayed a much broader inversion of their ascribed gender status" (13).

40. Ibid., 326–27 ("By the 1920s, gay men had become a conspicuous part of New York City's nightlife. They had been visible since the late nineteenth century in some of the city's immigrant and working-class neighborhoods, since the 1910s in the Bohemian enclave of Greenwich Village. But in the 1920s they moved into the center of the city's most prestigious entertainment district [Broadway and Times Square], became the subject of plays, films, novels, and newspaper headlines, and attracted thousands of spectators to Harlem's largest ballrooms").

41. See Chauncey, *Gay New York,* 131–49.

42. Ibid., 131–49, 179–205. The disorderly conduct law, for example, "was one of the omnibus legal measures used by the state to try to impose a certain conception

of public order on the city's streets, and in particular, to control the large numbers of immigrants from Ireland and southern and eastern Europe, as well as African-American migrants from the South—the so-called 'dangerous classes' many bourgeois Anglo-Americans found frightening" (172).

43. Ibid., 203.

44. Ibid., 172.

45. As Chauncey notes, "Only people who had not been successfully normalized by the dominant gender culture, such as gay men or lesbians (though not limited to them, but including, in different ways, for instance, working-class or minority men or women) were likely to face the more overt and brutal policing that occurred at the boundaries of the gender order, because only they came close to these boundaries" (*Gay New York,* 346).

46. Ibid., 105.

47. Ibid., 103.

48. Ibid., 101.

49. Ibid., 100.

50. In fact, the assumption that our contemporary understanding of homosexuality is self-evidently "enlightened" and "true" has become so pervasive that lesbian and gay scholars routinely assert that lesbians and gay men who were in fact gender nonconforming (not to mention those who still are) were suffering from a kind of false consciousness, based on their susceptibilities to cultural stereotypes. See, for example, Gilbert Herdt, *Same Sex, Different Cultures* (Boulder, CO: Westview, 1997), 54 ("It may be hard for us, looking back, to see to what extent the public refused to accept that people who seemed so 'normal and natural' in every other respect, especially their gender roles, could be homosexual. This refusal was no doubt due to the strength of the inversion stereotype left over from the nineteenth century—a magical belief so powerful that many gays and lesbians had learned it and made the belief part of their self-concepts"); Lillian Faderman, *Odd Girls and Twilight Lovers: A History of Lesbian Life in the Twentieth Century* (New York: Columbia University Press, 1991), 60 ("Perhaps these theories [about 'inversion'] even seemed accurate to women who desired to be active, strong, ambitious, and aggressive and to enjoy physical relationships with other women; since their society adamantly identified all these attributes as male, they internalized that definition and did indeed think of themselves as having been born men trapped in women's bodies").

51. Chauncey, *Gay New York,* 106.

52. Ibid., 105–6.

53. Nor does Chauncey make this claim for himself: "The transition from the world of fairies and men to the world of homosexuals and heterosexuals was a complex, uneven process, marked by substantial class and ethnic differences. Sex, gender, and sexuality continued to stand in volatile relationship to one another throughout the twentieth century, the very boundaries between them contested" (*Gay New York,* 127). In fact, it is probably misleading to describe our dominant contemporary model of homosexuality as "modern," if this is taken to imply, as it often is, that cultures, communities, and individuals for whom gender status is still very much a part of what it means to be lesbian or gay are somehow "backward" or reactionary.

54. See, for example, Marshall Kirk and Hunter Madsen, *After the Ball: How America Will Conquer Its Fear and Hatred of Gays* (New York: Doubleday, 1989), 379 (proposing a "marketing strategy" to overcome homophobic prejudice by consistently projecting the public image that lesbians and gay men are "just like everyone else" and that we "look, feel, and act just as they [i.e., heterosexual people] do"); Bawer, "Notes on Stonewall," 24 (defending the decision to exclude transgender people from the title of Stonewall 25 on the grounds that "gay America [should not] continue to be defined largely by its fringe" and concluding that "many of the people who were at the Stonewall bar on that night twenty-five years ago represent an anachronistic politics that largely has ceased to have salience for gay America today").

55. Vaid, *Virtual Equality*, 43.

56. Faderman, *Odd Girls and Twilight Lovers*, 168 ("Despite heterosexuals' single stereotype of the 'lesbian,' lesbian subcultures based on class . . . not only had little in common with each other, but their members often distrusted and even disliked one another. The conflict went beyond what was usual in class . . . antagonisms, since each subculture had a firm notion of what lesbian life should be and felt that its conception was compromised by another group that shared the same minority status").

57. Ibid. ("Being neither butch nor femme was not an option if one wanted to be part of the . . . working-class lesbian subculture").

58. Ibid., 169 (noting that "butch/femme style of dress was not much different from working-class male and female style").

59. Ibid., 175–87. Faderman notes that the rules governing appropriately feminine attire "were as vital to the middle-class lesbian subculture as the rule of butch/femme was to their working class counterparts. . . . It was crucial in the middle-class subculture to behave with sufficient, though never excessive, femininity and never to call attention to oneself as a lesbian in any way" (181).

60. Ibid., 182 (citing a middle-class lesbian recalling her reaction to working-class lesbians in an Omaha bar in the 1950s). See also Chauncey, *Gay New York*, 106 ("one source of middle-class gay men's distaste for the fairy's style of self-presentation was that its very brashness marked it in their minds as lower class—and its display automatically preempted social advancement").

61. Faderman, *Odd Girls and Twilight Lovers*, 180.

62. Ibid. (citing *The Ladder* [Journal of the Daughters of Bilitis, 1956]). Cf. Stryker and Van Buskirk, *Gay by the Bay*, 41 (noting that "the pages of the DOB journal *The Ladder* were filled with advice on how women who loved women could attain middle-class respectability if they gave up butch/femme styles associated with the more working-class lesbian bar culture"). See also Nestle, *Restricted Country*, 101–2 (explaining that "the writing in *The Ladder* was bringing to the surface years of pain, . . . giving a voice to an 'obscene' population in a decade of McCarthy witch hunts. To survive meant to take a public stance of societal cleanliness. But in the pages of the journal itself, all dimensions of Lesbian life were explored including butch-femme relationships. *The Ladder* brought off a unique balancing act for the 1950s. It gave nourishment to a secret and subversive life while it flew the flag of assimilation").

63. See, for example, Leslie Feinberg, *Stone Butch Blues* (Ithaca, NY: Firebrand Books, 1993), 135 (dramatizing the characterization of butch lesbians as "male

chauvinist pigs" by some lesbian feminists); Joan Nestle, "The Fem Question," in *Pleasure and Danger: Exploring Female Sexuality,* ed. Carole S. Vance (London: Pandora, 1991), 232, 236 ("The message to fems throughout the 1970s was that we were the Uncle Toms of the [lesbian feminist] movement"); Rose Jordan, "A Question of Culture: Mirror without Image," in *Lavender Culture,* ed. Karla Jay and Allen Young (New York: Jove Publications, 1978), 445, 450 (criticizing butch/femme identities as "role-playing in which one person is dominant and the other subservient").

64. Esther Newton and Shirley Walton, "The Misunderstanding: Toward a More Precise Sexual Vocabulary," in Vance, *Pleasure and Danger,* 242, 249. See also Nestle, *Restricted Country,* 100–109 (arguing that lesbian-feminists' vilification of butch and femme women was rooted in middle-class norms of respectability); Lyndall MacCowan, "Re-collecting History, Renaming Lives: Femme Stigma and the Feminist Seventies and Eighties," in *The Persistent Desire: A Femme-Butch Reader,* ed. Joan Nestle (New York: Alyson Publications, 1991), 299 (analyzing the anti-working-class bias in popular lesbian-feminist texts of the 1970s and 1980s); Cherríe Moraga, *Loving in the War Years* (Boston: South End, 1983), 120 (analyzing the racism implicit in the lesbian-feminist rejection of butch-femme roles).

65. See Paisley Currah, "Defending Genders: Sex and Gender Non-Conformity: The Civil Rights Strategies of Sexual Minorities," *Hastings Law Journal* 48 (1997): 1363 (describing the historical exclusion of gender-variant people, practices, and identities from mainstream gay rights advocacy).

66. Cf. Bolin, "Transcending and Transgendering," 447; Dave King, "Gender Blending: Medical Perspectives and Technology," in Ekins and King, *Blending Genders,* 79.

67. In acknowledging the importance of recognizing transsexualism as a medical condition, I do not mean to endorse the facile and unfortunately still-all-too-common notion that transsexuals are the unwitting dupes of reactionary medical authorities. See, for example, Janice Raymond, *Transsexual Empire* (Boston: Beacon Press, 1979); Dwight Billings and Thomas Urban, "The Socio-Medical Construction of Transsexualism: An Interpretation and Critique," in Ekins and King, *Blending Genders,* 99 (purporting to "show that transsexualism is a socially constructed reality which only exists in and through medical practice").

68. For example, a transsexual was by definition not a drag queen or a transvestite or a self-loathing homosexual but a "normal" heterosexual woman or man "trapped" in the wrong kind of body. See Denny, "Transgender in the United States," 9–10.

69. See Lou Sullivan, *Information for the Female to Male Cross Dresser and Transsexual* (Seattle: Ingersoll Gender Center, 1985), 78–83 (describing his lifelong battle to convince medical providers that some female-to-male transsexuals are gay men). Even now, in fact, some transsexual people who are married are required to get a divorce as a prerequisite for obtaining medical treatment (Denny, "Transgender in the United States," 10).

70. See Denny, "Transgender in the United States," 9–10.

71. Ki Namaste, "Tragic Misreadings: Queer Theory's Erasure of Transgender Subjectivity," in *Queer Studies,* ed. Brett Beemyn and Mickey Eliason (New York: New York University Press, 1996), 183, 197.

72. Kate Bornstein, *Gender Outlaw: On Men, Women, and the Rest of Us* (New York: Routledge, 1994), 121.

73. Sandy Stone, "The Empire Strikes Back: A Posttranssexual Manifesto," in *Body Guards: The Culture Politics of Gender Ambiguity*, ed. Julia Epstein and Kristin Straub (New York: Routledge, 1991), 280.

74. Jamison Green, introduction to Currah and Minter, *Transgender Equality*, 7.

75. See International Bill of Gender Rights, International Conference on Transgender Law and Policy, ITCLEP Rep. 7, August–October 1995.

76. See Dallas Denny, "Transgender: Some Historical, Cross-Cultural, and Contemporary Models and Methods of Coping and Treatment," in *Gender Blending*, ed. Bonnie Bullough, Vern L. Bullough, and James Elias (Amherst, MA: Prometheus Books, 1997), 33, 39 (describing the "paradigm shift" from a psychiatric model that defines transsexuals and transvestites as discrete clinical entities to a unified transgender sensibility); Bolin, "Transcending and Transgendering," 460–82 (noting the emergence of a politicized transgender community that "has supplanted the [previous] dichotomy of transsexual and transvestite"); Stryker and Van Buskirk, *Gay by the Bay*, 126–27 (noting that "the old divisions between drags, butches, transsexuals, and transvestites [have melded] into a provocative 'transgender' style"); Bornstein, *Gender Outlaw*, 118–21 (rejecting a narrow medical definition of transsexualism); Feinberg, *Transgender Warriors*, 98 (emphasizing the diversity of identities within the transgender movement).

77. See, for example, Whittle, "Gender Fucking or Fucking Gender?" in Ekins and King, *Blending Genders*, 202 ("During the 1990s many [transgendered people], including those who have apparently made the transition successfully and would not consider themselves to be lesbian or gay in their new gender-role, are staking a claim as actually belonging to and being a part, and an essential part at that, of the gay community"); Stryker and Van Buskirk, *Gay by the Bay*, 126–27 (describing the "shifting status of transgender identities and practices in the contemporary gay and lesbian community" and noting that "transsexuals in particular quickly seized the political opportunities they saw in the midst of . . . boundary-collapses within queer culture").

78. See, for example, Bornstein, *Gender Outlaw*, 104.

79. Ibid., 135. See also Frye, "Facing Discrimination," 451 (arguing that sexual orientation is a subset of gender identity).

80. Rotello, "Transgendered Like Me," 88.

81. Ibid.

82. Ibid.

83. Ibid. Rotello bases much of his argument on "the growing body of research into the 'cause' of sexual orientation" and the hypothesis that homosexuality and transgenderism have some common biological or genetic propensity to "exhibit 'sex-atypical' characteristics" (ibid.). For a critique of research purporting to find a biological basis for gender-typed behavior and a compelling analysis of the reactionary political implications of this type of research, see Ann-Fausto Sterling, *Myths of Gender: Biological Theories about Women and Men* (New York: Basic Books, 1992).

84. For a recent account of this history, see Karla Jay, *Tales of the Lavender Menace: A Memoir of Liberation* (New York: Basic Books, 1999).

85. See ibid.

86. Eve Kosofsky Sedgwick, *The Epistemology of the Closet* (Berkeley: University of California Press, 1990), 36.

87. Adrienne Rich, "Compulsory Heterosexuality and Lesbian Existence," in *Women, Sex, and Sexuality,* ed. Catherine R. Stimpson and Ethel Spector Person (Chicago: University of Chicago Press, 1980), 62.

88. See Jill Johnston, *Lesbian Nation: The Feminist Solution* (New York: Simon and Schuster, 1974) (arguing that all women are potential lesbians and that lesbianism is the ultimate feminist solution to sexism).

89. Radicalesbians, "The Woman-Identified-Woman," reprinted in *Out of the Closets: Voices of Gay Liberation,* ed. Karla Jay and Allen Young (New York: Douglas, 1977), 172 (originally published as a manifesto by the New York Radicalesbians in 1970).

90. See, for example, "Gay Revolution Party Women's Caucus, Realesbians and Politicalesbians," reprinted in Jay and Young, *Out of the Closets,* 177–78, 180 (condemning heterosexual women for "seeking a personal solution to a political problem" and bisexual women for "retaining their definition by men and the social privileges accruing from this").

91. See, for example, Minnie Bruce Pratt, *S/HE* (Ithaca: Firebrand Books, 1995), 18–19 (describing the disapproval directed at butch and femme lesbians by some lesbian feminists).

92. See, for example, Marilyn Frye, "Lesbian Feminism and the Gay Rights Movement: Another View of Male Supremacy, Another Separatism," in *The Politics of Reality: Essays in Feminist Theory* (Trumansburg, NY: Crossing, 1983), 129, 130–32 (rejecting any political affiliation between lesbians and gay men and concluding that "gay men generally are in significant ways, perhaps in all important ways, only more loyal to masculinity and male supremacy than other men").

93. See Raymond, *Transsexual Empire,* 149 (describing sex reassignment as "science at the service of a patriarchal ideology of sex-role conformity"); Denny, "Transgender in the United States," 10 (describing Raymond's campaign to deny transsexuals the right to hormone therapy and sex reassignment surgeries).

94. Halley, "Intersections," 103 (questioning whether there can be a political alliance between gay people and transsexuals and maintaining that "transsexuals—particularly male-to-female transsexuals—have . . . insisted that gender is conflated with bodily sex"); Judith Butler, *Bodies That Matter* (New York: Routledge, 1993), 124–33 (disagreeing with Janice Raymond's belief that gay male drag is inherently misogynist but concurring that transsexualism, at least in the case of the particular transsexual women she analyzes, attributes "false privilege" to women and amounts to "an uncritical miming of hegemonic norms"); Donna Minkowitz, "On Trial: Gay? Straight? Boy? Girl? Sex? Rape?" *OUT* 26 (1995): 99, 100 (describing Brandon Teena, a female-to-male transsexual who was raped and murdered in Nebraska after local authorities disclosed his transgender identity, as a self-hating butch lesbian).

95. See, for example, Stryker and Van Buskirk, *Gay by the Bay,* 58 ("The consolidation of a feminist alliance between lesbians and straight women depended on a gender ideology that regarded gender itself as inherently oppressive. . . . One of the

repercussions . . . was the marginalization of traditional butch/femme roles in the lesbian community and the disparagement of drag among gay men").

96. Esther Newton, "The Mythic Mannish Lesbian: Radclyffe Hall and the New Woman," in Duberman, Vicinus, and Chauncey, *Hidden from History,* 281 ("Thinking, acting, or looking like a man contradicts lesbian feminism's first principle: The lesbian is a 'woman-identified woman'"); Pratt, *S/HE,* 19 ("Often a lesbian considered 'too butch' was assumed to be, at least in part, a male chauvinist. She might get thrown out of her lesbian collective for this, or refused admittance to a lesbian bar").

97. Pratt, *S/HE,* 19 ("Frequently, a lesbian who was 'too femme' was perceived as a woman who had not liberated her mind or her body").

98. Faderman, *Odd Girls and Twilight Lovers,* 267. For a critical response to Faderman's disdain for contemporary butch and femme identities, see Sherrie Innes and Michele E. Lloyd, "G.I. Joes in Barbie Land," in *Queer Studies: A Lesbian, Gay, Bisexual, and Transgender Anthology,* ed. Brett Beemyn and Mickey Eliason (New York: New York University Press, 1996), 9–34.

99. See, for example, William G. Hawkeswood, *One of the Children: Gay Black Men in Harlem* (Berkeley: University of California Press, 1996); Leon E. Pettiway, *Honey, Honey, Miss Thang: Being Black, Gay, and on the Streets* (Philadelphia: Temple University Press, 1996).

100. Cf. Michael P. Jacobs, "Do Gay Men Have a Stake in Male Privilege?" in *Homo Economics: Capitalism, Community, and Lesbian and Gay Life,* ed. Amy Gluckman and Betsy Reed (New York: Routledge, 1997), 178 (arguing that while feminism and gay liberation overlap substantially, "gay activism should neither be conflated with, nor attempt to substitute for, a strong political movement that confronts women's subordination in all its forms").

101. As Kate Bornstein has rightly remarked, "The choice between two of something is not a choice at all, but rather the opportunity to subscribe to the value system which holds the two presented choices as mutually exclusive alternatives" (*Gender Outlaw,* 101).

102. This does not mean we should never use umbrella terms like *gay* or *transgender,* but it does mean that we should not mistake any of them for "the" new truth about the unilateral source of our oppression.

103. See, for example, Darren Lenard Hutchinson, "'Gay Rights' for 'Gay Whites'? Race, Sexual Identity, and Equal Protection Discourse," *Cornell Law Review* 85 (2000): 1358, 1365 (arguing that gay rights advocates must adopt a multidimensional perspective that is "attuned to the racial and gender dimensions of heterosexist structures").

104. Ibid. See also Darren Lenard Hutchinson, "Out Yet Unseen: A Racial Critique of Gay and Lesbian Legal Theory and Political Discourse," *Connecticut Law Review* 29 (1997): 561.

105. *Romer v. Evans,* 517 U.S. 620 (1996) (striking down Amendment 2, a proposed amendment to the Colorado Constitution that would have repealed all local and state laws or policies prohibiting antigay discrimination and prohibited the enactment of any such laws or policies in the future).

106. Ibid., 631.

107. *Baker v. State,* 744 A. 2d 864, 889 (Vt. 1999) (holding that same-sex couples must be afforded all of the rights and benefits given to married couples under Vermont state law).

108. *Lawrence v. Texas,* 539 U.S. 558 (2003).

109. Ibid. at 574.

110. Matt Coles, "Making the Case for Transgender Inclusion," *Southern Voice,* April 26, 2001.

9. Transgender Communities of the United States in the Late Twentieth Century

Dallas Denny

From prehistoric times to the present, individuals whom today we might call transgendered and transsexual have played prominent roles in many societies, including our own.[1] It is only in the second half of the twentieth century, however, that previously distinct and disparate segments within the transgendered and transsexual population began to write and organize around their mutual oppressions. By the end of the century and the close of the millennium, these various communities had merged—or were at least communicating—and had established a political voice and begun to achieve limited political victories.

What were the historical roots of these transgender communities, and how did they arise and grow so quickly? What kept these communities apart for so many years, and what eventually brought them together?

A Community of Cross-Dressers

By the late 1950s small numbers of male cross-dressers were secretly meeting in Los Angeles and the northeastern United States.[2] These cross-dressing clubs consisted exclusively of heterosexual men and, when they could be convinced to participate, their female partners. Charles (later Virginia) Prince was the founder of Los Angeles's Hose and Heels Club, which was perhaps the first formal support group in the United States for heterosexual cross-dressers. Prince also founded the Foundation for Full Personality Expression (FPE), a national organization for heterosexual cross-dressers, and was co-founder of Tri-Ess, the Society for the Second Self, which replaced FPE. She

171

was the author of several books about cross-dressing[3] and editor of *Transvestia*, the first nationally circulated magazine for cross-dressers.[4]

In the pages of *Transvestia*, Prince developed a model of male heterosexual cross-dressing that downplayed the importance of eroticism and sexuality in male cross-dressing and described the evolution of a nonsexual "girl within," a social woman with male anatomy. At the time (the 1950s and 1960s), both scientists and the general public assumed that cross-dressers were universally homosexual. Prince demonstrated that this was not so by surveying her readers and publishing the results not only in *Transvestia* but also in professional journals.[5]

Largely because of tireless educational efforts by Prince, the small, underground community of heterosexual cross-dressers grew and became more visible; by the 1970s, members of Tri-Ess were engineering newspaper articles and appearances on television to popularize and depathologize cross-dressing and help isolated heterosexual cross-dressers and their wives obtain support.

This support took the form of magazines, newsletters, and regional "sororities" that held meetings for socialization and mutual support of both cross-dressers and their female partners. Members cross-dressed at meetings and would venture out for meals and shopping at locations known to be safe. Newcomers were coached so they could learn to present a credible appearance; invited speakers would educate attendees on hair, makeup, clothing, voice, and mannerisms. Several conferences, notably Dream, on the West Coast, and Fantasia Fair, on Cape Cod, provided male cross-dressers with settings in which they could live safely *en rôle* for as long as ten days.

Unfortunately, Prince enforced her heterosexual model of cross-dressing by excluding homosexuals and transsexuals from her organizations. For more than forty years, those who disagreed with Prince's philosophy and those who were open about their inclinations toward homosexuality or transsexualism were routinely dismissed from the cross-dressing organizations she had founded or cofounded.[6] "When pressed . . . Prince would admit that some homosexual transvestites existed, but she excluded them from her definition of transvestism and, whenever possible, from her groups."[7] This policy effectively kept gay cross-dressers and transsexuals out of one of the only two visible communities of gender-variant people. (The other group was the drag community.) Those who did remain tended to keep their issues of sexuality and gender identity to themselves or to act covertly on those feelings. Denny, citing data from a Tri-Ess survey, has argued that this may have included the majority of members.[8] Certainly, many members of the various cross-dressing clubs—including Prince herself—went on to live full-time as members of the nonnatal sex, and some eventually came to identify as transsexual.[9] As of this writing, however, Tri-Ess, the predominant U.S. organization for male cross-dressers, still does not allow full membership for gay men or male-to-female transsexuals.

Gender-Variant Men and Women in the Gay and Lesbian Community

Throughout the twentieth century, many gender-variant individuals found a home in gay and lesbian bars, clubs, and other milieux. Unfortunately, they have left relatively little in the way of published accounts.[10] However, a rich visual history exists of transgendered entertainers in the form of films, photographs, and program books and playbills from nightclubs and the theater. Publicity shots of professional impersonators are sought after by private collectors, and many images of cross-dressed males and females are now part of larger gay and lesbian archives. Roger Baker and F. Michael Moore have written histories of female impersonation on the stage and screen; Homer Dickens, Desmond Montmorency, Avery Willard, and others have collected photographs and biographic information of notable female (and, occasionally, male) impersonators.[11] Less is known about the thousands of gender-variant individuals, male and female, who did not entertain, or who did shows but did not win fame. Present-day collectors often know little about those pictured in old photographs and promotional brochures.[12] The subjects of biographies and autobiographies are usually more well known and affluent.[13] We have Don Paulson's study of Seattle's Garden of Allah, and Esther Newton, a sociologist, studied what we might today call transgendered "club kids," but scholarly accounts of the drag community are relatively rare.[14]

The Clubs

Historically, the gay and lesbian community has been a haven for transgendered individuals and has looked to them for entertainment and fund-raising. Not all gay and lesbian clubs, however, have been receptive to gender-variant patrons.[15] Women's bars frequently have excluded those who presented as women but who were judged to be men, and some gay men's clubs, even those featuring female impersonation, had "no drag" policies. Bar owners often would enforce the "three items" rule, requiring even their own entertainers to wear three items that clearly reflected their natal gender. This was an attempt to stay clear of law enforcement agencies that routinely raided gay and lesbian bars, but the policy persisted long after the police raids had ceased. Throughout the 1970s, for instance, I often was denied entrance to Nashville's drag bars because I was in drag.

The exclusion of gender-variant people from the clubs increased in the immediate post-Stonewall period.[16] A new gay and lesbian culture emerged, in which stereotypes of feminine gay males and mannish lesbians were replaced by new social constructions of homosexuality in which many gay men embraced masculine dress and demeanor, and many lesbians rejected butch identities. Almost immediately, the very gender-variant individuals who had instigated the fighting at the Stonewall Inn were marginalized by the movement because they were visually different from emerging notions of straight-looking, straight-acting gay men and woman-identified lesbians.[17] Some gay men and lesbians have argued that gender-variant people are embarrassments to the movement, holding it back,[18] that transsexuals have no commonalities with the gay and lesbian community,[19] or, conversely, that they are gay men or lesbians in denial,[20] or are tools of the patriarchy.[21] Gender-variant men and women of my acquaintance report being routinely spat on by gay and lesbian patrons of bars in Atlanta before the mid-1980s. Nevertheless, many transgendered and transsexual people found welcome space in gay and lesbian bars. In some instances, they were welcomed as themselves; in others, they were pressured or otherwise found it expedient to adopt public identities as gay men or lesbians. Drag was always popular, but feminine gay men were often the butt of jokes. For natal females, there was a thin line between being fashionably butch and "too" butch; if their presentations grew too masculine, and particularly if they declared themselves female-to-male transsexuals, they would be accused of selling out and branded as undesirable.[22]

The 1990s brought a new acceptance of transgendered people in the gay/lesbian/bisexual community. By the early 2000s, most national GLB organizations, including Parents, Families, and Friends of Lesbians and Gays, the National Gay and Lesbian Task Force, and the Human Rights Campaign, had adopted trans-inclusive mission statements and begun to work actively for transgender rights. Gay and lesbian historical organizations have begun to organize and display their transgender-related materials and have indicated their commitment by adding transgender to their names.[23] Still, bars are uncertain havens for transgendered and transsexual people. While they are rarely denied admission, and while they are valued members in some gay and lesbian settings, they receive only grudging acceptance in others.

Enter Christine Jorgensen

During the first half of the twentieth century a few individuals began quietly enlisting the aid of physicians to help them alter their bodies to more closely resemble those of the nonnatal sex.[24] In the early 1950s ex-G.I. George Jorgensen sought such medical assistance in Denmark. In 1953 Jorgensen returned to the United States as the glamorous Christine. News of her sex reassignment caused a media sensation, and the idea that it might be possible for a human being to change sex became immediately and firmly rooted in the popular imagination.[25]

Jorgensen's was not the first "sex change," as male genitals had been surgically altered since ancient times,[26] and sex reassignment using modern surgical techniques had been attempted as early as the 1930s.[27] Small numbers of people, including Michael Dillon and Roberta Cowell,[28] were Jorgensen's contemporaries, and Dillon had actually preceded Jorgensen in sex reassignment, but without achieving the latter's level of notoriety.

To thousands of desperate men and women struggling with gender identity issues, Jorgensen served as a role model. Following the news of her sex reassignment, hundreds wrote to request sex reassignment.[29] Harry Benjamin, a New York endocrinologist, began treating many of those seeking sex reassignment, providing hormonal therapy and referrals for surgery. By the late 1950s he was calling his gender-variant patients "transsexuals."[30] In 1966 he published a text, *The Transsexual Phenomenon,* in which he defined the syndrome of transsexualism.[31] Benjamin, an empathetic soul who seemed to really like his transsexual patients, described them as profoundly miserable in their genders of original assignment, so much so that they were often unable to function in society and were at considerable risk of taking their own lives. Benjamin noted that medical science was unable to rid them of their compelling desires to change their sex or give them peace of mind in their original bodies. Surely, he argued, the humane thing in select cases was to give transsexuals relief from their suffering by altering their bodies with hormones and surgery and helping them to live as members of the other sex. To justify his argument, Benjamin pointed to the success of his own patients who had had sex reassignment.

It should be noted that both the physicians and transsexuals of the time tended to follow Benjamin's model, interpreting the experience of transsexualism almost entirely in terms of misery and anguish. While many transgendered persons still struggle with guilt and shame and fear, fewer of today's transsexuals view their experiences in this way. In an age of ready information, transsexuals are less likely to suffer in isolation until they can stand it no longer; more and more, they research their options and present to medical and psychological professionals not as desperate and uninformed but as thoughtful and knowledgeable consumers.

In 1966 the prestigious Johns Hopkins University announced a program for the treatment of persons with gender identity issues.[32] Three years later, in 1969, Richard Green and John Money published an edited textbook that established a medical protocol for sex reassignment, based on their experiences at Hopkins.[33] Now there was not only a model for transsexualism but a protocol for sex reassignment from one of the most prestigious medical schools in the United States. Other university-affiliated gender programs soon sprang up, following the Hopkins model; within ten years, there were more than forty such clinics scattered across the United States,[34] accepting small numbers of patients for sex reassignment and producing a prodigious number of journal articles.

However, following the 1979 release of a report by Jon Meyer and Donna Reter that showed "no objective improvement" following male-to-female sex reassignment, the universities disassociated themselves from their programs in the early 1980s.[35] Meyer and Reter's report came under immediate attack[36] and was eventually revealed to be contrived and possibly fraudulent.[37] According to an investigative report in the *Baltimore City Paper:* "The ending of surgery at the GIC now appears to have been orchestrated by certain figures at Hopkins who, for personal rather than scientific reasons, staunchly opposed any form of sex reassignment."[38]

Except for several clinics that continued as private for-profit centers, the clinics nonetheless closed, as did the program at the University of Minnesota, which came under the control of the Program for Human Sexuality after its original departmental sponsor decided to close the program. The only university-based gender program to have continued seems to have been at the University of Virginia, apparently persisting until the late 1980s.

The closing of the clinics resulted in the development of a market-driven sex-change industry,[39] in which transsexuals sought services like hormonal therapy, plastic surgery, and genital reconstructive surgery from enterprising private providers. This made sex reassignment more widely available than ever before, frustrating those like the psychiatrist Paul McHugh, who had had a hand in orchestrating the closing of the gender programs in hopes of doing away with sex reassignment in the United States: "It was my intention, when I arrived in Baltimore in 1975, to help end [sex reassignment surgery at Hopkins]."[40]

McHugh achieved his goal—but his scheme ultimately backfired, as the closing of the gender clinics led to the development of the market economy that has made professional services available to practically anyone in the United States who has the desire and the financial means to change his or her sex.

Being a "Good" Transsexual

The Benjamin model resulted in a narrow definition of transsexualism. Those who varied from the prescribed characteristics were at risk of not getting treatment—in fact, of being declared nontranssexual by medical professionals and by their peers.[41] This persisted in many gender programs throughout the

1990s and doubtless endures today in some quarters.[42] To qualify for treatment, it was important that applicants report that their gender dysphorias manifested at an early age; that they have a history of playing with dolls as a child, if born male, or trucks and guns, if born female; that their sexual attractions were exclusively to the same biological sex; that they have a history of failure at endeavors undertaken while in the original gender role; and that they pass or had potential to pass successfully as a member of the desired sex.[43] Applicants were turned away or denied hormones or surgery for reasons that today seem ridiculous: because they were "too successful" in their natal gender roles, because they were married, because they had read too much about transsexualism, because they had the "wrong" sexual orientation, because clinic staff didn't consider them sexually attractive in the cross-gender role, or because they wouldn't comply with lifestyle requirements imposed on them by the clinics. According to one transsexual woman, Margaux, quoted in *Chrysalis Quarterly:*

> Finally, it was time to hear the results of all the tests. I went into the room and sat down. The staff was making small talk. It was as if I weren't there. They were good at making you feel like you didn't exist. Finally, the head guy cleared his throat and said, "Frankly, we're worried because you've read so much on the subject of transsexualism. We have grave doubts as to whether, by seeking a sex change, you're embarking on the right course. Also, you'll have trouble passing. Because of that, and because of your age (I was eighteen), we do not feel comfortable with prescribing hormones for you.[44]

Those who were accepted for treatment were often counseled or even required to avoid socializing with other transsexuals.[45] After surgery, the clinic doctors told them that they were now normal men and women and should blend into society; most did.[46] Those who were turned away by the gender programs had no sources for treatment other than the black market, with its questionable hormones and surgeries. This rejection resulted in small groups of transsexuals who shared knowledge and strategies for gaining access to the clinics.[47]

The psychomedical literature of the period reflected these practices of the gender clinics, which in turn mirrored the biases and often-unsubstantiated assumptions of their staffs: it reported that transsexuals were manipulative and had high levels of psychopathology;[48] had narrow and stereotyped notions of masculinity and femininity and conformed to those stereotypes in their personal presentations; had a desire to disappear into the larger society after surgery, passing as nontranssexual; and viewed themselves as having been born into the wrong body because of some sort of birth defect or horrible joke of nature.[49] Money and Primrose even reported that transsexuals had a tendency to read up on transsexualism, as if that were a symptom of their psychopathology.[50]

Most transsexuals do not, of course, display the astonishing variety of personality and character disturbances attributed to them. The literature that suggests that they do reflects the bias and sexism of the psychologists and physicians who wrote it in keeping with the values of the dominant culture of the time.[51] Consider the following by Leslie Lothstein, one of the worst offenders:

> The severity and intensity of some patients' psychopathology and acting out were...revealed within the group, for example, two members brought loaded guns into the group (One member had to be forcibly restrained from using it!); auto- and mutual masturbation; exposure of breasts; an attempted kidnapping; several near-violent confrontations among group members which carried over outside the group (in which patients threatened each other physically and one patient drew a knife); innumerable sexual overtures to the therapists; patients bringing in pets (two dogs and a menagerie of land crabs); serious psychosomatic symptoms (including ulcerative, arthritic, hyperventilative, and cardiac distress).[52]

Lothstein describes a veritable circus and attributes it to "the severity and intensity of some patients' psychopathology and acting out"; more likely, the troubles of the group were due to poor management skills on the part of the facilitators and the draconian selection criteria of Case Western Reserve Gender Identity Clinic.[53]

Challenges to the Benjamin Model

Although the Benjamin model of transsexualism was attacked on several fronts, those who challenged it didn't offer suitable alternative models, and it held supreme until the early 1990s. Attacks came from psychiatrists like Charles Socarides,[54] who argued bitterly that the proper way to treat a mental illness was by curing it, not giving in to it; from feminists, who considered it patriarchal and antiwoman;[55] and from those who identified the cultural bias and sexism inherent in a dichotomous understanding of gender.[56] Perhaps the most cogent critic was Sandy Stone, whose 1991 essay "The *Empire* Strikes Back: A Posttranssexual Manifesto" questioned the accuracy of the clinical literature that stereotyped transsexuals. Stone pointed out that because clinicians were looking for "true transsexuals" who fit narrow diagnostic criteria, transsexuals learned to lie to their doctors, telling them whatever was necessary in order to qualify for medical treatment. Transsexuals, Stone argued, worked hard to fit the description of what they were supposed to be—by following a transsexual script, as it were. This had also been recognized and discussed in detail by Suzanne Kessler and Wendy McKenna, and Anne Bolin.[57]

The medical model of transsexualism supposed that there were but two sexes, and that the only alternative to remaining unhappily in the original gender role was to work hard to conform to the only available alternative. That is, one "changed sex," going from male to female or from female to male. The model didn't question the society that created such restrictive gender roles or examine the possibility of living somewhere outside those binary roles. Those who weren't interested in going from one polar extreme to the other were typically diagnosed as nontranssexual and presumed to be cross-dressers, even when they were profoundly gender dysphoric.[58] Transsexualism itself was considered a liminal state, a transitory phase, to be negotiated as rapidly as possible on one's way to becoming a "normal" man or "normal" woman.

The Transgender Paradigm Shift

Under the medical/psychological model of transsexualism, communication among transsexuals in gender programs had been discouraged because of considerations of confidentiality and because of the pressure to assimilate after surgery (i.e., pass as nontranssexual in the larger society). This kept transsexuals from communicating with each other and ensured there were no transsexual elders to pass on their accumulated wisdom.

Things began to change with the closing of the university-affiliated gender clinics, when transsexuals began to interact with other transsexuals and nontranssexual transgendered people. As soon as they established the necessary level of comfort, many transsexuals began to admit to one another that they were less than politically correct by the standards of the psychomedical community.

The establishment of the International Foundation for Gender Education (IFGE) in 1984 marked the first time transsexuals and cross-dressers came together in significant numbers, at the organization's annual conference and in the pages of IFGE's journal *Tapestry* (now *Transgender Tapestry Journal*). IFGE and other open organizations of the late 1980s—including the Phoenix Transgender Support Group in Asheville, North Carolina; Denver's Gender Identity Center; Seattle's Ingersoll Gender Center; and groups in New York and San Francisco—welcomed both transsexuals and cross-dressers, as did the Midwest's Be All You Can Be conference. For the first time, not only did transsexuals and cross-dressers come into regular communication, but transsexuals, who had been largely unwelcome in the gay/lesbian and heterosexual cross-dressing communities, came into communication with one another in person and in the pages of *Tapestry* and innumerable newsletters.

Within five years, these new interactions had resulted in the development of a continent-wide transgender community and had led to the emergence of a new model of gender variance. By 1990 both cross-dressers and transsexuals were questioning the accuracy of their diagnostic labels, and there was ongoing dialogue about descriptive terminology. The American Educational Gender Information Service, IFGE, Renaissance Transgender Association, and many other transgender community organizations—too numerous to list here—actively encouraged new ways of looking at cross-dressing and transsexualism. From this crucible there soon emerged a new way of thinking about those who were differently gendered—a paradigm shift.[59]

The change of viewpoint was both rapid and pervasive. In the late 1980s, the anthropologist Anne Bolin had studied a transgender support group in the American Midwest.[60] She found members were required to declare whether they were cross-dressers or transsexuals. There were no other available options, and members were expected to follow the script dictated by their labels: transsexuals were to pursue counseling, hormonal therapy, cross-living, and eventually sex reassignment surgery; cross-dressers were dissuaded from following such a transsexual "career path."

In 1994, barely five years after her initial report, Bolin published a paper noting profound changes in the transgender community.[61] She discovered the cross-dresser/transsexual dichotomy had been replaced by a model in which individuals could structure their lives, appearances, and genders along a continuum, according to their individual wishes. New options were available. Bolin was describing the result of a revolution in thinking within the community of gender-variant people. As with other paradigm shifts, there were multiple causative factors, but a 1991 article by Holly Boswell, published simultaneously in the journals *Chrysalis Quarterly* and *Tapestry,* was seminal.[62]

Boswell argued that the best "fit" for many gender-variant people was a path between cross-dressing and transsexualism. Boswell's article provided a starting point for a new model of gender variance, one that came not from the medical community but direct from the source—transgendered and transsexual people themselves. By postulating an essential transgender essence—a healthy need to vary from often unhealthy gender stereotypes and norms—the model broke both from the medical model of transsexualism and from Prince's model of heterosexual cross-dressing.

Boswell was not the first to use the term *transgender*—Prince had coined the word in the 1970s, to describe her personal accommodation to her transvestism—but after the publication of Boswell's article, and books by Kate Bornstein and Martine Rothblatt,[63] the term *transgender,* which had until then been used only sporadically, came into widespread use. Soon it was appearing not only in magazines and newsletters for cross-dressers and trans-sexuals but in gay and lesbian newspapers and, by 1995 or so, in mainstream publications.

The transgender model minimized the differences between gay and straight cross-dressers and transsexuals and helped the transgender community confront and work through its not inconsiderable homophobia. The model was brought to the attention of the gay, lesbian, and bisexual community by an awakening transgender political movement; by the publication of Leslie Feinberg's 1993 novel *Stone Butch Blues,* in which the protagonist rejected transsexualism in favor of an essential transgender identity; and by political demands for transgender inclusion at the Michigan Womyn's Music Festival, the 1993 March on Washington, and the Gay Games.[64] Feinberg's work, especially, resonated with lesbians. A number of prominent gay authors acknowledged, embraced, and wrote about their female sides.[65] Moreover, the transgender model reverberated with the renewed interest in butch-femme identities and aesthetics in the late 1990s.[66]

By the opening of the new century, the transgender model had been integrated into the sensibilities of hundreds of thousands of gender-variant and non-gender-variant people in the United States, and had begun to impact gender-variant communities outside the United States.[67] The electronic journal of the Harry Benjamin International Gender Dysphoria Association (http://www.symposion.com/ijt) had been named "The International Journal of Transgenderism," transgender studies had become an accepted field in a number of U.S. colleges and universities,[68] and all major U.S. gay and lesbian organizations had included transgender either in their names or mission statements. Although there's still confusion in some quarters about this relatively new term, it's clear *transgender* is here to stay.

Even though the term has met with widespread acceptance, not everyone favors it. Some transsexuals resent a descriptor that places them in the company of cross-dressers. Other transsexuals simply consider transgender short-hand for "transgressively gendered,"[69] which aptly describes both cross-dressers and transsexuals. In deference to transsexuals who don't identify as transgendered, the Gender Identity Project of the New York Gay, Lesbian, Bisexual, and Transgender Community Center uses the inclusive "transsexual and transgendered"—as do I, much of the time.

The Impact of the Transgender Model

By the mid-1990s, many gender-variant people in the United States were looking at themselves in a new way. Rather than being ashamed and guilt-ridden, they were taking pride in the very fact of their difference and shifting the locus of pathology from themselves to a society that could not accept difference. The term *transgender* had emerged as an umbrella for the entire constellation of differently gendered people, including cross-dressers, transgenderists, and transsexuals, who comprised what had come to be known as the transgender community.

Many of those who subscribe to the transgender model tend to see themselves as both man and woman, or neither, or as something else entirely. Moreover, there is no "proper" sexual orientation. Most important, the transgender model allows both transsexuals and nontranssexual transgendered people to view themselves as healthy and whole. The transgender model legitimized those who had not fit comfortably into the limited number of categories that had been open to them previously. Gender-variant people were no longer forced to choose restrictive transsexual or cross-dresser or drag queen/king roles, each with its own behavioral script. Suddenly it was possible to transition gender roles without a goal of genital surgery, to acknowledge one's gender dysphoria and yet remain in one's original gender role, to take hormones for a while and then stop, to be a woman with breasts and a penis or a man with a vagina, to blend genders as if from a palette. It was possible, and even preferable, to be out and proud, rather than fearful and closeted. Not surprisingly, this new and improved self-concept soon led to demands for political equality and justice.

Boundaries Blur

Soon, transgender had become an identity in and of itself. Individuals who formerly identified as cross-dressers or as transsexual now called themselves transgendered, or, in some cases, transgenders or simply trans. With a sensibility that now transcended the binary male/female gender system and was no longer divided along the issue of sexual orientation, the various transgender communities began to socialize and work with one another toward a common political end. Transgendered and transsexual men and women began to take leadership roles not previously open to them—no longer limited to transgender-specific organizations, they began to participate in nominally gay and lesbian organizations such as Pride and HIV organizations in a variety of cities and national organizations like the National Gay and Lesbian Task Force.

The 1990s saw several watershed events that altered transgender consciousness and brought organized response. The first was the 1991 expulsion from the Michigan Womyn's Music Festival of Nancy Burkholder, a postoperative transsexual woman.[70] This resulted in "Camp Trans," a site outside the festival proper, in which transgender education classes were held, and in challenges at the gate and within the festival proper.[71] In 1992, for instance, transgender activists passed out to festivalgoers thousands of buttons that read "I might be transsexual."[72]

Two other galvanizing events were the deaths of Brandon Teena and Tyra Hunter. Teena was murdered in 1995 in Humboldt, Nebraska;[73] Hunter was denied medical treatment by D.C. firefighters when they cut away her clothing and saw her penis.[74] The deaths shocked and angered the transgender community; Hunter's case, in particular, resulted in the formation of an alliance of social justice groups, of which transgender activists were an integral part. Teena's murder resulted in several books and films, including Kimberly Peirce's *Boys Don't Cry* (1999), which resulted in an Academy Award for Best Actress for Hilary Swank.

By the mid-1990s, transgendered individuals and groups were protesting when their peers were murdered, lobbying Capitol Hill and state legislatures for civil rights previously denied them, and engaging in vigorous letter-writing campaigns and political demonstrations when they were slandered or slighted by those in power.[75] The Washington lobbying effort was spearheaded by Phyllis Frye and Jane Fee; the fall 1998 cover of *Transgender Tapestry Journal* featured more than one hundred transsexual and transgendered lobbyists on the steps of the U.S. Capitol. Positive television, film, and print coverage of transgender political issues increased dramatically.[76] By the end of 2003, civil rights protections for transgendered people had been achieved in four states and more than sixty cities throughout the United States.[77]

The 1990s also saw the appearance of transgender voices in the professional literature; they had previously been excluded.[78] Especially notable was the previously mentioned essay by Sandy Stone, which addressed the psychomedical treatment of transsexualism.[79] Transsexuals began to run for and be elected to public office,[80] and transsexuals and nontranssexual transgendered men and women in prominent positions in a variety of professions embraced their gender-variant statuses and were valued for it.[81] For instance, Susan Kimberly, who had been prominent in St. Paul city government before her sex reassignment, was appointed to an important post by a conservative mayor whose prime consideration was that she was the right person for the job.[82] Academicians such as Michael Gilbert, Deirdre McCloskey, and Jacob Hale received positive press coverage,[83] and colleges and universities began to be responsive to the needs of their transgendered and transsexual students.[84]

The 1990s saw the emergence of homosexuality as a mainstream political issue. President Bill Clinton's attempt to end the gay ban in the U.S. military was a widely heard shot in what Supreme Court justice Antonin Scalia has called a Kulturkampf.[85] On one side of this cultural divide are the radical

Christian right and other traditionalists; on the other side are the newly combined gay, lesbian, bisexual, and transgender community and its allies. Since the struggle for gay and lesbian civil rights took the main stage in American politics, battles have raged along a number of fronts: gays in the military, gay and lesbian marriage, sodomy laws, ordinances banning discrimination against gender and sexual minorities, hate crimes laws, and custody, adoption, and inheritance issues.[86] Transsexual and other transgender identities have been intimately entwined with these issues of gay rights.

The transgender communities have begun to redefine the issues, in particular changing the locus of the "problem" from the individual to a hostile and unaccepting society. Transgender activists work at grassroots, state, and national levels to change laws and policies.

Transsexuals have begun to criticize the medical literature that has and often still does view them as mentally ill, and many transsexuals reject the medical model of transsexualism that has been in the public consciousness for the more than fifty years since the news of Christine Jorgensen's sex reassignment shocked the world. At issue is the Gender Identity Disorders section of the DSM-IV-TR.[87] The call for reform of the diagnostic category Gender Identity Disorder of Childhood has been of particular concern, since it is sometimes used to institutionalize gender-variant homosexual boys and girls.[88] Also at issue are the Harry Benjamin Standards of Care, which place restrictions on access to body-altering medical treatment even though there is no empirical evidence that such restrictions are necessary or even advisable.[89]

The rise of the transgender model and postmodern gender theory[90] has provided a new lexicon for the discussion of transgender issues.[91] The careful reader will notice that throughout this section there has been no mention of gender identity disorder (except when naming the diagnostic categories in the DSM) or other language that would dispose the reader to view transsexual and other transgendered persons as mentally ill or otherwise deficient. When resorting to the traditional medical model, it is virtually impossible to discuss gender-variant people or their issues without the use of terms that overtly state or at least imply pathology and reinforce the omnipotence of the medical professional.

It's notable that the transgender model arose not from the medical community, which had been studying cross-dressers and transsexuals for 150 years, but from the transgender community, and only five years after its inception. The labels *transvestite* and *transsexual, gender dysphoria,* and *gender identity disorder* were bestowed by the medical community and are in a sense slave names;[92] the word *transgender* was coined by a gender-variant individual, and the transgender model has been popularized by gender-variant people. Despite its grassroots origin, however, the transgender model makes great sense from a treatment standpoint, as it doesn't require intrusive medical procedures the individual does not want.[93]

Many professionals have embraced the new model. Talks on the transgender model by Holly (now Aaron) Devor and Walter Williams set the tone for the Fifteenth Harry Benjamin International Gender Dysphoria Association Symposium in Vancouver, British Columbia, in 1997.[94] Conversely, it must be noted that as recently as 1997, medical and psychological professionals have been held liable by persons who received sex reassignment surgery and later regretted that decision. Given this precedent, it's unlikely that self-protective professional standards will be eliminated in the near future. Full freedom of gender expression (and free access to medical services that foster it) will come as transsexuals succeed in gaining recognition from society as fully autonomous, personally responsible adults.

As the twenty-first century gets under way, one is struck by the degree to which gender roles and sartorial styles have changed in only one hundred years. From an era in which women wore nearly twenty pounds of clothing, were not allowed to vote, and were routinely arrested if they appeared on the streets wearing trousers,[95] we have arrived at a time in which the gender norms of 1900 are transgressed daily by practically every American citizen, including those stridently opposed to those who are pushing the frontiers of social acceptability today. Perhaps we will eventually arrive at a time in which people can wear whatever they want and alter their bodies in whatever way they wish without causing a fuss.

Notes

1. See V. L. Bullough and B. Bullough, *Cross-Dressing, Sex, and Gender* (Philadelphia: University of Pennsylvania Press, 1993); R. J. Dekker and L. C. van de Pol, *The Tradition of Female Transvestism in Early Modern Europe* (New York: St. Martin's, 1989); L. Feinberg, *Transgender Warriors: Making History from Joan of Arc to RuPaul* (Boston: Beacon, 1996); R. Green, "Mythological, Historical, and Cross Cultural Aspects of Transsexualism," in *Transsexualism and Sex Reassignment,* ed. R. Green and J. Money (Baltimore, MD: Johns Hopkins University Press, 1969), 173–86; R. Green, "Transsexualism: Mythological, Historical, and Cross-Cultural Aspects," in *Current Concepts in Transgender Identity,* ed. D. Denny (New York: Garland, 1998), 3–14, originally published in *Transsexualism and Sex Reassignment,* ed. R. Green and J. Money (Baltimore, MD: Johns Hopkins University Press, 1969), 173–86; G. Herdt, ed., *Third Sex, Third Gender: Essays from Anthropology and Social History* (New York: Zone Books, 1994); M. Hirschfeld, *Die Transvestiten: Eine Untersuchung über den Erotischen Verkleidungstrieb* (Berlin: Medicinisher Verlag Alfred Pulvermacher, 1910);

M. Hirschfeld, *Transvestites: The Erotic Drive to Cross Dress,* trans. Michael A. Lombardi-Nash (Buffalo, NY: Prometheus Books, 1991); R. von Krafft-Ebing, *Psychopathia Sexualis,* trans. C. G. Chaddock (Philadelphia: Davis, 1894); W. Roscoe, ed., *Living the Spirit: A Gay American Indian Anthology* (New York: St. Martin's, 1988); Roscoe, *The Zuni Man-Woman* (Albuquerque: University of New Mexico Press, 1990); Roscoe, "Priests of the Goddess: Gender Transgression in the Ancient World" (presentation, 109th annual meeting of the American Historical Association, San Francisco, December 1988); Roscoe, *Changing Ones: Third and Fourth Genders in Native North America* (New York: St. Martin's, 1998); T. Taylor, *The Prehistory of Sex: Four Million Years of Human Sexual Culture* (New York: Bantam Books, 1996); and W. L. Williams, *The Spirit and the Flesh: Sexual Diversity in American Indian Culture* (Boston: Beacon, 1986).

2. C. V. Prince, "The Life and Times of Virginia," *Transvestia* 17, no. 100 (1979). For outsiders' perspectives, see H. G. Beigel, "A Weekend in Alice's Wonderland," *Journal of Sex Research* 5, no. 2 (1969): 108–22; and D. Raynor, *A Year among the Girls* (New York: Lyle Stuart, 1966).

3. V. Prince, *The Transvestite and His Wife* (Los Angeles: Chevalier Publications, 1962); Prince, *How to Be a Woman though Male* (Los Angeles: Chevalier Publications, 1971); Prince, *Understanding Cross-Dressing* (Los Angeles: Chevalier Publications, 1976).

4. Bullough and Bullough, *Cross-Dressing, Sex, and Gender,* chap. 12.

5. V. Prince, "Homosexuality, Transvestism, and Transsexualism: Reflections on Their Etiology and Differentiation," *American Journal of Psychotherapy* 11 (1957): 80–85; P. M. Bentler and C. Prince, "Personality Characteristics of Male Transvestites: III," *Journal of Abnormal Psychology* 74, no. 2 (1969): 140–43.

6. D. Denny, "Heteropocrisy: The Myth of the Heterosexual Cross-Dresser," *Chrysalis: The Journal of Transgressive Gender Issues* 2, no. 3 (May 1996): 23–30; Raynor, *Year among the Girls.*

7. Bullough and Bullough, *Cross-Dressing, Sex, and Gender,* 281.

8. Denny, "Heteropocrisy," 23–30.

9. K. Cummings, *Katherine's Diary: The Story of a Transsexual* (Port Melbourne, Australia: Heinemann, 1992).

10. But see Roberts's manual for drag performers: P. Roberts, *Female Impersonator's Handbook* (Newark, NJ: Capri, 1967).

11. R. Baker, *Drag: A History of Female Impersonation on the Stage* (London: Trinton Books, 1968); R. Baker, P. Burton, and R. Smith, *Drag: A History of Female Impersonation in the Performing Arts* (New York: New York University Press, 1994); and F. M. Moore, *Drag! Male and Female Impersonators on Stage, Screen, and Television* (Jefferson, NC: McFarland, 1994); H. Dickens, *What a Drag: Men as Women and Women as Men in Movies* (New York: Quill, 1984); D. Montmorency, *The Drag Scene: Secrets of Female Impersonators* (London: Luxor, 1970); and A. Willard, *Female Impersonators* (New York: Regiment Publications, 1971).

12. B. Davis, "Regina Antiqua," *Transgender Community News,* December 2003, 24.

13. For example, D. Byng, *As You Were: Reminiscences* (London: Duckworth, 1976); M. Costa, *Reverse Sex: The Life of Jacqueline Charlotte DuFresnoy,* trans. J. Block (London: Challenge Publications, 1960); S. Maitland, *Vesta Tilley* (London: Virago, 1986);

A. Slide, *Great Pretenders: A History of Female and Male Impersonation in the Performing Arts* (Lombardi, IL: Wallace-Homestead Book, 1986).

14. D. Paulson and R. Simpson, *An Evening at the Garden of Allah: A Gay Cabaret in Seattle* (New York: Columbia University Press, 1996); E. Newton, *Mother Camp: Female Impersonators in America* (Chicago: University of Chicago Press, 1979).

15. Viviane K. Namaste, *Invisible Lives: The Erasure of Transsexual and Transgendered People* (Chicago: University of Chicago Press, 2000), 10–13.

16. M. B. Duberman, *Stonewall* (New York: Dutton, 1993).

17. L. Brewster, editorial, *Drag* 1, no. 1 (1970): 3.

18. Ibid.

19. E. Hunter, "Transgender Agenda Rides Gay-Rights Coattails," *Cincinnati CityBeat,* September 4–10, 1997, http://www.citybeat.com/archives/1997/issue342/newsarticle4.html.

20. See P. Varnell, "'Woman Trapped as a Man'—or Unable to Accept Being Gay?" *Pittsburgh's Out,* December 1996, 18.

21. J. Raymond, *The Transsexual Empire: The Making of the She-Male* (Boston: Beacon, 1979). This was reissued in 1994 with a new introduction by Teacher's College Press.

22. J. Halberstam, "Transgender Butch/FTM BorderWars and the Masculine Continuum," *GLQ* 4, no. 2 (1998): 287–310.

23. See C. King, "Gallery Night: Opening the Country's First GLBT History Museum," *Transgender Tapestry* 1, no. 104 (2003): 32–33.

24. F. Abraham, "Genitalumwandlung an Zwei Männlichen Transvestiten" (Genital Alteration in Two Male Transvestites), *Zeitschrift Sexualwissenschaft* 18 (1931): 223–26; L. Hodgkinson, *Michael nee Laura: The Story of the World's First Female-to-Male Transsexual* (London: Columbus Books, 1989).

25. "Ex-GI Becomes Blonde Beauty: Operations Transform Bronx Youth," *New York Daily News,* December 1, 1952; see also Bullough and Bullough, *Cross-Dressing, Sex, and Gender* ; B. Bullough and V. L. Bullough, "Transsexualism: Historical Perspectives, 1952 to Present," in *Current Concepts in Transgender Identity,* ed. D. Denny (New York: Garland, 1998), 15–34; and D. Denny, "Black Telephones, White Refrigerators: Rethinking Christine Jorgensen," in Denny, *Current Concepts in Transgender Identity,* 35–44.

26. M. O'Hartigan, "The Gallae of the Magna Mater," *Chrysalis Quarterly* 1, no. 6 (1993): 11–13; Roscoe, "Priests of the Goddess."

27. Abraham, "Genitalumwandlung"; N. Hoyer, *Man into Woman: An Authentic Record of a Change of Sex: The True Story of the Miraculous Transformation of the Danish Painter, Einar Wegener (Andreas Sparrer)* (New York: Dutton, 1933); for a thorough history of sex change in the first eight decades of the twentieth century, see J. Meyerowitz, *How Sex Changed: A History of Transsexuality in the United States* (Cambridge, MA: Harvard University Press, 2002).

28. R. Cowell, *Roberta Cowell's Story* (London: Heinemann, 1954); M. Dillon, *Self: A Study in Ethics and Endocrinology* (London: Heinemann, 1946); Hodgkinson, *Michael nee Laura.*

29. C. Hamburger, "The Desire for Change of Sex as Shown by Personal Letters from 465 Men and Women," *Acta Endocrinologica* 14 (1953): 361–75.

30. H. Benjamin, "Trans-sexualism and Transvestism," in *Transvestism: Men in Female Dress,* ed. D. O. Cauldwell (New York: Sexology Corporation, 1956), 15–22.

31. H. Benjamin, *The Transsexual Phenomenon: A Scientific Report on Transsexualism and Sex Conversion in the Human Male and Female* (New York: Julian, 1966).

32. J. Money and F. Schwartz, "Public Opinion and Social Issues in Transsexualism," in *Transsexualism and Sex Reassignment,* ed. R. Green and J. Money (Baltimore, MD: Johns Hopkins University Press, 1969), 253–69.

33. Green and Money, *Transsexualism and Sex Reassignment.*

34. D. Denny, "The Politics of Diagnosis and a Diagnosis of Politics: The University-Affiliated Gender Clinics, and How They Failed to Meet the Needs of Transsexual People," *Chrysalis Quarterly* 1, no. 3 (1992): 9–20. Reprinted in *Transgender Tapestry Journal* 1, no. 98 (2002): 17–27.

35. J. K. Meyer and D. Reter, "Sex Reassignment: Follow-up," *Archives of General Psychiatry* 36, no. 9 (1979): 1010–15.

36. M. Fleming, C. Steinman, and G. Bocknek, "Methodological Problems in Assessing Sex-Reassignment: A Reply to Meyer and Reter," *Archives of Sexual Behavior* 9, no. 5 (1980): 451–56.

37. Denny, "Politics of Diagnosis," 9–20; P. R. McHugh, "Psychiatric Misadventures," *American Scholar* 61, no. 4 (1992): 497–510.

38. O. Ogas, "Spare Parts: New Information Reignites a Controversy Surrounding the Hopkins Gender Identity Clinic," *City Paper* (Baltimore), March 9, 1994, 10.

39. Denny, "Politics of Diagnosis," 9–20.

40. McHugh, "Psychiatric Misadventures," 497–510; Ogas, "Spare Parts," 10.

41. L. E. Newman and R. J. Stoller, "Nontranssexual Men Who Seek Sex Reassignment," *American Journal of Psychiatry* 131, no. 4 (1974): 437–41.

42. M. A. Petersen and R. Dickey, "Surgical Sex Reassignment: A Comparative Survey of International Centers," *Archives of Sexual Behavior* 24, no. 2 (1995): 135–56.

43. Denny, "Politics of Diagnosis," 9–20.

44. Ibid., 15.

45. Ibid., 9–20.

46. Ibid.

47. A. R. Stone (as Sandy Stone), "The *Empire* Strikes Back: A Postranssexual Manifesto," in *Body Guards: The Cultural Politics of Gender Ambiguity,* ed. J. Epstein and K. Straub (New York: Routledge, 1991), 280–304.

48. C. B. Stone, "Psychiatric Screening for Transsexual Surgery," *Psychosomatics* 18, no. 1 (1977): 25–27.

49. See A. Bolin, *In Search of Eve: Transsexual Rites of Passage* (South Hadley, MA: Bergin & Garvey, 1988).

50. J. Money and C. Primrose, "Sexual Dimorphism and Dissociation in the Psychology of Male Transsexuals," *Journal of Nervous and Mental Disease* 147, no. 5 (1968): 472–86.

51. D. Denny, "Needed: A New Literature for a New Century" (unpublished manuscript, 1998).

52. L. M. Lothstein, "Group Therapy with Gender-Dysphoric Patients," *American Journal of Psychotherapy* 33, no. 1 (1979): 73.

53. L. Lothstein, *Female-to-Male Transsexualism: Historical, Clinical, and Theoretical Issues* (Boston: Routledge & Kegan Paul, 1983), 87–91; reproduced in Denny, "Politics of Diagnosis," 10–11.

54. Charles Socarides, "The Desire for Sexual Transformation: A Psychiatric Evaluation of Transsexualism," *American Journal of Psychiatry* 125, no. 10 (1969): 1419–25.

55. See especially Raymond, *Transsexual Empire.*

56. S. J. Kessler and W. McKenna, *Gender: An Ethnomethodological Approach* (New York: Wiley & Sons, 1978).

57. Ibid.; and Bolin, *In Search of Eve.*

58. Newman and Stoller, "Nontranssexual Men,"437–41.

59. T. S. Kuhn, *The Structure of Scientific Revolutions* (Chicago: University of Chicago Press, 1962); D. Denny, "The Paradigm Shift Is Here!" *AEGIS News* 1, no. 4 (1995): 1.

60. Bolin, *In Search of Eve.*

61. A. E. Bolin, "Transcending and Transgendering: Male-to-Female Transsexuals, Dichotomy, and Diversity," in Herdt, *Third Sex, Third Gender,* 447–85.

62. H. Boswell, "The Transgender Alternative," *Chrysalis Quarterly* 1, no. 2 (1991): 29–31.

63. K. Bornstein, *Gender Outlaw: On Men, Women, and the Rest of Us* (New York: Routledge, 1994); and M. Rothblatt, *The Apartheid of Sex: A Manifesto on the Freedom of Gender* (New York: Crown, 1994).

64. "Masked Skaters and Trans Protests Mar Gay Games Opening," *Southern Voice,* August 6, 1998.

65. See W. J. Blumenfeld, "Back into the Future: Transphobia Is My Issue Too," *The Speaker* 25, no. 1 (1997); *The Speaker* is the journal of the Gay, Lesbian, and Bisexual Speakers Bureau of Boston. G. Rotello, "Transgendered Like Me," *The Advocate,* December 10, 1996, 88.

66. L. Burana, Roxxie, and L. Due, eds., *Dagger: On Butch Women* (New York: Cleis, 1994); J. Nestle, *A Restricted Country* (Ithaca, NY: Firebrand, 1987).

67. J. Wickman, *Transgender Politics: The Construction and Deconstruction of Binary Gender in the Finnish Transgender Community* (Abo, Finland: Abo Akademi University Press, 2001).

68. R. Wilson, "Transgendered Scholars Defy Convention, Seeking to Be Heard and Seen in Academe: A Growing Movement Demands Protection in Anti-Bias Policies and Attention for Their Ideas," *Chronicle of Higher Education,* February 6, 1998.

69. See Bornstein, *Gender Outlaw.*

70. "Transsexuals Expelled from Women's Music Festival," *Query,* August 27, 1993.

71. R. Wilchins, "The Menace in Michigan," *Village Voice,* September 6, 1994.

72. J. Walworth, "Results of 1992 Gender Survey Conducted at Michigan Womyn's Festival," *TransSisters,* November–December 1993, 13–14.

73. E. Konigsberg, "Death of a Deceiver," *Playboy,* February 1995, 92–94, 193–99.

74. S. Bowles, "A Death Robbed of Dignity Mobilizes a Community," *Washington Post,* December 10, 1996.

75. See http://www.gender.org/remember for a litany of transgender dead.

76. *Transsexual Menace,* directed by Rosa von Praunheim (USA/Germany: Video Data Bank, 1996).

77. See P. Currah, S. Minter, and J. Green, *Transgender Equality: A Handbook for Activists and Policymakers* (Washington, DC: National Gay and Lesbian Task Force, 2000), http://www.ngltf.org/downloads/transeq.pdf; for an updated list of legal protections, see http://www.transgenderlaw.org/ndlaws/.

78. See D. Denny, "Coming of Age in a Land of Two Genders," in *Personal Stories of "How I Got into Sex": Leading Researchers, Sex Therapists, Educators, Prostitutes, Sex Toy Designers, Sex Surrogates, Transsexuals, Criminologists, Clergy, and More...*, ed. B. Bullough et al. (Amherst, NY: Prometheus, 1997), 75–86.

79. Stone, "*Empire* Strikes Back," 280–304.

80. E. Bingham, "Sex-Switch Not Crucial in Beyer Victory," *New Zealand Herald*, November 29, 1999.

81. Wilson, "Transgendered Scholars."

82. D. Grow, "A Change of Heart for Deputy Mayor: Transgendered Appointee Has Found Happiness, New Politics," *Star Tribune* (Minneapolis, MN), December 20, 1998; V. Rybin, "Making Her Way: Susan Kimberly Has Completed an Important Personal Journey, but She Has Not Yet Reached a Destination in Her Quest for a Political Identity," *St. Paul Pioneer Press*, January 3, 1999.

83. Wilson, "Transgendered Scholars."

84. B. Beemyn, "Serving the Needs of Transgender College Students," *Journal of Gay and Lesbian Issues in Education* 1, no. 1 (2003): 33–50.

85. United Press International, "Supreme Court Goes Out with a Bang," July 1, 2001.

86. See K. Blackwood, "A Woman Scorned," *Pitchweekly*, November 29–December 5, 2001; K. Doering, "Judge Rules in Favor of Transgender Dad, Victory in Kantaras," *National Center for Lesbian Rights* (and *Equality Florida*), February 21, 2003; "Alleged Will of Hemingway's Transgendered Daughter Contested," *The Advocate*, August 20, 2003.

87. American Psychiatric Association, *Diagnostic and Statistical Manual of Mental Disorders*, 4th. ed., text rev. (Washington, DC: American Psychiatric Association, 2000).

88. See P. Burke, *Gender Shock: Exploding the Myths of Male and Female* (New York: Doubleday, 1996); and D. Scholinski, *The Last Time I Wore a Dress* (New York: Riverhead Books, 1997).

89. See http://www.hbigda.org.

90. See Judith Butler, *Gender Trouble: Feminism and the Subversion of Identity* (New York: Routledge, 1990); Butler, *Bodies That Matter: On the Discursive Limits of "Sex"* (New York: Routledge, 1993); Michel Foucault, *The History of Sexuality* (London: Allen Lane, 1979).

91. R. Wilchins, *Read My Lips: Sexual Subversion and the End of Gender* (Ithaca, NY: Firebrand Books, 1997).

92. D. Denny, "Beyond Our Slave Names" (keynote address, Southern Comfort Conference, Atlanta, GA, September 22–25, 1999).

93. Under the Benjamin model, transsexuals were often required to have genital surgery as a condition for acceptance to gender programs; that is, one had to commit to invasive genital surgery in order to obtain more benign and less intrusive medical treatments such as hormones; see Denny, "Politics of Diagnosis."

94. H. Devor, "A Social Context for Gender Dysphoria" (paper presented at the XV Harry Benjamin International Gender Dysphoria Association Symposium: The State of Our Art and the State of Our Science, Vancouver, British Columbia, 1997); W. Williams, "Two-Spirit Gender Variant Roles in Native American, Polynesian, and Southeast Asian Cultures" (paper presented at the XV Harry Benjamin International Gender Dysphoria Association Symposium: The State of Our Art and the State of Our Science, Vancouver, British Columbia, 1997).

95. See "Girl Dressed in Male Attire Escorted to Club for Drink," *Atlanta Constitution,* February 20, 1911; and "Dressed in Men's Clothes, Chorus Speeders Arrested," *Atlanta Constitution,* February 26, 1911.

10. Public Health Gains of the Transgender Community in San Francisco: Grassroots Organizing and Community-Based Research

Willy Wilkinson

The Transgender Community's Myriad Health Issues

Transgendered individuals face a multitude of issues that heighten their risks for serious health concerns and contribute to difficulties when accessing health care services. Beginning in early childhood and continuing throughout adulthood, multiple sociopolitical forces, and the resulting psychological and sometimes physical trauma, limit a transgendered person's ability to participate equally in society. The result is an alarming public health crisis within a population that has historically fallen through the cracks of service delivery.

Many members of the transgender community struggle to access stable employment, housing, and health care, the essential triad that directly affects one's ability to maintain health and well-being. Most transgendered people have experienced societal stigma, ridicule, and family rejection from the time they were small children, making it difficult to access basic educational opportunities. In addition, many have left home to flee family violence and harassment, only to encounter employers who refuse to hire them, throwing many trans people into dire economic straits. All races and socioeconomic statuses are affected, though health risks increase considerably when compounded by other layers of marginalization. For example, transgendered immigrants to the United States—often fleeing persecution in their homelands—and transgendered people of color have experienced tremendous difficulty securing gainful employment.[1] A Los Angeles study found a direct correlation between low-income status and experience with transgender-related violence.[2]

Transgendered persons are discriminated against when seeking housing, leaving many of them homeless or marginally housed in crime-ridden neighborhoods.[3] Furthermore, trans people are often mistreated while walking down the street and denied service in public accommodations such as restaurants, retail establishments, and bathrooms.[4] Trans people are often the targets of hate violence—at least one transgendered person is murdered per month in the United States; untold others face daily harassment and assault on the streets, at work, and in their homes.[5] Legal protections are limited, for police harassment is epidemic, especially targeting transgendered people of color, often for simply "Walking While Transgendered."[6]

As a result of institutional and societal discrimination against transgendered people, members of this community struggle with fluctuating self-esteem, substance abuse, and mental health problems, including suicide. A San Francisco study found that fully one-third of both male-to-female (MTF) and female-to-male (FTM) participants had attempted suicide.[7] In sexual situations, transgendered people struggle with issues of disclosure of transgender status, negotiation of sexual parameters, and rejection. Potential sexual partners who are nontransgendered often do not accept trans bodies once transgender status becomes known; thus, both transwomen and transmen have reported engaging in sexual risk-taking in order to have the opportunity to sexually express their respective femininity and masculinity.[8] Because of these myriad socioeconomic issues, some segments of the population have alarmingly high rates of HIV infection, sexually transmitted diseases, and tuberculosis.[9]

One important segment of the population with critical needs is MTF sex workers, many of whom have had to resort to commercial sex work out of economic necessity. Despite concerns about HIV risk and low compensation, MTF sex workers report engaging in unprotected sexual activity out of dire hunger and basic survival needs.[10] Individuals with limited English-language capabilities, immigration concerns, and experiences with racial discrimination are particularly at risk. Other transgender-related factors play a part in perpetuating a vicious cycle; both MTF and FTM transgendered individuals report participating in sex work because the attention from paying customers makes them feel validated for their gender identity and boosts their self-esteem. Some engage in sex work to support their drug addictions, and others describe using drugs to cope with sex work.[11]

This multilayered system of marginalization begs for competent health care delivery and a multitiered response from public health and social service providers. Yet when many transgendered individuals seek health care, they often encounter providers who are ignorant and insensitive to their health needs. A Boston study of barriers to health access for transgendered individuals described providers who insisted on referring to trans clients with the inappropriate pronoun, were unnecessarily focused on transgender status when treating nontrans ailments, and were confused about the relevance of their clients' transgender status to mental health and substance abuse treatment. The study highlighted the unfamiliarity among many providers about routine transgender and transsexual health needs, such as hormone use, gynecological care, and HIV prevention counseling. Moreover, study participants described being routinely denied health insurance coverage.[12]

Until recent years, this population has been unacknowledged and underserved. Transgender communities throughout the United States have remained marginalized in public health programming, social service provisions, and discrimination protections. Trans people have been invisible in health data collection, such as HIV reporting, and programs have not focused on transgender health needs. Furthermore, the transgender community has historically not been consulted for assistance in addressing its own health concerns. Nonetheless, over time, communities have awakened to the urgency and devastation, and responded to the public health crisis in the transgender community.

San Francisco's Response

During the past decade, the transgender community in San Francisco has experienced tremendous gains in public health policy and access to health care. The perseverance of countless activists, in coordination with the San Francisco Department of Public Health (DPH), has produced trans-inclusive health and prevention services, discrimination protection, data collection protocol, and improved cultural competency among service providers. As members of the transgender community organized to define our needs and enact policy changes, we have built community capacity and improved health outcomes. This chapter describes the history of the transgender community in San Francisco as it worked with the city health department to prioritize its needs, conduct community-based participatory research, and enhance service provision.

Early HIV Prevention Efforts

Since many transgendered individuals in San Francisco have been tragically affected by the AIDS epidemic, much of the public health gains have been centered on HIV prevention and services. With the HIV/AIDS crisis in the 1980s, street outreach efforts began to address the public health needs of individuals at risk for drug and sexual transmission by providing bleach, condoms, and AIDS education. Some male-to-female transgendered sex workers received services as part of larger outreach efforts, though their needs were not specifically addressed until years later. In the early years, there were few transgendered people employed as public health service providers, and input from the larger transgender community was not solicited. Consequently, transgender health needs were usually ill defined and poorly addressed by nontrans researchers and program administrators who were unaware of the languages and practices of diverse trans communities.

During my years as a community health outreach worker in San Francisco's Tenderloin District in the late 1980s, my agency referred to transgendered clients as "queens," the term most often used on the street, and documented them in a "third gender" catchall category. Concerns about HIV risk centered on sexual activity and needle sharing, both from injection drugs and hormone use. The city did not track AIDS cases among male-to-female transgendered persons, instead recording them as gay men or biological women. Similarly, the few transwomen who participated in HIV-related studies were usually listed as female, often skewing the risk picture for biological females, as well as making transgender data invisible. The existence of female-to-male transgendered persons was not acknowledged or documented in any way.

Access to Health Care

In the early 1990s we saw a transformation in San Francisco as transgendered people began to define our own public health needs and demand that they be addressed. At the time, transgendered patients were routinely being turned away from San Francisco General Hospital and other health care facilities because of ignorance and mistreatment. Angered by the insensitivity of health care workers, activists pushed for health care services that would provide not only hormone treatment therapy but primary care as well. In December 1993, with input from a variety of communities, including transgendered people, advocates, consumers, and providers, and assistance from liaison Dr. Barry Zevin, the city-funded Tom Waddell Health Center began a program called "Transgender Tuesdays," a four-hour-per-week primary care clinic providing multidisciplinary health care for self-defined transgendered people.

The Tom Waddell Health Center is a large community health center that specifically serves homeless people and other severely underserved populations within a multidisciplinary model of health care. San Francisco residents who are poor or uninsured receive care for free or based on a sliding-scale fee schedule. The Transgender Tuesdays clinic was initially established in response to the many transgendered people who were either living in single-room occupancy hotels (SROs) or completely homeless. This population was suffering the most severe health care discrimination: many were simply not getting any medical care; others were being discriminated against in medical settings. While it was not surprising that homeless transgendered people, like other homeless populations, had little or no access to medical care, providers at Tom Waddell later reported that their transgender clientele was in fact more diverse than initially expected:

> I think what we didn't count on was the level of non-access to care in all popula-
> tions throughout San Francisco. And that in fact we have a very mixed population.
> In total 13 percent in a snapshot were completely homeless in shelters or on the
> street. Another 32 percent were in SRO minimal kind of housing. On the other
> hand 48 percent lived with a roommate or a partner in an apartment.[13]

Transgender Tuesdays continues to serve hundreds of clients and educate medical providers on hormone treatment protocol, including the spectrum of treatment options, from low dose to full transition. In addition, there are now several other San Francisco clinics that provide primary and transgender care for transgendered clients.

The Changing Picture of HIV Prevention for Transgendered Individuals

In the early 1990s, nonmedical services for transgendered people were limited to assistance with immediate survival needs at a Tenderloin nonprofit, and mental health services through a DPH mental health agency. Transgendered individuals did not have specific programs at HIV prevention agencies, but continued to be served as part of larger outreach efforts. While community health outreach workers had provided services to transgendered MTF sex workers and drug users since the mid-1980s, especially in the Tenderloin, the low-income San Francisco neighborhood with the highest visible transgender population, it wasn't until the early 1990s that trans-specific programs were put into place and transgender-identified outreach workers were hired.

In 1993, following a mandate from the Centers for Disease Control and Prevention (CDC) that all states develop an HIV prevention plan, the California State Office of AIDS mandated that all city and county health departments develop their own plans. The HIV Prevention Planning Council (HPPC) was established in San Francisco to prioritize and allocate funding. Risk behaviors were ranked in order of high risk, and populations were allocated funding accordingly. Following strong advocacy from transgender community leaders, the HPPC eventually prioritized pre-op MTFs and genital post-op FTMs who have sex with men and who inject drugs. HIV prevention funding was allocated for transgendered individuals, and small transgender programs popped up in ethnic-specific agencies and neighborhood programs (though some continued to rely on funding for gay men or drug users). The numbers of transgendered people providing street outreach and crisis management to transgendered clients increased.

Discrimination Protection

Clearly, marginalization in public health services was only part of the problem. In response to the legacy of egregious civil rights violations directed toward trans people, the San Francisco community was also organizing an effort to enact discrimination protections during this time. Between 1989 and 1994, the Human Rights Commission processed over forty complaints of harassment, violence, denial of services, and unfair treatment of transgendered individuals in housing, employment, public accommodations, health care, and education. In 1993 the Lesbian/Gay/Bisexual Advisory Committee of the Human Rights Commission organized a Transgender Task Force as a subcommittee, which conducted a series of educational presentations on transgender issues to the Advisory Committee. In early 1994 the Advisory Committee added Transgender to its name and voted to hold a public hearing to investigate discrimination against the transgender community.

On May 12, 1994, over three hundred people attended this historic public hearing at City Hall to provide testimony and support for gender protections in housing, employment, health care, education, and public accommodations. Seventy speakers provided oral testimony and fifteen provided written testimony. Transgendered individuals, business representatives, and providers from community and social service organizations educated the commissioners on transgender issues and described appalling acts of discrimination. In September 1994 the Human Rights Commission produced a lengthy report with their findings and the recommendation that the City and County of San Francisco develop and enact legislation amending the City's Human Rights Ordinances to add "gender identity" as a protected class.[14]

On January 30, 1995, the law took effect. The community celebrated as then mayor Frank Jordan proclaimed the day Transgender Day in San Francisco. Prior to San Francisco adding gender identity as a protected class, there had been only three other U.S. cities to provide gender protections: Minneapolis (1974), Seattle (1986), and Santa Cruz (1992), and the state of Minnesota (1993). (In 2003, the passage of AB 196 in California amended the Fair Employment and Housing Act to include protection from discrimination based on gender identity and expression; a number of other states, counties, and cities have added laws protecting transgendered people.[15] In December 2003, the San Francisco Human Rights Commission adopted the newly named "Rules and Regulations Regarding Gender Identity Discrimination," which clarified key points concerning gender identity discrimination, specifically that gender identity is an individual's own sense of self in terms of masculinity and/or femininity, and that this identity is not dependent on body modification through hormones or surgical interventions, or the gender marker on one's identification.)[16]

San Francisco's Anti-Discrimination Ordinance has helped trans people tremendously by holding individuals and institutions accountable for discrimination in employment, housing, health care, education, and public accommodations. As the chair of the Transgender Task Force at that time stated:

> It started with grassroots activism, not funded through an agency or grant, but just old-fashioned activism—getting in people's faces and making nuisances of ourselves. We deserved the same services as everybody else in a competent, sensitive, supportive way. Since that time, fifty-seven municipalities have added gender identity as a protected class, though none have been as comprehensive to include more people on the [gender] spectrum.[17]

The fight for discrimination protections set the stage for the community to push for public health services. Though it was known anecdotally that HIV/AIDS was devastating transgender communities, in the mid-1990s there was still little epidemiological data on this population. To address this limitation, the San Francisco DPH and the transgender community worked together to conduct the first large-scale quantitative study of the transgender community: the Transgender Community Health Project.

Community-Based Participatory Action Research in the Transgender Community

Much of the literature on so-called hidden populations describes gaining access by identifying and hiring indigenous community members to serve the researcher's traditional research agenda.[18] The most marginalized populations are rarely considered capable of participating in the planning, design, and implementation of research on their own communities. Historically, what little data that existed on the transgender community involved outside researchers coming into the community to act on a specific agenda with little, if any, community involvement. Because the transgender community had been so marginalized and lacking in resources, researchers tended to infantilize the community's leadership and disregard the community's problem-solving abilities and expertise. And, frankly, because of ignorance and prejudice toward the community as a whole, past researchers had not treated transgendered individuals as equals capable of collaboration.

Participatory action research is the systematic investigation of a population—in respectful collaboration with the community being studied—for the purposes of knowledge development, self-determination, and social change. The Transgender Community Health Project (TCHP) was the first true participatory collaboration between members of the transgender community and the San Francisco Department of Public Health AIDS Office. This project honored and respected community voices, and involved the community at every step of the process. The effect on the community in San Francisco and throughout the country has been tremendous. I speak from the perspective of both a public health professional and member of the transgender community and participant in the study.

From the beginning, it was the community that first defined the need for research and the problem that needed to be studied. Though the study itself took place in 1997–98, its roots began in 1994. At the time, Kiki Whitlock was the only out transgendered person of the thirty-seven members on San Francisco's HIV Prevention Planning Council. As the program coordinator of the transgender program at Asian AIDS Project, she was concerned about the high-risk activity that she saw among MTF sex workers. She and other transgendered activists pushed for an HIV prevalence and risk behavior study, and in 1995 the HPPC prioritized such an epidemiologic study. That year community members formed a Transgender Advisory Group, which, in collaboration with AIDS Office staff, developed a research grant application.[19]

In 1996 the California State Office of AIDS funded the quantitative study and the CDC augmented the funds. The seventeen-member Transgender Advisory Group proposed that the San Francisco AIDS Office conduct focus groups as formative research for the quantitative study. In collaboration with the AIDS Office epidemiologist Kristen Clements-Nolle (a heterosexual Caucasian woman who is not transgendered), eleven focus groups were conducted on the transgender community in San Francisco. Other formative research included thirty key informant interviews and neighborhood mapping. Researchers spent four months conducting ethnographic mapping in neighborhoods known to have high concentrations of transgendered individuals, in order to develop an understanding about the appropriate time and place for study recruitment and interviews.[20]

At this time very little research existed on transgendered persons in San Francisco or elsewhere in the country. The community was eager to correct past research that had been conducted by outsiders with limited understanding of and respect for community concerns. As Clements-Nolle, the principal investigator, said, "The community wanted *good data*."[21] I was the transgendered qualitative data analyst who, along with the project director and a nontrans-gendered coconsultant, coded and analyzed the data from the focus groups and wrote the report.

One hundred transgendered individuals participated in the focus group study. The Transgender Advisory Group worked with AIDS Office staff to determine appropriate focus group questions, and each group was cofacilitated by a member of the community and an AIDS Office staff person. While participants were primarily male-to-female, they were racially and ethnically diverse, and self-disclosed both HIV-negative and HIV-positive serostatuses. A monolingual Spanish group was conducted, and there was one FTM-only focus group.

It was clear from this qualitative study that HIV was one of many problems affecting the transgender community, and the community had a tremendous need for services. Focus group participants were concerned about high rates of unprotected sex, commercial sex work, and injection drug use, with low self-esteem, substance abuse, and economic necessity cited as common barriers to safer behaviors. They described the need for job skills, housing, employment, transgender-sensitive health care, and mental health treatment, among other issues. Participants felt that discrimination and the insensitivity of service providers were the primary factors that kept them and other transgender community members from accessing HIV prevention and health services.[22]

Based on the data from this focus group study, the Transgender Advisory Group and the AIDS Office developed recommendations that included implementing a peer-based approach to service provision, training HIV prevention and health service providers in transgender cultural competence and standards of care, coordinating existing services, and ensuring documentation of services provided. Still, the community needed quantitative data on HIV infection and risk behavior; the process by which it was obtained was key to community empowerment, self-determination, and policy change.

Working in Collaboration on Design, Data Collection, Analysis, and Dissemination

In early 1997 a thirty-two member Community Advisory Board (CAB) was established to guide the study. The CAB was multiracial and multilingual, displayed a range of gender expression and identity (MTF as well as FTM), and consisted of transgendered health and social service providers, sex workers, homeless, and other interested individuals. The degree of involvement of the CAB demonstrated the AIDS Office commitment to truly participatory research. The group agreed on a name for the project—symbolic itself in terms of establishing community participation and ownership—and eligibility criteria for the study. The CAB developed protocols, sampling plans, survey instruments, and the Human Subjects application, and pilot-tested instruments. CAB members assisted in interviewing and hiring transgendered individuals for TCHP staff research positions, getting collaborating agencies and sites on board, overseeing participant recruitment and interviewing, and developing transgender-specific educational and referral materials.

The research team was an ethnically diverse group of six transgendered individuals. There were three transwomen (African American, Filipina, and Latina) and three people on the FTM spectrum (Vietnamese, Caucasian Jewish, and Caucasian). They had strong ties to their transgender ethnic communities, and those from communities with language-access issues were bilingual in their respective languages. The Caucasian FTM had equally important connections to the trannyfag community (FTMs who have sex with men). Beginning in mid-1997 the research associates recruited and interviewed participants in English, Spanish, Vietnamese, and Tagalog, and provided oral HIV testing (using the OraSure method) and referrals. They worked with CAB members to develop long-awaited transgender-specific HIV prevention educational and referral materials. They also conducted numerous trainings for local service providers, with the intent that referred agencies would have a more developed knowledge base and skill set in order to appropriately address transgender health needs.[23]

By the end of 1997 and continuing into 1998, the research associates presented preliminary findings to collaborating agencies, participants, the HPPC, the HIV Services Council, university classes, and local and national conferences. In 1998 the CAB met monthly to assist in the analysis plan and to review and interpret the data. TCHP staff continued to provide in-service trainings, expanding well beyond initial agency referrals. In 1999, when the study results were finalized, the research associates, in coordination with the CAB, presented the findings at a large community forum. In 2000 and 2001 additional members joined the CAB and original members dropped out. This eighteen-member CAB met to ensure the wide distribution of results and the implementation of new HIV services, and to develop appropriate data collection categories and a behavioral risk assessment.

Sharing Power

Nina Wallerstein, a community-based researcher, emphasizes that "lack of power and control has been identified as an over-arching disease risk factor, a barrier to research findings being used for policy change, and . . . a barrier to collaborative community-based research."[24] Similarly, Patricia Maguire argues that "the principle of shared power is central to participatory research" and that "involving research subjects as partners in the entire research process also increases the potential to distribute the benefits of the research process more equitably."[25] The TCHP study provided opportunities for community members to get involved and learn, share ideas, and feel that they were experts on their lives. This organic process of idea development and implementation contributed to community ownership of the study, the data, and subsequent accomplishments. Whitlock, one of the community members involved in every step of the TCHP research, stated:

> I think that it was a very good process. It doesn't mean that it couldn't have been improved, but overall I'd say that it was quite remarkable because our health issues and needs were addressed. I really didn't feel like there was an AIDS Office agenda that was different from what the community wanted. I feel that they did it right. I really do.[26]

As Adela Vasquez, a TCHP CAB member, proudly stated, "This time we weren't the clowns, we were the researchers. We weren't asked to do a show or be in a float."[27] Indeed, one of the dynamic, far-reaching impacts of this study was the way in which people in the community found their voices and were listened to. The CAB spent hours defining the criteria for the study (who fit into the umbrella of "transgender") and determining gender and behavioral categories for the survey instrument. As a CAB member, I remember the feeling of excitement and commitment that permeated the room. For the first time ever, the responsibility to define and document our community's needs was in our hands, and we were going to do whatever it took to do it right, even if it meant frustration, struggle, and disagreement along the way. This process of community empowerment and self-determination cannot be forced or faked; it came because we were given the opportunity to meet as a community and grapple to define our lived realities.

Yet the AIDS Office has the reputation of being an entity with which communities often struggle. Why was this study different? I asked community members for their thoughts on the process. Again and again, they pointed to Clements-Nolle and her commitment and patience as principal investigator. "I didn't set out to do a participatory action research study. I just did what I thought was right," Clements-Nolle humbly commented.[28] Said one of the research associates: "Kristen has really good ethics. She pushed for the study without a lot of support initially and did a lot of hard work to make it participatory. I think it was pretty revolutionary. Other AIDS Office studies use CABs, but they aren't participatory."[29]

The participatory action researchers Andrea Cornwall and Rachel Jewkes describe the continuum along which participation can take place as ranging from contractual to consultative, collaborative, and truly collegiate. Participation in the TCHP study exemplified a collegiate relationship in that "researchers and local people work(ed) together as colleagues with different skills to offer, in a process of mutual learning where local people have control over the process."[30] To their credit, the AIDS Office staff sought out, trusted, and honored the community's expertise on traditionally unappreciated topics, such as sex work, gender transition and identity, and monolingual immigrant communities.

Challenges

Prior to TCHP and the fight for discrimination protections, the transgender community was not particularly cohesive socially or politically. Though informational and social networks were established, MTFs and FTMs functioned, for the most part, in separate worlds. Furthermore, the community did not trust that our health needs would be heard and taken seriously. One of the biggest challenges of TCHP was in rallying the community around its health concerns, as Whitlock, a CAB member, describes:

> If we weren't able to [get participation] as community leaders and activists, we wouldn't have had the buy-in from the community that we needed to make the project successful. If the study didn't work, it could've hurt the community in the future. So convincing the community that we needed to get it together here— especially in a bureaucratic environment like the DPH or any other government agency—helped to fuel the study.[31]

In any working community group, there are issues of inclusion, influence, and competing priorities. Communities are never monolithic, and, fortunately for us, the transgender community is rich with vibrancy and color. The CAB was a highly diverse group of MTF and FTM individuals with varying needs, agendas, and personalities. Though the two groups share common issues of self-esteem, validation for our chosen gender expressions, and disclosure, in many ways MTF and FTM health needs differ considerably. MTF folks on the CAB were concerned about discrimination and the lack of employment opportunities, as well as the high prevalence of commercial sex work and HIV infection in their community. FTMs were concerned about the sexual risk-taking that was occurring among members of their community in order to be seen, and validated, as sexual men.[32] Because this was the first time that we had the opportunity to define and address our health needs as a community, we were often overwhelmed by our excitement and need to be heard. But we worked it out. Harnessing and focusing the various viewpoints required patience and time, and, fortunately, the AIDS Office staff was committed to the process. Ari Bachrach, a research associate, commented, "I have a lot of respect for their [the AIDS Office] leadership. Kristen showed more patience in working with the community than I could ever dream of. There were twelve opinions for ten people in the room."[33]

While the community worked enthusiastically on all the other aspects of the research process, participation in the CAB dropped off considerably when it came time for quantitative data analysis. People were much less interested in analyzing the data than they were in obtaining it. The principal investigator tried to solicit participation, but CAB meetings began to dwindle to two attendees. People felt that they could trust her to sort out the data. Once the results were ready, participation again surged when it came time for dissemination, because the community was proud of its work.

Other challenges involved the question of who got left out of the study. Though media promotion was extensive, and recruitment hit numerous venues around the city, the study was less successful in reaching certain population groups. "Mainstreamed trannies," or transgendered persons who have transitioned and blended into society, are often less interested in participating in the transgender community. MTF respondents drew heavily from sex worker populations—an important risk group—though not representative of the MTF population as a whole. In addition, those of us who were FTMs of color grappled from the beginning with how to ensure that this segment of the FTM community was represented in the study. At the time, there was little in the way of organized avenues of support for this population, and many had "woodworked," or mainstreamed. Because much of the FTM recruitment centered on Female-to-Male International, an organization that is perceived as disproportionately white and middle class, FTM respondents reflected this selection bias.

Once results were disseminated, some members of the FTM community suggested that the study did not serve their needs. Said Bachrach: "People wanted it to show a different reality because the reality we found didn't advocate for services for FTMs. The study suggested that FTMs weren't as high risk as they really are, though it brought validity to looking at FTMs who have sex with men."[34] Indeed, research on a large, diverse community can produce results that are controversial or inconclusive.[35] A community process will invariably leave someone out or be unsatisfactory to someone.

In the end, the community had taken the plunge to organize itself, define its needs, work diligently on the process, and enact change at the policy level. For these accomplishments, the community was proud. Though the work had its challenges, the project was enthusiastically claimed and supported by many.

Giving Back to the Community

Control of knowledge and its dissemination is critical to the self-determination of traditionally marginalized peoples. The objective of participatory action research, therefore, is at least twofold: to empower people through constructing their own knowledge, and to create knowledge and action useful for socio-political action. The TCHP study gave back to the community by generating much-needed data on the population, as well as by being a tool of consciousness development, economic empowerment, skills development, and mobilization for change.

Clearly, the community needed "hard data" to justify the need for health and social services. Over five hundred respondents (392 MTFs and 123 FTMs) were interviewed and tested for HIV, making TCHP by far the largest study of a transgender community anywhere in the world. The data showed alarming HIV-seroprevalence rates among the MTF population (35 percent) and, in particular, an astounding 63 percent seroprevalence among the African American MTF population. Although HIV prevalence among FTM participants was much lower (2 percent), risk behavior for FTMs who have sex with men showed a high incidence of unprotected vaginal-receptive intercourse (64 percent) and unprotected anal-receptive intercourse (28 percent). Two-thirds of MTF participants and over half of FTM participants were classified as depressed, and 32 percent of both populations had attempted suicide.[36] These numbers told the story that individuals could not tell alone: transgendered persons were at risk for HIV infection and were in dire need of support services.

The study process had other benefits—the enhancement of community capacity and competence. Through involvement in TCHP, community members learned research and advocacy skills, and health education and public health principles. Most of all, participants were able to take the expertise that they had on their lives *to the bank,* so to speak. As one study participant stated, "I was working the streets before the study. Now I'm a health educator."[37] Research associates were respected and financially compensated for work that had been previously volunteered, and they developed skills that led to higher-level employment.

In addition, study participants were paid for each of two interviews, as well as for bringing in up to five more participants, at a maximum of seventy-five dollars per person. For many who were struggling financially, that compensation helped ease, in a small way, the dailiness of poverty while validating their experiences.

The research team, CAB members, and study participants benefited from the study's socially supportive environment, which honored and normalized transgender expression and language. For some, this study provided the first opportunity they had had to fully present their transgender selves on a professional level.[38] CAB members and research associates also gained from the experience of meeting with each other monthly. The time before and after meetings was filled with the loud buzz of community sharing, catching up, and the exchange of resources.

Many TCHP participants experienced a process of coming into our own power and the power of our community as we transformed our private individual experiences into a larger community experience that commanded visibility and public concern. Moreover, the TCHP study gave back to the transgender community by giving us the power to create change in our lives. As Meredith Minkler and Nina Wallerstein assert, "Closely related to the concept of empowerment is the notion of community competence or problem-solving ability as a central goal and outcome of community organization practice."[39]

Transforming Research into Action

As a result of this research project and the community's activism, the transgender community has made tremendous gains in public health services and data collection, as well as greater discrimination protections based on gender identity and expression. The widespread provider training that the TCHP research associates conducted has resulted in increased cultural competency among service providers and improved services. Moreover, city funding for transgender trainings has been augmented. In addition, the TCHP study paved the way for additional studies on the transgender community in San Francisco.[40]

More transgendered persons are employed and have taken leadership in public health throughout the city. Whereas in earlier years there were very few transgendered service providers, now there are many. As one transgendered provider commented,

> When I first got involved in these types of workshops and forums five years ago, the transgender persons were there strictly as consumers, as clients, as patients. You know, there is a big power differential there. So today a lot of us are here as peers of other care providers, which I think is really important.[41]

Preliminary results of the study helped to immediately secure supplemental CDC funding for HIV prevention programs and health services that targeted African American and Latina MTFs. Subsequently, the DPH and community-based organizations used the data to secure additional local and national funding. The data illuminated the prevention needs of transgendered persons by highlighting specific risk behaviors that could be addressed in interventions. New programs for MTF transgendered individuals were developed and existing ones augmented. In addition, recommendations from the focus group study and the TCHP risk data underscored the need for at least one HIV prevention program for FTMs. In 2000, in coordination with the larger female-to-male community, I launched the Trannyfags Project at STOP AIDS Project, the first HIV prevention program for FTMs who have sex with men.

As a result of the Transgender Community Health Project and the work of the CAB, the HPPC was convinced of the need to adopt new gender categories for classifying transgendered persons for data collection and service provision. City-funded community-based HIV agencies and many large data-reporting systems in the city now report HIV/AIDS data separately for transgendered persons. This new way of categorizing transgendered people has resulted in increased funding for transgender populations.

In addition, the Transgender Advisory Group, an offshoot of the CAB, worked with the health department to develop a transgender-specific behavioral risk-assessment instrument in English and Spanish for use by HIV agencies serving transgendered clients. In 2001 the prominent ethnic-specific HIV agencies and a Tenderloin agency initially implemented the behavioral risk assessment, which helped evaluate and develop their interventions, and secure additional funding.[42] In 2002 and 2003 additional agencies that serve transgendered individuals followed suit. During both phases, agencies received training in interviewing skills, research ethics, and human subjects protection.

Finally, the Transgender Community Health Project helped transgendered city employees secure unprecedented health insurance coverage. The San Francisco Health Systems Board used TCHP data on health needs and gender confirmation surgery to make the April 2001 landmark decision to offer limited transition-related health benefits, including sexual-reassignment surgery, to all city employees.[43] As of July 1, 2004, the city removed transgender exclusions in its health insurance policies, so that the HMOs Health Net, Blue Cross/Blue Shield, and Kaiser now offer surgical benefits for transgendered employees, retirees, and their dependents.[44] San Francisco is the only governmental entity in the nation to recognize and respect the health needs of its transgender citizens by treating them equally in the city health plan.

Far-Reaching Social and Policy Change

In addition to the programmatic successes in San Francisco, cities around the country have used the TCHP data to secure funding for their programs and assist in other advocacy efforts. Researchers in Los Angeles, New York, Boston, and Seattle have networked with TCHP researchers to develop and conduct similar studies in their areas.[45] Other cities have utilized some of the tools developed for TCHP, such as the study's system for gender classification,[46] in their own studies.[47] These needs assessments have influenced local programming and discrimination protections by illuminating local health needs, as well as by painting a larger picture of transgender health needs throughout the country.

I asked activists and researchers from around the country to speak about how they conducted their own transgender health studies, the effects of these studies, and if they had been impacted by TCHP. Health studies on the transgender community have varied in size, scope, community involvement, and perceived ability to effect change. Many have not been widely distributed or published, because of limited funding, less-supportive public health departments, or lack of academic connections.[48] Some indicated a frustration that their study or studies did not have the impact they had hoped for. Yet there were indications that, as a result of conducting these studies, each city's transgender community had received more attention to its needs, augmented its credibility with city officials, and felt growing strength as a community that had become better equipped to advocate for transgender rights.

A number of individuals felt that the San Francisco TCHP study helped or inspired them to conduct their own research. In 1998 researchers in Los Angeles began collecting data for the Los Angeles Transgender Health Study, a large epidemiological study that involved 244 transgendered participants and included OraSure HIV testing. The coprincipal investigator Cathy Reback felt that the L.A. study benefited considerably from the research in San Francisco, because Clements-Nolle shared the TCHP survey instrument, which served as a model for theirs. Said Reback, "Kristen was incredibly helpful and generous. It saved us six months of time to have a starting base."[49] Emilia Lombardi, a transgendered consultant on this project as well as principal investigator on a study funded by the National Institute for Drug Abuse (NIDA) to examine substance use and substance abuse treatment in the transgender community in L.A., felt that TCHP was important for many reasons:

> Most of all, it was the first that actually included trans people in the design process and as such it was based more in the real lives of trans people and not a particular researcher's agenda. This is especially the case in how the data was subsequently presented. It was also the first to include FTMs, a first not only in HIV/AIDS related studies, [but in other transgender studies]. It formed the basis for many health studies including my own. The data from that study enabled other researchers to show to funders and others that there is a need and that more work is still needed. I still cite it in many of my works.[50]

Other cities have conducted research efforts on transgender populations with community input and growing support from their health departments. In Philadelphia, two quantitative needs assessments of the transgender community were conducted between 1995 and 1997. In the latter, the transgender community, in collaboration with local agencies and a university, provided input into survey design, recruitment, and data collection. Though the results of these two studies were not widely distributed, the community process was ultimately helpful in securing funding for local programming. Recently, in an unprecedented show of support, the Philadelphia Department of Public Health funded trainings in association with a CDC-funded transgender harm-reduction program, "their largest funding commitment to local trans programming thus far," according to the transgendered activist Ben Singer.[51]

Researchers later replicated the Philadelphia assessment of transgender health and social service needs in Chicago after receiving funding from the University of Illinois. This 2001 quantitative needs assessment documented face-to-face interviews of 111 participants and was the first large-scale community-based study of the transgender community in Chicago.[52] The survey instrument used in Philadelphia was augmented with feedback from the local transgender community, and trans people conducted the interviews. The results were delivered to the community immediately. Soon afterward, the Chicago Department of Public Health conducted a qualitative study. Gretchen Kenagy, the project investigator, said that she was inspired by TCHP.

> I use it all the time. It's helpful because it was the largest by a longshot and included a broad spectrum of people. It may not be well-documented, but connections with people around the country who did needs assessments have an effect on each other. It helps to have a continuity of questions that were asked, to know that people have been asking the same things.[53]

Boston has been well supported by the Massachusetts Department of Public Health and has experienced important gains as a result of transgender community efforts. The 2000 study of barriers to health care access highlighted the insensitivity and ignorance of many health care providers on transgender health needs and demonstrated the importance of eliminating barriers to access in the public health model, including health care, employment, and housing as a triad toward stability. Transgendered activists helped determine the appropriate structure for this focus group study, and transgendered community members facilitated the groups. Results of the study have helped secure additional funding for transgender programs and were instrumental in helping pass the 2002 Boston ordinance that provides discrimination protection on the basis of gender identity and expression in housing, employment, public accommodations, educational opportunities, and lending.[54]

While many whom I spoke with expressed disappointment that their study findings had not appeared to directly effect policy change and secure public health funds, everyone described a process of community organizing and community building that led to systemic change. Though Reback was disappointed that "the L.A. study was not as effective as we had hoped with changing policy and in providing more monies for transgender-specific services," there have been many benefits. This study brought the transgender community together for the first time, and since then, L.A. has had more funding and attention to trans youth issues, formed an additional Transgender Task Force, and has received funding for additional studies.[55]

Indeed, nothing occurs in a vacuum. As studies draw attention to the health needs of transgendered individuals, so do people who are able to make appeals to city officials on a personal level. Carrie Davis, a transgendered activist from New York, said that while trans services are nominally funded in New York City, their qualitative needs assessment led to advocacy efforts, including passage of the 2002 amendment to the New York City human rights law to include protection from discrimination in housing and public accommodations based on gender identity and expression.

> The effect has been an ever-expanding network of trans providers and allies who are interested in advocating for different paradigms for recognizing and working with the transgender community in New York State. The gist of it is that we would not have so many politically-active people in the transgender community if not for this [needs assessment and the HIV Prevention Planning Group]. The result is that we have a core of individuals who are tough, strong, and loud.[56]

Looking to the Future

By engaging participants in a collaborative, reciprocal process, San Francisco's Transgender Community Health Project set an example for participatory action research at its finest. Because of the dedicated activism of countless community members and the pro–human rights attitude of public health professionals, the San Francisco Department of Public Health is the first city health department to enact policies that prioritize transgender health needs and provide transgender-specific services in a competent and supportive way. As the transgender community in San Francisco makes strides in public health and civil rights, transgender communities in cities across the country and throughout the world are embarking on their own successes—new public health programs, additional funding, and discrimination protections. As the numerous leaders and dedicated activists of the transgender movement continue to educate and advocate for equal treatment and services, the momentum of each new victory energizes and inspires us to continue to push the boundaries of public health service provision for the transgender community.

Notes

The author would like to thank the many individuals who took the time to provide information and share their experiences, including Marcus Arana, Ari Bachrach, Kristen Clements-Nolle, Carrie Davis, Mara Keisling, Gretchen Kenagy, Emilia Lombardi, Samuel Lurie, Cathy Reback, Diego Sanchez, Pablo Santos, and Ben Singer.

1. C. J. Reback, P. A. Simon, C. C. Bemis, and B. Gatson, *The Los Angeles Transgender Health Study: Community Report,* May 2001. Study participants were primarily people of color (85 percent), many of them immigrants from Asian and Latin American countries. Fifty percent were low income (less than $12,000 annually). Fifty percent reported that sex work was a major source of income in the previous six months.

2. E. L. Lombardi, R. Wilchins, D. Priesing, and D. Malouf, "Gender Violence: Transgender Experiences with Violence and Discrimination," *Journal of Homosexuality* 42, no. 1 (2001): 89–101.

3. A number of studies show that housing is of serious concern, especially among MTFs. In the San Francisco study, nearly half of MTF participants reported living in unstable housing, including single-room occupancy hotels, homeless on the streets or in shelters, and "crashing" with friends and relatives. See K. Clements-Nolle, R. Marx, R. Guzman, and M. Katz, "HIV Prevalence, Risk Behaviors, Health Care Use, and Mental Health Status of Transgendered Persons in San Francisco: Implications for Public Health Intervention," *American Journal of Public Health* 91, no. 6 (2001): 915–21. See also Kelly C. McGowan, *Transgender Needs Assessment,* HIV Prevention Planning Unit, New York City Department of Health, 1999.

4. K. Clements-Nolle, W. Wilkinson, K. Kitano, and R. Marx, "HIV Prevention and Health Service Needs of the Transgender Community in San Francisco," in *Transgender and HIV: Risks, Prevention, and Care,* ed. W. Bockting and S. Kirk (New York: Hayworth, 2001), 69–89.

5. "Remembering Our Dead," Gender Education and Advocacy, http://www.rememberingourdead.org.

6. C. Daley, E. Kugler, and J. Hirschmann, *Walking While Transgendered,* Ella Baker Center for Human Rights/TransAction, San Francisco, April 2000.

7. Clements-Nolle et al., "HIV Prevalence."

8. Clements-Nolle et al., "HIV Prevention."

9. A number of studies have documented high rates of HIV infection, including Clements-Nolle et al., "HIV Prevalence"; and C. J. Reback and E. L. Lombardi, "HIV Risk Behaviors of Male-to-Female Transgenders in a Community-Based Harm Reduction Program," in *Transgender and HIV: Risks, Prevention, and Care,* ed. W. Bockting and S. Kirk (New York: Hayworth, 2001), 59–68. This L.A. study also documented high STD rates. See also Centers for Disease Control and Prevention, *HIV-Related Tuberculosis in a Transgender Network—Baltimore, Maryland, and New York City Area, 1998–2000,* http://www.cdc.gov/mmwr/preview/mmwrhtml/mm4915a1.htm.

10. Clements-Nolle et al., "HIV Prevention." See also McGowan, *Transgender Needs Assessment,* 1999.

11. Ibid.

12. JSI Research and Training Institute, "Access to Health Care for Transgendered People in Greater Boston," July 2000, http://www.glbthealth.org/transaccess.pdf, 20, 22. Participants described egregious behavior on the part of providers once their transsexual status became known, such as the doctor who told the transwoman that she needed to see a veterinarian because doctors were "for people," or the FTM youth who was turned away from the emergency room when the doctor stated that he did not treat people like him.

13. B. Zevin, "Demographics of the Transgender Clinic at San Francisco's Tom Waddell Health Center" (Transgender Care Conference, San Francisco, May 5, 2000).

14. J. Green, *Investigation into Discrimination against Transgendered People,* Human Rights Commission, City and County of San Francisco, September 1994.

15. At press time, there are currently seventy-seven jurisdictions that prohibit discrimination on the basis of gender identity or expression: sixty-one cities, ten counties, and seven states, including California, Hawai'i, Illinois, Maine, Rhode Island, Minnesota, and New Mexico. For current updates on discrimination protections, see www.nctequality.org.

16. M. Arana, e-mail message to author, July 2, 2004. Facilities must make reasonable accommodations to allow an individual access to the facility that is most appropriate for the individual's gender identity. The regulations strongly urge that all single-use bathroom facilities in the city be designated as "gender-neutral" and clarifies that people must be allowed to use the bathroom that is appropriate to their gender identities, regardless of hormonal or surgical status, or the gender marker on their IDs.

17. P. Santos, telephone conversation with author, January 16, 2003.

18. See J. K. Watters and P. Biernacki, "Targeted Sampling: Options for the Study of Hidden Populations," *Social Problems* 36, no. 4 (October 1989): 416–30.

19. K. Whitlock, telephone conversation with author, April 23, 2000.

20. K. Clements-Nolle and A. Bachrach, "Community Based Participatory Research with a Hidden Population: The Transgender Community Health Project," in *Community-Based Participatory Research for Health,* ed. M. Minkler and N. Wallerstein (San Francisco: Jossey-Bass, 2003), 332–43.

21. K. Clements-Nolle, "Case Study: PAR with Hidden Populations: The Transgender Community Health Study" (panel presentation, Transgender Community Health Project, Participatory Action Research Class, University of California, Berkeley, School of Public Health, March 7, 2000).

22. Clements-Nolle et al., "HIV Prevention."

23. Clements-Nolle and Bachrach, "Community Based Participatory Research."

24. N. Wallerstein, "Power between Evaluator and Community: Research Relationships with New Mexico's Healthier Communities," *Social Science and Medicine* 49 (1999): 39–53.

25. P. Maguire, *Doing Participatory Research: A Feminist Approach* (Amherst, Center for International Education, School of Education, University of Massachusetts, 1987), 38–39, 74–105.

26. Whitlock, telephone conversation with author.

27. A. Vasquez, "Case Study: PAR with Hidden Populations: The Transgender Community Health Study" (panel presentation, Transgender Community Health Project, Participatory Action Research Class, University of California, Berkeley, School of Public Health, March 7, 2000).

28. K. Clements-Nolle, telephone conversation with author, February 2000.

29. A. Bachrach, telephone conversation with author, April 23, 2000.

30. A. Cornwall and R. Jewkes, "What Is Participatory Research?" *Social Science Medicine* 41, no. 12 (1995): 1667–76.

31. Whitlock, telephone conversation with author.

32. Clements-Nolle and Bachrach, "Community Based Participatory Research."

33. Bachrach, telephone conversation with author.

34. Ibid.

35. J. Schensul, "Organizing Community Research Partnerships in the Struggle against AIDS," *Health Education and Behavior* 26, no. 2 (April 1998): 266–83.

36. Clements-Nolle et al., "HIV Prevalence."

37. K. Aguilar, "Case Study: PAR with Hidden Populations: The Transgender Community Health Study" (panel presentation, Transgender Community Health Project, Participatory Action Research Class, University of California, Berkeley, School of Public Health, March 7, 2000).

38. Clements-Nolle and Bachrach, "Community Based Participatory Research."

39. M. Minkler and N. Wallerstein, "Improving Health through Community Organization and Community Building, a Health Education Perspective," in *Community Organizing and Community Building for Health,* ed. M. Minkler (New Brunswick, NJ: Rutgers University Press, 1997), 30–52.

40. A number of studies have been conducted on MTFs, including HIV risk behaviors of MTFs of color, by the Centers for AIDS Prevention Studies, University of California at San Francisco (http://www.caps.ucsf.edu). The San Francisco Department of Public Health conducted an HIV testing survey (http://www.dph.sf.ca.us).

41. Andrea Pasillas, "Addressing Psychosocial Issues in the Transgender Client," (Transgender Care Conference, San Francisco, May 5, 2000).

42. Transgender Advisory Group, "History and Future Directions" (presentation to the HIV Prevention Planning Council regarding the Transgender Behavioral Risk Assessment, 2001).

43. Clements-Nolle and Bachrach, "Community Based Participatory Research."

44. Arana, e-mail message to author. Affecting roughly eighty thousand consumers, this change will create the actuarial information that will prove that this is not an expensive benefit and that it will not be overly or spuriously utilized, thus hopefully expanding coverage for all other employees in the future.

45. Clements-Nolle and Bachrach, "Community Based Participatory Research."

46. K. Clements-Nolle, personal communication, July 2, 2004. Participants were eligible for TCHP if they self-identified as transgender, transsexual, bigender, transvestite, or a gender other than that assigned at birth. The categories were somewhat restrictive in order to satisfy the CDC concern about drawing a clear distinction between transgendered individuals and gay men.

47. B. Singer, telephone conversation with author, October 3, 2003.

48. "An Overview of the Top U.S. Transgender Health Priorities," a meta-analysis of available research on U.S. transgender populations, not all of which has been published in journals, can be found at http://www.nctequality.org/HealthPriorities.pdf.

49. C. Reback, telephone conversation with author, October 8, 2003.

50. E. Lombardi, e-mail message to author, October 8, 2003.

51. Singer, telephone conversation with author.

52. G. Kenagy, "HIV among Transgendered People," *AIDS Care* 14, no. 1 (2002): 127–34. See http://www.hawaii.edu/hivandaids/HIV Among Transgendered People.pdf.

53. G. Kenagy, telephone conversation with author, October 8, 2003.

54. D. Sanchez, telephone conversation with author, October 10, 2003.

55. Reback, telephone conversation with author.

56. C. Davis, telephone conversation with author, October 10, 2003.

PART III. POLITICS

11. Compliance Is Gendered: Struggling for Gender Self-Determination in a Hostile Economy

Dean Spade

> I think capitalism is not just inegalitarian, not just full of
> maldistributions of wealth, not just wasteful of certain
> kinds of human energies and natural resources, not just
> producing for profit rather than human need, but also that
> it's a form of political economy that is fundamentally
> undemocratic, that it is full of forms of domination
> which prevent us from being able to organize the
> possibilities of our own lives.
>
> —**Wendy Brown**, *The Anti-Capitalism Reader*

Since the emergence of poor-relief programs in sixteenth-century Europe, governments have developed varying strategies of social welfare to quell resistance among those who inhabit the necessary lowest level of the capitalist economy: the pool of unemployed whose presence keeps wages low and profit margins high.[1] Throughout their history, relief systems have been characterized by their insistence on work requirements for recipients, their vilification of recipients of relief, and their ability to paint the necessary failures of the economic systems they prop up as moral failures of the individuals who are most negatively affected by those systems.[2]

Feminist theorists have provided vital insight into how public relief systems have also operated through moralistic understandings of sexuality and family structure to force recipients into compliance with sexist and heterosexist notions of womanhood and motherhood. The creation of coercive policies requiring this compliance have usually been mobilized by appeals to white supremacist notions of white motherhood and racial purity, as well as depictions of black women as oversexualized, lazy, and morally loose. Feminist theorists have provided a picture of how the day-to-day surveillance of low-income people and the rigid and punitive rule systems used in social services create a highly regulated context for the gender expression, sexuality, and family structure of low-income women who often rely on these systems to get out of economically dependent relationships with men. This fits into a broader analysis of how gendered models of citizenship, and gender and race hierarchies in the economy, operate to dominate the lives of low-income people most forcefully and directly affect the ability of all people to determine and express our gender, sexuality, and reproduction.

Unfortunately, this analysis has not yet been applied to examine how gender regulation of the poor applies to those who face some of the most dire consequences of a coercive binary gendered economy, those who transgress the basic principles of binary gender. Much feminist analysis of binary gender transgression has focused on the pathologizing medical discourses that have defined popular understandings of gender role distress to reinscribe meaning into rigid notions of "male" and "female."[3] However, as transgender liberation movements proliferate, and feminist analysis of gender transgression becomes more nuanced and sophisticated, it is essential that we bring along the feminist analysis of gender regulation in work and public assistance systems in order to account for the extreme economic consequences that gender-transgressive people face because of our gender identities and expressions.

Similarly, many lesbian, gay, and bi activists and theorists have tended to miss the vital connection between economic and anticapitalist analysis and the regulation of sexual and gender expression and behavior. The most well-publicized and well-funded LGB organizations have notoriously marginalized low-income people and people of color, and framed political agendas that have reflected concern for economic opportunity and family recognition for well-resourced and disproportionately white LGB populations. Feminist, anticapitalist, and antiracist analysis has been notably absent from mainstream discourses about LGBT rights, and low-income people, people of color, and gender-transgressive people have been notoriously underrepresented from leadership and decision-making power in these movements.[4]

This is particularly distressing given the economic realities that people who transgress gender norms face. Economic and educational opportunity remain inaccessible to gender transgressive people because of severe and persistent discrimination, much of which remains legal,[5] but for low-income people caught up in the especially gender-regulating public relief systems and criminal justice systems that dominate the lives of the poor, the gender regulation of the economy is felt even more sharply.

Many trans people start out their lives with the obstacle of abuse or harassment at home, or being kicked out of their homes because of their gender identities or expressions. Some turn to foster care, but often end up homeless when they experience harassment and violence at the hands of staff and other residents in foster care facilities (most of which are sex segregated and place trans youth according to birth sex designation).[6] The adult homeless shelter system, similarly, is inaccessible because of the fact that most facilities are sex segregated and will either turn down a trans person outright or refuse to house them according to their lived gender identity.[7] Similarly, harassment and violence against trans and gender nonconforming students is rampant in schools, and many drop out before finishing or are kicked out. Many trans people also do not pursue higher education because of fears about having to apply to schools and having their paperwork reveal their old name and birth sex because they have not been able to change these on their documents. Furthermore, trans people face severe discrimination in the job market and are routinely fired for transitioning on the job or when their gender identities or expressions come to their supervisor's attention.[8]

Trans people also have a difficult time accessing the entitlements that exist, though in a reduced and diminished format, to support poor people. Discrimination on the basis of gender identity occurs in welfare offices, on workfare job sites, in Medicaid offices, in Administrative Law Hearings for welfare, Medicaid, and Social Security Disability benefits. These benefit programs have been decimated in the last ten years and are generally operated with a punitive approach that includes frequent illegal termination of benefits and the failure to provide people their entitlements. For most people seeking to access these programs consistently during a time of need, the availability of an attorney or advocate to help navigate the hearings process has been essential to maintaining benefits. Unfortunately, most poverty attorneys and advocacy organizations are still severely lacking in basic information about serving trans clients and may reject cases on the basis of a person's gender identity or create such an unwelcoming environment that a trans client will not return for services. Based on community awareness of this problem, many trans people will not even seek these services, expecting that they will be subjected to humiliating and unhelpful treatment. The resulting lack of access to even the remaining shreds of the welfare system leaves a disproportionate number of trans people in severe poverty and dependent on criminalized work such as prostitution or the drug economy to survive. This, in turn, results in large numbers of trans people being entangled in the juvenile and adult criminal justice systems where they are subjected to extreme harassment and violence.

Given these conditions, the need for an understanding of the operations of gender regulation on gender-transgressive people in the context of poverty is urgent. In this chapter, I want to begin to suggest how we could reexamine what we know from feminist and LGB analysis of gender, sexual, and reproductive regulation, to see how this applies to the lives of low-income transgender, transsexual, intersex, and other gender-transgressive people. I come to these questions as a poverty lawyer working for these populations, and I want to use feminist, queer, and anticapitalist analysis of the operation of poverty alleviation programs and other methods of controlling and exploiting poor people to contextualize case studies from the day-to-day lives of my clients. I want to begin a conversation about what it means that almost all of the institutions and programs that exist to control and exploit poor people and people of color in the United States are sex segregated, especially in a context where membership in a sexual category is still determined with regard to access to medical technologies that are prohibitively expensive to all but the most well-resourced gender-transgressive people. It is my hope that by inviting such analysis we can begin to think about how emergent movements for gender self-determination can avoid the pitfalls of mainstream gay and lesbian rights movements by centralizing the concerns of those who face the most extreme consequences of gender and sexual regulation: those who face manifestations of institutionalized racism and bear the brunt of capitalism while struggling against coercive binary gender systems. It seems that now, as gender rights movements increasingly institutionalize and gain broader visibility, we should take stock of the possibilities for real alliances and collaborations with feminist, welfare rights, and antiprison advocates, and see how those allies can extend the scope of their inquiries to include gender-transgressive people.

Now is the time to recognize that no project of gender and sexual self-determination will be meaningful if it fails to engage resistance to an inherently violent and hierarchical capitalist economic system that grounds its control over workers and the poor in oppressive understandings of race, sex, gender, ability, and nationality.[9] To address homophobic and transphobic domination in pursuit of a better world, we need to start from an understanding of the experiences of those who face the intersection of multiple oppressions, centralize the analysis that this intersectionality fosters, and think concretely about what strategies a movement dedicated to these principles would engage.

Capitalism, Access to Income, and the Use of Social Welfare Policies to Regulate Gender and Sexuality and Promote White Supremacy

Access to participation in the U.S. economy has always been conditioned on the ability of each individual to comply with norms of gendered behavior and expression, and the U.S. economy has always been shaped by explicit incentives that coerce people into normative gender and sexual structures, identities, and behaviors. At the same time the U.S. economy has, since its inception, been structured to recognize and maintain access to wealth for white people and to exploit the labor, land, and resources of native people, immigrants, and people of color. Property ownership itself has been a raced and gendered right throughout U.S. history, and an individual's race, gender, and sexuality have operated as forms of property themselves.[10] Similarly, interventions that would appear to seek to remedy the exploitative and damaging outcomes of our economic system have often been structured to control gendered behavior and expression and incentivize misogynist and heterosexist family norms. These interventions have typically been mobilized by white supremacy and the desire to benefit white workers and families to the disadvantage of people of color and immigrants. For example, the first wage and hour laws in the United States were passed under a notion of protectionism for women, the logic being that since women really did not belong in the workplace anyway, if they had to work outside the home, it was the state's role to intervene in their labor contracts to protect them from exploitation.[11] Similarly, since the inception of poor relief in the United States, programs have been structured to support gendered divisions of labor and promote heterosexual family structure and have been mobilized by discourses of racial purity.[12] As Gwendolyn Mink describes, the first social welfare program in the United States, the pension system for Union Army veterans, emerged out of notions of American citizenship that were grounded in "independence, industry and virtue" and rewarded military service to the republic.[13] These notions of citizenship were overtly gendered, with male citizenship reliant on civic participation, and women's citizenship defined by their marriages to men who had rights to civic participation that they lacked, including suffrage, the right to serve on juries, and the right to claim American nationality independent of marital status.[14] The first legal advancements in women's civil status, such as the Married Women's Property acts and maternal child custody preference, were intimately tied to the construction of women's roles as mother, wife, and caregiver of children.[15] The cultural understanding of female citizenship, Mink further articulates, was also intimately tied to the assertion that white women were protectors of white American racial purity. The first relief programs were shaped by the concern that the woman citizen be supported in her role as the ensurer of the "well-being of the race."[16] The formation of U.S. social programs was shaped around maintaining existent power structures with regard to gender and race despite the fact that these were changing because of the influences of industrialization and immigration.

> The gender-biased social welfare innovations of the pre–New Deal period tackled problems of poverty through a focus on dependent motherhood and sought solutions to dilemmas of ethnic and racial diversity in the regulation of motherhood. The interweaving of race and gender during the process of the welfare state's formation gendered citizenship, produced paternalist policies that benefited some women, opened the state to other women, and allowed the assimilation of "lesser races" into the system while assuring their continued subordination within it. It created a welfare state that tied the woman citizen to women's place and that institutionalized political ambivalence toward universal social citizenship.[17]

Anyone who has lived through the last ten years of "welfare reform" rhetoric in the United States will notice that racist and sexist rhetoric and policy in the realm of welfare is still strongly with us. Such rhetoric is still being used to formulate welfare policies that control the gender and sexual behavior and expression of women and firmly tie economic survival and advantage to racial status. The most recent well-publicized massive overhaul of the welfare system, the "welfare reform" of the mid-1990s, was motivated, structured, and sold to the American public through racist and sexist understandings of poverty, work, and family structure. Its results have lived up to its intentions, with poor women of color suffering horribly under the new system.[18] Holloway Sparks writes about how the changes in welfare policy in the mid-1990s were based on a concept of contractual citizenship in which low-income people needed to be obligated to work and meet certain moral standards in order to earn their rights to public benefits.[19] Public benefits recipients were cast in the media as pathological, amoral people caught in a "cycle of dependency." Welfare mothers were depicted as people who couldn't stop having more and more children and committing welfare fraud.[20] The media uproar focused on racist and sexist images of black "welfare queens" and irresponsible teenage mothers. The mobilization of these images was an essential part of the creation of the Personal Responsibility and Work Opportunity Reconciliation Act of 1996 (PRWORA).[21]

The purpose and result of vilifying welfare recipients and focusing on sexual morality and gender role transgression is the creation of coercive policies designed to force poor people to obey rigid gender and family norms. Marriage incentives and requirements that mothers disclose the paternity of their children are only the most explicit examples of how the moral performance on which benefit receipt is conditional is fundamentally a requirement that poor women rigidly obey conservative notions of gender role and family structure. As countless critics have pointed out, these requirements create horrendous obstacles to women struggling with domestic violence who cannot safely disclose paternity or comply with other aspects of the "maintenance and sustenance of two-parent families" dictated by welfare policy.[22] Additionally, for lesbian mothers the rigidity with which family structure is viewed and regulated by welfare policies and rules makes benefits inaccessible or dependent on remaining closeted.[23]

Perhaps the most insidious problem with the "work + morality = rights" view of contractual citizenship through which the "welfare reform" attacks on welfare were justified is that it is a selectively applied contract.[24] While conservatives portray care-giving work that poor mothers do at home as not being work at all, and demand that as a condition of receiving welfare, mothers engage in workfare programs where they are assigned to work outside the home, gendered home-based work is given value as "real work" for upper-class women. The same week that the PRWORA was passed, Congress granted stay-at-home wives the right to establish IRAs, essentially giving a tax break to nonpoor women who work in the home and recognizing this work as work.[25] Similarly, Sparks points out that the Survivor's Insurance program has provided unstigmatized and far more generous benefits to mothers with children than AFDC/TANF benefits.[26] SI benefits support the decision of a widowed mother to work inside the home caring for children, while the welfare benefits we have seen decimated under the PRWORA utterly devalue this work and characterize it as pathological laziness. As Mink observes, it is no coincidence that SI recipients have been disproportionately white and AFDC/TANF participants have been disproportionately black.[27] The proper performance of gendered citizenship and work for upper-class and disproportionately white women is measured by a different standard than that of poor and disproportionately nonwhite women.

The example of the PRWORA passage, as well as more recent activity around reauthorizing PRWORA, which has included increasing discussion of "healthy marriage promotion,"[28] demonstrates that social welfare programs are explicitly designed to promote oppressive and racialized understandings of gender, sexuality, and family structure. The depiction of the lives of poor women that motivated the PRWORA, and behind which both Democrats and Republicans rallied, made it clear that poor women were responsible for their poverty and that the only remedy was to coerce them into marriage and work. These morality-based understandings of poverty play out in the day-to-day operation of social services programs that emphasize surveillance and gender regulation of poor people.

Failing to Comply

The climate of vilification of the poor and pathologization of the conditions and consequences of poverty produce and operate through day-to-day punitive and coercive structures within poverty service provision. These programs often focus on notions of "compliance" and "noncompliance" among participants. Feminist theorists have provided helpful analysis in this area, examining the ways that access to homeless and domestic violence shelters is mediated through punitive processes where those looking for assistance are treated as morally and intellectually deficient and subjected to humiliating violations of privacy as an integral part of the disincentification of receiving services.[29] Navigating benefits systems, shelter systems, essential medical services, and entanglement with the criminal justice system that is now a central aspect of low-income existence in order to survive is increasingly tied to the ability of each person to meet highly gendered and raced behavioral and expression requirements.[30] While feminist analysis has exposed the hidden agendas of poverty policies to shape women's work and family structure and inhibit the ability of women to be economically independent and escape violent relationships, this analysis has not extended to examine the effects of this system on poor people who also transgress the coercive binary gender system that maintains sexism.

The following two stories from my work with low-income gender-transgressive people illustrate the particular ways in which the incorporation of rigid binary gender expectations into social service provision and the criminal justice system operate in the lives of gender-transgressive people.

Jim's Story

Jim is an intersex person.[31] He was raised as a girl, but during adolescence began to identify as male. To his family, he remained female identified, but in the world he identified as male. The stress of living a "double life" was immense, but he knew it was the only way to maintain a relationship with his family, with whom he was very close. When Jim was nineteen, he was involved in a robbery for which he received a sentence of five years' probation. During the second year of that probation period, Jim was arrested for drug possession and was sentenced to eighteen months of residential drug treatment. Jim was sent to a male residential facility. In a purportedly therapeutic environment, Jim discussed his intersex status with his therapist. His confidentiality was broken, and soon the entire staff and residential population were aware that

Jim was intersex. Jim was facing such severe rape threat with no support or protection from staff that he ultimately ran away from the facility. I met Jim after he had turned himself in, wanting to deal with his criminal justice status so that he could safely apply to college and get on with his life. Jim was in a Brooklyn men's jail, again facing severe rape threat because the jail refused to continue his testosterone treatments, which caused him to menstruate, and when he was strip-searched while menstruating other inmates and staff learned of his status. Jim and I worked together to try to convince the judge in his case that Jim could safely access drug treatment services only in an outpatient setting because of the rape threat he continually faced in residential settings. Even when we had convinced the judge of this, though, we faced the fact that most programs were gender segregated and would not be a safe place for Jim to be known as intersex. When I contacted facilities to find a place for Jim, staff at all levels would ask me questions like "Does he pee sitting or standing?" and "Does he have a penis?" indicating to me that Jim would be treated as a novelty and his intersex status would be a source of gossip. Even the few lesbian and gay drug treatment programs I identified seemed inappropriate because Jim did not identify as gay and was, in fact, quite unfamiliar with gay and lesbian communities and somewhat uncomfortable in queer spaces. Eventually, the judge agreed to let Jim try outpatient treatment, but on a "zero tolerance" policy, where a single relapse would result in jail time. Jim was under enormous stress, engaged in treatment where he was always afraid he might be outed and where his participation in the daily hours of group therapy required hiding his identity. He relapsed and was sentenced to two years in state prison. When I went before the judge to request that Jim be placed in women's prison because of his well-founded fear of sexual assault in men's facilities, the judge's response was "He can't have it both ways." Once again, Jim's intersex status, and his inability to successfully navigate the gender requirements of the extremely violent system in which he was entangled because of involvement in nonviolent poverty-related crimes, was considered part of his criminality and a blameworthy status.

Bianca's Story

Bianca is a transgender woman. In 1999 she was attending high school in the Bronx. After struggling with an internal understanding of herself as a woman for several years, Bianca eventually mustered the courage to come out to her peers and teachers at school. She and another transgender student who were close friends decided to come out together, and arrived at school one day dressed to reflect their female gender identities. They were stopped at the front office and not allowed to enter school. Eventually, they were told to leave and not come back. When their parents called the school to follow up and find out what to do next, their calls were never returned. They were given no referrals to other schools, and no official suspension or expulsion documents. Because of their families' poverty and language barriers, they were never able to successfully get documentation or services from the schools. I met Bianca three years later. She had been trying to find an attorney to take the case and had never found one, and when I met her and began investigating the possibility of bringing a lawsuit, I discovered that the statute of limitations had run out, and she no longer had a claim. When I met Bianca, she was homeless and unemployed and was trying to escape from an abusive relationship. She was afraid to go to the police both because of the retaliation of her boyfriend and because she rightly feared that the police would react badly to her because of her transgender status. Her IDs all said her male name and gender, and there would be no way for her to seek police protection without being identified as transgender. As we searched for places for Bianca to live, we ran up against the fact that all the homeless shelters would only place her according to birth gender, so she would be a woman in an all-men's facility, which she rightly feared would be unsafe and uncomfortable. Women's shelters for domestic violence survivors were unwilling to take her because they did not recognize her as a woman. When Bianca went to apply for welfare she was given an assignment to attend a job center to be placed in a workfare program. When she tried to access the job center, she was severely harassed outside, and when she entered she was outed and humiliated by staff when she attempted to use the women's restroom. Ultimately, she felt too unsafe to return, and her benefits were terminated. Bianca's total lack of income also meant that she had no access to the hormone treatments that she used to maintain a feminine appearance, which was both emotionally necessary for her and kept her safe from some of the harassment and violence she faced when she was identifiable as a trans woman on the street. Bianca felt that her only option for finding income sufficient to pay for the hormones she bought on the street (it would have been more expensive from a doctor, since Medicaid would not cover it even if she could successfully apply for Medicaid) was to engage in illegal sex work. This put her in further danger of police violence, arrest, and private violence. Additionally, because she was accessing injectable hormones through street economies, she was at greater risk of HIV infection and other communicable diseases.

These two cases are typical of my clients in that almost everyone who comes to the Sylvia Rivera Law Project for services is facing serious consequences of failing to fit within a rigid binary gender structure in multiple systems and institutions: welfare, adult or juvenile justice, public education, voluntary or mandated drug treatment, homeless services, and mental and physical health care. "Compliance" is a central issue that my clients face in these systems. They are unable to "comply" or "rehabilitate" because to do either means to match stereotypes associated with their birth genders. Some are kicked off welfare because they fail to wear birth-gender appropriate clothing to "job training" programs that require them to.[32] Others are labeled "sex offenders" in juvenile justice simply because of their transgender identities despite the fact that their criminal offenses were not sex-related, and forced to wear sex offender jumpsuits while locked up and attend sex offender therapy groups. If they cannot or will not remedy their gender transgressions, they cannot complete the rehabilitation process required for release. Some clients lose housing at youth or adult shelters because staff argue that their failures to dress according to birth gender means they are not seriously job hunting, a requirement of the program to maintain housing. The ways that these systems apply rigid gendered expectations to poor people, which are notably not applied to nonpoor people, are manifold, because these systems operate through detailed surveillance coupled with extensive discretion on the part of individual caseworkers and administrators. I find my clients serving the role of example, particularly in adult and juvenile justice contexts, by being humiliated, harassed, or assaulted because of their gender transgressions in a way that communicates clearly to others entangled in those systems exactly what is expected of them. For many transgender, transsexual, or intersex people, this violence results in long-term severe injuries and in death.[33]

The other vitally important component to the inability of gender-transgressive poor people to access benefits and services is the fact that gender segregation remains a central organizing strategy of systems of social control. Employed people with stable housing are subjected to far fewer gender-segregated facilities on a daily basis than poor or homeless people. While we all must contend with bathrooms or locker rooms that are gender segregated, those of us with homes and jobs may even be able to avoid those a good deal of the time, as opposed to homeless people who must always use public facilities that are likely to be segregated and highly policed. Additionally, all the essential services and coercive control institutions (jails, homeless shelters, group homes, drug treatment facilities, foster care facilities, domestic violence shelters, juvenile justice facilities, housing for the mentally ill) that increasingly dominate the lives of poor people and disproportionately of people of color use gender segregation as a part of the gendered social control they maintain.[34] For the most part, these institutions recognize only birth gender, or rely on identity documents such as birth certificates to determine gender. In every state in the United States that allows people to change their gender markers on their birth certificates, evidence of sex reassignment surgery is required.[35]

As I have written elsewhere,[36] the reliance on medical evidence in all legal contexts in which transgender and other gender-transgressive people struggle for recognition or rights is highly problematic. Whether seeking to prove our marriages valid so that we can keep our parental rights or access our spouse's estate,[37] or attempting to change our names and gender on our identity documents so that we can apply for educational or employment opportunities,[38] or when attempting to access sex-segregated facilities of various kinds,[39] medical evidence remains the defining factor in determining our rights. This is problematic because access to gender-related medical intervention is usually conditioned on successful performance of rigidly defined and harshly enforced understandings of binary gender,[40] because many gender-transgressive people may not wish to undergo medical intervention, and because medical care of all kinds, but particularly gender-related medical care, remains extremely inaccessible to most low-income gender-transgressive people.[41]

The combination of the disproportionate poverty of gender-transgressive people resulting from widespread discrimination, the overincarceration of the poor, the inaccessibility of social services and alternatives to incarceration to gender-transgressive people because of a gender segregation of these services and sex designation change requiring medical evidence of inaccessible procedures, and the heightened danger of criminal justice entanglement for those who cannot or will not comply with the gender coercion of criminal justice systems is especially deadly when coupled with the utter lack of individual or policy advocacy for low-income gender-transgressive people. Surviving on public assistance, using social services, and dealing with criminal justice system entanglement increasingly requires access to legal services.[42] For gender-transgressive people, finding a legal advocate can be especially difficult. My clients consistently report experiencing extreme disrespect when attempting to access legal services, having their cases rejected or ignored by the agencies they turn to, and feeling so unwelcome and humiliated that they often do not return for services. Non-LGBT social/legal services agencies, for the most part, are completely unprepared to provide respectful or effective advocacy to gender-transgressive people.[43] At the same time, LGBT organizations typically do not provide these services.

Asking for More

The most well-funded organizations in the lesbian and gay movement do not provide direct legal services to low-income people, but instead focus their resources on high-profile impact litigation cases and policy efforts. Most of these efforts have traditionally focused on concerns central to the lives of nonpoor lesbian and gay people and have ignored the most pressing issues in the lives of poor people, people of color, and transgender people. The "gay agenda" has been about passing our apartments to each other when we die, not about increasing affordable housing or opposing illegal eviction. It has been about getting our partnerships recognized so our partners can share our private health benefits, not about defending Medicaid rights or demanding universal health care. It has been about getting our young sons into Boy Scouts, not about advocating for the countless/uncounted queer and trans youth struggling against a growing industry of youth incarceration. It has been about working to put more punishment power in the hands of an overtly racist criminal system with passage of hate crimes laws, not about opposing the mass incarceration of a generation of men of color, or fighting the abuse of queer and trans people in adult and juvenile justice settings.

The debates about gender identity inclusion in the federal Employment Non-Discrimination Act (ENDA)[44] or the exclusion of gender identity protection from New York State's Sexual Orientation Non-Discrimination Act (SONDA)[45] are only the most blatant examples of the mainstream lesbian and gay movement's lack of commitment to gender-transgressive populations, but the failure of "LGBT" dollars, services, and resources to reach the lives of low-income people is even more widespread. What it means in the lives of low-income gender-transgressive people is that not only do they lack essential legal protections, they cannot find effective advocacy to access the fair treatment, services, or benefits they are entitled to. Unfortunately, the trend in gender rights litigation toward the recognition of gender identity change only in the context of medicalization maintains this imbalance. The history of gender rights litigation seems to be progressing with increasing recognition of membership in the "new" gender category, but only for those transgender people who have undergone medical intervention. The vast majority of gender-transgressive people who will either not want or not be able to afford such intervention remain unprotected. No doubt, the structure of our legal system is partially responsible for this result. Lawyers, in general, will pick the most favorable plaintiff for any case they want to bring, and bring the most conservative claims they can to win for the client they are representing. In fact, it is a part of our ethical obligation to represent the interests of our client above all else, including above our obligations to a movement or to a broader set of plaintiffs who will not be served if gender expression rights are made reliant on medical intervention.

On a broader level, though, the distribution of resources (services, policy and legislative advocacy, direct representation) is something that our movements can be more responsible about than they have been. Transgender and gender-transgressive movements are at a moment of building and expansion, and in some senses institutionalization. We are increasingly forming organizations, we are seeking funding, we are forming a growing national and international conversation seeking an end to the inequality and oppression we have struggled against. It is in this moment that it is most urgent for us to examine where our resources have been going, and what unintentional consequences may result from following the model of the lesbian and gay rights movement. Inevitably, given the context of capitalism in which transliberation activism occurs, and the economic/educational privilege that usually accompanies the ability to secure paid "movement leader" jobs in nonprofits and to raise money to start and maintain movement organizations, the voices of low-income people and people of color will remain underincluded without a serious commitment to intervention.[46] As long as our agendas are determined by those with access to these resources, and those individuals prioritize struggles in which they can see themselves (i.e., employment discrimination for white-collar workers, private health-care discrimination, housing discrimination in the private market, inheritance issues relating to marriage rights) while ignoring or marginalizing struggles that are not a common part of their lives and the lives of those of their class status (welfare, Medicaid, incarceration, police brutality, illegal eviction, institutionalization for mental illness), we will fail to see meaningful change in the lives of those who suffer the most acute effects of the coercive binary gender system. A central concern must be the balancing of resources between legislative efforts, impact litigation, and direct legal representation and advocacy and organizing.

Wendy Brown's recent writing on the role of notions of tolerance in civil rights struggles is helpful here. Brown describes how

> tolerance involves a retreat from larger justice projects on the part of liberals and leftists. . . . Tolerance as a primary political virtue involves a very thin notion of citizenship, a passive notion of co-existence. More importantly, it casts differences as given—not as products of inequality or domination, but as intrinsic and something we have to bear in the social and political world; also as something we would rather not bear—you only tolerate that which you wish you didn't have to. Tolerance is also part of a complex shell game that liberalism plays with equality and difference—tolerance is extended by the state whenever equality is refused or attenuated.[47]

As Brown articulates, tolerance is a far lesser demand than equality and is based on a shallower analysis of how hierarchy and oppression operate than a demand for equality is. It obscures the meaning of oppression and hierarchy and replaces it with a power-neutral concept of difference that makes characteristics of social organization like race, gender, or ability into personal qualities that should be tolerated. It erases the possibility of a systemic understanding of power and eclipses the possibilities of more meaningful systemic remedies. Similarly, tolerance enters our civil rights struggles at some points as a struggle merely for nondiscrimination, not for actual equality. In the context of gender expression rights, the demand for nondiscrimination operates as a lesser demand than gender self-determination, and the shortcomings of this demand can be seen in the lives of those who are supposedly legally protected against gender identity discrimination but still suffer extreme oppression because of their gender transgressions. Even in those jurisdictions that have nondiscrimination policies that cover a variety of contexts such as employment, education, housing, and public accommodations, this coverage frequently offers no assistance to gender-transgressive people in the context of sex-segregated facilities, either because of preexisting carve-outs for sex-segregated facilities in the law,[48] or because judges refuse to enforce nondiscrimination when sex-segregated facilities are at issue.[49] Beyond that, nondiscrimination policies do not speak to the day-to-day struggles that gender-transgressive people, and in particular low-income gender-transgressive people, face with sex segregation and the gendering of legal identity. For the most part, they do nothing to resolve issues like incarceration according to birth gender, the requirement of proving genital surgery in order to get birth certificate sex designation changed, or incorrect placement in gender-segregated facilities such as homeless shelters, group homes, bathrooms, and locker rooms.[50] While nondiscrimination policies may provide remedies in some important contexts, they do not address the broader problem that prevents gender self-determination and creates daily dangerous and deadly situations for poor, gender-transgressive people: the existence of legal gender classification. The choice to pursue nondiscrimination policies (to the extent that LGBT movements have included gender identity in the nondiscrimination legislation they have drafted at all) rather than to pursue a strategy of deregulating gender in state agencies, with service providers, and with regard to government-issued identification suggests an adoption of this lesser demand. This choice, most importantly, ignores the daily struggles that disproportionately impact low-income gender-transgressive people and fails to meaningfully oppose the state regulation of gender that, as I mentioned above, tends to make room only for those gender-transgressive people who can afford medical intervention to bring them into line with the state's construction of male or female gender.

The notion that we should put our movement resources into a struggle for gender identity nondiscrimination in employment, but not concern ourselves with the fact that there is no one to represent struggling gender-transgressive people being harassed on workfare jobsites or raped in prisons or falsely arrested for prostitution, indicates a problem in terms of the depth and breadth of liberation we are seeking. LGBT movement activists have the power to determine whether the liberation we pursue will follow a tolerance model, making room for those who can access private employment and housing to not experience discrimination there because of their gender identities (and possibly conditioned on medical intervention), or we can quest for a broader liberation that demands gender self-determination for all people regardless of their positions in capitalist economies. To make the latter real, we need to strategize beyond a notion that if we win rights for the most sympathetic and normal of our lot first, the others will be protected in time. Instead, we should be concerned that the breadth of our vision will determine the victories we obtain. If we want to end oppression on the basis of gender identity and expression for all people, we need to examine how the rigid regulation of binary gender is a core element of participation in our capitalist economy, how the hyperregulation of poor people's gender and sexuality has propped up that system, and how this has resulted in disproportionate poverty and incarceration for poor, gender-transgressive people. Starting from that analysis, we can undertake strategies to combat these problems and make sure that our activism does not further entrench this regulation by relying on pathologization and medicalization to articulate gender rights.

Is it politically viable to work toward gender self-determination rather than just nondiscrimination? Yes. Policy change toward gender self-determination requires many of the same strategies as nondiscrimination. We need to change law and policy state by state to reduce medical evidence requirements for changing gender designation on birth certificates and drivers' licenses, and work toward eliminating gender markers on these documents altogether. We need to prioritize sex-segregated facilities in our nondiscrimination laws, explicitly stating that as part of nondiscrimination, no one can be forced to use facilities that do not comport with their gender identities. We need to expand resources for trainings and build political alliances so that domestic violence shelter providers and activists, homeless shelter providers and activists, welfare rights activists, the prison abolition movement, and others whose work is intimately tied to the fates of poor, gender-transgressive people come to understand gender self-determination and the elimination of sex segregation as a core component of the equality and justice their work seeks.

Even more broadly, we need to transfer resources toward direct services for low-income people struggling with systems that have been unremarked on by a mainstream gay and lesbian rights movement that has focused too much attention toward equality for middle- and high-income people. Our political agendas come from what our leaders know about our communities and communicate to media and decision makers. To make those agendas meaningfully inclusive of those most marginalized by the sexual and gender regulation that dominates our lives under capitalism, we need to change where that knowledge is coming from. This requires changing who our leaders are and combating the race, education, gender, and class privilege that operates to make paid and resourced LGBT activism predominately white, upper-class, nongender transgressive, nonimmigrant, able-bodied, and educationally privileged. It also requires putting resources toward directly assisting those most in need, so that we can have as full an understanding as possible of the obstacles they are facing and the strategies that justice requires.

Single-issue politics has left people who struggle against connecting and overlapping oppressions out in the cold for too long. It is not too much to ask that anticapitalist movements engage principles of gender and sexual deregulation and antiracism in their analysis and activism, and prioritize those who face extreme consequences of a capitalist system that they fall to the bottom of because of heterosexism, binary gender rigidity, and racism. At the same time, movements focused on heterosexism and transphobia must be held accountable to those who struggle with systems motivated by antipoor and racist cultural understandings. Sexual and gender liberation will never be meaningful if it is contingent on economic privilege, racial privilege, or genital status.

Times are no doubt changing. The consolidation of global capital and the boldness of imperial conquests are rising to new heights. At the same time, the number of people distressed and endangered by these trends grows daily, and with that the potential for victorious resistance. Gender-transgressive people are part of the majority of people worldwide who are disserved and endangered by the economic arrangements designed to siphon resources away from the masses for the benefit of the few. Our analysis, and our power, should come from the understanding of our position within that majority and within that resistance. Our struggles and concerns have been marginalized and forgotten too often when we have depended on purported allies whose failure to engage questions of racial and economic oppression exclude us from reaping benefits from their work. Now is the time to forge new alliances, demand accountability from movements that purport to represent us, and create and pursue a broad, daring vision of the change we are seeking.

Notes

Many people generously provided editorial advice for this chapter. Thanks to Craig Willse, Paisley Currah, Danny McGee, Franklin Romeo, Jenny Robertson, Bridge Joyce, and Richard M. Juang for their help. The asterisks that appear with page numbers in these notes refer to screen page numbers from a database.

1. Frances Fox Piven and Richard Clower, *Regulating the Poor* (New York: Vintage, 1993).

2. Ibid.

3. Janice Raymond, *The Transsexual Empire* (New York: Teachers College Press, 1994); Dwight B. Billings and Thomas Urban, "The Socio-Medical Construction of Transsexualism: An Interpretation and Critique," *Social Problems* 29 (1982): 266, 276. Billings and Urban are engaged in an anticapitalist critique of the gender-regulating process of sex reassignment therapy and the adoption of norm-supporting narratives by patients seeking medical interventions. However, rather than focusing on the problems of a coercive system that demands the performance of rigid gender norms by people seeking body alteration, they vilify transgender people for performing these narratives. The resulting analysis paints trans subjects as clueless gender upholders, who are buying our way out of our gender distress and ruining any radical potential for disrupting gender norms. For more on the strategic uses of medical narratives by trans subjects, and the attribution of oppressive medical understandings of gender to trans people, see Dean Spade, "Mutilating Gender," *makezine* (spring 2002), http://makezine.org/mutilate.html.

4. Theorists and activists who produce intersectional and multi-issue queer and trans analysis and activism continually critique these failures. See, for example, Eli Clare, *Exile and Pride* (Cambridge, MA: South End, 1999); Amber Hollibaugh, "Queers without Money," *Village Voice*, June 2001; Cathy Cohen, "Punks, Bulldaggers, and Welfare Queens: The Radical Potential of Queer Politics?" *GLQ* 3 (1997): 437; Craig Willse and Dean Spade, "Confronting the Limits of Gay Hate Crimes Activism: A Radical Critique," *Chicano-Latino Law Review* 21 (2000): 38–49; Sylvia Rivera, "Queens in Exile, the Forgotten Ones," in *Genderqueer: Voices from Beyond the Binary*, ed. Joan Nestle et al. (New York: Alyson, 2002), 67–85; Richard E. Blum, Barbara Ann Perina, and Joseph Nicholas DeFilippis, "Why Welfare Is a Queer Issue," *NYU Review of Law and Social Change* 26 (2001): 207.

5. According to the National Gay and Lesbian Task Force, 76 percent of the U.S. population lives in jurisdictions that are not covered by antidiscrimination laws that include prohibitions on gender identity discrimination. See L. Mottet, "Populations of Jurisdictions with Explicitly Transgender Anti-Discrimination Laws" (Washington, DC: National Gay and Lesbian Task Force, 2003), http://ngltf.org/downloads/TransIncPops.pdf. Even those who are covered may find these laws ineffectual when they try to enforce their rights before biased judges. See *Goins v. West Group*, 635 N.W.2d 717 (Minn. 2001) (finding that an employer's refusal to allow a transgender employee access to the women's bathroom was not gender identity discrimination); *Hispanic AIDS Forum v. Bruno*, 792 N.Y.S. 2d 43 (2005). Further, even for those who live in jurisdictions where gender identity discrimination is prohibited, seeking redress may be difficult because of a lack of attorneys willing to take cases with transgender

plaintiffs and because of the failure of city governments to enforce these provisions. See *Local Laws of the City of New York* 3, 2002, http://www.council.nyc.ny.us/pdf_files/bills/law02003.pdf; Duncan Osborne, "Trans Advocates Allege Foot-Dragging," *Gay City News*, June 17, 2004; Cyd Zeigler Jr., "Trans Protection Compromised?" *New York Blade*, May 28, 2004.

6. *Doe v. Bell*, 2003 WL 355603 at *1–2 (N.Y. Sup. Ct. 2003) (finding that group home's policy forbidding transgender youth from dressing in skirts and dresses was illegal).

7. L. Mottet and J. Ohle, *Transitioning Our Shelters: A Guide to Making Homeless Shelters Safe for Transgender People* (Washington, DC: National Gay and Lesbian Task Force, 2003). In 2006 transgender advocates succeeded in winning a written policy in the Department of Homeless Service of New York City addressing the rights of transgender people seeking shelter in the city's facilities. The policy explicitly states that transgender people may not be placed in shelters that do not comport with their self-identified gender and may not be forced to wear clothing associated with their birth gender. Years of advocacy were required to put this policy, which is not yet being enforced as of this writing, in place. A handful of cities in North America, including Boston, San Francisco, and Toronto, have policies addressing the discrimination and exclusion transgender people face in shelter systems. For more information on these policies, see www.srlp.org.

8. *Oiler v. Winn-Dixie Louisiana, Inc.*, 2002 WL 31098541 at *1 (September 16, 2002) (where a grocery store loader and truck driver was fired for cross-dressing off the job).

9. I use the term *gender self-determination* throughout this chapter, and more broadly in my political work, as a tool to express opposition to the coercive mechanisms of the binary gender system (everything from assignment of birth gender to gender segregation of bathrooms to targeting of trans people by police). I use this term strategically while also recognizing that any notion of self-determination is bound up in understandings of individuality that support capitalist concepts like individual "freedom to sell labor" that obscure the mechanisms of oppression we are seeking to overcome. While I want to think past and reconceptualize articulations of individuality and replace them with understandings of community-centered change, mobilizing around ending coercive gender within a political framework where we still experience ourselves through heavily entrenched concepts of individuality and freedom requires strategic employment of ideas like self-determination.

10. See Cheryl I. Harris, "Whiteness as Property," in *Critical Race Theory Reader*, ed. Kimberlè Crenshaw, Neil Gotanda, Garry Peller, and Kendall Thomas (New York: New Press, 1996), 276–91. Harris traces the racial origins of property ownership, both in terms of how race has defined property status—with one's ability to own property or to be property of another determined by race—and in terms of how racial identity itself has been attributed a property status through libel and slander laws. She argues that racial identity still has property value recognized and protected by American law. Gender and sexual orientation have also, at times, had property status protected in various ways in the law. In the case of gender, clearly the right to own property has at times been a gender-based right, and, additionally, we see value being assigned to sexuality in tort claims of Loss of Consortium, typically brought by spouses claiming

that they have been damaged by the loss of sexual service from their spouses because of whatever tort was committed. Additionally, defamation cases regarding false accusations of homosexuality similarly indicate a legal protection of heterosexual identity. See E. Yatar, "Defamation, Privacy, and the Changing Social Status of Homosexuality: Re-Thinking Supreme Court Gay Rights Jurisprudence," *Law and Sexuality* 12 (2003): 119–56.

11. The court decisions establishing protection for women laborers are based on this protectionist logic: "It is manifest that this established principle is peculiarly applicable in relation to the employment of women in whose protection the state has a special interest. That phase of the subject received elaborate consideration in *Muller v. Oregon* (1908) 208 U.S. 412, 28 S.Ct. 324, 326, 52 L.Ed. 551, 13 Ann.Cas. 957, where the constitutional authority of the state to limit the working hours of women was sustained. We emphasized the consideration that 'woman's physical structure and the performance of maternal functions place her at a disadvantage in the struggle for subsistence' and that her physical well being 'becomes an object of public interest and care in order to preserve the strength and vigor of the race.' We emphasized the need of protecting women against oppression despite her possession of contractual rights. We said that 'though limitations upon personal and contractual rights may be removed by legislation, there is that in her disposition and habits of life which will operate against a full assertion of those rights. She will still be where some legislation to protect her seems necessary to secure a real equality of right.' Hence she was 'properly placed in a class by herself, and legislation designed for her protection may be sustained, even when like legislation is not necessary for men, and could not be sustained'" (*West Coast Hotel v. Parrish*, 57 S.Ct. 578, at 583 [upholding Washington State's minimum wage law for women]).

12. Gwendolyn Mink, "The Lady and the Tramp: Gender, Race, and the Origins of the American Welfare State," in *Women, the State, and Welfare*, ed. Linda Gordon (Madison: University of Wisconsin Press, 1990), 92–122.

13. Ibid., 94.

14. Ibid.

15. Ibid., 97.

16. Ibid., 99.

17. Ibid., 114.

18. See J. Heinz and N. Folbre, *The Ultimate Field Guide to the U.S. Economy: A Compact and Irreverent Guide to Economic Life in America* (New York: New Press, 2000).

19. Holloway Sparks, "Queens, Teens, and Model Mothers: Race, Gender, and the Discourse of Welfare Reform," in *Race and the Politics of Welfare Reform*, ed. Sanford F. Schram, Joe Soss, and Richard C. Fording (Ann Arbor: University of Michigan Press, 2003), 188–89.

20. See Susan James and Beth Harris, "Gimme Shelter: Battering and Poverty," in *For Crying Out Loud: Women's Poverty in the United States*, ed. Diane Dujon and Ann Withorn (Boston: South End, 1996), 57–66.

21. Sparks, "Queens, Teens, and Model Mothers," 171. Then senator John Ashcroft utilized the contractual view of citizenship described by Sparks during one of the final debates on welfare reform in the 104th Congress: "I think it is time for us to limit the amount of time that people can be on welfare. It is time for us to provide

disincentives to bear children out of wedlock. It is time for us to provide powerful incentives for people to go to work. It is time for us to say that, if you are on welfare, you
should be off drugs. It is time for us to say that, if you are on welfare, your children
should be in school. . . . You have to be responsible for what you are doing. We are not
going to continue to support you in a way in which you abdicate, you simply run
from, you hide from, your responsibility as a citizen" (quoted in Sparks, "Queens,
Teens, and Model Mothers," 190).

22. Sparks, "Queens, Teens, and Model Mothers," 189.

23. See Blum, Perina, and DeFilippis, "Why Welfare Is a Queer Issue," 207.

24. Sparks, "Queens, Teens, and Model Mothers," 190.

25. Gwendolyn Mink, *Welfare's End* (Ithaca, NY: Cornell University Press,
1998), 134.

26. Sparks, "Queens, Teens, and Model Mothers," 191.

27. Mink, *Welfare's End*, 28.

28. Current Republican proposals for the reauthorization include an increase in
work requirements to forty hours a week and $200 million in federal grants plus $100
million in state matching grants for marriage promotion programs. See Jonathan Ris-
kind, "House Set to Revisit Welfare Reform This Week: Legislators to Vote on Bill
Very Similar to One Passed in May," *Columbus Dispatch*, February 12, 2003. See also
Sharon Tubbs and Thomas C. Tobin, "When Government Wants Marriage Reform,"
St. Petersburg Times, February 8, 2003; Sharon Lerner, "Marriage on the Mind: The
Bush Administration's Misguided Poverty Cure," *The Nation*, July 5, 2004.

29. See Roofless Women's Action Research Mobilization, "A Hole in My Soul:
Experiences of Homeless Women," ed. Marie Kennedy, in Dujon and Withorn, *For
Crying Out Loud*, 41–56.

30. I recently participated in a bar association panel about queer and trans youth
in juvenile justice and foster care at which a youth service provider smilingly described
continued efforts to not let the transgender youth leave the residence she supervised
looking like "hos." Her determination that an aspect of receiving housing at her facility
should include compliance with particular expressions of femininity, and her use of a
racialized term to indicate the prohibited expression, exemplifies the type of race/gen-
der expression management that typically becomes the concern of poverty service
providers measuring compliance.

31. Intersex people are people who have physical conditions that make their bodies
difficult to classify under current medical understandings of what constitutes a "male"
or "female" body. Intersex activists are working to stop the infant and childhood surgeries that intersex people are frequently subjected to as doctors attempt to bring
their bodies into line with medical expectations of what a male or female body should
look like. For more information on intersex conditions and intersex activism, see the
Web site of the Intersex Society of North America, www.isna.org.

32. Blum, Perina, and DeFilippis, "Why Welfare Is a Queer Issue," 213.

33. See Remembering Our Dead, http://www.rememberingourdead.org.

34. A common response to questions about the wisdom of sex segregation in jails,
prisons, shelters, and other contexts is a concern for women's safety and a suggestion
that sex segregation exists to prevent violence against women. While women's safety
should be of paramount concern to service providers and corrections staff, there is not

sufficient evidence that sex segregation policies are motivated by concern for women's safety or that women are safe in these institutions. In fact, systemic sexual assault and violence against women are more often than not a fundamental part of the coercive control exercised over poor women in these institutions. Examining the violence against women and gender-transgressive people in these settings should be a project that advocates for women's safety are deeply engaged in with advocates for gender self-determination, as these two populations are frequently targets for related violence. The first step may be to acknowledge that control of low-income people, not safety, is the aim of these institutions. See R. Ralph, "Nowhere to Hide: Retaliation against Women in Michigan State Prisons," *Human Rights Watch* 10 (1998), http://hrw.org/reports98/women/.

35. See *Ala. Code* § 22–9A-19 (2002) (order of court of competent jurisdiction and surgery required); *Ariz. Rev. Stat.* § 36–326 (2001) (change may be made based on sworn statement from licensed physician attesting to either surgical operation or chromosomal count, although registrar may require further evidence); *Ark. Code Ann.* § 20–18–307 (2002) (order of court of competent jurisdiction and surgery required); *Cal. Health & Safety Code* § 103425, 103430 (2002 Supp.) (court order and surgery apparently required); *Colo. Rev. Stat. Ann.* § 25–2-115 (2002) (same); *D.C. Code Ann.* § 7–217 (2002) (same); *Ga. Code Ann.* § 31–10–23 (2002) (same); *Haw. Rev. Stat.* § 338–17.7 (2002) (physician affidavit and surgery required; registrar can require additional information); 410 *Ill. Comp. Stat.* 535/17 (2002) (same); *Iowa Code* § 144.23 (2002) (physician affidavit and surgery "or other treatment"); *La. Rev. Stat. Ann.* § 40: 62 (2002) (order of court of competent jurisdiction and surgery required); *Mass. Ann. Laws* chap. 46, § 13 (2002) (same); *Mich. Comp. Laws* § 333.2831 (2002) (affidavit of physician certifying sex reassignment surgery); *Miss. Code Ann.* § 41–57–21 (2001) (registrar may correct certificate that contains incorrect sex on affidavit of two persons having personal knowledge of facts; not clear whether restricted to initial error in certificate or includes gender change); *Mo. Rev. Stat* § 193.215 (2001) (order of court of competent jurisdiction and surgery required); *Neb. Rev. Stat.* § 71–604.1 (2002) (affidavit of physician as to sex reassignment surgery and order of court of competent jurisdiction changing name required); *N.J. Stat. Ann.* 26:8–40.12 (2002) (certificate from physician attesting to surgery and order of court of competent jurisdiction changing name); *N.M. Stat. Ann.* § 24–14–25 (2002) (same); *N.C. Gen. Stat.* 130A-118 (2001) (affidavit of physician attesting to sex reassignment surgery); *Or. Rev. Stat.* § 432.235 (2001) (order of court of competent jurisdiction and surgery required); *Utah Code Ann.* § 26-2-11 (2002) (order of Utah District Court or court of competent jurisdiction of another state required; no specific requirement of surgery); *Va. Code Ann.* § 32.1–269 (2002) (order of court of competent jurisdiction indicating sex has been changed by "medical procedure"); *Wis. Stat.* § 69.15 (2001) (order of court or administrative order) cited in *Matter of Heilig*, 2003 WL 282856 at *15 n.8 (Md. 2003). See also Lambda Legal Defense and Education Fund, Resources: Transgender Issues, http://www.lambdalegal.org/cgi-bin/iowa/documents/record?record=1162 (November 12, 2002) (accessed March 30, 2003).

36. Dean Spade, "Resisting Medicine, Re/modeling Gender," *Berkeley Women's Law Journal* 18 (2003): 16–26.

37. *In re Estate of Gardiner,* 42 P.3d 120 (Kan. 2002); *Kantaras v. Kantaras,* Case No. 98–5375CA (Circuit Court of the Sixth Judicial Circuit, Pasco County, Florida, February 19, 2003).

38. See, for example, *In re Rivera,* 165 Misc.2d 307, 627 N.Y.S.2d 241 (Civ. Ct. Bx. Co. 1995); *Application of Anonymous,* 155 Misc.2d 241, 587 N.Y.S.2d 548 (N.Y.City Civ.Ct., August 27, 1992); *Matter of Anonymous,* 153 Misc.2d 893, 582 N.Y.S.2d 941 (N.Y.City Civ.Ct., March 27, 1992); but see, *In re Guido,* 2003 WL 22471153, 2003 N.Y. Slip Op. 23821 (N.Y. Civ.Ct., October 24, 2003).

39. See Jody Marksamer and Dylan Vade, "Gender Neutral Bathroom Survey," http://www.transgenderlawcenter.org/documents/safe_WC_survey_results.html (2001) (accessed March 30, 2003). See Dean Spade, "2 Legit 2 Quit, Piss & Vinegar," http://www.makezine.org/2legit.html (accessed March 14, 2003).

40. See Spade, "Resisting Medicine," 16–26, for a broader discussion of the gender regulation accomplished by medical approaches to gender role distress.

41. Most states in the United States still explicitly exclude "sex reassignment related care" from Medicaid coverage, and most medical insurance companies still exclude this care from coverage. See *Smith v. Rasmussen,* 249 F.3d 755 (8th Cir. 2001) (reversing district court's ruling and holding that Iowa's rule denying coverage for SRS was not arbitrary or inconsistent with the Medicaid Act); *Rush v. Parham,* 625 F.2d 1150 (5th Cir. 1980) (reversing district court's ruling that Georgia's Medicaid program could not categorically deny coverage for SRS); 18 NYCRR § 505.2(l). See N.Y. St. Reg. (March 25, 1998) at 5; Ill. Admin. Code tit. 89 at 140.6(1); 55 Pa. Code at 1163.59(a)(1); Alaska Admin. Code tit. 7, at 43.385(a)(1); Medicare Program: National Coverage Decisions, 54 Fed. Reg. 34555, 34572 (August 21, 1989); 32 C.F.R. at 199.4(e)(7) (excluding sex reassignment surgeries from the Civilian Health and Medical Program of the Uniformed Services); but see *J.D. v. Lackner,* 80 Cal. App. 3d 90 (Cal. Ct. App. 1978).

42. In the context of welfare reform, illegal termination of benefits has been a significant strategy on the part of government agencies looking to "slash the rolls." When benefits are illegally terminated, recipients are entitled to a hearing. In New York City, these hearings, ironically called "fair hearings," are estimated to average less than two minutes, and recipients without representation typically are not permitted to utter a word before the hearing is over. With representation, however, these hearings can frequently be won because the basis for these terminations and the procedures for them are usually executed in violation of federal and state regulations and city policies. In this context, maintaining benefits for any period of time, and sometimes even just getting through the application process, will require access to an advocate who knows the applicable law and can argue on behalf of a wronged recipient. Similarly, accessing basic social services, including housing programs, often requires outside advocacy. My clients are frequently rejected from housing programs on the basis of their gender identities, and only through advocacy can a facility be convinced that this is illegal discrimination. In the criminal justice context, my clients consistently report that their assigned attorneys are blatantly transphobic toward them, refuse to return their calls, advocate against their interests in situations where they are facing sentencing to sex-segregated facilities of one kind or another, and are generally very disrespectful.

43. A good example of this ineffective advocacy came from one of my trainings for criminal attorneys. An attorney who attended described an incident in which she was representing two transgender women that, after sitting through most of the training, she was concerned she had handled badly. She said that she had never spoken to her clients about their gender identities, although she was aware that they were transgender, because she did not know how. When they came before the judge, he asked her what gender her clients were, and she said, "I don't know." The court clerk piped in that they were male according to their criminal records. The judge told the lawyer that he wanted to sentence them to women's drug treatment because they appeared to be women, and asked what the lawyer thought of this. The lawyer responded that she did not think he could do that. Clearly, the fact that she had never discussed gender identity with her clients, or addressed the fact that they were facing sentencing in sex-segregated facilities, caused her to miss a rare opportunity to work with a judge who may have provided her clients with a safer option than they ultimately got. In fact, her input seems in this anecdote to have harmed her clients' chances at a beneficial determination by the judge. I hear stories like this repeatedly in trainings, suggesting that even well-meaning providers are so unprepared to assist gender-transgressive clients that they may actually harm their clients.

44. See L. Mottet, *Partial Equality* (Washington, DC: National Gay and Lesbian Task Force, 2003), http://www.ngltf.org/library/partialeq.htm.

45. H. Humm, "Unity Eludes SONDA Advocates, Gender Identity Divides Duane, Pride Agenda," *Gay City News,* December 13, 2002, http://www.gaycitynews.com/gcn29/unity.html; K. Krawchuk, "SONDA Bill Heads to Senate," *Capital News 9* (Albany, NY), 2002, http://www.capitalnews9.com/content/headlines/?SecID=33& ArID=7580.

46. Significant inequalities in access to education persist. In 1997 less than 75 percent of African Americans and less than 55 percent of Latinos had completed four years of high school, and less than 14 percent of either group had completed four years of college. Cuts in financial aid for college students have reinforced a decline in the percentage of low-income high school graduates going to college (Heinz and Folbre, *Ultimate Field Guide to the U.S. Economy,* 74). Further, the end of affirmative action policies in higher education and new rules making people with drug convictions ineligible for federal financial aid have reduced access to higher education for poor communities and communities that are overexposed to police enforcement.

47. Charlie Bertsch, "Interview with Wendy Brown," in *The Anti-Capitalism Reader: Imagining a Geography of Opposition,* ed. Joel Schalit (New York: Akashic Books, 2002), 209.

48. In New York City, while we have celebrated the success of the passage of Local Law 3 expanding protection of the city's Human Rights Law to include gender identity discrimination, we have also been very concerned about our ability to use this law effectively when trans people face discrimination in sex-segregated housing, because of a preexisting carve-out in section 8–107 of the city's administrative code. It reads: "(k) Applicability; dormitory-type housing accommodations. The provisions of this subdivision which prohibit distinctions on the basis of gender and whether children are, may be or would be residing with a person shall not apply to dormitory-type

housing accommodations including, but not limited to, shelters for the homeless where such distinctions are intended to recognize generally accepted values of personal modesty and privacy or to protect the health, safety or welfare of families with children." No doubt, many other jurisdictions will face similar problems with carve-outs that preexist gender identity protection but seriously impair the ability of advocates to argue that gender-transgressive people should be able to access sex-segregated facilities according to our lived genders rather than birth gender. The existence of these carve-outs may undermine the effectiveness of these laws in circumstances that are among the most dire for many transgender people, such as homeless shelters, group homes, and assisted-living facilities.

49. *Goins v. West Group,* 635 N.W.2d 717 (Minn. 2001).

50. In Boston, activists achieved a rare victory regarding sex-segregated facilities with the passage of an antidiscrimination ordinance that protects the rights of transgender people to access facilities in accordance with gender identity rather than birth gender. See Gay and Lesbian Advocates and Defenders, http://glad.org/Rights/Boston_TG_Ordinance.pdf.

12. Transgendering the Politics of Recognition

Richard M. Juang

Being recognized within a liberal democracy means being valued, having one's dignity protected, and possessing some access to public self-expression. The struggle for recognition's key components—value, dignity, and self-expression—is a cornerstone of modern U.S. political, social, and cultural activity. Despite its unquantifiability, recognition's importance can be measured by the consequences of its absence: an unvalued person readily becomes a target or a scapegoat for the hatred of others and begins to see himself or herself only through the lens of such hatred. An existence restricted to purely private expressions of the self, to the closet, becomes corrosive.

Although recognition is insufficient as a political goal—recognition alone will not solve serious problems of economic inequality—it is also an inevitable and indispensable part of the transgender movement. The only acceptable vision of a just society includes equal recognition for transgender and nontransgender persons alike. While short-term, tactical compromises in the struggle for our rights are inevitable (e.g., allowing employers to require a consistent gender presentation in order to gain the right to determine for oneself what that gender presentation will be), a society in which we finally settle for anything short of the full array of rights and privileges enjoyed by nontrans citizens will remain an unjust society. Such an ethical horizon is not a utopian fantasy but is inherent in the very idea of justice. As John Rawls observes, inherent to a concept of justice is the principle that "each person possesses an inviolability founded on justice that even the welfare of society as a whole cannot override. For this reason justice denies that the loss of freedom for some is made right by a greater good shared by others. It does not allow that the sacrifices imposed on a few are outweighed by the larger sum of advantages enjoyed by many."[1]

To encompass all trans persons, a robust transgender politics of recognition should address the discriminations and prejudices targeted not only against gender but against racial and ethnic differences. Present discussions of transgender issues in the classroom, mass media, and everyday conversation separate out transphobia, heterosexism, and misogyny from racism, ethnocentrism, and Eurocentrism. This separation misrepresents how oppressive forces intersect in practice: racism is frequently gendered, while gender discrimination is often shaped by racism. In the first half of this chapter, I hope to outline some of the ways that antitransgender discrimination and violence are often accompanied by racial and ethnic discriminations, and, conversely, situations interpreted as instances of racial and ethnic injustice often also involve a policing of gender and sexual boundaries. Rather than provide a wide survey of examples, I focus on two seemingly unconnected events separated by over a decade: the deaths of Tyra Hunter and Vincent Chin. In turn, our ability to address hate violence more generally depends on an expanded politics of recognition.

Articulating a web of connections does not mean that we ignore the complex differences among identities and forms of discrimination. Indeed, accuracy demands that we attend to the different origins, histories, and consequences of structures of oppression. While strategically useful in many instances, the representation of broad ranges of racial and gender identities under rubrics such as "persons of color" and "transgender" risks ignoring substantial cultural and economic realities that define and shape identities. One risks, in essence, the very kind of nonrecognition that a politics of recognition intentionally seeks to avoid. While this essay cannot offer an overarching strategy for a robust transgender politics of recognition, it will close in on a narrower question raised by an intersectional analysis: the use of cross-cultural comparisons in asserting the legitimacy of transgender identities. A self-critical, multiculturalist ethics may be useful in avoiding an "imperializing" politics of recognition. In terms of a broader political strategy, I would simply note that direct political and cultural efforts toward recognition have been and will probably continue to be as heterogeneous as transgender persons and communities themselves.

Recognition and Intersectionality

Conventional discussions of rights and equality, including sex equality, have excluded transgender persons as aberrant cases, and a simple assimilation of trans persons into existing paradigms for civil equality is inadequate. Put crudely, it has not been enough, historically, to claim in theoretical terms that transgender persons are deserving of rights because we are "just like everyone else," when the definition of "everyone" has been established, in practice, through the exclusion of transgender persons.

A politics of recognition consists of more than just disseminating positive images for a group. For Charles Taylor, recognition is shorthand for how value is attributed to both persons and groups. Its conceptual origins are in the classical liberal philosophies of the eighteenth century that predicated political life on a principle of equal dignity. Ideally, such a principle accords value to persons by virtue of their individual humanness, rather than by exterior considerations such as family, social rank, or wealth.[2] At stake in the contemporary idea of recognition is not the complete elimination of differences. Such assimilation would mean the forcible repression or purging of human difference and diversity in favor of a single idealized norm. Rather, the goal of much of the contemporary politics of recognition is to make illegitimate the use of racial, cultural, sexual, or physical difference as a basis for "disrespect, domination, and inequality."[3]

The emergence of democracy as a political system, Taylor notes, "has ushered in a politics of equal recognition, which has taken various forms over the years, and has now returned in the form of demands for the equal status of cultures and of genders."[4] Taylor's use of "genders" rather than "men and women" is telling in its open-endedness. Although he does not seem to intentionally include transgender persons, the openness of Taylor's language fits well with an understanding of democratic politics that demands a constant vigilance against a priori exclusions from the realm of rights and civic participation. One should not have to "earn" a conferral of equal value. Rather, the equal valuation of persons is the *basis* for a democratic system of politics and rights. Furthermore, the assigning of unequal status as a precondition for civic and political participation, as in the case of racially segregated systems of education, is illegitimate.

Critical to a politics of recognition is both an attention to material conditions of inequality and to the semiotics of inequality. In regard to *Brown v. Board of Education*, Charles Lawrence has argued that "read most narrowly, the case is about the rights of Black children to equal educational opportunity. But *Brown* can also be read more broadly to articulate a principle central to any substantive understanding of the equal protection clause, the foundation on which all anti-discrimination law rests. This is the principle of equal citizenship. Under that principle, 'Every individual is presumptively entitled to be treated by the organized society as a respected, responsible, and participating member.'"[5] *Brown*, Lawrence argues, is simultaneously about ending unequal access to education and about dismantling the systems of signification that sanction white racial supremacy. Systems of meaning and valuation interact with material and economic practices in ways that complement, reinforce, or even guide those practices: "*Brown* held that segregation was unconstitutional not simply because the physical separation of Black and white children is bad or because resources were distributed unequally among Black and white schools. *Brown* held that segregated schools were unconstitutional primarily because of the *message* segregation conveys—the message that Black children are an untouchable caste, unfit to be educated with white children."[6]

Analytically, the concept of recognition is useful as a starting point, but not as an end in itself. The refusal of recognition is often not simply the consequence of a single form of discrimination but often precedes or extends out of a constellation of social forces. Indeed, as Frank Wu observes, for opponents of desegregation, *Brown* "was thought to be the harbinger of a sexual calamity," with, for example, Judge Thomas Brady of Mississippi "predict[ing] that white Southern men would fight to the death to preserve racial purity, defined as whiteness and the honor of their women."[7] For understanding such ideologies, Kimberlé Crenshaw's concept of intersectionality becomes useful. Crenshaw provides a way to articulate how constellations of forces operate such that racial hierarchies can both define and be defined by sexual policing. Analytically distinctive structures of oppression and privilege can manifest, in practice, simultaneously in complex patterns of collusion and antagonism.[8] For Crenshaw and subsequent critical race theorists, analyzing an instance of injustice as *solely* racial, gendered, or economic in nature is likely to result in an inadequate understanding of causes, injuries, and solutions. Sumi K. Cho observes that "in light of the prevalent and converging racial and gender stereotypes of Asian Pacific American Women as politically passive and sexually exotic and compliant, serious attention must be given to the problem of racialized sexual harassment. . . . The law's current dichotomous categorization of racial discrimination and sexual harassment as separate spheres of injury is inadequate to respond to racialized sexual harassment."[9] Stereotypes such as the hyperfemininity and sexual submissiveness of Asian American men and women, for example, are not merely a problem of negative images that can be remedied by creating more positive portraits. When a belief in the sexual submissiveness of Asian Americans is taken to imply a broader social submissiveness, Asian Americans are not simply misrepresented but become more readily the target of sexual harassment and employment discrimination because perpetrators believe that we are unlikely to fight back. Alternately, one might see the intersectional translation of racial privilege into heterosexism and male privilege when whiteness appears to entitle young men to engage in homophobic violence as an extension of their masculinity ("boys will be boys") in situations where racial supremacist violence would be far less tolerated, such as in schools, and where violence by men of color would be interpreted as an indication of simple criminality.

Crenshaw's work has at least three further implications. First, specific constellations of racial and gendered discrimination result in unique kinds of physical and representational violence. Second, seemingly disparate acts of violence and discrimination may also be linked to one another by what Cho observes as the pattern of "synergism" that "results when sexualized racial stereotypes combine with racialized gender stereotypes."[10] Third, no single particular form of oppression is necessarily the root cause for, or automatically more urgent to address, than another.

Theorizing Transgender Recognition: Patricia Williams's *The Alchemy of Race and Rights*

In the United States, the history and structures of antiblack racism stand as an intellectual touchstone for understanding how and why recognition is refused. This necessarily leads to the question, what is the connective tissue between transphobia and racism? A sufficient answer to the question is more subtle than simply saying that both are forms of unjust discrimination. In her ground-breaking work *The Alchemy of Race and Rights,* Patricia Williams writes of meeting S., a white transsexual woman and law student. Intending to transition, S. "wanted to talk to me before anyone else at the school because I was black and might be more understanding. I had never thought about transsexuality at all and found myself lost for words."[11] Williams's ambivalent silence should not be read, I think, as a signal of unconscious transphobia but as the sign of an important experiential difference between the racism experienced by nontrans persons of color and the transphobia faced by white transgender persons.

Not surprising, S. was met, Williams recalls, with antagonism over what bathroom she should use; her fellow students asserted their proprietorship over public facilities, over the meaning of those facilities, and even over the significance of S.'s body when she enters "their" space:

> After the sex-change operation, S. began to use the ladies' room. There was an enormous outcry from women students of all political persuasions, who "felt raped," in addition to the more academic assertions of some who "feared rape." In a complicated storm of homophobia, the men of the student body let it be known that they too "feared rape" and vowed to chase her out of any and all men's rooms. The oppositional forces of men and women reached a compromise: S. should use

the dean's bathroom. Alas, in the dean's bathroom no resolution was to be found, for the suggestion had not been an honest one but merely an integration of the fears of each side. Then, in his turn the dean, circumspection having gotten him this far in life, expressed polite, well-modulated fears about the appearance of impropriety in having students visit his inner sanctum, and many other things most likely related to his fear of a real compromise of hierarchy...

At the vortex of this torment, S. as human being who needed to go to the bathroom was lost. Devoured by others, she carved and shaped herself to be definitionally acceptable. She aspired to a notion of women set like jewels in grammatical mountings, fragile and display-cased. She had not learned what society's tricksters and its dark fringes have had to learn in order to survive: to invert, to stretch, meaning rather than oneself. She to whom words meant so much was not given the room to appropriate them. S. as "transsexual," S. as "not homosexual," thus became a mere floating signifier, a deconstructive polymorph par excellence.[12]

Through their phobic responses, S.'s classmates and their dean transform bathrooms from a ubiquitous public convenience into extensions of their own genders, sexualities, and institutional positions. S., Williams observes, attempted to adapt to the phobic "logic" of the situation by protesting that she was not homosexual, and thus not a sexual threat. However, this attempt at accommodation fails. The conceptual framework erected against S. denies her claim to self-definition in the first place by prohibiting her access to a public space in which the self-definition of one's sex is a symbolic part of the act of entry.

It might seem strange, then, that in arrogating such power to themselves, S.'s classmates would then imagine themselves the *victims* of sexual assault. But in conceiving of bathroom spaces as extensions of their sexed personhood, they transform the bathrooms from a place of passive "urinary segregation," in which entry and exit occur with minimal thought, into spaces requiring a vigilant and active patrolling of sex definition and their own bodies. In the transphobic imagination, the bathroom becomes the extension of a genital narcissism (which could be expressed, roughly, as "my body is how sex should be defined for all other bodies" and "the presence of other kinds of body violates the sex of my own body").

At the same time, being black and nontrans is not the same as being transsexual and white, and the privileges of whiteness have a complicated relationship to the encounter with transphobia. We see in Williams's account at least three levels of complication. The structures of racism and transphobia do not emanate from the same historical space or set of ethical assumptions; nontrans persons who would likely balk at racial restrictions on bathroom use often see no problem with excluding persons based on their gender expressions or transgender identities. At the same time, among the privileges of whiteness in predominantly white institutions is the ability to take inclusion for granted; it is, arguably, this sense of automatic belonging that S. finds betrayed by her classmates. Lastly, the simple projection of kinship threatens an act of *mis*-recognition in which Williams would be reduced to the status of a pure victim while her racial identity is enlisted into S.'s search for legitimacy: "Initially it felt as if she were seeking in me the comfort of another nobody; I was a bit put off by the implication that my distinctive somebody-ness was being ignored—I was being used, rendered invisible by her refusal to see all of me."[13] The incautious use of the gains made by persons of color into furthering the social and political inclusion of white persons demands a certain degree of critical skepticism. In the context of LGBT political organizing, Allan Bérubé notes that

> dramatic race-analogy scenarios performed by white activists beg some serious questions. Are actual, rather than "virtual," people of color present as major actors in these scenarios, and if not, why not? What are they saying or how are they being silenced? How is their actual leadership being supported or not supported by the white people who are enacting this racialized history?[14]

The need for caution does not deny the existence of a connective tissue, however. For Williams, the link between herself, a black nontrans woman and law professor, and S., a white transsexual woman and student, lies in the ideological framework revealed by the refusal of material and symbolic recognition:

> In retrospect, I see clearly the connection between S.'s fate and my being black, her coming to me because I was black. S.'s experience was a sort of Jim Crow mentality applied to gender. Many men, women, blacks, and certainly anyone who identifies with the term "white" are caught up in the perpetuation and invisible privilege of this game; for "black," "female," "male," and "white" are every bit as much properties as the buses, private clubs, neighborhoods, and schools that provide the extracorporeal battlegrounds of their expression. S.'s experience, indeed, was a reminder of the extent to which property is nothing more than the mind's enhancement of the body's limitation.[15]

To Williams, S. was cut off from the natural act of claiming an identity (linguistically, one might imagine such an act as the simple but foundational grammatical act of speaking in the first person: "I am . . ."). The persons around S. relegated her a priori to the status of a nonperson; they laid claim to an exclusive ownership of gendered and sexual identities. For Williams, her connection to S. extends out of the understanding that ideologies of segregation work through both material and symbolic exclusions. Segregation is material in nature insofar as public spaces are physically cordoned off and defended as the private reserve of certain privileged subjectivities. Segregation is also symbolic insofar as the material act of exclusion attempts to convey the message and bolster the illusion that the boundaries of proper identities and the attribution of value, as well as dignity, are fully and solely in the hands of those privileged subjects.

In spirit, if not explicitly, transgender scholars have followed Williams's work by providing increasingly nuanced analyses of the differences in identities and experiences *among* trans persons. In Williams's account, the students who decried S. as a "rapist" echoed a long-standing stereotype of transsexual women as secret sexual predators. Judith Halberstam has argued that trans men and masculine women are, in contrast, more likely to be imagined as targets than as threats. Halberstam notes that "the codes that dominate within the women's bathroom are primarily gender codes; in the men's room, they are sexual codes."[16] In turn, gender policing in bathrooms intersects with the asymmetries that structure the cultural ideals of the divide between public (coded as a space of masculine sexual privilege) and private (coded as feminine domesticity). Because of these intersections, "The perils for passing FTMs in the men's room are very different from the perils of passing MTFs in the women's room. On the one hand, the FTM in the men's room is likely to be less scrutinized because men are not quite as vigilant about intruders for obvious reasons. On the other hand, if caught, the FTM may face some version of gender panic from the man who discovers him, and it is quite reasonable to expect and fear violence in the wake of such a discovery. The MTF, by comparison, will be more scrutinized in the women's room but possibly less open to punishment if caught."[17] Masculine and androgynous women in the women's room receive intensified scrutiny and face the demand by law enforcement to confirm their sex in ways that feminine men or androgynous persons in the men's room typically do not. These are, of course, interpretively useful generalizations, not absolutes. One can refine the analysis of gender policing further by exploring the ways that persons are scrutinized also for skin color, class, age, body art, and other features.

Susan Stryker describes our contemporary moment as a "wild profusion of gendered subject positions, spawned by the rupture of 'woman' and 'man' like an archipelago of identities rising from the sea: FTM, MTF, eonist, invert, androgyne, butch, femme, nellie, queen, third sex, hermaphrodite, tomboy, sissy, drag king, female impersonator, she-male, he-she, boy-dyke, girlfag, transsexual, transvestite, transgender, cross-dresser."[18] This proliferation does not mark a momentary cultural confusion that will subside into some more simple model of sex, gender, and sexuality later; on the contrary, such nuanced self-definitions indicate that such complexity is, as C. Jacob Hale argues, phenomenologically real.[19] What is politically critical is the understanding that no single type of gender policing is exemplary of all other forms at the same time that these multiple experiences of gender policing are also experientially real and function as preludes to the denial of recognition.

Social Death: Tyra Hunter and Vincent Chin

On August 7, 1995, Tyra Hunter, a black transgender woman, was struck by a car. As the emergency medical technician at the scene began to administer aid, he suddenly exclaimed, "This bitch ain't no girl . . . it's a nigger, he's got a dick!" and walked away. Witnesses later reported that, while Hunter was possibly still conscious, the EMT stood "laughing and telling jokes" with his fellow technicians for several minutes. Hunter would subsequently die of her injuries at Washington, DC, General Hospital.[20]

On June 19, 1982, Vincent Chin, a nontransgender Chinese American, was clubbed to death by Ronald Ebens and his stepson, Michael Nitz. In a national and local atmosphere poisoned by the media's heavy-handed Japan-bashing, Chin's attackers blamed him for taking away "American" jobs. Both men were charged with manslaughter and released on probation with a three-thousand-dollar fine. Wayne County Circuit Court chief justice Charles Kaufman defended his light sentencing by noting, "We're talking here about a man who's held down a responsible job with the same company for 17 or 18 years, and his son who is employed and a part-time student. These men are not going to go out and harm somebody else. I just didn't think that putting them in prison would do any good for them or for society. You don't make the punishment fit the crime; you make the punishment fit the individual."[21]

These two instances of discriminatory behavior seem separated by different kinds of conduct, perpetrators, victims, and motives. Nevertheless, they are, I would suggest, two faces of one ideological coin. The deaths of a black transgender woman and a nontrans Chinese American man are connected through acts of injustice predicated on gross refusals of civil and human recognition. In the first instance, the EMT's marked hostility toward women as a whole—"this bitch"—colluded, in his eyes, with Hunter's "failure" to meet his sexualized and gendered expectations of a black woman. Misogyny, racism, homophobia, and transphobia are all *simultaneously* audible in the EMT's statement. Regarded as an "it," Hunter is rendered socially dead, such that, lying injured on the ground, she is left to die, treated by the technicians at the scene as if she were already dead.[22] The display of callousness and arrogance on the part of the perpetrators is not incidental; rather, it arises from their implicit beliefs that they possessed the right to either withhold or grant recognition in the form of medical care according to racialized, gendered, and sexual criteria.

In the second instance, a similar arrogance is visible in Judge Kaufman's explanation of his light sentencing. In effect, he absolves Chin's attackers of their violent racism because they were "responsible" family men. Kaufman imagines himself as the defender not of racist killers but of well-employed, heterosexual heads-of-households whose personal well-being and society's welfare are imagined to be one and the same. Kaufman gives voice to a discourse that equates whiteness with middle-class heterosexual masculinity and with society in general. For Kaufman, a challenge to Ebens's and Nitz's racially motivated violence, legible as an assertion of supremacism, would threaten their socially sanctioned gender and class roles. In turn, Chin, while also employed and about to get married, has no standing as a man, a worker, or as a properly familial heterosexual. Although there is no clear reason why another attack on an Asian American would *not* occur, Chin and Detroit's Asian American community are dismissed from view as merely "somebody else," a referent without content.

My contention that these two instances of injustice are connected through their enactment of an exclusionary and *simultaneous* policing of race, gender, and sexuality may seem overbroad. Nonetheless, I would suggest that neither Hunter's nor Chin's deaths are intelligible without reference to broader patterns of bias and exclusion. Barbara Perry has argued that hate crimes, understood as assaults against the communities to which an individual appears to belong, are significantly oriented toward creating a *spectacle* of subordination, as well as physical harm. Hate crimes, Perry argues, are intended as a message to the communities who bear witness, as well as the immediate victims, to get back "in their place."[23] The "messages" conveyed by acts of hate violence are not idiosyncratic personal expressions but attempts to reinforce publicly available discourses that support the subordination of historically marginalized groups. In short, even though the bulk of hate crimes are *not* committed by organized hate groups, acts of transphobic or racist violence are nonetheless attempts to turn beliefs in transgender deviance or white supremacy into concrete realities.

Hunter and Chin faced different historical legacies, to be sure. The intense demand to be "properly" gendered imposed on Hunter might be reckoned, in part, to be a consequence of the nineteenth-century construction of "womanhood" as white and centered in the domestic sphere; in contrast to such a standard, Cheryl Harris argues, "Black women functioned as important regulatory symbols: by representing everything that 'woman' was not.... Indeed, through the rigid construction of the virgin/whore dichotomy along racial lines, the conception of womanhood was deeply wedded to slavery and patriarchy and the conduct of all women was policed in accordance with patriarchal norms and in furtherance of white male power."[24] Chin and Asian Americans stand in the shadow cast by a different history. As Frank Wu and others have noted, we have been painted as "perpetual foreigners" whose presence in the United States is regarded as transitory or even parasitical.[25] These historical differences do not mean that Hunter's and Chin's deaths are isolated from one another, however. Taken together, the EMT's regard of black trans women as sexually deviant and socially dead and Judge Kaufman's claim that white heterosexual family men are preeminently valuable are interlocking and mutually reinforcing. As a mass of beliefs, they echo historically enduring hierarchies of race, gender, and sexuality.

Here, it becomes important to address the distinction between a politics of recognition and economic or redistributive justice. The severe economic vulnerability of trans persons makes us vulnerable to abuse in many settings, from the workplace to the criminal justice system. Nondiscrimination laws alone are simply inadequate. In historical perspective, as Derrick Bell has argued, the gains made toward racial equality since *Brown* have been regularly undermined by the structuring of economic interests in parallel with racism. Economic justice remains a necessary part of civil and human rights struggles, Bell argues, stressing the need to develop strategies that will "dilute both the financial and psychological benefits" of discriminatory behavior.[26] Recognition is, generally, an insecure achievement when it relies on the largesse of those with the power to grant or deny it or when it pits self-interest against moral persuasion.

Yet, to the extent that discriminatory actions have their roots in phobic beliefs that are *not* economically motivated, an emphasis on recognition remains essential. Hate violence does not correlate readily to economic disparities, and "hatemongers are not all alienated deprived youth. It is also the case that hate crimes know no class boundaries.... Hate crime is increasingly likely to occur in places of privilege such as the workplace and college campuses."[27] The beliefs surrounding Hunter's or Chin's deaths, or the student S.'s exclusion from bathrooms, had less to do with economic disparities than with the systematic devaluation of their personhoods and communities. Such devaluation took place in terms of cultural and social, rather than material, worth. In all three cases, the question that became visible was not whether they could afford fair treatment but whether they deserved fairness in the first place. Economic equality, whether measured in terms of income or more complex quality-of-life measurements, does not safeguard against the perception that one's life, identity, psychological integrity, and communities are of no *inherent* value.

Transphobia and Hate-Motivated Violence

Hate-motivated violence deserves an extended consideration insofar as it is one of the areas in which an expansion of our current politics of recognition is particularly needed. From the schoolyard thug to the bully with a badge, both opportunistic violence and state-sanctioned violence are a barbed-wire cage that keeps us from full cultural, economic, and political participation. While violence is by no means the only civil rights concern of trans persons or persons of color, it is, nonetheless, the most direct means by which we have been warded off from attempting to make rights claims or pointing out unjust inequalities.

The relationship between the refusal of recognition and hate violence is multilayered. Most evident, nonrecognition promotes hate crimes by allowing perpetrators to regard victims as targets who "deserve" to be hated. Beneath this causal relationship are at least three other pernicious consequences of nonrecognition. Nonrecognition renders invisible the frequency of those crimes. For example, neither transgender persons nor perceptions of gender identity appear as categories of persons or motives in the FBI's hate crime statistics.[28] Nonrecognition further leads to a dismissive attitude by the criminal justice system, the media, and the public toward the consequences of hatred for its victims and to victims being blamed for "bringing it on themselves." Most perniciously, perhaps, when victims receive inadequate support, it becomes possible to accept such attitudes and to resign oneself to the "inevitability" of being hated. Often, then, the consequence is that hate crimes go unreported and unaddressed, thus creating a cycle of suppression and silence.

Trans persons are systematically misrepresented both within the mass media and within the criminal justice system. We are regarded as persons whose identities are not simply "deviant" but actively deceptive and criminal. As I write this essay, a mistrial has occurred in the prosecution of Gwen Araujo's killers. Araujo was a seventeen-year-old trans woman who was tortured and strangled by four men. Even when, because of pressures brought by family, friends, and transgender activists, the attention of the media and criminal justice system are sympathetic to the victims of antitransgender hate crimes, trans persons can end up represented in ways that undermine the equal recognition implicit in hate crime laws. Both prosecution and defense relied on rhetorical ploys that have no actual ethical or legal basis. To the prosecutor, Araujo had committed "the sin of deception"[29] even as he closed his case by arguing that "the provocation [for murder] did not flow from Eddie [Gwen] Araujo."[30] The defense, in its turn, accused Araujo of "sexual fraud."[31]

The mass media bear a significant responsibility for misrepresenting trans persons and the scale of violence that we face. Trans activists have changed, to be sure, the quality of non-LGBT press coverage, especially since Brandon Teena's murder. We are less frequently represented as exotic perverts in order to create sensationalistic copy. Nonetheless, reporters still have trouble with names, genders, and, most important perhaps, context. (Indeed, I should note that the significance of turning Teena's life into a movie, *Boys Don't Cry*, remains to be seen; I have met a number of persons who, after seeing the film, did not know that he was an actual person.) In September 2003, for example, *Newsweek* reported sympathetically on the murders of Ukea Davis, Bella Evangelista, Kiera Spaulding, Stephanie Thomas, and Mimi Young over a one-year period. However, the tendency to blame the victim for the crime still persisted; Evangelista is implied to have been complicit in her death by deceiving unsuspecting heterosexual men: "[Evangelista] occasionally resorted to an especially risky form of prostitution—soliciting straight men on the street without telling them her true gender." The chilling larger context of violence against trans persons is relegated to a parenthetical comment: "Evangelista's killing was gruesome, but it wasn't unique. In the past year, four other transgender men have been found brutally murdered in the Washington area. Another was attacked and narrowly survived. Police say that so far, they have found no connection between the crimes. . . . (Nationwide, nine other transgenders have been murdered in the past 12 months, according to Remembering Our Dead, a San Francisco–based activist group)."[32] Among the consistent features of non-LGBT reporting on antitrans hate crimes is the tendency for journalists to portray such crimes as a shocking new development or a sudden surge. In fact, it would have been more accurate to describe the violence in Washington as the continued expansion of an epidemic. Kylar Broadus observes that roughly two killings a month of trans persons are recorded each year. Furthermore, any number taken from currently available sources is likely to be low because of a combination of underreporting and misreporting, "because the individual victim is not identified as transgendered—because [authorities] will ignore the victims' transgender name and identity and state, 'It was a man,' or say, 'It was a gay man in drag' that was killed."[33]

Phrases such as "sins of deception" and "sexual fraud" have no ethical or legal basis; they are strictly rhetorical stratagems. Their effectiveness rests not only on widespread stereotypes and misconceptions but on an a priori negation of transgender identity. Just as persons of color in the nineteenth century were excluded from testifying against white persons in court because their color presumptively negated the legitimacy of their testimony in a white supremacist juridical context, transgender persons are rendered "unreal" in a rigidly binaristic and heterosexist cultural environment.

Toward a Critical Multiculturalism

The need for portraits of subjectivity that do not simply assimilate existing culturally dominant standards of normalcy and that enable a critical assessment of the United States' particular sex-gender system has lead many to search for alternative sex-gender systems in which gender nonconformity is valued. Indeed, I recall reading Walter Williams's influential *The Spirit and the Flesh: Sexual Diversity in American Indian Culture* for the first time as an undergraduate. With embarrassing hubris, I walked into Robert Warrior's office, the professor for my Native American literature class, and asked why gender and sexuality were not more prominent topics in the class? Gently but firmly, he asked me if I had learned anything yet about water rights, education issues, or sovereignty. The question made clear that while gender and sexual identity were not unimportant areas of inquiry, they should not be detached from the concerns over survival and justice for the communities in which those systems of gender and sexuality emerged.

What are the benefits and risks of writing about apparently transgender aspects of cultures "outside" the West as a source of cultural legitimacy in the United States? This question might seem an odd departure from my explorations of Patricia Williams's and Kimberlé Crenshaw's works and the deaths of Tyra Hunter and Vincent Chin. However, as Derrick Bell and others have noted, U.S. black and Native American struggles over rights and self-determination were watched intensely by those engaged in decolonization in Africa, Asia, Latin America, and the Caribbean. For some observers, U.S. civil rights struggles were an extension inward of anticolonialism. No less, whether or not early transgender activists considered themselves part of a broader liberation movement, they were part of a milieu steeped in racial civil rights struggles, labor organizing, antiwar and peace movements, and second-wave feminism. One might argue that postwar civil rights struggles generally cannot be read in terms of strictly national beliefs and actors.

This broader historical intersectionality requires us to attend to one of the key strategies of legitimation in transgender politics: the representation of cultures in which apparently "third sexes or genders" have a positive role and of cultures with different taxonomies for embodiment and sexual life more generally. The precedent of such intellectual work has been set by feminist and, more recently, gay and lesbian historians and anthropologists who have sought worldviews in which gender relations are not organized around patriarchy and domesticity, and sexuality is not defined in terms of mutually exclusive heterosexual and homosexual identities. Indeed, as Patrick Califia-Rice has noted, the archive of cross-cultural comparisons of gender and sexuality often undermines attempts to demarcate cleanly between transgender and gay-lesbian historiography.[34]

Transgender writers have referred to cultural systems in which so-called third genders or sexes have an established role in order to develop a critique of the fixity and universality of contemporary Western taxonomies of gender and sex.[35] One relatively moderate argument that can be made based on cross-cultural comparisons is that transgender identities do not herald the decay and end of civilization but are simply one of many cultural possibilities. The existence of other cultural taxonomies is part of a larger body of evidence supporting the claim that Western models of sex, gender, and sexuality do not reflect some bedrock cultural necessity but one of several roads of historical development that are open to future change. For trans persons, knowledge of other cultural systems lends credence to the idea that transphobia and rigid gender roles are neither a permanent nor an organic feature of societies and offers the possibility that there might well be a future in which transgender persons possess cultural and social legitimacy despite or even because of their identities.

The benefits of cross-cultural comparisons entail an equivalent degree of ethical danger. At the outset, transgender or third sex/gender are labels that might well be rejected or culturally unintelligible if applied. The act of misrepresentation or mistranslation is not trivial. In prioritizing sex or gender over other dimensions of cultural reality or in isolating sex and gender from their cultural milieu, it is easy to treat other cultures and persons in a fashion similar to the way that U.S. trans persons have been regarded by, for example, medical and psychiatric institutions that have tended to be interested in us primarily as case studies of a "condition." When transgender writers are located within the United States, the danger of misrepresentation is compounded by the problem of taking on an imperialistic approach to political and intellectual work. To be sure, trans persons typically have neither the financial nor the cultural capital to be a neocolonial vanguard; there is nothing to be gained by rehearsing the facile metaphors central to Janice Raymond's vitriolic *Transsexual Empire*. The risk in using other cultures for our own political ends is an erosion of ethical consciousness in which we come to regard both "trans" and nontrans persons as mere instruments in struggles that they have had little voice in shaping and whose fruits they are unlikely to share.

By no means is the problem of cross-cultural representation faced by transgender writers alone. How transphobia intersects with the act of cross-cultural representation in the so-called mainstream of Western mass media is instructive about the uses to which the representations of other cultures can be put. One cornerstone of transphobic representation works through a radical constriction of the norms against which sex and gender expressions are interpreted and evaluated. Take, for example, a short review of a travel book from the *Economist:* "It is, one imagines, every sex-tourist's nightmare: the go-go bar, the tuk-tuk, the hotel room and then . . . the discovery that there is rather more to the lovely lady than had been bargained for. Thailand's ladyboys have struck again."[36]

Within a few brief sentences, the *Economist* imagines transgender subjectivity as nothing more (or less) than a threat to heterosexual genital security. "Thailand's ladyboys," Thai *kathoeys,* are depicted strictly with regard to whether they conform to the desires of the heterosexual European sex-tourist, presented here as the standard of normalcy and the "one" whose subjectivity should be "imagined" by the reader. Whether Thai *kathoeys* are represented in a positive or negative light in this instance is, to some extent, irrelevant; more important, I think, is the fact that *kathoey* identity is represented as dependent on, and subordinate to, the presumptive gender expectations and heterosexuality of the narrator. The *kathoey* becomes nothing more or less than the extension of a sexual "nightmare." At the same time, the author invokes the common stereotype of the devious and cunning Asian: in effect, *kathoeys* are Fu Manchu posing as Madame Butterfly.

Writing for the *New Internationalist,* Urvashi Butalia offers an alternative and far more expansive mode of representation in a profile of Mona, an Indian *hijra:*

> Mona Ahmed's visiting card currently lists five names. Apart from Mona, which is how I know her, there is Ahmad Bhai, Saraswati, Ahmed Iqbal and Radharani. These names are a mix of Hindu (Saraswati, Radharani), Muslim (Ahmed Bhai, Ahmed Iqbal) and Christian (Mona), but they also combine different genders. Mona, Saraswati, and Radharani are female names. Ahmed Bhai and Ahmed Iqbal are male names. This is entirely appropriate—with Mona it's difficult to tell from one moment to the next which gender she will assume. . . .
>
> As a eunuch she has limited ways of making a living: eunuchs live on the fringes of Indian society and can't easily find jobs. The group to which she belongs make their living by blessing newborn children in return for money—an act which plays on people's fear of the "evil eye" and is the reason families willingly oblige. . . .

There are times when Mona yearns to be what she calls "normal." But that normality doesn't have to do with sex. Instead, it's a longing to be a part of main-stream society. It has to do with acceptability, with respect—all of which elude her simply because she cannot be classed as one or other of the two genders avail-able us. At other times she laughs at the trap of "normal" society. Years ago she adopted a little girl when she felt a strong urge to motherhood which for her has nothing to do with biology.[37]

The difference here is qualitative, not merely quantitative. Mona's identity cannot be reduced to either her physicality or her gender, but must be seen within the cultural, religious, and economic structures specific to India as a modern nation. Mona's identity, while understood relationally, is not repre-sented as a subordinate extension of another's reality. Celebratory representa-tion need not be a central concern here. Rather, the "positive" quality of Butalia's representation of Mona extends from how she depicts Mona's reality as composed through the complex relationships among her personal agency, the social and economic possibilities surrounding her, and the larger, evolving communities and histories within modern Indian society.

On the one hand, when portrayed as strange and deviant, different sys-tems of sex and gender relations can be used to reaffirm the belief that the West's culturally dominant understanding of sex and gender identity is natural and superior. On the other hand, placed in a broader cultural and historical context, the depiction of a different sex and gender system can also be used to demonstrate that the binary and heterocentric understanding of "normal" sex and gender identity in the United States is not a fact of nature but the product of a specific historical legacy, one reinforced not by the force of nature but by relations of privilege and exclusion. The desire to engage in comparative thought should not be dismissed merely as a search for Shangri-la. Instead, the use of cross-cultural comparisons as a strategy of legitimation requires a heightened awareness of the ethical stakes involved.

A multiculturalist ethics provides a useful vantage point. In the United States, multiculturalism has been, typically, an attempt to challenge ethnocen-trism through education after the demise of overt racial and ethnic suprema-cism. At its weakest, multiculturalism descends into the tokenistic and easily forgotten celebration of cosmetic cultural differences. Ideally, more serious changes in ways of thinking can take place through a rigorous, critical multi-culturalism in which education focuses "on the material historical productions of difference rather than on 'culture' as a ready-made thing" and explores how specific systems of identification, discrimination, and privilege become forged over time.

A critical multiculturalist approach toward representing cultural differences in transgender intellectual work has at least three dimensions: elaborating historical context, defining the purposes and limits of cross-cultural comparison, and establishing reciprocity rather than parasitism. The representation of Native American cultures by trans persons, particularly the idea of two-spiritedness, provides a useful vantage point. When speaking of gender systems, we should not mistake the idea of a system or a structure as meaning historical immobility or indicating a machinelike creation of identity categories. In the case of Navajo categories of gender, Wesley Thomas argues that "gender formulation and reformulation are ongoing processes that have been affected by the influence of Euro-American cultures. The Navajo world has always evolved by synthesizing traditional ideas and practices with new ones."[38] Cultures should be recognized not as templates but as dynamic systems containing internal debates, tensions, and contradictions. Awareness of this internal autonomy and self-reflexivity is analytically vital. Robert Warrior notes that "American Indian intellectual discourse can now ground itself in its own history the way that African-American, feminist, and other oppositional discourses have ... far from engaging in some new and novel practice that belongs necessarily to the process of assimilating and enculturating non-Native values, we are doing something that Natives have done for hundreds of years—something that can be and has been an important part of resistance to assimilation and survival."[39] Second, information about another culture constitutes a critical vantage point from which to see one's own culture from a different perspective; it does not enable one to claim those identity categories as one's own. As Gary Bowen observes, "There are many 'magpies' who are drawn to latch onto the bright shiny aspects of Native culture, who misappropriate Native culture, customs, and artifacts in the belief that they are 'honoring' Native people by imitating them without understanding them."[40] Finally, substantive cross-cultural work requires that one understand and value the stakes central to other communities' struggles. In short, a transgender politics of recognition requires that we recognize others, even as we demand recognition for ourselves.

Notes

1. John Rawls, *A Theory of Justice* (Cambridge, MA: Harvard University Press, 1999), 3.

2. Charles Taylor, *Multiculturalism: The Politics of Recognition*, ed. Amy Gutmann (Princeton, NJ: Princeton University Press, 1994), 27.

3. Seyla Benhabib, *The Claims of Culture: Equality and Diversity in the Global Era* (Princeton, NJ: Princeton University Press, 2002), 8.

4. Taylor, *Multiculturalism*, 27.

5. Charles Lawrence III, "If He Hollers Let Him Go: Regulating Racist Speech on Campus," in *Words That Wound: Critical Race Theory, Assaultive Speech, and the First Amendment*, ed. Mari J. Matsuda and Charles Lawrence III (Boulder, CO: Westview, 1993), 59.

6. Ibid.

7. Frank H. Wu, *Yellow* (New York: Basic Books, 2002), 265–66.

8. Kimberlé Crenshaw, "Beyond Racism and Misogyny: Black Feminism and 2 Live Crew," in Matsuda and Lawrence, *Words That Wound,* 111–32. Crenshaw distinguishes among three kinds of intersectionality: structural, "to refer to the way in which women of color are situated within overlapping structures of subordination"; political, "to refer to the different ways in which political and discursive practices relating to race and gender interrelate, often erasing women of color"; and representational, "referring to the way that race and gender images, readily available to our culture, converge to create unique and specific narratives deemed appropriate for women of color. Not surprisingly, the clearest convergences are those involving sexuality, perhaps because it is through sexuality that images of minorities and women are most sharply focused" (114–16).

9. Sumi K. Cho, "Converging Stereotypes in Racialized Sexual Harassment: Where the Model Minority Meets Suzie Wong," in *Critical Race Feminism,* ed. Adrien Katherine Wing (New York: New York University Press, 1997), 212.

10. Ibid., 205.

11. Patricia J. Williams, *The Alchemy of Race and Rights* (Cambridge, MA: Harvard University Press, 1991), 123.

12. Ibid., 123–24.

13. Ibid., 124.

14. Allan Bérubé, "How Gay Stays White and What Kind of White It Stays," in *The Making and Unmaking of Whiteness,* ed. Birget Brander Rasmussen, Eric Klinenberg, Irene J. Nexica, and Matt Wray (Durham, NC: Duke University Press, 2001), 245–46.

15. Williams, *Alchemy of Race and Rights,* 124.

16. Judith Halberstam, *Female Masculinity* (Durham, NC: Duke University Press, 1998), 24.

17. Ibid., 25.

18. Susan Stryker, "The Transgender Issue: An Introduction," *GLQ* 4, no. 2 (1998): 148.

19. C. Jacob Hale, "Leatherdyke Boys and Their Daddies: How to Have Sex without Women or Men," *Social Text* 52, no. 3 (1997): 230.

20. Scott Bowles, "A Death Robbed of Dignity Mobilizes a Community," *Washington Post,* December 10, 1995.

21. Judith Cummings, "Detroit Asian-Americans Protest Lenient Penalties for Murder," *New York Times,* April 26, 1983.

22. In his comparative study of systems of slavery, Orlando Patterson argues that slaves are regarded as "socially dead," insofar as they are considered by the slave-owning culture to be cut off from family, kinship, and community, and lack both honor and power (*Slavery and Social Death* [Cambridge, MA: Harvard University Press, 1982], 1–3).

23. Perry emphasizes the ideological and semiotic dimension of hate crimes and argues that a hate crime "involves acts of violence and intimidation, usually directed toward already stigmatized and marginalized groups. It attempts to re-create simultaneously the threatened (real or imagined) hegemony of the perpetrator's group and the 'appropriate' subordinate identity of the victim's group. It is a means of marking both the self and the other in such a way as to reestablish their 'proper' relative positions, as given and reproduced by broader ideologies and patterns of social and political inequality" (Barbara Perry, *In the Name of Hate: Understanding Hate Crime* [New York: Routledge, 2001], 10).

24. Cheryl I. Harris, "Finding Sojourner's Truth: Race, Gender, and the Institution of Property," *Cardozo Law Review,* November 18, 1996, 315.

25. Wu, *Yellow,* 79, 95.

26. Derrick Bell, *Faces at the Bottom of the Well: The Permanence of Racism* (New York: Basic Books, 1992), 61.

27. Perry, *In the Name of Hate,* 38. For a discussion of the relationship between economic or redistributive justice and recognition, see Iris Marion Young, "Unruly Categories: A Critique of Nancy Fraser's Dual Systems Theory," in *Theorizing Multiculturalism: A Guide to the Current Debate,* ed. Cynthia Willett (Oxford: Blackwell, 1998), 50–67.

28. Federal Bureau of Investigation, *Uniform Crime Report,* Hate Crime Statistics, 2002, http://www.fbi.gov/ucr/hatecrime2002.pdf.

29. Chris Lamiero, quoted in "Prosecutor: Transgender Teen 'Executed,'" Michelle Locke, Associated Press, April 14, 2004, http://www.guardian.co.uk/uslatest/story/0,1282,-3978164,00.html.

30. See http://www.nbc11.com/news/3378630/detail/html.

31. Ibid.

32. Holly Bailey, "Targeting Transgenders," *Newsweek,* September 8, 2003, 53.

33. Quoted in Cei Bell, "Danger across Genders," *Philadephia Enquirer,* April 14, 2003, http://www.philly.com/mld/inquirer/news/editorial/5627384.html.

34. Patrick Califia-Rice, *Sex Changes: The Politics of Transgenderism* (San Francisco: Cleis, 1997).

35. Leslie Feinberg, *Transgender Warriors: Making History from Joan of Arc to RuPaul* (Boston: Beacon, 1996).

36. "Skirting Pain," review of *The Third Sex: Kathoey, Thailand's Ladyboys,* by Richard Totman, *Economist,* June 14–20, 2003, 82.

37. Urvashi Butalia, "The Third Sex," *New Internationalist,* October 2002, 5.

38. Wesley Thomas, "Navajo Cultural Constructions of Gender and Sexuality," in *Two-Spirit People: Native American Gender Identity, Sexuality, and Spirituality,* ed. Sue-Ellen Jacobs, Wesley Thomas, and Sabine Lang (Urbana: University of Illinois Press, 1997), 169.

39. Robert Warrior (Osage), *Tribal Secrets: Recovering American Indian Intellectual Traditions* (Minneapolis: University of Minnesota Press, 1995), 2.

40. Cited in Leslie Feinberg, *Trans Liberation: Beyond Pink or Blue* (Boston: Beacon, 1998), 66.

13. (Trans)Sexual Citizenship in Contemporary Argentina

Mauro Cabral (A. I. Grinspan) and Paula Viturro

Toward the end of April 2005, a news story shocked Argentinean public opinion. For the first time in the history of the Argentinean legal system, a judge allowed a legal name and sex change for a trans man who also received judicial authorization to surgically modify his body. These surgeries had to be performed within six months of the decision. Ten days before that, *travesti* activist Alejandra Galicio, beaten up by strangers, had died.

This chapter aims to briefly introduce a series of ethical-political issues about the sexual citizenship of trans persons in Argentina.[1] By *sexual citizenship*, we refer to that which enunciates, facilitates, defends, and promotes the effective access of citizens to the exercise of both sexual and reproductive rights and to a political subjectivity that has not been diminished by inequalities based on characteristics associated with sex, gender, and reproductive capacity.[2] Throughout, this chapter affirms that (trans)sexual citizenship in Argentina may be identified as a diminished, decreased citizenship and that the nature of such diminution seriously compromises not only the *citizen* status of trans persons but also, and centrally, their *human* status. We focus, here, specifically on the juridical anthropology of the transsexual that surrounds the legal economy of sex change in Argentina.[3]

Undoubtedly, our focus leaves unanalyzed two important aspects of that same diminished citizenship: the difficulties faced by trans persons in gaining access to essential health services, including endocrinology and surgery, and the specific consequences of judicial decisions, sometimes ill-fated, for the civil and political status of trans persons.[4] We believe, however, that our approach allows us to critically introduce the fundamental aspects that shape our understanding of the current map of (trans)sexual citizenship in Argentina: the ethical-political consequences of the reduction of transsexuality to a principle of sex change and the way ideas of binary sexual difference function both as a value and as a moral justification with terrible normative effectiveness.[5] The combination of both these aspects produces a particular ethical-political effect: the language of rights for trans persons yields a prescriptive set of demands placed on trans persons, particularly in corporeal terms, as a requirement for achieving legal recognition of their gender identities. The affirmation of such rights, predicated on the demand for such corporeal requirements, creates a diminished ethical-political status.

In contrast to countries such as Germany, Italy, the Netherlands, or Sweden, Argentina does not have a law that states the terms on which a person may change his or her legal sex and name. Similar to France, Argentinean law demands a specific judicial authorization for any intervention destined to modify a person's bodily identity markers or reproductive capacity. The sexual body, far from being identified with personal individuality and subjectivity—and, in particular, with the person's decisional autonomy—is, instead, considered a subject of state regulation, in which the state must guarantee certainty as to the true identity of the person, a certainty that is considered a fundamental social and political good.[6]

According to different judicial decisions during the last several years and the legal and bioethical architectures surrounding them, it is possible to access such judicial authorization only through the petitioner's identification as a "true" transsexual. With reference to a descriptive and prescriptive canonic definition of transsexuality, access to legal recognition of a gender identity different from the one assigned at birth takes place within the exhaustive exercise of a judicial verification of "authentic" transsexuality. The foundational act of such verification is the repeated gesture of differentiation: in Argentinean law, transsexuals must be clearly differentiated from members of other, well-defined sexual species—thus invoking, at the same moment in which transsexual difference is being delineated, the danger of categorical contamination. Transsexuals must be extensively distinguished from homosexuals, intersexed persons, and *travestis*, and wedged into a precise ensemble of defining characteristics and traits.

The development of a strongly stereotyped autobiographical narrative is considered indispensable evidence of transsexual authenticity. The transsexual autobiography, according to Argentina's legal and bioethical corpus, must tie its development to a stable ensemble of narrative topoi that constitute its diagnosed specificity: a stable and continuous gender identity opposed to the one assigned at birth and sustained without modifications throughout life; a subjectivity damaged by a permanent incongruence between the sexed body and the gendered self; clearly dysphoric manifestations of the person's bodily experience; a strongly stereotyped and undisputed expression of gender roles; a plainly heterosexual sexual orientation, but exercised with difficulty. Thus, for example, the Quilmes Tribunal declared,

> In order to decide upon the request for sex change, it must be analyzed whether the petitioner, during the course of his life, has seen a substantial transformation of his original sexual assignation leading to the opposite sex. . . . in case of an external morphological examination carried out by the expert doctor it appears that there are feminine sexual traits due to the surgical intervention of ablation of the masculine organs and additionally he has lived as a woman since adolescence and from the evaluation of the expert psychologist it appears that from that point of view, the petitioner is a woman and is free from psycho-pathological symptoms and there are not traces of problems in his psycho-sexual identification which is plainly feminine.[7]

A fundamental part of this verification is that the affirmation of transsexuality centers on a heteronomy: no person who is truly transsexual would make his or her demands for modification based on an unfounded *election* rather than on an existential imperative, usually described in pathological terms. Heteronomy appears inextricably tied to suffering—no person who is truly transsexual, according to this line of thought, would base such a demand in desire or pleasure. On the contrary, it is a heteronomous imposition of suffering that, even as it obligates, authentically constitutes the individual as transsexual and thus renders his or her demands legally viable. As the jurist Carlos Fernández Sessarego writes, for example:

> Contrary to homosexuals or *travestis,* the transsexual is a tormented being who may not oppose an irresistible, uncontrollable force, higher than his/her will. . . . Without denying the possibility to admit the new sex attribution, it was necessary to impede . . . the mere caprice of the subject, which could be utilized to mere utilitarian or perverse purposes.[8]

Or, as in the terms offered by the Quilmes Tribunal in 1994:

> The sex change petitioner has traveled a different path to that which was . . . assigned by his/her nature without this being the fruit of a free and individual decision. . . . having decided to undergo a surgical operation for masculine genital ablation and the insertion of a false vagina not as an act of free disposition, but as a need to put an end to such transformation.[9]

These judicial verifications, destined to confirm the presence of "real" subjective transsexual traits—which function as a transsexual anthropology put in circulation by Argentinean law and which originate in its canonic formulas—do not provide, however, sufficient evidence to obtain a legal sex and name change through the judiciary. In addition, the verification of a *transsexed* body becomes the indispensable, unequivocal manifestation, for the law, of the incarnated transsexual biography. The predominant legal and cultural position surrounding the relationship between embodiment and identity is that which anchors the "sexual identity" of the persons (including the legal one) in genital appearance and functionality. In the case of persons who seek to modify their legal names and sex, this position establishes the obligation of a transsexed body, capable of sustaining three fundamental corporeal pillars: morphological resemblance, sterility, and the irreversibility of the modifications. Normative heterosexuality, which is a central part of the canonic definition of transsexuality, works both as an assumption and a justification.

Once the expert verification of an authentic transsexual subjectivity is obtained, the genital surgical modification is presented as a de facto matter, more so than a requisite. As Fernández Sessarego writes, "It is legally valid that the transsexual, due to a demand that corresponds to a medically originated state, undergoes a surgical intervention of sexual adaptation, the only open way to enjoy the right to health. From there, in the case of an *authentic* transsexual such operation is not prohibited by the legal system."[10]

The concern for legality is displaced onto an evaluation of the hypothetical capacity of the surgically removed genitals to sustain the remedied identity. Through a line of argument that locates the "truth" of identity in genitals, defining them, in turn, through a strong normative standard, only a transsexed genitality capable of accurately reaching the female or male genital standard could then justify legal recognition of a sex change.[11]

However, the logic of resemblance, articulated on the basis of available technical possibilities, raises the problem of achieving a paradigmatic sexual individuation through the necessary genital modification: to obtain a legal sex change it is necessary to demonstrate not only the reconstruction of the sexual organs of the "opposite sex" but also the removal of any appearance of the "original sex" that might create a shadow of uncertainty or ambiguity with respect to identity or, even worse, that might install a "hermaphrodite" anatomy.[12] The so-called arrival sex of transsexed genitals must not only be similar to the standard male or female genitals, but that similarity also must be potentially tied, from the expert's perspective, to the possibilities of a "successful" genitally oriented heterosexuality, equally stereotypical. The legal economy of transsexuality therefore produces a continuous knowledge that amply exceeds the restricted frame of transsexual anthropology and reaches out to a general ordering of genitalized and stereotyped human sexuality.

The possibility of people who, having modified their sex, would retain their original reproductive capacities haunts the legal discourse on transsexuality.[13] In this, Argentinean law is not exceptional. According to Stephen Whittle, this anxiety must be interpreted in eugenicist terms—where there is the pathologization of transsexuality, transsexual reproduction becomes socially undesirable. Within the context of Argentina, sterilization is a requirement for obtaining a legal name and sex change and has two normative bases. First, as we discussed above, the standard sexed bodies of men and women are seen as a point of origin, as sexual difference in its normative dimensions. Second, however, lurks the potential threat to the psycho-physical well-being of the possible biological sons and daughters of transsexuals, who are subject to the double threat of a materpaternity that is simultaneously transsexual and homosexual. For example, Matilde Zabala de González warns, "Should civil sex change be admitted without a surgical modification that eliminates the possibility to procreate, there is the risk that, for example, a genetically feminized transsexual may generate children who will not have a father and a mother but two mothers!"[14]

It is possible to agree that the judicial authorization granted in April 2005, mentioned at the beginning of this chapter, constitutes a personal victory for the one who requested it and a fundamental advance for those in the community who require access to specific health and legal resources associated with sex change. However, such a decision may and must be read within the ethical-political terms in which corporeality, sexuality, and identity are tied together. The de facto association of masculinity and femininity with standard paradigms of embodiment makes invisible the same sexual difference as a normative ideal; against this, the sexual and reproductive rights of trans persons represent nothing.

Legal recognition of gender identities that differ from a person's sex assigned at birth require that one inhabit a reduced and prescriptive anthropology, with the sexual and reproductive body as the price for access to citizenship. Within the regulatory politics of identity and recognition endorsed by Argentinean law, then, the very concept of the transsexual becomes one of perpetual ethical and political foreignness and exile. Those surgical and hormonal procedures that can be pursued by trans people by virtue of their decisional autonomies become, under the legal economy of sex changing, part of the inhuman procedures of (in)corporation to the body of the state.[15]

Travesti Community

It is not possible to conclude this introduction to the complexities of (trans) sexual citizenship in Argentina without referring to the current situation of one of the most vulnerable trans communities: the *travesti* community.

The death of Alejandra Galicio represented the last step of an uninterrupted ladder of violence that permanently oppresses Argentinean and Latin American *travesti* communities. The same stories of exclusion, discrimination, harassment, arbitrary detentions, tortures, and murders are reproduced far and wide throughout the continent. Throughout the last several years, and in a strongly repressive sociopolitical context, the criminalization of the wearing of clothes usually worn by the other sex was introduced in the legal system. Joined by decrees that penalize "incitement to prostitution, prowling and public scandal," clothing regulations are constantly used as instruments of social control over *travesti* communities, persisting as part of, and sometimes reinforcing, Argentina's authoritarian legacies.

The construction of a *travesti* sexual citizenship or of a *travesti* citizenship in general are tasks that have been taken up by various activism groups such as ALITT (Association for the Struggle for Travesti and Transsexual Identity), Futuro Transgenerico (Transgender Future), ATTTA (Association of Travestis, Transsexuals, and Transgenders in Argentina), Asociación Gondolin, and others. The construction of this citizenship faces enormous challenges. Argentinean *travestis* are marginalized from the school and labor system, stigmatized and hypersexualized, and reified as objects of media consumption or theoretical critique. Consequently, Argentinean *travestis* find themselves in a sustained struggle to create their own political subjectivities.[16]

The political organization of the *travesti* community continues to have a profound impact on the dismantling of the repressive state in Argentina, as well as on exposing human rights violations based on gender identity and gender expression. The Argentinean *travesti* movement has had a fundamental role in introducing critical positions in the sexual rights and reproductive agendas at regional and national levels.

Within the context of Argentinean law, *travestism* is simply understood through a heteronormative lens as a perversion or—in the best of all cases— as a sexual orientation.[17] In the case of the *travestis,* because what is imagined is an altered natural order that gives precedence to the transsexual, the figure of the hermaphrodite gives way to proper moral order and the incorporation (though partial) of the transsexual within it. What is imagined is a crude syllogism in which the "victims" are replaced by "autonomous subjects" who have the corporeal possibility of living according to the natural order, but do not do so, and thus deserve adverse life conditions and persecution.[18] Here, the retributive discourse is equivalent to the one surrounding the delinquent in modern criminal law. This is not coincidental, given that most of the legal fictions and legal representations of *travestis* are created through the institutions of the police and the criminal justice system. In fact, the Argentinean *travesti* community is most persecuted by such institutions. The basis of prohibitions against the use of clothing usually worn by the opposite sex is the "protection of third parties who may be deceived in their good faith" and the protection of "morality and good manners."[19]

The procedural systems through which these bodies are coercively normalized may be one of the following two types: (1) the police chief dictates the rules and conventions, and the police ensure their strict observance and apply penalties for nonobservance; (2) the provincial legislative organ promulgates procedural and substantive norms that the judicial authority uses to prosecute and condemn persons who violate those norms. The first type of system is more frequent and obviously does not respect any of the due process guarantees set forth in international human rights instruments. The second one, while objectively better than the first, does not necessarily improve the *travestis'* situations, given that the substantive norms are based on their criminalization. The paradigmatic example is the city of Buenos Aires, where the police edict was supplanted by a written code, which mandates that infractions be judged by courts and which guarantees due process. As a result, this code constructed the mere presence of *travestis* in the streets as scandalous and criminal. Therefore, within public space—the natural space for the exercise of citizenship—*travestis* find themselves constantly threatened by the state's coercive order.

In the field of civil law, legal discourse does not lack a categorization of *travestism*. In fact, there have been a number of stories about requests for legal recognition by the ALITT. This association's purposes are

> a) to fight for state and society acceptance of *travestism* as a proper identity; b) to achieve that *travestis* and transsexual persons become subjects of rights; c) to achieve a better quality of life for *travestis* and transsexual persons; d) to implement a campaign under the motto "Building *travesti*-transsexual citizenship," and demanding the right to education, work, housing and other social benefits; e) to facilitate spaces for thought, information campaigns and assessment contributing to the stated objectives; and f) to foster participation of the organization in national and international summits related to issues of human rights.[20]

The ALITT petition was rejected by the General Justice Inspection, an administrative organ of the Minister of Justice and Human Rights. They argued that the association does not have the common good as a goal, because it does not appear that the "fight for state and social acceptance of *travestism* as a proper identity" . . . nor the "construction of a *travesti*-transsexual citizenship" offer a valuable frame for the development of coexistence, and the integration of spiritual patrimony and community culture. . . . the authorization given by the state to civic associations that present themselves implies that such principles are followed by the association and I don't believe—beyond the allusions made by the presenters about the necessity to combat the discrimination to which they are subject, which they may well achieve without the authorization that they are demanding—that acceptance of *travestism* as a proper identity or the building of a *travesti*-transsexual citizenship constitutes a State objective, according to the express purposes which have inspired its founding.[21]

Faced with this denial, the association judicially appealed. Section K of the civil National Chamber confirmed the denial by asserting that,

from the objective that society accepts *travestis* or transsexuals as equals, members of the same human community, it is not evident that a general public good extending to all of society will follow, but instead, that it is only a particular group will benefit. . . . there is nothing that impedes each person from exercising his/her right to develop and debate new ideas and principles related to human rights and recommending their acceptance, but without the guarantee that state recognition implies . . . to implement campaigns demanding the right to health, education, work and housing, and other social benefits to such persons, to facilitate spaces to think, information campaigns and assessment in sexual rights and anti-discrimination matters are goals that do not lead toward the common good.[22]

The Chamber decision was appealed in the Supreme Court of the Nation, which is the last competent judicial instance in the national context.

In the meantime, articles circulated characterizing *travestism* and transsexuality as perverse lifestyles that generated the negative social consequences suffered by *travesties* and transsexuals:

No one would doubt to grant legal recognition to an association whose object was promoting scientific investigations into cancer treatment and prevention or cardiovascular afflictions. Because unfortunately we are *all* exposed to be reached at any moment by such illnesses.[23]

No "common good" provision—an essential condition for such a "blessing"—has, or can have, consistently, the acceptance of such beings on behalf of society, as if they were normal men and women. . . . these are individuals whose customs, activities and *modus vivendi* in general, present, without any pejorative intention, deviations.[24]

Deviant foreigners and strange aliens within the corpus of Argentinean citizenship, trans communities and their allies are committed to the task of contamination—just as foreigners have been doing in every place and at every time.

Notes

Dedicated to Lohana Berkins and her invincible and joyful strength.

1. Throughout the present essay, we utilize the *trans* concept as an umbrella term, that is, alluding to all those persons who identify themselves in a gender different from that which was assigned to them at birth, whatever their transitional or legal status. The term *travesti* will be utilized according to its regional specificity; that is, alluding to all those persons who, having been assigned the masculine gender at birth, identify themselves in different versions of femininity, and who may or may not surgically or hormonally modify their bodies. The term *travesti* possesses a particular political specificity, in that it unites a generalized condition of social vulnerability, an association with sexual work, the exclusion of basic rights, and the recognition of the same as a political identity. See, for example, Lohana Berkins, "Eternamente atrapadas por el sexo" ("Externally Trapped by Sex"), in *Cuerpos ineludibles: Un dialogo a partir de las sexualidades en America Latina (Ineludible Bodies: A Dialogue as from Sexualities in South America),* ed. Josefina Fernández, Monica D'Uva, and Paula Viturro (Buenos Aires: Ediciones Ají de Pollo, 2004); Lohana Berkins, "Itinerario politico del travestismo" ("Transvestism's Political Itinerary"), in *Sexualidades migrantes: Género y transgénero (Migrant Sexualities: Gender and Transgender),* ed. Diana Maffía (Buenos Aires: Feminaria, 2003). Other literature on the topic, not cited directly in this chapter, includes Marina Camps Merlo, "Aproximación a la problemática jurídica del 'cambio de sexo'" ("A First Approach to Legal Issues concerning Sex Changes"), *El Derecho Journal,* October 13, 2001; Santos Cifuentes, *Derechos personalísimos (Individual Rights)* (Buenos Aires: Astrea, 1998); Pedro Hooft, *Bioética y derechos humanos (Bioethics and Human Rights)* (Buenos Aires: Depalma, 1999); Graciela Ignacio, "Transexualismo, cambio de sexo y derecho a contraer matrimonio" ("Transsexualism, Sex Change, and the Right to Marry"), *Argentinean Jurisprudence* (1999): I-868; Ignacio Adrián Lerer and Hernán Víctor Gullco, "Denegación de pedido de cambio de sexo: Una sentencia con fundamentos equivocados" ("Rejection of an Application for a Change of Sex: An Erroneously Substantiated Court Decision"), *Argentinean Jurisprudence* (1990): III-831; Ricardo Rabinovich-Berkman, *Derecho civil parte general (Civil Law: Introduction)* (Buenos Aires: Astrea, 1998); Rabinovich-Berkman, *Vida, cuerpo y derecho (Life, Body, and the Law)* (Buenos Aires: Dunken, 1998); Florencia Abbate, *El, Ella, ¿Ella? Apuntes sobre transexualidad masculina (He, She, She? Notes on Masculine Transsexuality)* (Buenos Aires: Perfil, 1998); Kate Bornstein, *Gender Outlaws: On Men, Women, and the Rest of Us* (New York: Routledge, 1994); Henry Frignet, *El transexualismo (Transsexualism)* (Buenos Aires: Nueva Visión, 2003); Beatriz Preciado, *Manifiesto contra-sexual (Countersexual Manifesto)* (Madrid: Opera Prima, 2002).

2. Diana Maffía, "Ciudadanía sexual: Aspectos personales, legales y políticos de los derechos reproductivos como derechos humanos" ("Sexual Citizenship: Personal,

Legal, and Political Aspects of Reproductive Rights as Human Rights"), in *Feminaria* 14, nos. 26–27 (Buenos Aires: Feminaria, 2001): 2–3; Susana Rance, "Ciudadanía sexual" ("Sexual Citizenship"), *Conciencia Latinoamericana* 13, no. 3 (2001): 2–3.

3. We use the term *sex change (cambio de sexo)* according to the social understanding, *doxica*, of the expression it has in Argentina. Persons are identified as one sex or the other at birth, and that information appears on the birth certificate as well on as the personal identification that each Argentinean citizen must carry at all times. Changing sex, therefore, is associated with both the modification of the legal identity markers as well as the corporal changes demanded for a legal change of sex.

4. Two examples: a sentence establishes the need to publicize the sex change through the press over a two-month period, thus ending any hopes for privacy for trans persons. Another sentence bars the petitioner from marrying for life, making him or her, for the purposes of marriage, civilly dead.

5. This reduction also appears in the different legislative projects currently under discussion. Since all persons who demand either to modify their sexed bodies or to alter their legal names and sex or to do both—the most common possibility—are transsexuals, identifying "true" transsexuals with this preestablished formula unavoidably integrates the realization of genital reconstruction surgeries with the legal recognition of sex change.

6. On the one hand, articles 19, numbers 4 and 20 of law 17–132, which regulates the exercise of medicine, prohibit, in the first case, such interventions that may modify the sexual organs of a person and, in the second case, the practice of sterilizing interventions. Both articles additionally introduce the possibility of carrying out such interventions through judicial authorization. On the other hand, article 91 of the Criminal Code still codifies modifications that prevent a person from using the organs or affecting the reproductive capacity as "grave injuries."

7. *La Ley* (1997), 1032, our translation.

8. Carlos Fernández Sessarego, *Derecho a la identidad personal (Right to Personal Identity)* (Buenos Aires: Astrea, 1992), 331, our translation.

9. *La Ley*, 1031.

10. Carlos Fernández Sessarego, "Apuntes sobre el derecho a la identidad sexual" ("Notes on the Right to Sexual Identity"), *Argentinean Jurisprudence, Especial de Bioética* (1999): 20.

11. As Augusto Belluscio explains, "If, as a consequence of a medical-surgical treatment, a person who presents the transsexualism syndrome does not already have all the characteristics of his/her sex origin and has achieved a physical appearance which approximates the other sex, which corresponds to his/her sexual behavior, the principle of due respect to private life justifies that his/her civil state registration indicates the sex which corresponds to his/her appearance" ("Transexualidad: Derecho de los transexuales a casarse" ["Transsexuality: Transsexuals' Right to Marry"], *La Ley* [2001], 3).

12. For example, to be legally recognized as a man, it is not only necessary to have a phalloplasty but to have the vagina occluded. See Stephen Whittle, *Respect and Equality: Transsexual and Transgender Rights* (London: Cavendish, 2002); and Paula Viturro, "Ficciones de hembra" ("Female Fictions"), in *Filosofía, política y derecho: Homenaje a Enrique Marí (Philosophy, Politics, and the Law: Tribute to Enrique Mari)*, ed. Roberto Bergalli and Claudio Martyniuk (Buenos Aires: Prometeo, 2003).

13. Whittle, *Respect and Equality.*

14. Matilde Zabala de González, *Resarcimiento de daños (Indemnification for Damages),* vol. 2 (Buenos Aires: Hammurabi, 2000), 305.

15. The key judicial sentences and court commentaries on the ruling *(notas a fallo)* include: *La Ley* (1966), 23–603, with a commentary by Carlos Fontán Balestra, "La responsabilidad por lesiones en los casos de supuesto cambio de sexo"; *La Ley* (1975), A-479, with a commentary by Arturo R. Yurgano; *Argentinean Jurisprudence* 3 (1997); Bidart Campos, "El cambio de identidad civil de los transexuales quirúrgicamente transformados," *Argentinean Jurisprudence* (1990): 111–117; *El Derecho Journal* 151 (1992); *El Derecho Journal* 12 (1993), with a commentary by Julio César Rivera, "Europa condena a Francia y la Casación cambia su jurisprudencia"; *La Ley* (Buenos Aires, 1994), with commentaries by Santos Cifuentes, "Soluciones para el pseudohermafroditismo y la transexualidad," and by Julio César Rivera, "Ratificación del derecho a la identidad sexual de un caso de hermafroditismo"; *La Ley* (Córdoba, 2001), with the following commentary by Ana María Chechile, "Transexualidad y matrimonio" ("Transsexuality and Marriage"), *La Ley* (Córdoba, 2002); Héctor E. Sabelli, "Derecho y transexualidad" ("Law and Transsexuality"), *La Ley Suplemento de Derecho Constitucional* (2002).

16. Berkins, "Itinerario politico del travestismo"; Berkins, "Eternamente atrapadas por el sexo"; Berkins, Scott Long, and Alejandra Sarda, "The Rights of Transvestites in Argentina: A Report to United Nations Special Rapporteurs at the 57th Meeting of the UN Commission on Human Rights" (New York: International Gay and Lesbian Human Rights Commission, 2001), http://www.iglhrc.org/files/iglhrc/reports/Argentina_trans.pdf.

17. According to Adriana M. Wagmaister and Cristina Mourelle de Tamborenea, "In travestism there is no profound desire to modify the sex, but rather, that a psychical need has simply been established in the subject to dress with clothes of the other sex as a necessary condition to reach sexual excitement" ("Derecho a la identidad del transexual" ["Transsexual's Right to Identity"], *Argentinean Jurisprudence* [1999]: VI-960, 69; Fernandez Sessarego writes, "It is worth noting that it is not possible to mix up transsexuality, which is an existential problem, with isosexuality, be it homosexuality or lesbianism, nor with '*travestism*'" ("Apuntes sobre el derecho a la identidad sexual," *Argentinean Jurisprudence, Especial de Bioética* [1999]: 16).

18. Here we must point out that it is impossible to make explicit, in a few pages, the complex discrimination suffered by Argentinean *travestis,* given that it is based not only on gender but also for reasons of class and ethnic origin. See Josefina Fernández, *Cuerpos desobedientes (Disobedient Bodies)* (Buenos Aires: Edhasa, 2004).

19. Given the early age in which *travesti* girls are expelled from their homes, their schooling is often interrupted. Faced with economic exclusion, they turn to prostitution to survive.

20. Article 2 of the social statute of the Asociatión Lucha por la Identitad Travesti y Transexual (ALITT), a *travesti* advocacy group in Buenos Aires.

21. Conf. Resolución I.G.J. No. 001142.

22. Conf. Expte. 92673/03—"ALITT Asociación Lucha por la Identidad Travesti-Transexual c/IPJ 1720574 s/recurso contencioso administrativo," CNCIV– SALA K, April 19, 2004.

23. Omar U. Barbero, "Transexualismo: Travestismo, personería juridical, bien común" ("Transsexualism: Travestism, Judicial Personhood, Common Good"), *El Derecho Journal*, May 7, 2004, 2.

24. Ricardo Wetzler Malbrán, "Correcta resolución de un caso absurdo: La 'personalidad jurídica' de los travestis y transexuales" ("Correct Outcome in an Absurd Case: The 'Juridical Personhood' of Travesties and Transsexuals"), *El Derecho Journal*, May 7, 2004, 3.

14. Undiagnosing Gender

Judith Butler

In recent years there have been debates about the status of the DSM diagnosis of gender identity disorder and, in particular, whether there are good reasons to keep the diagnosis on the books, or whether there are no longer very many good reasons. On the one hand, those within the GLBQTI community who want to keep the diagnosis argue that it offers certification for a condition and facilitates access to medical and technological means for transitioning. Moreover, some insurance companies will absorb some of the high costs of sex change only if they first can establish that the change is "medically necessitated." It's important, for these reasons, not to understand sex change surgery or hormonal usage as "elective surgery." Although one might want to say that it is a choice, even a choice of a dramatic and profound kind, it has to, for the purpose of the insurance allocation, be a medically conditioned choice. We can surely think for quite some time on what a medically conditioned choice actually is, but for this argument it's important to distinguish between a choice conditioned by a diagnosis and one that is not. In the latter case, the choice to transition can include some or all of the following: the choice to live as another gender, to take hormonal surgery, to find and declare a name, to secure new legal status for one's gender, and to undergo surgery. If it is determined by psychological or medical professionals to be necessitated, that is, if it is determined that not undergoing this transition produces distress, maladaptation, and other forms of suffering, then it would seem to follow that the choice to transition is conceived as one that is embraced and condoned by medical professionals who have the person's ultimate well-being at issue. The "diagnosis" can operate in several ways, but one way it can and does operate, especially in the hands of those who are transphobic, is as an instrument of pathologization. To be diagnosed with gender identity disorder is to be found, in some way, to be ill, sick, wrong, out of order, abnormal, and to suffer a certain stigmatization as a consequence of the diagnosis being given at all. As a result, some activist psychiatrists and trans people have argued that the diagnosis should be eliminated altogether, that transsexuality is not a disorder, and ought not to be conceived of as one, and that trans people ought to be understood as engaged in a practice of self-determination, an exercise of autonomy. Thus, on the one hand, the diagnosis continues to be valued because it facilitates an economically feasible way of transitioning. On the other hand, the diagnosis is adamantly opposed because it continues to pathologize as a mental disorder what ought to be understood instead as one among many human possibilities of determining one's gender for oneself.

One can see from the above sketch that is, for the sake of opening this chapter, cast in terms that are perhaps too simple, that there is a tension in this debate between those who are, for the purposes of the debate, trying to gain entitlement and financial assistance and those who seek to ground the practice of transsexuality in autonomy. We might well hesitate at once and ask whether these two views are actually in opposition to one another. After all, one might argue, and people surely have, that the way that the diagnosis facilitates certain entitlements, to insurance benefits,[1] to medical treatment, and to legal status, actually works in the service of what we might call trans-autonomy. After all, if I want to transition, I may well need the diagnosis to help me achieve my goal, and achieving my goal is precisely an exercise of my autonomy. Indeed, we can argue that no one achieves autonomy without the assistance or support of a community, especially if one is making a brave and difficult choice such as transitioning. But then we have to ask whether the diagnosis is unambiguously part of the "support" that individuals need in order to exercise self-determination with respect to gender. After all, the diagnosis makes many assumptions that undercut trans-autonomy. It subscribes to forms of psychological assessment that assume that the diagnosed person is affected by forces he or she does not understand; it assumes that there is delusion or dysphoria in such people; it assumes that certain gender norms have not been properly embodied and that an error and a failure have taken place; it makes assumptions about fathers and mothers, and what normal family life is and should have been; it assumes the language of correction, adaptation, and normalization; it seeks to uphold the gender norms of the world as it is currently constituted and tends to pathologize any effort to produce gender in ways that fail to conform to existing norms (or to a certain dominant fantasy of what existing norms actually are). It is also a diagnosis, we have to remember, that has been given to people against their will, and it is a diagnosis that has effectively broken the will of many people, especially queer and trans youth.

So it would seem that the debate is a complex one, and that, in a way, those who want to keep the diagnosis want to do so because it helps them achieve their aims and, in that sense, realize their autonomies. And those who want to do away with the diagnosis want to do so because it might make for a world in which they might be regarded and treated in nonpathological ways, therefore enhancing their autonomies in important ways. On the face of it, it would seem that there are two different approaches to autonomy, but here is where it seems important to note that this is not only a philosophical problem to be answered in the abstract. To understand the difference between these views, we have to ask how the diagnosis is actually lived. What does it mean to live with it?[2] Does it help some people to live, to achieve a life that feels worth living? And does it also hinder some people from living, make them feel in a stigmatized position and, in some cases, contribute to a suicidal conclusion? On the one hand, we ought not to underestimate the benefits that the diagnosis has brought, especially to trans people of limited economic means who, without the assistance of medical insurance, could not have achieved their goals. On the other hand, we ought not to underestimate the pathologizing force of the diagnosis, especially on young people who may not have the critical resources to resist its pathologizing force. In these cases, the diagnosis can be debilitating, if not murderous. And sometimes it murders the soul, and sometimes it becomes a contributing factor in suicide. So the stakes of this debate are high, since it would seem, in the end, to be a matter of life and death, and for some the diagnosis seems to mean life, and for others, the diagnosis seems to mean death. For others, too, it may well seem to be an ambivalent blessing or, indeed, an ambivalent curse.

To understand how these two understandable positions have emerged, let's consider first what the diagnosis consists of in the United States and understand something of its history and present usages. A "diagnosis" of gender disorder has to conform to the way that the DSM-IV defines gender dysphoria.[3] The last revision to that set of definitions was instituted in 1994. For a diagnosis to be complete, however, psychological tests are needed along with "letters" from therapists providing a diagnosis and vouching that the individual in question can live and thrive in the new sexed identity. The 1994 definition is the result of several revisions, and probably needs to be understood as well in light of the American Psychiatric Association's decision in 1973 to get rid of the "diagnosis" of homosexuality as a disorder and its 1987 decision to delete "ego dystonic homosexuality," a remaining vestige from the earlier definition. Some have argued that the gender identity disorder diagnosis took over some of the work that the earlier homosexuality diagnosis performed, and that GID became an indirect way of diagnosing homosexuality as a gender identity problem. In this way, the GID continued the APA's tradition of homophobia, but in a less explicit way. In fact, conservative groups that seek to "correct" homosexuality, such as the National Association of Research and Therapy of Homosexuality, argue that if you can identify GID in a child, there's a 75 percent chance that you can predict homosexuality in that person as an adult, a result that, for them, is a clear abnormality and tragedy. Thus the diagnosis of GID is in most cases a diagnosis of homosexuality, and the disorder attached to the diagnosis implies that homosexuality remains a disorder as well.

The very way that groups such as these conceptualize the relationship between GID and homosexuality is problematic. If we are to understand GID as based on the perception of enduring gendered traits of the opposite sex, that is, boys with "feminine" attributes and girls with "masculine" attributes, then the assumption remains that boy traits will lead to a desire for women, and girl traits will lead to a desire for men. In both of these cases, heterosexual desire is presumed, where presumably opposites attract. But this is to argue, effectively, that homosexuality is to be understood as gender inversion and that the "sexual" part remains heterosexual, although inverted. It is apparently rare, according to this conceptualization, that boy traits in a boy lead to desire for other boys and that girl traits in a girl lead to desire for other girls. So the 75 percent of those diagnosed with GID are considered homosexual only if we understand homosexuality on the model of gender inversion, and sexuality on the model of heterosexual desire. Boys are still always desiring girls, and girls are still always desiring boys. If 25 percent of those diagnosed with GID do not become homosexual, that would seem to mean that they do not conform to the gender inversion model. But because the gender inversion model can only understand sexuality as heterosexuality, it would seem that the remaining 25 percent would be homosexual, that is, nonconforming to the model of homosexuality as inverted heterosexuality. Thus, we could argue, somewhat facetiously, that 100 percent of those diagnosed with GID turn out to be homosexual!

Although the joke is irresistible to me only because it would so alarm the National Association of Research and Therapy of Homosexuality, it is important to consider, more seriously, how the map of sexuality and gender is radically misdescribed by those who think within these terms. Indeed, the correlations between gender identity and sexual orientation are murky at best: we cannot predict on the basis of what gender a person is what kind of gender identity that person will have, and what direction(s) of desire he or she will ultimately entertain and pursue. Although John Money and other so-called transpositionalists think that sexual orientation tends to follow from gender identity, it would be a huge mistake to assume that gender identity causes sexual orientation or that sexuality references in some necessary way a prior gender identity. As I'll try to show, even if one could accept as unproblematic what "feminine" traits are, and what "masculine" traits are, it would not follow that the "feminine" is attracted to the masculine, and the "masculine" to the feminine. That would only follow if we used an exclusively heterosexual matrix to understand desire. And actually, that matrix would misrepresent some of the queer crossings in heterosexuality, when for instance a feminized heterosexual man wants a feminized woman, in order that the two might well be "girls together." Or when masculine heterosexual women want their boys to be both girls and boys for them. The same queer crossings happen in lesbian and gay life, when butch on butch produces a specifically lesbian mode of male homosexuality. And bisexuality, as I've said before, can't be reducible to two heterosexual desires, understood as a feminine side wanting a masculine object, or a masculine side wanting a feminine one. Those crossings are as complex as anything that happens within heterosexuality or homosexuality. These kinds of crossings happen more often than is generally noted, and it makes a mockery of the transpositionalist claim that gender identity is a predictor of sexual orientation. Indeed, sometimes it is the very disjunction between gender identity and sexual orientation—the disorientation of the transpositionalist model itself—that constitutes for some people what is most erotic and exciting.

The way that the disorder has been taken up by researchers with homophobic aims presupposes the tacit thesis that homosexuality is the damage that will follow from such a change, but it is most important to argue that it is not a disorder and that there is a whole range of complex relations to cross-gendered life; some of them may involve dressing in another gender, some of them may involve living in another gender, some of them may involve hormones, and surgery, and most of them involve one or more of the above. Sometimes this implies a change in so-called object choice, but sometimes not. One can become a transman and want boys (and become a male homosexual), or one can become a transman and want girls (and become a heterosexual), or one can become a transman and undergo a set of shifts in sexual orientation that constitute a very specific life history and narrative. That narrative is not capturable by a category, or it may be capturable by a category only for a time. Life histories are histories of becoming, and categories can sometimes act to freeze that process. Shifts in sexual persuasion can be in response to particular partners, so that lives, trans or not, don't always emerge as coherently heterosexual or homosexual, and the very meaning and lived experience of bisexuality can also shift through time, forming a particular history that reflects certain kinds of experiences rather than others.

The diagnosis of gender dysphoria requires that a life takes on a more or less definite shape over time; a life can only be diagnosed if it meets the test of time.[4] One has to show that one has wanted for a long time to live life as the other gender; it also requires that one prove that one has a practical and livable plan to live life for a long time as the other gender. The diagnosis, in this way, wants to establish that gender is a relatively permanent phenomenon. It won't do, for instance, to walk into a clinic and say that it was only after you read a book by Kate Bornstein that you realized what you wanted to do, but that it wasn't really conscious for you until that time. It can't be that cultural life changed, that words were written and exchanged, that you went to events and to clubs, and saw that certain ways of living were really possible and desirable, and something about your own possibilities became clear to you in ways that they had not been before. You would be ill-advised to say that you believe that the norms that govern what is a recognizable and livable life are changeable, and that within your lifetime, new cultural efforts were made to broaden those norms, so that people like yourself might well live within supportive communities as a transsexual, and that it was precisely this shift in the public norms, and the presence of a supportive community, that allowed you to feel that transitioning has become for you possible and desirable. In this sense, you cannot explicitly subscribe to a view that changes in gendered experience follow on changes in social norms, since that would not suffice to satisfy the Harry Benjamin standard rules for the care of gender identity disorder. Indeed, those rules presume, as does the GID, that we all more or less "know" already what the norms for gender—"masculine" and "feminine"—are, and that all we really need to do is figure out whether they are being embodied in this instance or some other. But what if those terms no longer do the descriptive work that we need them to do? What if that only operates in unwieldy ways to describe the experience of gender that someone has? And if the norms for care and the measures for the diagnosis assume that we are permanently constituted in one way or another, what happens to gender as a mode of becoming? Are we stopped in time, made more regular and coherent than we necessarily want to be, when we submit to the norms in order to achieve the entitlements one needs, and the status one desires?

Although there are strong criticisms to be made of the diagnosis—and I will detail some of them below when I turn to the text itself—it would nevertheless be wrong to call for its eradication without first putting into place a set of structures through which transitioning can be paid for and legal status attained. In other words, if the diagnosis is now the instrument through which benefits and status can be achieved, it cannot be simply disposed of without finding other, durable ways to achieve those same results.

One obvious response to this dilemma is to argue that one should approach the diagnosis *strategically*. One could then reject the truth-claims that the diagnosis makes, that is, reject the description it offers of transsexuality but nevertheless make use of the diagnosis as a pure instrument, a vehicle for achieving one's goals. One would, then, ironically or facetiously, or half-heartedly submit to the diagnosis, even as one inwardly maintains that there is nothing "pathological" about the desire to transition and the resolve to realize that desire. But here we have to ask whether submitting to the diagnosis does not involve, more or less consciously, a certain subjection to the diagnosis such that one does end up internalizing some aspect of the diagnosis, conceiving of oneself as mentally ill or "failing" in normality, or both, even as one seeks to take a purely instrumental attitude toward these terms.

The more important point in support of this last argument has to do with children and young adults, since when we ask who it is who would be able to sustain a purely instrumental relation to the diagnosis, it tends to be shrewd and savvy adults, ones who have other discourses available for understanding who they are and want to be. But are children and teens always capable of effecting the distance necessary to sustain a purely instrumental approach to being subjected to a diagnosis?

Richard Isay gives as the primary reason to get rid of the diagnosis altogether its effect on children. The diagnosis itself, he writes, "may cause emotional damage by injuring the self-esteem of a child who has no mental disorder."[5] Isay, a doctor, accepts the claim that many young gay boys prefer so-called feminine behavior as children, playing with their mother's clothes, refusing rough-and-tumble activities, but he argues that the problem here is not with the traits but with "parental admonitions . . . aimed at modifying this behavior [which] deleteriously affect[s] these boys' self-regard." His solution is for parents to learn to be supportive of what he calls "gender atypical traits." Isay's contribution is important in many respects, but one clear contribution it makes is that it calls for reconceptualizing the phenomenon that refuses pathologizing language: he refuses to elevate typical gender attributes to a standard of psychological normality or to relegate atypical traits to abnormality. Instead, he substitutes the language of typicality for normality altogether. Physicians who argue against Isay not only insist that the disorder *is* a disorder, and that the presentation of persistently atypical gender traits in children is a "psychopathology,"[6] but they couch this insistence on pathologization with a paternalistic concern for the afflicted, citing how the diagnosis is necessary for insurance benefits and other entitlements. Indeed, they exploit the clear and indisputable need that poor, working-class, and middle-class trans-aspirants have for medical insurance and legal support to argue not only in favor of keeping the diagnosis on the books but in favor of their view that this is a pathology that must be corrected. So even if the diagnosis is approached as an instrument or vehicle for accomplishing the end goal of transitioning, the diagnosis can still (1) instill a sense of mental disorder on those whom it diagnoses, (2) entrench the power of the diagnosis to conceptualize transsexuality as a pathology, and (3) be used as a rationale by those who are in well-funded research institutes whose aim it is to keep transsexuality within the sphere of mental pathology.

Some other solutions have been proposed that seek to ameliorate the pathological effects of the diagnosis by taking it out of the hands of the mental health profession altogether. Jacob Hale argues that psychologists and psychiatrists should not mediate this matter; the question of whether and how to gain access to medical and technological resources should be a matter between client and medical doctor exclusively.[7] His view is that one goes to the doctor for other kinds of reconstructive surgeries or on other occasions where taking hormones may prove felicitous, and no one asks you a host of questions about your earliest fantasies or childhood practices of play. The certification of stable mental health is not required for breast reduction or menopausal ingestion of estrogen. The required intervention of a mental health professional on the occasion in which one wants to transition inserts a paternalistic structure into the process and undermines the very autonomy that is the basis for the claim of entitlement to begin with. A therapist is asked to worry about whether you will be able, psychologically, to integrate into an established social world characterized by large-scale conformity to accepted gender norms, but the therapist is not asked to say whether you are brave enough or have enough community support to live a transgendered life when the threat of violence and discrimination against you will be heightened. The therapist is not asked whether your way of living gender will help to produce a world of fewer constrictions on gender, and whether you are up to that important task. The therapist is asked to predict whether your choice will lead to postoperative regret, and here your desire is examined for its persistence and tenacity, but little attention is given to what happens to one's persistent and tenacious desires when the social world, and the diagnosis itself, demeans them as psychic disorders.[8]

I began this chapter by suggesting that the view one takes on keeping or opposing the diagnosis depends in part on how one conceives the conditions for autonomy. From Isay, we see an argument that claims that the diagnosis not only undermines the autonomy of children but mistakes their autonomies for pathology. In the argument that Hale offers, we see that the diagnosis itself takes on a different meaning if mental health professionals no longer use it. The question remains, though, whether medical practitioners with no particular background in mental health will nevertheless use mental health criteria to make decisions that could be no less favorable than those made by mental health practitioners. If Hale is arguing, though, that it ought to be shifted to medical doctors as part of a drive to redefine the diagnosis so that it no longer contains mental health criteria in it, then he is also proposing a new diagnosis or no diagnosis, since the DSM-IV rendition cannot be voided of its mental health criteria. To answer the question of whether the shift to medical doctors would be propitious, we would have to ask whether the inclinations of medical practitioners are generally to be trusted with this responsibility, or whether the world of progressive therapists offers a better chance for humane and successful passage through the process of diagnosis. Although I do not have a sociologically grounded answer to this question, I consider that it has to be pursued before one can judge the appropriateness of Hale's recommendation. The great benefit of his view is that it treats the patient as a client who is exercising consumer autonomy within the medical domain. That autonomy is assumed, and it is also posited as the ultimate goal and meaning of transitioning itself.

But this raises the question of how autonomy ought to be conceived in this debate, and whether revisions in the diagnosis itself might provide a way around the apparent stand-off between those who wish to have the diagnosis deleted and those who wish to keep it for the instrumental value it provides, especially for those in financial need. There are two different conceptions of autonomy at work in this debate. The view that opposes the diagnosis altogether tends to be individualist, if not libertarian, and the views that argue in favor of keeping the diagnosis tend to acknowledge that there are material conditions for the exercise of liberty. The view that worries that the diagnosis may well be internalized or damaging suggests that the psychological conditions for autonomy can be undermined, and have been undermined, and that youth are at higher risk for this compromised and damaged sense of self.

Autonomy, liberty, and freedom are all related terms, and they also imply certain kinds of legal protections and entitlements. After all, the U.S. Constitution guarantees the pursuit of liberty, and it could be argued that restrictive conditions imposed on transsexual and transgendered individuals to exercise a liberty proper to that identity and practice are discriminatory. Paradoxically, the insurance companies demean the notion of liberty when they distinguish, say, between mastectomies that are "medically necessitated" and those that constitute "elective surgery." The former are conceived as operations that no one readily chooses, that are imposed on individuals by medical circumstance, usually cancer. But even that conceptualization misrepresents the kinds of choices that informed patients make about how to approach cancer, where possible treatments include radiation, chemotherapy, arimidex, lumpectomy, partial and full mastectomy. Women will make different choices about treatment depending on how they feel about their breasts and the prospects of further cancer, and the range of choices made is significantly broad. Some women will struggle to keep their breasts no matter what; others let them go without much difficulty. Some will choose reconstruction and make some choices about prospective breasts, and others choose not to.

A rather butch lesbian in San Francisco recently had cancer in one breast and decided, in consultation with her doctor, to have a full mastectomy. She thought it was a good idea to have the other breast removed as well, since she wanted to minimize the chances of a recurrence. This choice was made easier for her because she had no strong emotional attachment to her breasts: they did not form an important part of her gendered or sexual self-understanding. Whereas her insurance company agreed to pay for the first mastectomy, they worried that the second breast was "elective surgery" and that, if they paid for that, it would be setting a precedent for covering elective transsexual surgery. The insurance company thus wanted to limit both consumer autonomy in medical decision making (understanding the woman as someone who wanted for medical reasons to have the second breast removed) and to dismiss autonomy as the basis for a transsexual operation (understanding the woman as a possible transitioner). At the same time, a friend of mine recovering from a mastectomy sought to understand what possibilities existed for her for reconstructive surgery. She was referred by her doctor to transsexual clients who could introduce her to various technologies and the relative aesthetic merits of those options. Although I'm not aware of coalitions of breast-cancer survivors and transsexuals, I can see how a movement could easily emerge whose main demand would be to petition insurance companies to recognize the role of autonomy in producing and maintaining primary and secondary sex characteristics. All this seems less strange, I would suggest, when we understand cosmetic surgery on a continuum with all the other practices that humans engage in to maintain and cultivate primary- and secondary-sex characteristics for cultural and social reasons. I gather that men who want penile augmentation or women who want breast augmentation and

reduction are not sent to psychiatrists for certification. It is, of course, interesting to consider in light of current gender norms why a woman who wants
breast reduction requires no psychological certification, but a man who wants
penile reduction may well. There is no presumption of mental malfunction-
ing for women who take estrogen or men who take Viagra. This is because, I
presume, they are operating within the norm to the extent that they are seeking to enhance the "natural," making readjustments within acceptable norms,
and sometimes even confirming and strengthening traditional gender norms.

The butch, nearly trans, person who wanted her cancerous and non-
cancerous breasts removed understood that the only way she could gain the
benefits of a mastectomy was to get cancer in her other breast or to subject
her own gender desires to medical and psychiatric review. Although she didn't
consider herself trans, she understood that she could present as trans in order
to qualify for the GID and insurance benefits. Sometimes reconstructive breast
surgery is covered by medical insurance, even if done for elective reasons, but
mastectomy is not included as elective surgeries covered by insurance. In the
world of insurance, it appears to make sense that a woman might want less
breast, but no sense that she would want no breast. Wanting no breast puts
into question whether she still wants to be a woman. It is as if the butch's
desire to have the breast removed is not quite plausible as a healthy option
unless it is the sign of a gender disorder or some other medical urgency.

But why is it that we do accept these other choices as choices, regardless of what we take their social meanings to be? Society doesn't consider
itself to have a right to stop a woman from enlarging or diminishing her
breasts, and we don't consider penile enhancement to be a problem, unless it
is being done by an illegitimate doctor who botches the results, as it sometimes sadly is. No one gets sent to a psychiatrist because they announce their
plans to cut or grow their hair or to go on a diet, unless one is at risk for
anorexia, and yet these practices are part of the daily habits of cultivating
secondary-sex characteristics, if we expand that category to mean all the various bodily indicators or "cues" of sex. If the bodily traits "indicate" sex, then
sex is not quite the same as the means by which it is indicated. Sex is made
understandable through the signs that indicate how it should be read or understood. These bodily indicators are the cultural means by which the sexed
body is read. They are themselves bodily, and they operate as signs, so there is
no easy way to distinguish between what is "materially" true and what is "culturally" true about a sexed body. I don't mean to suggest that purely cultural
signs produce a material body, but only that the body does not become sexually readable without those signs, and that those signs are irreducibly cultural
and material at once.

So what are the versions of autonomy at work in these various approaches to the DSM diagnosis of gender identity disorder? And how might we conceive of autonomy in such a way that we might find a way of thinking through the reasonable disagreements that have emerged on whether to preserve or eradicate the diagnosis? Although it is obvious that not all individuals diagnosed with GID are or wish to become transsexual, they are nevertheless affected by the use of the diagnosis to further the aims of transsexuals, since to use the diagnosis is to strengthen its status as a useful instrument. This is no reason not to use it, but it does imply a certain risk, and certain implications. A strengthened diagnosis can have effects that its users do not intend or condone. And though it may well serve an individual's important needs to secure status and funding for a transition, it may well be used by the medical and psychiatric establishments to extend their pathologizing influences on populations of transsexuals, trans youth, and lesbian, bi, and gay youth as well. From the point of view of the individual, the diagnosis can be regarded as an instrument by which to further one's self-expression and self-determination; indeed, it can be counted among the fundamental instruments one needs to make a transition that makes life livable and that provides the grounds for one's flourishing as an embodied subject. On the other hand, the instrument takes on a life of its own, and it can work to make life harder for those who suffer by being pathologized and who lose certain rights and liberties, including child custody, employment, and housing, by virtue of the stigma attached to the diagnosis or, more precisely, by virtue of the stigma that the diagnosis strengthens and furthers. Whereas it would no doubt be best to live in a world in which there was no such stigma, and no such diagnosis, we do not yet live in such a world; and the profound suspicion about the mental health of those who transgress gender norms structures the majority of psychological discourses and institutions, medical approaches to gender, and legal and financial institutions that regulate questions of status and possibilities for financial assistance and medical benefits.

There is an important argument to be made from the perspective of freedom, and yet it is important to remember that the specific forms that freedom takes depend on the social conditions and social institutions that govern human options at this time. Those who claim that transsexuality is, and should be, a matter of choice, an exercise of freedom, are surely right, and they are right as well to point out that the various obstacles posed by the psychological and psychiatric professions are paternalistic forms of power by which a basic human freedom is being suppressed. Underlying some of these positions is a libertarian approach to sex transformation. Richard Green, the president of the Harry Benjamin International Gender Dysphoria Association, and a strong advocate for transsexual rights, including the rights of transsexual parents, cites John Stuart Mill, arguing on behalf of this issue as a matter of personal freedom and of privacy. He writes that Mill "argued forcefully that adults should be able to do with their bodies as they wish providing that it did not bring harm to another. Therefore, if the third gender, the transsexual, or the would-be limb amputee can continue to shoulder social responsibilities post-surgery, then the surgical requests are not society's business."[9] Although Green makes this claim, one he himself calls "philosophical," he notes that it comes into conflict with the question of who will pay, and whether society has an obligation to pay for a procedure being defended as a matter of personal liberty.

I don't find many people writing in this area, except from within the discourse of the Christian Right, whose response to GID is to embrace it wholeheartedly and say, "Don't take this diagnosis away from me! Pathologize me, please!" There are, surely, many psychiatrists and psychologists who insist on GID as a pathology. And there is a well-funded and impossibly prolific professor of neuropsychiatry and behavioral science at the University of South Carolina, George Rekers, who combines a polemical political conservatism with an effort to intensify and extend the use of this diagnosis.[10] His main concern seems to be about boys, boys becoming men, and men becoming strong fathers in the context of heterosexual marriage. He also traces the rise of GID to the breakdown of the family, the loss of strong father figures for boys, and the subsequent "disturbance" that it is said to cause. His manifest concern about the emergence of homosexuality in boys is clear from his discussion as well, citing as he does the 1994 DSM conclusion that 75 percent of GID youth turn out to be homosexual as adults. Rekers has published loads of studies strewn with "data" presented within the context of empirical research protocols. Although intensely polemical, he understands himself as a scientist and an empiricist, and he attributes ideological bias to his opponents. He writes that "in a generation confused by radical ideologies on male and female roles, we need solid research on men and women who are well adjusted examples of a secure male identity and a secure female identity."[11] His "solid research" is intended to show the benefits of distinguishing clearly between gender norms and their pathologies "for family life and the larger culture." In this vein, Rekers also notes that "preliminary findings have been published in the literature which report on the positive therapeutic effects of religious conversion for curing transsexualism ... and on the positive therapeutic effect of a church ministry to repentant homosexuals."[12] He seems to be relatively unconcerned with girls, which impresses me as entirely symptomatic of his preoccupation with patriarchal authority and his inability to see the threat that women of all kinds might pose to the presumptions he makes about male power. The fate of masculinity absorbs this study because masculinity, a fragile and fallible construct, needs the social support of marriage and stable family life in order to find its right path. Indeed, masculinity by itself tends to falter, in his view, and needs to be housed and propped up by various social supports, suggesting that masculinity is itself a function of these social organizations and has no intrinsic meaning outside them. In any case, there are people like Rekers who make an adamant and highly polemical case, not only for retaining the diagnosis but for strengthening it, and they give highly conservative political reasons for strengthening the diagnosis so that the structures that support normalcy can be strengthened.

Ironically, it is these very structures that support normalcy that compel the need for the diagnosis to begin with, including its benefits for those who need it in order to effect a transition. It's with some irony, then, that those who suffer under the diagnosis also find that there is not much hope for doing without it. The fact is, that under current conditions, a number of people have reason to worry about the consequences of having their diagnosis taken away or failing to establish eligibility for the diagnosis. Perhaps the rich will be able to shell out the tens of thousands of dollars that an FTM transformation entails, including double mastectomy and a very good phalloplasty, but most people, especially poor and working-class trannies, will not be able to foot the bill. At least in the United States where socialized medicine is largely understood as a communist plot, it won't be an option to have the state or insurance companies pay for these procedures without first establishing that there are serious and enduring medical and psychiatric reasons for doing so. A conflict has to be established; there has to be enormous suffering; there has to be persistent ideation of oneself in the other gender; there has to be a trial period of cross-dressing throughout the day to see if adaptation can be predicted; there have to be therapy sessions, and letters attesting to the balanced state of one's mind. In other words, one must be subjected to a regulatory apparatus, as Foucault would have called it, in order to get to the point where something like an exercise in freedom becomes possible. One has to submit to labels and names, to incursions, to invasions, one has to be gauged against measures of normalcy, and one has to pass the test. So sometimes what this means is that one needs to become very savvy about these standards and know how to present oneself in such a way that one comes across as a plausible candidate. And sometimes therapists find themselves in a bind, being asked to supply a letter for someone they want to help, but abhorring the very fact that they have to write this letter, in the language of diagnosis, in order to help produce the life that their client wants to have. In a sense, the regulatory discourse surrounding the diagnosis takes on a life of its own: it may not actually describe the patient who uses the language to get what he or she wants; it may not reflect the beliefs of the therapist who nevertheless signs her name to the diagnosis and passes it along. Approaching the diagnosis strategically involves a series of individuals not quite believing what they say, signing on to language that does not represent the reality it is or should be. The price of using the diagnosis to get what one wants is that one cannot use language to say what one really thinks is true. One pays for one's freedom, as it were, by sacrificing one's claim to use language truthfully. In other words, one purchases one sort of freedom only by giving up another.

So perhaps this brings us closer to understanding the quandary of autonomy that the diagnosis introduces and the specific problem of how freedom is to be understood as conditioned and articulated through specific social means. The only way to secure the means by which to start this transformation is by learning how to present yourself in a discourse that is not yours, a discourse that effaces you in the act of representing you, a discourse that denies the language you might want to use to describe who you are, how you get here, and what you want from this life, denies all this at the same time that it holds out the promise, if not the blackmail, that you will get this life, you stand a chance of getting your life, the body and the gender you want, if you agree to falsify yourself and, in so doing, support and ratify the power of this diagnosis over many more people in the future.

If one comes out in favor of choice, and against diagnosis, it would seem that one has to deal with the enormous financial consequences of this decision for those who cannot pay for the resources at hand and whose insurance, if there is insurance, will not honor this choice as one that is to be included as a covered elective treatment. And even when local laws are passed, offering insurance to city workers who seek such treatments, as is the case now in San Francisco, there are still diagnostic tests to pass, so choice is clearly bought at a price, sometimes at the price of truth itself.

The way things are set up, if we want to support the poor and the uninsured in this area, it would seem that we have to support efforts to extend insurance coverage, and to work within the diagnostic categories accepted by the AMA and the APA, codified in the DSM-IV. The call to have matters of gender identity depathologized and for elective surgery and hormone treatment to be covered as a legitimate set of elective procedures seems bound to fail, only because most medical, insurance, and legal practitioners are committed to supporting access to sex change technologies only if we are talking about a disorder. Arguments to the effect that there is an overwhelming and legitimate human demand here are bound to prove inadequate. Examples of the kinds of justifications that ideally would make sense and should have a claim on insurance companies include: this transition will allow someone to realize certain human possibilities that will help this life to flourish, or this will allow someone to emerge from fear and shame and paralysis into a situation of enhanced self-esteem and the ability to form close ties with others, or this transition will help alleviate a source of enormous suffering or give reality to a fundamental human desire to assume a bodily form that expresses a fundamental sense of selfhood. Though some gender identity clinics, like the one at the University of Minnesota run by William Bockting, do make such arguments, and do provide supportive therapeutic contexts for people disposed to make a choice on this issue, whether it be to live as transgendered or transsexual, whether to be third sex, whether to consider the process as one of a becoming whose end is not in sight, and may never be.[13] But even that clinic has to supply materials to insurance companies that comply with DSM-IV.[14]

The exercise of freedom that is performed through a strategic approach to the diagnosis involves one in a measure of unfreedom, since the diagnosis itself demeans the self-determining capacities of those it diagnoses, but whose self-determinations, paradoxically, it sometimes furthers. When the diagnosis can be used strategically, and when it undermines its own presumption that the individual diagnosed is afflicted with a condition over which no choice can be exercised, the use of the diagnosis can subvert the aims of the diagnosis. On the other hand, to pass the test, one must submit to the language of the diagnosis. Although the stated aim of the diagnosis is it wants to know whether an individual can successfully conform to living according to the norms of another gender, it seems that the real test that the GID poses is whether one can conform to the language of the diagnosis. In other words, it may not be a matter of whether one can conform to the norms that govern life as another gender, but whether one can conform to the *psychological discourse* that stipulates what these norms are.

Let's take a look at that language. The GID section of the DSM starts by making clear that there are two parts of this diagnosis. The first is that "there must be strong and persistent cross-gender identification." This would be difficult to ascertain, I would think, since identifications do not always appear as such: they can remain aspects of hidden fantasy, or parts of dreams, or inchoate structures of behavior. But the DSM asks us to be a bit more positivist in our approach to identification, assuming that we can read off of behavior what identifications are at work in any given person's psychic life. Cross-gender identification is defined as "the desire to be" the other sex, "or the insistence that one is." The "or" in this line is significant, since it implies that one might desire to be the other sex—and we have to suspend for the moment what "the other sex" is and, by the way, in my mind, it is not quite clear—without necessarily insisting on it. These are two separate criteria. They do not have to emerge in tandem. So if there is a way to determine that someone has this "desire to be" even though they do not insist on it, that would seem to be satisfactory grounds for concluding that cross-gender identification is happening. And if there is "an insistence that one is" the other sex, then that would function as a separate criterion which, if fulfilled, would warrant the conclusion that cross-gender identification is happening. In the second instance, an act of speech is required in which someone insists that one is the other sex, an insistence understood as a way of laying claim to the other sex in one's own speech and of attributing that other sex to oneself. So certain expressions of this "desire to be" and "insistence that I am" are precluded as viable evidence for the claim. "This must not merely be a desire for any per-ceived cultural advantages of being the other sex." Now, this is a moment for pause, since the diagnosis assumes that we can have an experience of sex without considering what the cultural advantages of being a given sex are. Is this, in fact, possible? If sex is experienced by us within a cultural matrix of meanings, if it comes to have its significance and meaning in reference to a wider social world, then can we separate the experience of "sex" from its social meanings, including the way in which power functions throughout those meanings? *Sex* is a term that applies to people across the board, so that it is difficult to refer to my "sex" as if it were radically singular. If it is, gener-ally speaking, then, never only "my sex" or "your sex" that is at issue, but a way in which the category of "sex" exceeds the personal appropriations of it, then it would seem to be impossible to perceive sex outside this cultural matrix and to understand this cultural matrix outside the possible advantages it may afford. Indeed, when we think about cultural advantages, whether we are doing something—anything—for the cultural advantage it affords, we have to ask whether what we do is advantageous for me, that is, whether it furthers or satisfies my desires and my aspirations. Now there are crude analyses that suggest that FTM happens only because it is easier to be a man in society than a woman. But those analyses don't ask whether it is easier to be *trans* than to be in a perceived bio-gender, that is, a gender that seems to "follow" from natal sex. If social advantage were ruling all these decisions unilaterally, then the forces in favor of social conformity would probably win the day. On the other hand, there are arguments that could be made that it is more ad-vantageous to be a woman if you want to wear fabulous red scarves and tight skirts on the street at night. In some places in the world, that is obviously true, although bio-women, those in drag, transgendered, and transwomen share certain risks on the street, especially if any of them is perceived as a prostitute. Similarly, one might say, it is generally more culturally advantageous to be a man if you want to be taken seriously in a philosophy seminar. This seems to be true, but some men are at no advantage at all, if they cannot talk the talk, and being a man is no sufficient condition for being able to talk that talk. So I wonder whether it is possible to consider becoming one sex or the other without considering the cultural advantage it might afford, since the cultural advantage it might afford will be the advantage it affords to someone who has certain kinds of desires, who wants to be in a position to take advantage of certain cultural opportunities. If GID insists that the desire to be another sex or the insistence that one is the other sex has to be evaluated without reference to cultural advantage, it may be that GID misunderstands some of the cultural forces that go into making and sustaining certain desires of this sort. And then GID would also have to respond to the epistemological question of whether sex can be perceived *at all* outside the cultural matrix of power relations in which relative advantage and disadvantage would be part of that matrix.

The diagnosis also requires that there be "persistent discomfort" about one's assigned sex or "inappropriateness," and here is where the discourse of "not getting it right" comes in. The assumption is that there is an appropriate sense that people can and do have, a sense that this gender is appropriate for me, to me. And that there is a comfort that I would have, could have, and that it could be had if it were the right norm. In an important sense, the diagnosis assumes that gender norms are relatively fixed and that the problem is making sure that you find the right one, the one that will allow you to feel appropriate where you are, comfortable in the gender that you are. There must be evidence of "distress"—yes, certainly, distress. And if there is not "distress," then there should be "impairment." Here it makes sense to ask where all this comes from: the distress and the impairment, the not being able to function well at the workplace or in handling certain daily chores. The diagnosis presumes that one feels distress and discomfort and inappropriateness because one is in the wrong gender, and that conforming to a different gender norm, if viable for the person in question, will make one feel much better. But the diagnosis does not ask whether there is a problem with the gender norms that it takes as fixed and intransigent, whether these norms produce distress and discomfort, whether they impede one's ability to function, whether they generate sources of suffering for some people or for many people, and what the conditions are in which they provide a sense of comfort, or belonging, or, even, become the site for realizing certain human possibilities that let a person feel possibility, futurity, life, and well-being.

The diagnosis seeks to establish criteria by which a cross-gendered person might be identified, but the diagnosis, in articulating criteria, articulates a rigid version of gender norms. It offers the following account of gender norms (the emphases are mine) in the language of simple description: "In boys, cross-gendered identification is manifested by a marked preoccupation with traditionally feminine activities. They may have a preference for dressing in girls' or women's clothes *or may improvise such items from available materials* when genuine materials are unavailable. Towels, aprons, and scarves are often used to represent long hair or skirts." The description seems to be based on a history of collected and summarized observations; someone has seen boys doing this and reported it, and others have done the same, and those reports are collected, and generalizations are derived from the observable data. But who is observing, and through what grid of observation? This we do not know. And though we are told that in boys this identification is "marked" by a preoccupation with "traditionally feminine activities," we are not told in what this mark consists. And it seems important, since the "mark" will be what selects the observation as evidence for the thesis at hand. In fact, what follows from this claim seems to undermine the claim itself, since what the boys are said to do is to engage in a series of substitutions and improvisations. We are told that they may have a preference for dressing in girls' or women's clothes, but we're not told whether the preference manifests itself in actually dressing in them. We are left with a vague notion of "preference" that could simply describe a supposed mental state, or internal disposition, or it may be inferred by practice. This last seems open to interpretation. But what we are told is that one practice they do engage in is improvisation, taking items that are available and making them work as feminine clothing. Feminine clothing is called "genuine clothing," which leaves us to conclude that the materials with which these boys are improvising is less than genuine, other than genuine, if not ingenuine and "false." "Towels, aprons, and scarves are often used to represent long hair or skirts." So there is a certain imaginary play, and a capacity to transfigure one item into another through improvisation and substitution. In other words, there is an art practice at work here, one that would be difficult to name, simply, as the simple act of conforming to a norm. Something is being made, something is being made from something else, something is being tried out. And if it is an improvisation, it is not fully scripted in advance.

Although the description goes on to insist on the fascination of these boys with "stereotypical female-type dolls"—and "Barbie" is mentioned by name—and "female fantasy figures" also seem prominent, we are not really given an account of the place that dolls and fantasy have in formulating gender identification. For a given gender to be a site of fascination or, indeed, for a so-called stereotype to be a source of fascination may well involve several kinds of relations to the stereotype. It may be that the stereotype is fascinating because it is overdetermined, that it has become the site for a number of conflicting desires. But the DSM assumes that the doll you play with is the one you want to be. But maybe you want to be her friend, her rival, her lover. Maybe you want all this at once. Maybe you do some switching with her. Maybe playing with the doll, too, is a scene of improvisation that articulates a complex set of dispositions, and that something else is going on in this play besides a simple act of conforming to a norm. Perhaps the norm is itself being played, explored, even busted. We would need to take play as a more complex phenomenon than does the DSM if we were to begin to pose and pursue these kinds of questions.

The way you can tell that girls are having cross-gendered identification according to the DSM-IV is that they argue with their parents about wearing certain kinds of clothes. They prefer boys' clothing and short hair, apparently, and they have mainly boy friends, express a desire to become a boy, but also, oddly, "they are often misidentified by strangers as boys." I am trying to think through how it could be that evidence of one's cross-gendered identification is confirmed by being identified as a boy by a stranger. It would seem that random social assignment functions as evidence, as if the stranger knows something about the psychological makeup of that girl, or as if the girl has solicited that interpellation from the stranger. The DSM goes on to say that the girl "may ask to be called by a boy's name." But even there, it seems, she is first addressed as a boy and, only after being addressed, wants to take on a name that will confirm the rightness of the address itself. Here again, the very language that the DSM provides seems to undercut its own arguments, since it wants to be able to claim cross-gendered identification as part of gender identity disorder, and so as a psychological problem that can be addressed through treatment. It imagines that each individual has a relation to its "assigned sex" and that this relation is either one of discomfort and distress or a sense of comfort and being at peace. But even this notion of "assigned sex"— sex "assigned" at birth—implies that sex is socially produced and relayed, and that it comes to us not merely as a private reflection that each of us makes about ourselves but as a critical interrogation that each of us makes of a social category assigned to us, that exceeds us in its generality and power, but which also, consequentially, instances itself at the site of our bodies. It is interesting that the DSM seeks to establish gender as a set of more or less fixed and conventional norms, even as it keeps giving us evidence to the contrary, almost as if it is at cross-purposes with its own aims. Just as the boys who were improvising and substituting were doing something other than conforming to preestablished norms, so the girls seem to be understanding something about social assignment, about what might happen if someone starts to address you as a boy, and what that might make possible. I'm not sure that the girl who seizes on this stray and felicitous interpellation is giving evidence to a preestablished "disorder" of any kind, but noting that the very means by which sex comes to be, through assignment, opens up possibilities for reassignment that excite her sense of agency, play, and possibility. Just as the boys who are playing with scarves as if they were something else are already versing themselves in the world of props and improvisation, so the girls, seizing on the possibility of being called by another name, are exploring the possibilities of naming themselves in the context of that social world. They are not simply giving evidence to internal states but performing certain kinds of actions, and even engaging practices, practices that turn out to be essential to the making of gender itself.

The DSM offers a certain discourse of compassion, as many psychiatrists do, suggesting that to live with such a disorder is a cause of distress and unhappiness. The DSM has its own antipoetry on this subject: "In young children, distress is manifested by the stated unhappiness about their assigned sex." And here it seems that the only unhappiness is one created by an internal desire, not by the fact that there is no social support for such children, that the adults to whom they express their unhappiness are diagnosing and pathologizing them, that the norm of gender frames the conversation in which the expression of unhappiness takes place. At the same time that the DSM understands itself as diagnosing a distress that then becomes a candidate for alleviation as a result of the diagnosis, it also understands that "social pressure" can lead to "extreme isolation for such a child." The DSM does not talk about suicide, even though we know that the cruelty of adolescent peer pressure on transgendered youth can lead to suicide. The DSM does not talk about risks of death, generally, or murder, something that happened only miles from my home in California last week when a transgendered boy arrived at a teen party in a dress, and his body was found dead from beating and strangulation in the Sierra foothills. Apparently, the "distress" that comes from living in a world in which suicide and death by violence remain real issues is not part of the diagnosis of GID. So consider that the DSM remarks, after a brief discussion of the euphemistically called "peer teasing and rejection," that "children may refuse to attend school because of teasing or pressure to dress in attire stereotypical of their assigned sex." Here the language of the text seems to understand that there may be an impairment of ordinary functioning caused by the pressure of social norms. But then, in the next sentence, it domesticates the distress caused by social norms, by claiming that it is the person's own preoccupation with cross-gender wishes that often "interferes with ordinary activities" and ends up in situations of social isolation. In a way, the fact of social violence against transgendered youth is euphemized as teasing and pressure, and then the distress caused by that is recast as an internal problem, a sign of preoccupation, self-involvement, which seems to follow from the wishes themselves. Indeed, is the "isolation" noted here real, or are the communities of support eclipsed from the observation? And when there is isolation, is it, therefore, a sign of a pathology? Or is it, for some, the cost of expressing certain kinds of desires in public?

What is most worrisome, however, is how the diagnosis works as its own social pressure, causing distress, establishing wishes as pathological, intensifying the regulation and control of those who express them in institutional settings. Indeed, one has to ask whether the diagnosis of transgendered youth does not act precisely as peer pressure, as an elevated form of teasing, as a euphemized form of social violence. And if we conclude that it does act in such a way, standing for gender norms, seeking to produce adaptation to existing norms, then how do we return to the vexed issue of what the diagnosis also offers? If part of what the diagnosis offers is a form of social recognition, and if that is the form that social recognition takes, and if it is only through this kind of social recognition that third parties, including medical insurance, will be willing to pay for the medical and technological changes that are sometimes desired, is it really possible to do away with the diagnosis altogether? In a way, the dilemma with which we are faced in the end has to do with the terms by which social recognition is constrained. Since even if we are tempted by the civil libertarian position in which this is understood as a personal right, the fact is that personal rights are only protected by, and can only be exercised through social and political means; to assert a right is not the same as being empowered to exercise it. And in this case, the only recognizable right at hand is the "right to be treated for a disorder and to take advantage of medical and legal benefits that seek its rectification." One exercises this right only by submitting to a pathologizing discourse, and, in submitting to the discourse, one also gains a certain power, a certain freedom.

It is possible to say, necessary to say, that the diagnosis leads the way to the alleviation of suffering, and it is possible, necessary, to say that the diagnosis intensifies the very suffering that requires alleviation. Under present and entrenched social conditions in which gender norms are still articulated in conventional ways, and departures from the norm regarded as suspect, this is the paradox that autonomy is in.[15] Of course, it is possible to move to a country where the state will pay for sex reassignment surgery, to apply to a "transgender fund" that a broader community supplies to help those who cannot pay the high costs, or indeed to apply for a "grant" to individuals that covers "cosmetic surgery." And the movement for trans people to become the therapists and diagnosticians has and will surely help matters. These are all ways around the bind, until the bind goes away. But if the bind is to go away for the long run, the norms that govern how we understand the relation between gender identity and mental health would have to change radically, so that economic and legal institutions would recognize how essential becoming a gender is to one's very sense of personhood, one's sense of well-being, one's possibility to flourish as a bodily being. Until that time, freedom will require unfreedom, and autonomy is implicated in subjection. If the social world must change for autonomy to become possible, then individual choice will prove to have meaning only in the context of a more radical social change.

Notes

1. See Richard Friedman, "Gender Identity," *Psychiatric News,* January 1, 1998. This viewpoint, however, is one that accepts that the diagnosis does describe a pathology, so his view is not that the diagnosis should be kept only for instrumental reasons.

2. See Robert Pela, "Boys in the Dollhouse, Girls with Toy Trucks," *The Advocate,* November 11, 1997. He argues that "the American Psychiatric Association has invented mental health categories—specifically, gender identity disorder—that are meant to pathologize homosexuality and to continue the abuse of gay youth." He also cites Shannon Minter to the effect that "GID is just another way to express homophobia." See also Katherine Rachlin, "Transgender Individuals' Experiences of Psychotherapy" (paper presented at the American Psychological Association meetings, August 2001), http://www.symposion.com/ijt/ijtvo06no01_03.htm. She notes that "individuals may resent having to spend time and money for psychological services in order to obtain medical services. They may also have fears concerning speaking to someone who holds the power to grant or deny them access to the interventions they feel they need. This fear and resentment creates a dynamic between therapist and client which may have an impact on the process and outcome of treatment." See also Anne Vitale, "The Therapist versus the Client: How the Conflict Started and Some Thoughts on How to Resolve It" in *Transgender Care,* ed. Gianni E. Israel, Donald E. Tarver II, and Diane Shaffer (Philadelphia: Temple University Press, 1997), 251–55. Kate Bornstein offers a searing critique of therapy: "Here's how this one works: we're taught that we are literally sick, that we have an illness that can be diagnosed and maybe cured. As a result of the medicalization of our condition, transsexuals must see therapists in order to receive the medical seal of approval required to proceed with any gender reassignment surgery. Now, once we get to the doctor, we're told we'll be cured if we become members of one gender or another. We're not told to divulge our transsexual status, except in select cases requiring intimacy. Isn't that amazing? Transsexuals presenting themselves for therapy in this culture are channeled through a system that labels them as having a disease (transsexuality) for which the therapy is to lie,

hide, or otherwise remain silent. Transsexuality is the only condition for which the therapy is to lie" (*Gender Outlaw: On Men, Women, and the Rest of Us* [New York: Routledge, 1994], 62).

3. It is important to note that transsexualism was first diagnosed in 1980 in the DSM-III. In the DSM-IV, published in 1994, transsexualism does not appear, but is treated instead under the rubric of gender identity disorder, termed "GID" throughout this chapter as shorthand. The diagnosis as it currently stands requires that applicants for transsexual surgery and treatment show "evidence of a strong and persistent cross-gender identification, which is the desire to be, or the insistence that one is the other sex." Second, "this cross-identification must not be merely the desire for any perceived cultural advantages of being the other sex," but "there must also be evidence of persistent discomfort about one's assigned sex or a sense of inappropriateness in the gender role of that sex." The diagnosis "is not made if the individual has a concurrent physical intersex condition," and "to make the diagnosis, there must be evidence of clinically significant distress or impairment in social, occupational, or other important areas of functioning." For more information, see *Trans-health.com* 4, no. 1 (spring 2002); see the same online journal, volume 1, number 1 (summer 2001) for an important critique titled "The Medicalization of Transgenderism," a five-part work by Whitney Barnes (published in successive issues) that thoroughly and trenchantly covers pertinent issues related to the diagnostic category.

4. For a discussion on changes of nomenclature within the history of the diagnosis to differentiate those who are considered to be "gender dysphoric" from the start from those who arrive at this conclusion in time, see "The Development of a Nomenclature" in the Harry Benjamin International Gender Dysphoria Association's *The Standards of Care for Gender Identity Disorders*, 6th ed. (Düsseldorf: Symposion Publishing, 2001).

5. Richard Isay, "Remove Gender Identity Disorder from DSM," *Psychiatric News*, November 21, 1997.

6. Friedman, "Gender Identity."

7. Jacob Hale, "Medical Ethics and Transsexuality" (paper presented at the Seventeenth Harry Benjamin International Gender Dysphoria Association Symposium, Galveston, Texas, October 31–November 4, 2001), http://www.symposion.com/ijt/hbigda/2001/69_hale.htm. See also Richard Green's queries in the lecture cited below: "Should sex change be available on demand? That was hardly the issue in 1969, as the nearly insurmountable hurdle then was professionally endorsed reassignment. If gender patients can procure surgeons who do not require psychiatric or psychological referral, research should address outcome for those who are professionally referred versus the self-referred. Then an ethical issue could be, if success is less (or failure greater) among the self-referred, should otherwise competent adults have that autonomy of self-determination?" Later he asks, "Should there be a limit to a person's autonomy over body?" Green also applauds the fact that some transgendered individuals have now entered into the profession, so that they are the ones making the diagnosis and also electing the medical benefits.

8. For a discussion of the etiology of the diagnosis that covers recent psychological findings about postoperative regret and sex reassignment surgery's "success rates," see P. T. Cohen-Kettenis and L. J. G. Gooren, "Transsexualism: A Review of

Etiology, Diagnosis, and Treatment," National Library of Medicine, http://www.ncbi.nlm.nih.gov/entrez/query.fcgi?cmd=Retrieve&db=PubMed&dopt=Abstract&list_uids=99271590.

9. Richard Green, "Reflections on 'Transsexualism and Sex Reassignment,' 1966–1999" (presidential address to the Harry Benjamin International Gender Dysphoria Association, London, August 17–21, 1999), http://www.symposion.com/ijt/greenpresidential/green00.htm.

10. See, for example, George A. Rekers, "Gender Identity Disorder," *Journal of Family and Culture* 2, no. 3 (1986), http://www.leaderu.com/jhs/rekers.html, and revised in 1996 for the *Journal of Human Sexuality*, a Christian Leadership Ministries publication. He proposes conversion to Christianity as a "cure" for transsexuality and has provided a psychological guide for those "afflicted" and "repentant" with this condition in his *Handbook of Child and Adolescent Sexual Problems* (New York: Lexington Books, 1995).

11. Rekers, "Gender Identity Disorder."

12. Ibid.

13. See Walter O. Bockting and Charles Cesaretti, "Spirituality, Transgender Identity, and Coming Out," *Journal of Sex Education and Therapy* 26, no. 4 (2002); and Bockting, "From Construction to Context: Gender through the Eyes of the Transgendered," *Siecus Report* (October–November 1999). See also Kate Bornstein's enormously important conception of transitioning as a process of perpetual becoming in *Gender Outlaw*, especially "The Other Questions," 113–42.

14. For an impressive account of how that clinic works to provide a supportive environment for its clients at the same time that it seeks to secure benefits through use of the diagnosis, see Walter O. Bockting, "The Assessment and Treatment of Gender Dysphoria," in *Directions in Clinical and Counseling Psychology*, vol. 7 (New York: Hatherleigh, 1997), lesson 11, 3–22. For another impressive account, see Green, "Reflections on 'Transsexualism and Sex Reassignment.'"

15. Richard Green in the lecture cited above suggests that the paradox is not between autonomy and subjection, but implied by the fact that transsexualism is self-diagnosed. He writes, "It is difficult to find another psychiatric or medical condition in which the patient makes the diagnosis and prescribes the treatment."

15. Reinscribing Normality? The Law and Politics of Transgender Marriage

Ruthann Robson

Almost thirty years later, I still recall an episode of a television show I saw while I was in law school. I was sitting around with some of my classmates watching a small black-and-white TV, probably drinking and smoking, definitely stalling preparation for another boring class that seemed to have no connection with reality. So, perhaps not surprisingly, the show *Real People* seemed to be a student favorite, this precursor to "reality TV" and a spawn of *Candid Camera.* The show's concept, such as it was, seemed to be that truth is stranger than fiction. It not only provided diversion from unpleasant tasks such as studying fee simple and proximate cause, it invited the viewing audience to laugh at the show's subjects and meanwhile feel reinforced in our own normalcy.

The segment I remember centered on a married couple with children. The twist was that they were transgendered. The man-born one was transitioning to a woman; the woman-born one was transitioning to a man. Importantly, someone said (someone on TV? someone in the room? both?) the couple could still be husband and wife and the children would still have a mother and a father. The audience could laugh—isn't that strange?—but normalcy prevailed. And not merely the normalcy of the viewers, the normalcy of the world. If these two people wanted to "switch," well then, that would be fine. Nothing fundamental would be altered. We could get back to determining the ownership of private property and the liability of tortfeasors.

Recently, long past law school, I experienced déjà vu while reading *Trans-Sister Radio,* by Chris Bohjalian. The novel's plot revolves around the character Dana, transitioning from male to female. For most of the book, Dana is involved with a divorced woman, Allison, whom Dana first meets when he is her male professor. After an intense affair, Allison and the now-female Dana break up what is often described as their lesbian relationship. Dana uneasily dates a few women, but when she falls in love—and lust—it is with Allison's ex-husband. The "switch" from Allison as Dana's partner to her ex-husband as Dana's partner in the last pages of the novel reestablishes heterosexual normalcy.[1] Again, we are reassured that despite a small substitution, nothing fundamental has been altered.

This lack of fundamental alteration is what worries me about the legal discourse surrounding transgendered marriage. Like other movements, including other queer movements, transgendered legal reform has the potential to be merely accommodating, what I have called in other contexts domesticating. The legal discourse surrounding transgendered marriage too often serves to recapitulate and reinscribe the most traditional visions of marriage and heterosexuality. Like the cartoon image of a man and a woman used to represent humanity to alien beings who might discover that NASA launched Pioneer 10 spacecraft, what Michael Warner has termed "heteronormativity" is incessantly being equated with humanness itself.[2]

Perhaps the best known example of such heterosexual insistence occurs in *MT v. JT*, decided by a New Jersey court in 1976, in which the court upheld the marriage between M. T., born a male who transitioned to a woman, and J. T, born a male who remained so.[3] The court made explicit that in determining the validity of the marriage, it is "the sexual capacity of the individual which must be scrutinized. Sexual capacity or sexuality in this frame of reference requires the coalescence of both the physical ability and the emotional orientation to engage in sexual intercourse as either a male or a female."[4] On this view, it is heterosexual intercourse, rather than birth certificates, chromosomes, or expert testimony about gender dysphoria, that is the talisman for sex/gender identity.

Traditional heterosexual intercourse is also the shibboleth for marriage itself. While particular distinctions might be made, and the importance of procreation as an outcome of sexual intercourse is often stressed, various doctrines surrounding the marital relation establish that heterosexual intercourse is the underpinning of marriage. For example, generally a marriage can be annulled by one party if the other party does not have the capacity to engage in heterosexual intercourse.[5] Likewise, in states that require grounds for divorce, one party can divorce another on the grounds of "constructive abandonment" for failure to engage in traditional heterosexual intercourse, despite repeated requests to do so.[6] (Interestingly, if the request is for nontraditional heterosexual intercourse, then the refusal will be justified and will not constitute abandonment.)[7]

In one sense, *MT v. JT* can be theorized as upholding a functionalist rather than formalist perspective of marriage and gender identity. The formalist approach relies upon formal relationships dictated by law, while the functionalist approach emphasizes the functions or attributes or "realities" that are deemed to be operative. While this may be described as the difference between law and fact, it is more complex than that, because the argument is really that the law should take into account the "real" facts as opposed to mere formalities. For example, the legal definition of "family" is imbued with a functionalist hue in cases such as *Braschi,* in which New York's highest court interpreted a New York City rent-control regulation disallowing eviction of "either the surviving spouse of the deceased tenant or some other member of the deceased tenant's family."[8] In considering whether Braschi, the surviving partner in a gay relationship, fit into the statutory exemption, the court approvingly referred to factors such as the exclusivity and longevity of the relationship, the level of emotional and financial commitment, the manner in which they conducted their everyday lives and presented themselves, and the reliance they placed upon each other for "family services." The court relied upon underlying facts such as their cohabitation for ten years, their regular visits to each other's relatives, and their joint status as signatories on three safe deposit boxes, bank accounts, and credit cards. Similarly, in the parenting context, the formalist viewpoint rejects any visitation or custody claim of the member of a lesbian couple who has no legal relationship to the child (whether as birth mother or by adoption), since the woman is not a legal parent.[9] The functionalist perspective, on the other hand, is not content with the formal legal definition of "parent" and develops criteria to determine whether a person should be recognized by the law as a parent. These criteria generally include the fostering of the parent-child relationship by the legal parent, the nonlegal parent and child living in the same household, the nonlegal parent's assumption of the obligations of parenthood "by taking responsibility for the child's care, education, and development, including but not limited to financial contribution, and did not expect financial compensation," and the existence of the relationship for a sufficient amount of time to have produced bonding.[10]

A critique of the functionalist approach is that while it may seem more "liberal" than the formalist approach, it actually enshrines the most conservative versions of the categories it determines. It prescribes and enforces its concept of normalcy. For example, if Braschi had been a partner in an "open" relationship that was not sexually exclusive, this fact would have been used to argue that he was not a family member entitled to stay in his home, regardless of any understandings between Braschi and his lover. Likewise, if a lesbian partner agrees to coparent but maintains a separate residence, she will not be deemed a functional parent, again regardless of any understandings between the parents or the quality of relationship with the child.

In the transgender marriage context, the functionalist test employed by the court in *MT v. JT* also requires an application of the most traditional aspects of the functions at issue—here a "wife" or "husband" is judged by the function of heterosexual intercourse. Again, the understandings or sexual satisfactions of the parties are irrelevant.

The law may seem to be considering "reality," but it is imposing a singular and dominant reality. However, in another sense, the functionalist strategy is only necessary because the court is troubled by the formal legal status that would otherwise prevail. In the case of *MT v. JT*, the trial court would never have delved beyond the formal marital status (evidenced by a proper marriage certificate) had not JT argued that the marriage was void, which would release him from his financial obligations of support.

More recently, in *Littleton v. Prange*, the Texas Court of Appeals was also troubled by the formal marital status of Christie Littleton and her deceased husband, Jonathan Littleton.[11] In her medical malpractice suit against the physician who had treated her husband, it became known that Christie had been born male and had undergone sex reassignment surgery before entering into the otherwise valid marriage, again evinced by a proper marriage certificate. Unlike the court in *JT*, however, the Texas courts did not uphold the marriage. Instead, the appellate court resorted to another formalistic document— the birth certificate—to undermine the validity of the formal marriage certificate. According to the court, the original birth certificate, despite the fact that it had been amended to reflect a change of name and gender, was absolutely controlling. In the words of the court, it described things the way "they just are" as opposed to things the way one might "will into being."[12] Born male, Christie remained male, and she could therefore not be the wife of the deceased suing for wrongful death.

The Kansas Supreme Court has likewise refused to recognize a transgendered marriage in *In re Estate of Gardiner*, decided in 2002.[13] As in *MT* and *Littleton*, the court was faced with a challenge to the seemingly lawful marriage of a man to a woman who was MTF. Again, the stakes in *Gardiner* were economic: the challenge came from the estranged son of the man who died intestate, seeking to disinherit his stepmother, J'Noel Gardiner. Ms. Gardiner had been born male, had undergone sex reassignment surgery, had been issued a new birth certificate reflecting a change of name and gender, and several years later had met and married Marshall Gardiner. Invalidating the marriage, the court concluded that J'Noel is not a woman. However, more than the Texas court, the Supreme Court of Kansas recognized that J'Noel's sex/gender had changed. But not to female—to transsexual. This enabled the Kansas Supreme Court to invoke the Kansas so-called little-DOMA statute,[14] which defined the marriage contract as a civil contract between "two parties who are of opposite sex" and declared all other marriages contrary to public policy and void. The court interpreted the DOMA statute to exclude transsexuals. "The plain ordinary meaning of 'persons of the opposite sex' contemplates a biological man and a biological woman and not persons who are experiencing gender dysphoria."[15] Such an interpretation presumably precludes transgendered persons from marrying, since they would have no "opposite sex." However, as Julie Greenberg presciently argued, such a position is difficult to defend, given the current constitutional jurisprudence that marriage is a fundamental right and here, as distinct from the same-sex marriage cases, the person is being denied the right to marry "anyone at all."[16]

In both *Littleton* and *Gardiner,* the courts conclude, as a matter of law, that the sex/gender identity of each MTF is not female and thus the marriages to their husbands are invalid. This position is consistent with most of the other cases in the United States that have considered the issue and is now the majority view, although there is more diversity of opinion in other jurisdictions.[17] However, while the result in such cases differs from *MT v. JT,* in all of these cases the courts preserve the heterosexual matrix. In *MT v. JT,* heterosexual intercourse is established, and thus the marriage is valid. In *Littleton* and *Gardiner,* the judicial guardians of heterosexuality have dispatched the pretenders: Christie Littleton remained in reality a man, while J'Noel Gardiner had transitioned from male to transsexual.

It is tempting to argue against the formalistic decisions in *Littleton* and *Gardiner* by favoring the more functionalist approach displayed in *MT v. JT.* Yet such arguments serve to reestablish and reinvigorate the normalcy of heterosexuality. As Andrew Sharpe has demonstrated, judicial approaches to transgender marriage in common law countries have, despite their differences, displayed a concern to "insulate marriage from 'unnatural' homosexual incursion."[18] While Sharpe argues that at times the judicial concern in the non-U.S. context may not be focused on actual sexual functionality but can shift to aesthetic concerns—how the transgendered person appears when unclothed—he nevertheless links the concern with "homophobic anxiety."[19]

The judicial preoccupation with maintaining heterosexuality obviously impacts litigation strategy and also influences and mirrors theoretical and political positions. We may find ourselves objecting to the result in *Littleton* based upon our own preconceptions of the heterosexual arrangement of marriage: a characterization of Ms. Littleton as a "widow" conveys a certain pathos in a heterosexist and sexist society. While perhaps less sympathetic, Ms. Gardiner is also easily stereotyped in sexist and heterosexist terms: she is "hardly the first widow to be accused of marrying a man twice her age for money instead of love, with a stepson she first met at her husband's funeral trying to block her inheritance."[20] With relative ease, our understandings of the equities of these cases recapitulate our notions of normalcy and heterosexuality. A slight "switch" is required, but the fundamental social, legal, and political arrangements remain unaltered.

The potentially more subversive situation is the one in which one partner in an extant marriage changes gender. As the transgender theorist and activist Phyllis Randolph Frye has noted, powerful forces militated against such a possibility, given the refusal of the psychiatric and medical community to approve or provide genital surgery to married persons.[21] When such situations do occur, the unchanged spouse would most likely be able to procure a divorce, even in states that require grounds.[22] However, dissolving a valid marriage is quite different from declaring a marriage invalid. In the former instance, the legal recognition of the marriage occurs through terminating the legal relation by the divorce. In the latter instance, the marriage is declared void. It is not that the marriage is terminated; it is as if it never existed.

Yet doctrinally, the facts giving rise to the voided marriage occur at the time the marriage is entered into by the parties. Subsequent events may reveal such facts to the parties (e.g., the parties could learn that the husband's previous marriage was not dissolved and thus the current marriage is void for bigamy), but subsequent facts cannot retroactively void the marriage. The application of such well-settled doctrine to the subsequent gender transition of one of the parties to the marriage means, as Frye has argued, that "same-sex marriages" do exist in the United States.[23] Under the reasoning of *Littleton*, Frye is surely correct. However, given the subsequent judicial pronouncement of *Gardiner*, Frye's conclusion has been cast into doubt: the transgendered person is neither female nor male, and just as she or he has no *opposite* sex according to the court, she or he can have no *same* sex. Except, perhaps, for another transgendered person, presumably one who has transitioned in the same manner.

As a litigation strategy, Frye is surely astute in recommending that the nontransgendered spouse should initiate or join the litigation, although I am less sanguine that such a person could not "be cast into the role of the degenerate" by a religious or conservative court.[24] Nevertheless, an analogy can be drawn to the U.S. Supreme Court case of *Turner v. Safley*, authored by Justice Sandra Day O'Connor—not known for her liberal views—in which the

Court declared unconstitutional a prison regulation limiting marriage for inmates.[25] In a case that could have potentially more resonance than the oft-quoted *Loving v. Virginia* in which the Supreme Court finally declared miscegenation laws unconstitutional,[26] the Court in *Turner* de-emphasized heterosexual intercourse as a rationale of marriage. While the Court did include the eventual (heterosexual) consummation of the prison inmate's marriage as significant—implicitly precluding the notion of conjugal visits—the Court first noted the importance of marriage as an expression of "emotional support and public commitment," and next alluded to the religious and spiritual significance of marriage.[27] Additionally, after mentioning the sexual component, the Court recognized the tangible benefits of marriage, such as Social Security benefits and property rights, as well as intangible benefits, such as the legitimation of children.[28]

Yet assimilation to heterosexuality remains strong as a litigation strategy. As Frye notes, the evidence supporting the gender transition document, such as the amended birth certificate, which will be used to obtain the marriage certificate, should be sufficient to allow the conclusion that "she has a vagina, or he has a penis, and can be sexually penetrated as a female or can sexually penetrate as a male."[29] While such a view is consistent with *MT v. JT* in which the court upheld the marriage, like *MT*, it makes heterosexual intercourse the sine qua non of marriage. Such a theoretical and social position undermines claims to same-sex marriage.[30]

The larger question is whether marriage—whether heterosexual in fact, heterosexual by law, or even nonheterosexual—is consistent with a liberatory politic. The naturalist arguments for coupling and marriage that proclaim that such arrangements are "just the way things are" echo the *Littleton* court's pronouncement that Christie Littleton's gender just "is" the male gender assigned at birth. Moreover, such a coupling recapitulates and reinforces the dualism displayed by present male/female genders. The traditional model of marriage, as opposed to plural marriage, for example, supports a dyadic and binary mode of social arrangement. The NASA Pioneer spacecraft model of humanity as a "technological but benign Adam and Eve" becomes the theoretical construct and litigation position of this transgender politic.[31]

Moreover, the solution of marriage to the problems faced by MT, Christie Littleton, and J'Noel Gardiner is, at best, partial. As in same-sex marriage, the specter of benefits to spouses often appears as an advantage—and in these three cases, each putative wife sought an economic gain—yet the political, social, and legal arrangement of marriage can obscure other inequalities. Additionally, it allows the state to impose a bright line rule for the distribution and nondistribution of wealth, both private (as in these cases) and public. A regime of marriage allows the state to privatize problems of economic and other inequalities: the solution to a person not having medical care, for example, is not a government policy of universal health care but the individual becoming married to someone whose employer provides good health insurance. In other words, as a matter of reform, it may be expedient to argue for recognizing transgender marriages, but as a matter of critical change, even the success of the argument fails.

I remain convinced that transgendered people can develop a liberatory politic beyond marriage, just as I remain hopeful that lesbians and other queers can develop such a stance, despite what seems to me to be the essential conservatism of present same-sex marriage strategies and theoretical perspectives. In writing on the topic of transgendered marriage, I am cognizant that I am not situated within the transgendered movement, politic, or sensibility, and that my observations and analysis spring from my life as a lesbian and my work on lesbian legal issues, including marriage. Yet when I survey the transgender marriage cases, arguments, scholarship, and theorizing, I confront the same uneasiness I experienced thirty years ago watching shoddy television journalism or more recently reading a popular novel. I am worried that only a few of the characters will be switched. And that nothing fundamental will be altered.

Notes

The author expresses her appreciation to Shannon Minter and Paisley Currah for their inspiration and editorial guidance, not to mention their confidence in me when they solicited this piece; to Nicole Mandarano, CUNY 2004, for her research assistance; and to the CUNY School of Law Professional Development Committee for financial support for research assistance.

1. The author calls readers' attention to the "switch" character of this plot development by invoking Louisa May Alcott's novel *Little Women* and noting that Laurie, "the lad who lives next door to the March girls," had "spent years wooing the tomboy Jo March, and then, after she finally rebuffed him, he simply moved on to her kid sister Amy and married her. He believed he was destined to become part of the March clan" (Chris Bohjalian, *Trans-Sister Radio* [New York: Crown, 2000], 334–35).

2. See Michael Warner, introduction to *In Fear of a Queer Planet: Queer Politics and Social Theory,* ed. Michael Warner (Minneapolis: University of Minnesota Press, 1993).

3. 355 A.2d 204 (N.J. Superior Ct. Appellate Division 1976).

4. Ibid., 209.

5. For a general discussion of the doctrine, see *Incapacity for Sexual Intercourse as Ground for Annulment,* 52 A.L.R. 589 (1974).

6. For example, section 170 of the New York Domestic Relations Law, which includes as a ground for divorce "the abandonment of the plaintiff by the defendant for

a period of one of more years" (NY DRL § 170[2]). This abandonment may be actual or constructive, and it is "well-settled that to establish a cause of action for constructive abandonment, the spouse who claims to have been constructively abandoned must prove that the abandoning spouse refused to fulfill the basic obligations arising from the marriage contract." See *Silver v. Silver*, 253 A.2d 756, 757 (N.Y. App. Div. 1998) (citing cases). As the cases make clear, having heterosexual intercourse is a basic obligation of the marriage contract.

7. Again, as is well settled, the refusal to fulfill the basic marital obligation of sexual relations must be "unjustified, willful, and continue despite repeated requests." See *Silver v. Silver*, 757. In *George M. v. Mary Ann M.*, 171 A.D.2d 651 (N.Y. App. Div. 1991), the court held that the wife's refusal to engage in sexual intercourse was "entirely justified" because of the husband's "consistent and repeated demands for anal and oral sex, as well as his demands that his wife retire in erotic nightwear" (652).

8. *Braschi v. Stahl Associates*, 74 N.Y.2d 201, 543 N.E.2d 49, 544 N.Y.S.2d 784 (1989).

9. This formalist viewpoint is exemplified by *Alison D. v. Virginia M.*, 77 N.Y.2d 651, 569 N.Y.S.2d 586, 572 N.E.2d 27 (1991), in which the same court that decided *Braschi* rejected the lesbian coparent's claim to visitation based upon her de facto parent status, concluding that she had no "standing" to bring an action for visitation because she was not a parent.

10. See *In re Custody of H.S.H.-K. (Holtzman v. Knott)*, 193 Wis. 2d 649, 533 N.W.2d 419 (1995). See also *VC v. MJB*, 163 N.J. 200, 748 A.2d 539 (N.J. 2000).

11. *Littleton v. Prange*, 9 S.W.3rd 223 (Tex. Ct. App. 1999), *cert. denied*, 531 U.S. 872 (2000).

12. Ibid., 231.

13. 42 P.3d 120 (Kan. 2002).

14. In response to the Hawai'i Supreme Court's decision allowing room for debate on the subject of same-sex marriage, *Baehr v. Lewin*, 852 P.2d. 44 (Haw. 1993), and the potentiality of other states being compelled to recognize Hawai'i's same-sex marriages under the Constitution's full faith and credit clause, Const. Art. IV §1 ("Full Faith and Credit shall be given in each State to the public Acts, Records, and judicial Proceedings of every other State"), the United States Congress passed the Defense of Marriage Act, DOMA, PL 104–199, 110 Stat. 2419, codified at 28 U.S.C. §1738C (1996), which provides that federal law shall recognize only opposite-sex marriages and that states shall not be required to give effect to same-sex marriages from other states. The majority of states enacted their own DOMA statutes declaring that, under their own state laws and public policy, marriages were limited to those between a man and a woman, thus precluding their recognition of any same-sex marriages possibly entered into in Hawai'i or any other state, as well as preventing the judiciary from entertaining challenges to state opposite-sex marriage requirements or practices.

15. 42 P.3d at 135.

16. Julie Greenberg, "When Is a Man a Man, and When Is a Woman a Woman?" *Florida Law Review* 52 (2000): 745, 762 (discussion of *Littleton v. Prange*).

17. Other cases in the United States include *In re Ladrach*, 513 N.E.2d 828 (Ohio Probate Ct. 1987) (holding that there is "no authority in Ohio for the issuance of a

marriage license to consummate a marriage between a post-operative male to female transsexual person and a male person"); *Frances B. v. Mark B.*, 355 N.Y.S. 2d 712 (1974) (court stating that while the defendant may "function as a male in other situations and relationships," since he does not have male sexual organs or a "normal penis," he is not able to "function as a man"); *Anonymous v. Anonymous*, 325 N.Y.S.2d 499 (1971) (declaring marriage between a man and a transitioning MTF who had male sex organs at the time of marriage and whom husband believed to be a woman). For discussions of these cases, as well as cases from other nations, see Andrew N. Sharpe, *Transgender Jurisprudence: Dysphoric Bodies of Law* (London: Cavendish, 2002), 89–134 (discussing cases from the United States, Canada, New Zealand, Great Britain, and Australia); Mary Coombs, "Sexual Dis-Orientation: Transgendered People and Same-Sex Marriage," *UCLA Women's Law Journal* 8 (1998): 219.

18. Sharpe, *Transgender Jurisprudence*, 115.

19. Ibid., 127–28. Sharpe is discussing the Aortearoa/New Zealand case of *Attorney General v. Otahuhu Family Court* [1995], 1 NZLR 603. In this discussion, Sharpe argues that I have not previously made enough of the distinction between functionality and aesthetics, given the Otahuhu court's emphasis on the purpose of sex-reassignment surgery as being aesthetic (Sharpe, *Transgender Jurisprudence*). However, I would agree with Sharpe that "while an aesthetic concern over bodies is a consistent theme of transgender jurisprudence, it is usually masked, at least partially, by a preoccupation with heterosexual capacity" (ibid., 127). I also agree with Sharpe in his interpretation of *Otahuhu* that while the decision may "undermine a view of marriage as being the necessary locus of 'natural' heterosexual intercourse," it is nevertheless founded on "the hetero/homo dyad," and the characterization of any sex that does occur as heterosexual is crucial (128).

20. Jodi Wilgren, "Suit over Estate Claims a Widow Is Not a Woman," *New York Times*, January 13, 2002.

21. Phyllis Randolph Frye and Alyson Dodi Meiselman, "Same-Sex Marriages Have Existed in the United States for a Long Time Now," *Albany Law Review* 64 (2001): 1031, 1039–40 ("Until the 1990s, almost all married transgenders seeking sex reassignment were coerced into divorce by the medical profession").

22. See *Steinke v. Steinke*, 357 A.2d 674 (Super. Ct. Pa. 1975) (holding that wife had grounds for divorce given husband's exploration of the possibility of sex reassignment, including dressing as a woman and taking hormones, although husband did not undergo surgery and eventually "resumed living as a man").

23. Ibid. Frye further argues that same-sex marriage advocates should avail themselves of such transgender same-sex marriage situations as a "wedge issue" to promote same-sex marriage and concludes that their failure to do so is "incomprehensible" (Frye and Meiselman, "Same-Sex Marriages," 1045). Yet given the essential conservatism of the quest for marital recognition, this failure is easily comprehended. It is not only arguments on behalf of transgendered marriage that avail themselves of traditional functionalist strategies; arguments on behalf of same-sex marriage also employ the "we are essentially like you" rhetorical claim.

24. Frye and Meiselman, "Same-Sex Marriages," 1065.

25. *Turner v. Safley*, 482 U.S. 78 (1987).

26. *Loving v. Virginia*, 388 U.S. 1 (1967). The Court's decision in *Pace v. Alabama*, 106 U.S. 583, 585 (1883) was considered the precedent for allowing miscegenation statutes, and previous to *Loving*, the Court three times declined to review constitutional challenges to miscegenation statutes; see *Jackson v. Alabama*, 348 U.S. 888 (1954) (memorandum opinion denying certiorari to Alabama Supreme Court opinion upholding conviction for marital miscegenation against a fifth and fourteenth amendment challenge); *Naim v. Virginia*, 350 U.S. 891 (1955) (holding that the "inadequacy of the record as to the relationship of the parties to the Commonwealth of Virginia at the time of the marriage in North Carolina and upon their return to Virginia, and the failure of the parties to bring here all questions relevant to the disposition of the case, prevents the constitutional issue of the validity of the Virginia statute on miscegenation tendered here being considered 'in clean-cut and concrete form, unclouded' by such problems"); *Naim v. Virginia*, 350 U.S. 985 (1956) (memorandum opinion stating that federal question not properly presented). Three years before *Loving*, the Court declared unconstitutional a Florida statute criminalizing interracial cohabitation; see *McLaughlin v. Florida*, 379 U.S. 184 (1964).

27. *Turner v. Safley*, 95–96.

28. Ibid., 96.

29. Frye and Meiselman, "Same-Sex Marriages," 1063.

30. Thus, while "the courts in transsexual marriage cases struggle with the same concerns as the opponents to same-sex marriage—the relative significance to marriage of [heterosexual] intercourse and procreation" (Coombs, "Sexual Disorientation," 260), a litigation strategy on behalf of transgendered marriage that argues that the relationship does include heterosexual intercourse is one which accedes to the validity of heterosexual intercourse as definitional of marriage.

31. See Warner, *In Fear of a Queer Planet*, xxiii.

Afterword: Are Transgender Rights *In*human Rights?

Kendall Thomas

We must *(il faut)* more than ever stand on the side of
human rights. *We need (il faut) human rights.*
We are in need of them and they are in need, for there is
always a lack, a shortfall, a falling short, an insufficiency;
human rights are never sufficient.

—Jacques Derrida

What if what is "proper" to humankind were to be
inhabited by the inhuman?

—Jean-François Lyotard

The essays gathered in this volume offer us a wealth of historical, political, legal, and economic perspectives from which to frame the question of transgender rights. In this brief coda, I propose to revisit only one of them: whether and how the movement for transgender rights represents a demand to deepen and broaden the culture of what have come to be known as "human rights."[1] In his contribution to this book, Shannon Price Minter provides a useful point of entry into the human rights argument for transgender rights. Minter advances the arresting thesis that transgendered people should aspire not to "transgender rights" but "simply [to] human rights." The claim here (to adapt the famous Amnesty International poster campaign) is that "transgender rights *are* human rights." The power of this formulation lies precisely in the

attractive simplicity of its logic and in the moral and political intuition that sub-
tends it: transgender people are human beings who, as such, deserve the protections to which all human beings are entitled in any society that has committed itself to recognize and respect the modern regime of human rights.

For all its simplicity, however, the identification of transgender rights
with human rights immediately runs up against two difficulties. First, it is
obvious, once said, that we live at an historical moment when the concepts of
the "human" and of "rights" have become the object of "the most radical questioning possible."[2] The regime of "hard" and "soft" global human rights law
(within and across states) has never been more comprehensive and complex.
For all its complexity, however, a clear consensus over the interpretation and
application of contemporary human rights norms continues to elude us.
Indeed, even the once taken-for-granted notions bequeathed to us by the liberal humanist tradition—that of a sovereign, rational human subject; a shared
human condition; a common humanity; or the existence of inborn, inalien-
able human rights—are being challenged and criticized on theoretical as well
as practical grounds.[3] The already weakened foundations of the classic human
rights idea have been put under even greater stress by the contradictions of
global power politics and the transparent cynicism around such discourses as
those on genocide and "humanitarian" military intervention.

Second and equally important, the fiercely contested and conflictual
character of the modern human rights regime is compounded when we consider the contexts in which human rights advocacy by and on behalf of transgendered persons must operate. A reading of the writings in this volume
makes it distressingly clear that trans activists must contend with a social order
and a legal regime of "infrahumanity"[4] under which transgendered people
are viewed as "non-persons, with no right to marry, to work, to use a public
bathroom, or even to walk down the street in safety." In a real sense, the
human rights argument for transgendered people must reckon with the ugly
fact that in many places around the world, those whose gender identities and
gender expression do not conform to their assigned birth sex are not even
seen to count as human; they are not deemed, in other words, to be human in
the sense that "ordinary" humans are. The belief that the bodies and lives of
transgendered people "cannot be humanized"[5] has rendered them vulnerable
to the terrorisms of structural and physical violence.[6] The transgender rights
movement thus faces the daunting challenge of raising the question of
human rights under conditions in which the simple humanity of transgender
publics is continually being called into question.

In advancing a human rights argument for transgender rights, trans
activists could choose "simply" to ignore the complications of the double

predicament to which I am calling attention here. I do not mean to suggest that such a decision would be unwarranted. I do contend that the case can also be made for a strategic transgender human politics that critically and creatively enlists ("secures as a means of help and support") these twin dilemmas as a potentially positive resource. In their introduction, the editors of *Transgender Rights* rightly insist that the success of the transgender movement will depend on its ability to create "a culture in which trans people are not just a curiosity or a perversion of nature." While it does not deny the importance of acting within the formal institutional arenas of domestic and global governance, this is a vision of human rights practice that understands that politics involves more than the effort to influence the content of public policy through arguments about the requirements of public reason or appeals to the rule of public law. Politics is both a cultural form and a cultural force. To put the point another way, modern politics is "a matter of *fantasies,* in which the way people 'imagine' themselves [and others] occupies a crucial place."[7] Accordingly, effective struggle on behalf of the transgendered will entail (in the words of the editors) a kind of "cultural work" *at the level of collective political fantasy.* From this perspective, a successful transgender human rights strategy must find ways to enlarge the public imagination regarding the lives and aspirations of trans people.

How is this to be done? I am going to suggest, tentatively and rather counterintuitively, that the transgender movement ought perhaps to embrace and exploit the productive, positive possibilities that the "radical questioning" of the "human" in contemporary human rights discourse has opened up. Specifically, and more controversially—I shall contend that one important, indeed, crucial feature of a transgender human rights strategy ought to be a critical tactical engagement ("a doing battle with" in both the negative and positive senses of the term) with the very image-idea of infrahuman or "nonhuman living being"[8] through which the lives and bodies of trans people have been negatively marked by the politics of shame and stigma. I want to take the risk of asking the following set of overlapping questions about the possible futures of transgender human rights advocacy and activism: What might it mean for the transgender human rights movement to challenge the inhuman treatment of trans people by treating the notion of the inhuman not just as an obstacle but as an opportunity? What might it mean for trans activists and their allies to mobilize around a vision of transgender or, better, "transhuman" rights that affirmatively aligns itself with, rather than against, the idea of the *in*human? What might it mean to view the human rights culture we seek to create as one in which the call to social justice for transgendered people is voiced as a call to "stand on the side" of the inhuman? What might it mean for the transgender movement to conceive the justice it seeks not as a matter of simple inclusion into the existing institutions and ideology of human rights but as a transformation of human rights discourse, and a transfiguration of the human rights imaginary? What if trans human rights advocates began to advance the idea of a human right to *inhumanity*? Before I proceed further, I should add parenthetically that what is at stake here is not the desirability of substituting the idea of the human with the idea of the inhuman but of teasing out their tensed, mutual implication.

I must acknowledge straightaway the unease I feel in posing these questions in these terms. I am all too mindful that some readers may find it morally offensive and politically dangerous even to entertain this line of questioning, or respond to it with another: What possible good can come from equivocating about the full and equal humanity of transgendered people? Wouldn't it be irresponsible for transgender human rights discourse to abandon the "mobilization of shame" strategy to which the modern human rights movement owes so much of its success? Shouldn't the ethics of solidarity oblige transgender human rights advocates to fashion forms of argument and activism that are consistent with those advanced by the domestic and international feminist, gay and lesbian, disability, religious freedom, antiracist, refugee, and other movements? Doesn't this strategy run the risk of playing into the hands of those who oppose the movement for transgender human rights? Who is to say that it won't increase public indifference to, or worse, further entrench the current repressive state of affairs? How can the transgender human rights movement plausibly hope to make positive and empowering political use of terms that encapsulate the sad, sordid history of trans disempowerment and denigration? These are powerful and compelling questions. Nonetheless, I am going to put them on hold or, more precisely, address them only indirectly. This is not because they don't deserve careful consideration. Rather, I want to try to explain why I think the cluster of questions I have put on the table are still important questions to ask, even if that task is undertaken in another, less provocative vocabulary.

Since I'm trying to map a minefield here, let me make clear what I am *not* arguing. Like the other contributors to this volume, I am not interested in "defending or refuting any claims about *why* transgender people exist." What interests me, rather, is *how* transgender people exist, or, more precisely, how some important aspects of transgender existence stand in potential tension with an unmodified, humanist human rights argument for transgender rights. Riki Wilchins has argued that a transgender rights movement that is "unable to interrogate the fact of its own existence, will merely end up cementing the idea of a binary sex which I am presumed to somehow transgress or merely traverse."[9] Whatever one's view on the gender community's internal debate about the uses and limits of the idea of binary sex, it is hard to find fault with Wilchins's insistence that the transgender movement should not prematurely foreclose its examination. The same spirit of self-critical questioning should be brought to bear on the idea of humanity or, more precisely, on the presumption of a sharp and necessary distinction between *lives that are human* and *lives that are not.* This holds true as well for the moral categories and consequences that have historically turned on this distinction. The interrogatory imperative I am advancing here is this: a transgender rights movement that refuses to question the commonsense truths about human existence (its nature, scope, meaning, etc.) runs the risk of entrenching the rigid, repressive ideas about humanity and inhumanity from which trans people are fighting to be free.

The normative position on the links between transgender and human rights this sentence seeks to capture is connected to an important, but overlooked, dimension of the daily lives of transgender persons. As a strictly factual matter, anyone familiar with contemporary transgender communities cannot help but note how transgender existence may be said not only to "cross over, cut across, move between, or otherwise queer socially constructed *sex/gender* boundaries,"[10] but to do so in ways that test and contest the socially constructed boundaries of *human* ontology. This is the sense in which contemporary transgender identity and practice always embody a species of "transhuman" experience: to borrow a formulation that Giorgio Agamben has developed for a very different purpose, we might say that transgender people enact styles or modes of existence that "[mark] the threshold between the human and the inhuman."[11]

I noted earlier that the speculations I'm pursuing here about transgender human rights advocacy are motivated by an interest in some aspects of transgender culture and politics that seem to me to be experimenting with the intersections of human and nonhuman being in critical, creative, and, frankly, nonidentitarian ways. I eventually want to say something about two such moments. I'm going to spend most of my time, though, discussing a third that has haunted my own thinking about the possibilities and the risks of a "transhuman" human rights strategy. I am referring, of course, to the rampant incidence of physical violence against transgender people that has been provoked or justified by the discourse of *dehumanization.* I do so because I'm persuaded that an inquiry into the potentially positive uses of the "inhuman" has to start by reckoning with its less sanguine side.

Consider in this connection the tragic story of Chanelle Pickett, a young, black, transgender woman from New York City who was killed in November 1995. Her accused killer, William Palmer, had met Pickett at the Playland Café in Boston's Combat Zone, a bar in the city popular among drag queens and their admirers. Playland Café patrons later reported that Palmer was a frequent visitor, whose attraction to pre-op transsexuals was no secret. Indeed, witnesses reported that Palmer and Pickett had been seeing one another for some time. At Palmer's murder trial, the prosecution offered evidence that Pickett, Pickett's sister Gabrielle (also a transgender woman), and Palmer left the bar together, where they spent some time snorting cocaine at Pickett's apartment. Pickett and Palmer then left to spend the night at Palmer's home. A medical examiner testified for the prosecution that Pickett had been beaten about the head and then strangled for over eight minutes.

The defense strategy was to present Palmer, a white computer programmer, as a clean-cut all-American innocent whom Pickett had deceived. Palmer claimed that he had no clue Pickett was a pre-op transsexual when he invited her home, and only discovered that fact when the two started to have sex. According to Palmer, he had no choice but to defend himself after Pickett became violent. Palmer testified that Pickett went into a rage when Palmer rejected her. In Palmer's words: "All of a sudden *it* turned from a soft voice to not just a man but a crazed man who began banging walls and preaching. Crazy talk that made no sense whatsoever."[12] The defense strategy was to paint a mental image that asked the members of the jury to picture Chanelle Pickett as a devious and dangerous "gender shape-shifter," who could be a man, a woman, or, finally, little more than a nonhuman "it." Sadly, this tactical exercise in the politics of racist and transphobic fantasy paid off. Although the jury voted to convict Palmer of assault and battery, he was acquitted of the more serious charge of murder. At his sentencing hearing, the judge in the case told Palmer that he should "kiss the ground" his African American lawyer walked on.

Consider, too, the story, recounted by Richard M. Juang in his chapter for this volume, of Tyra Hunter. As Juang notes, Tyra Hunter was a transgender African American woman who lived in Washington, DC. In August 1993 Hunter was a victim in an automobile accident. As one of the firefighters who had arrived at the site of the accident was treating Hunter, he suddenly said within hearing distance of several witnesses, "This bitch ain't no girl... *it's* a nigger, he's got a dick!" and then walked away. Witnesses later testified that the firefighter spent several minutes at the scene "laughing and joking" about Hunter. Hunter was taken to the District's General Hospital, but the emergency room physician who was on duty offered her only the most cursory care. Hunter eventually died of her injuries. Juang rightly calls our attention to the condominia of racist, misogynistic, homophobic, and transphobic discourses that were at work in the deadly dehumanizing reduction of Tyra Hunter to an "it"—to the status and condition of abject, inhuman being.[13]

The stories of Chanelle Pickett and Tyra Hunter provide more than ample grounds for suspicion toward the claim that the transgender human rights movement can put, or should even consider trying to put, the notion of the "inhuman" to potentially positive use. Let me make it emphatically clear that I in no way mean to trivialize the senseless and deadly violence of which Pickett and Hunter were victims. The discourse of degradation that marked the bodies of Hunter and Pickett as "its" occupies a central place in the history of transgendered and intersexed people, as well as gay men and lesbians, bisexuals, and other sexual minorities. The deaths of Tyra Hunter, Chanelle Pickett, Marsha P. Johnson, Brandon Teena, F. C. Martinez, and so many unknown, unnamed transgendered people are an extreme instance and expression of the politics of trans dehumanization. As I suggested earlier, no viable investigation of the potentially positive uses of the "inhuman" can ignore what transgender violence teaches us about its seamy underside.

The first such lesson has to do with the continuities between the political ontology of transphobic violence and the ordinary, everyday life of transphobia. At a conceptual level (if one can call it that), the transphobic imagination unfolds through a certain "categorical miscegenation"[14] between normative ideas about gender and normative ideas about the human. We live in a world in which individual human identities are forged in and through constructs of gendered difference. In the West, the notion of human subjectivity (of the human subject *as such*) has been erected on the fictional foundation of two fixed, unified, and coherent genders in one of which we are all inserted (by force if necessary) at birth.[15] What I am underscoring here is an interarticulated ideological architecture in which normative gender identity and normative human identity are cross-buttressed: (normative) gendered embodiment is human embodiment and (normative) human being is gendered being. When transphobic violence inscribes itself on the bodies of trans people, its perpetrators do so not only in the name of a normative vision of the gendered body; they simultaneously mark those bodies "in the name of a normative notion of the human, a normative notion of what the body of a human must be."[16]

In the transphobic imaginary, human beings who abandon their birth sex in order to "cross over, cut across, move between, or otherwise queer socially constructed *sex/gender* boundaries" have, in effect, entered an indeterminate location somewhere between the human and the inhuman. For victims of transphobic violence, this "zone of indistinction"[17] between the human and the inhuman has all too often been a "zone of extinction." However, it is important to see that transphobic ideology's narrow visions of gender and humanity constrict the freedom of *all* transgender persons: those who "have staked out a space between"[18] male and female identity, as well as those who live as male or female in defiance of their designated birth sex. For a society in which "transgender" becomes the name for someone who is thought to lack a recognizable sexual identity (again we are talking about the transphobic imaginary), it is already also the name of someone who is seen to lack a human identity *as such*. Transgender existence represents a radical interrogation of the confident, commonsense distinction between male/female, masculinity/femininity, on the one hand, and the human and the inhuman, on the other. However, in exposing the social artifice of "gender" and "humanity," transgender existence brings both these concepts to crisis. The figure of the trans person confronts our transphobic society with its most deep-seated fears and anxieties. Terrified by that fact, the transphobic imagination exorcises that terror through acts of political terrorism against the transgendered. To adapt an image from Hannah Arendt's critique of human rights in *The Origins of Totalitarianism*, we are dealing here with a political regime under which a person who violates the rules of the (normative) gender contract is considered to have "lost the very qualities which make it possible for other people to treat him [*sic*] as a fellow [human being]."[19] The transgender person is thus caught in an impossible double bind. Recognizing the need to become more fully human, the transgender person realizes she or he must break free of the constricting bonds of "normal" gender. However, in renouncing normative gender, she or he must forfeit any right to recognition and respect as a "normal" human being.[20] Put another way, we might say that the transgendered person must either choose, or risk being forced, to "stand on the side" of the inhuman.

But this is not the only lesson the political ontology of transphobic violence teaches about the "inhuman" dimension of the "human condition." Consider in this connection the record in the murder trial that followed the death of Gwen Araujo, a young transgender woman from Newark, California, who was murdered in October 1992. One of the most interesting, and objectionable, aspects of the proceedings was the use of the so-called transpanic defense. The transpanic defense is best understood as a variation on the "gay panic" and "gay advance" defenses often raised by perpetrators of hate crimes against gay men and lesbians. The transpanic defense became an issue in the Araujo case when two of the three defendants argued that if they were guilty of killing Araujo, the crime for which they should be charged was not murder but the lesser offense of manslaughter. The defendants argued that mitigation of the murder charge was appropriate because they had killed Gwen Araujo "in the heat of passion."[21] They argued, in short, that they had done what they did because of the trauma triggered by their sudden discovery that Gwen Araujo, a transgender woman, was in fact biologically male. The transpanic defense was advanced even though evidence was presented that three of the four young men had had sex with Araujo prior to the night she was murdered. As one commentator has noted, the language of uncontrollable emotion figured prominently in the Araujo case:

> [The] defense counsel's heat of passion claim turned on the defendants' emotional reaction to discovering that their friend Gwen—with whom three of them had been sexually intimate—had male genitals. One lawyer explained that the men acted out of "shame and humiliation, shock and revulsion." Feelings of having been duped grounded [the] defendants' framing of the case as a story about "deception and betrayal."[22]

A memorandum filed on behalf of one of the defendants detailed two of the defendants' (alleged) immediate reactions when they realized Araujo's biological sex. One defendant, the brief contended, became "disillusioned" and had a "look in his eyes...like *his illusion as to normality and the way things are supposed to be* had been shattered." Another defendant supposedly broke into tears and "throughout all the events was very emotional." According to the brief, while killing Araujo, this defendant kept shouting, "I can't be fucking gay, I can't be fucking gay."[23]

When we imagine and narrate the idea of "inhumanity" in human rights discourse, we tend to do so in a consistent, but curious, way. In the ordinary language of human rights, discussion of cases of "inhuman or degrading treatment"[24] generally proceeds as though the question of the inhuman were always and only "on the side" of the victims of human rights violations that fall into this category. The image is of one or more human beings who, in violation of the norms of human rights law, engage in a course of action that cruelly "dehumanizes" other human beings. However, to my mind, the location of the inhumanity of "inhuman treatment" exclusively "on the side" of its victims provides only a partial picture of what is at stake. My purpose in reviewing the uses of the transpanic defense in the Araujo trial is to underscore the "blowback" effects of the inhuman institution of transphobic violence. I am not suggesting that the account offered by the defense in the Araujo case tells a true story of what went on in the minds of Araujo's killers that October night.[25] If the story is false, it betrays a cynicism of inhuman dimensions, not least on the part of the lawyers who decided to deploy that defense. If the story is even partially true, however, it forces the recognition that the dehumanizations of transphobic violence are implicated (albeit in distinct and divergent ways) *on both its sides*. Approached from its other side, it not only becomes possible but absolutely necessary to understand how transphobic violence functions as an institution to divest its agents of the very property interest that the brutal enforcement of normative gendered being is supposed to protect: their humanity. A social world in which the recovery of lost "illusions" about gender "normality and the way things are supposed to be" compels human beings to strip, kick, slap, choke, bind, beat, and bury what they take to be a nonhuman being is an *inhuman* world, or, rather, it is a world in which human beings are "constrained" into "becoming inhuman."[26] The point I am belaboring here is surely something we already know: those who perpetrate or try to excuse acts of "torture and other inhuman or degrading treatment" against trans persons must also, in one way or another, dehumanize themselves. The "human beings" who enact transphobic violence thus testify by their actions to the "inhumanitarianism" of the human. This is one way to construe Agamben's axiom that "human beings are human in so far as they bear witness to the inhuman."[27]

I hope by now to have said enough to indicate why the struggle of transpeople for freedom from normative conceptions of gender must in a real sense also entail battle with the regnant and repressive order of inhumanity. In the face of this recognition, the question then becomes: how can the transgender rights movement negotiate the language of human rights once we come to grasp the irreducible inhumanity of the human, an inhumanity that, far from being a simple negation of the human, seems to be a substance on which humanity thrives? I believe the beginnings of an answer to this question can be found in the new cultural and political forms that transgender people and other gender-nonconforming publics are fashioning for themselves. I want briefly to mention two aspects of contemporary transgender existence that, in my view, can be described as creative efforts by trans people to walk and work through the idea of the inhuman, in an effort to harness its potential, positive force.

In his chapter for this volume, Paisley Currah directs our attention to a paradoxical feature of contemporary transgender politics. Currah shows that movement work within the courts most often seems to rely on "seemingly fixed categories such as transgender or gender identity" rather than on "concepts less anchored to identity categories, such as gender expression." He notes, by contrast, that in the legislative realm, "the legal instantiation of a new identity category—transgender—is not the ultimate goal of the activists who deploy it," and points to several instances of formal institutional politics in which trans activists seem to have made a considered decision to mobilize support around more general notions such as "gender expression" or looser senses of "gender identity." In many instances, as drafted, the capacious language of antidiscrimination statutes functionally forecloses "any legally prescribed relationship between biological sex, gender identity and gender expression"; it does so, moreover, in terms that apply to every gender. One conclusion Currah draws from these developments is that "the ultimate goal of transgender rights does not seem to be to contain gender nonconforming identities and practices within slightly expanded yet still-normative constructions and arrangements." Drawing an analogy with U.S. constitutional jurisprudence on the Establishment Clause of the First Amendment, Currah observes that some trans activists are working hard for the adoption of policies that would "dis-establish" gender.[28] A "disestablishmentarian" legal regime would end "the state's authority to police the relation between one's legal sex assigned at birth, one's gender identity, and one's gender expression," and prohibit "the state's use of 'sex' as a marker of identity on identification documents," as well as state "reliance on sex as a legal category to distribute resources." For Currah, these developments indicate how the transgender movement can in a sense be characterized as "an identity politics movement that seeks the *dissolution of the very category under which it is organized*."[29] From this vantage point, the term *transgender* is a political rather than a social identity, or better, a political *strategy* that tries "to get *beyond* identity politics by invoking a term so broad and inclusive as to make room for multiple identities and expressions, and still refer to the specific oppressions that transpeople faced."[30]

I would underscore three aspects of the political landscape Currah describes. First, in its tactical register, though trans activist engagement with the state does not ignore the existing logics of law and politics, it remains keenly aware of the limits of institutional politics as a tool to achieve substantive transgender justice. Although trans activism is not afraid to deploy the language of formal gender equality and rights, its ultimate goal is not only the democratization of existing gender relations but a more liberatory and liberationist pluralization of the possibilities of gender itself. Second, at its best, trans activist political activism is not, as it were, "transnormative." The terms of transgender political discourse are informed by a deep understanding that the "bonds of gender," as Shane Phelan puts it, are a "burden and constriction" for some people, but a "crucial support" for the "personal identity and self-esteem" of others.[31] Thus, while there are certainly voices within transgender publics who hold that "it's the gender system itself—the idea of gender itself—that needs to be done away with,"[32] others take the view that there is an important and principled distinction to be made between the "gender system" and the concept of "gender" itself. For these activists, a trans democratic project ought not endorse a politics of compulsory resistance to gender assignment. What transdemocracy demands, rather, is the abolition of the regime of *compulsory* gender. Patrick Califia has put the point well: "If the concept of gender freedom is to have any meaning, it must be possible for some of us to cling to our biological sex and the gender we were assigned at birth while others wish to adapt the body to their gender of preference, and still others choose to question the very concept of polarized sexes."[33]

Trans activism can thus be seen to pursue a complex and sophisticated "double strategy." At one level, trans advocates are demanding that the state get out of the business of using "law to bring about gendered forms of being."[34] This is the "disestablishment" approach. On another (to extend the First Amendment analogy), trans activism is seeking a political order that guarantees the right to the "free exercise" of gender. Taken together, the "free exercise" and "disestablishment" strategies are aimed at multiplying the possibilities individuals have to "imagine" (and reimagine) their relationships to ideas about gender and gendered human being.

Third, and finally, transgender activism is informed by a realization that the continuing democratization of gender power relations requires the preservation of an "empty space" in the law. This political commitment may in part explain the decision to write nonidentitarian language into some of the more recently enacted trans antidiscrimination laws. As Currah notes, these laws protect persons of all genders. Importantly, these are also laws that, by their terms, not only address discrimination against persons because of their gender identity or expression but also speak to discrimination against persons who are perceived, or perceive themselves, as having no gender *at all.* Importantly, these laws recognize that the right to gender self-determination encompasses the right to *indetermination.* This means that protections against discrimination on the basis of gender "identity and expression" must extend to those "whose gender expressions are so complex they haven't even been named yet,"[35] to those who do not care if their gender identities are ever given a "name," and, at the limit, to those "gender atheists" whose gender cannot be named because they do not live their lives as gendered human beings. In this respect, these emerging antidiscrimination policies may reasonably be construed as gesturing toward a species of democratic "destabilization rights."[36] If consolidated, these destabilization rights might serve as an effective political tool for disentrenching public institutions and practices that undermine the continuing democratization of gender relations. Indeed, they might provide a vehicle for forging a future democratic consensus in favor of the "dissolution" (to use Currah's metaphor) of gendered human being as a publicly meaningful category and the abolition of gendered human being as a requirement for full, equal participation in the public sphere.

Not surprisingly, the fluid, experimental qualities we have observed in transgender political culture are also present in the transcultural politics with which trans activism is so obviously aligned. This brings us, finally and very briefly, to a second feature of contemporary transgender existence on which the transhuman rights movement might draw as a resource in rethinking the "human" in human rights around the axis of the "inhuman." With an energy and inventiveness of breathtaking scope, transgender communities are probing and pushing up against and across the boundaries of gender. A full account of the proliferation of transgender cultural production and practice in literature, film and video, the performance arts, 'zines, music, cultural activism, and in the everyday arts of transexistence would lead me too far from my brief. I will only say here that, through their bodily enactment of what gender is and might become, the drag kings, drag queens, cross-dressers, stone butches, transsexuals, transvestites, radical fairies, leather queens, transgender fags and transsexual lesbians, diesel dykes, banji gospel divas, genderqueer punk rockers, trannie festers, gender illusionists, and gender dissolutionists are forging a rich cultural "transimaginary" and a vibrant transmaterial culture. This cultural work represents nothing short of an ontological insurgency.

Let me end where I started. In the chapter I mentioned at the beginning of this afterword, Shannon Price Minter cautions those engaged in transgender analysis and activism not to assume "that gender is necessarily the only or even the most important frame of reference for transgender issues." Minter's cautionary advice bears remarking here. We should not presume that gender is the sole or even most significant point of reference for understanding the transgender cultural forms to which I've referred. To do so is to overlook one of transgender culture's central preoccupations: the political and social fantasy of nongendered transhuman existence. Here is one representative example. In the final pages of *Sex Changes: The Politics of Transgenderism*, Patrick Califia asks the reader to join him in a thought experiment.[37] Califia poses a number of increasingly provocative, but fascinating questions. "What would it be like," he asks, "to walk down the street, go to work, or attend a party and take it for granted that the gender of the people you met would not be the first thing you ascertained about them?" Califia then slowly raises the stakes: "What would it be like," he asks, "if you could take a vacation from gender?" What would it be like to "imagine the creation of Gender Free Zones"? Califia's questions are about the time and space of trans human being beyond the boundary of gender. I'm going to conclude by posing a couple of additional questions about the time and space of transgender being at, or over, the edge of humanity. What would it be like for a transgender woman to learn to fall "in love with [her] prosthesis"?[38] What would it be like for a gay, transgender leatherman to execute a disciplinary contract with a master who specializes in the "care and training of the human dog"?[39] It would be, I submit, very much like the transhuman world in which many transgender and other gender nonconforming people are already living.

This is a world in which transgender and other non–gender conforming people are exploring the affirmative and empowering potential of trans existence beyond gender. It is also a world whose participants are opening fresh, pacific possibilities that in a very real way gesture toward the horizon that lies beyond the human as we human beings have known it. This project of cultural invention is driving a wedge between the idea of inhumanity, on the one hand, and the practice of violence, on the other. The denizens of transgender publics are experimenting with a new art of the self and fashioning an insolent political aesthetics of affirmative inhuman being. The transgender human rights movement and its allies would do well to learn what it can from this cultural politics, not least that human rights, though necessary, are never enough.

Notes

1. The last decade has produced a prolific literature exploring the value of human rights analysis and advocacy on behalf of transgender, lesbian, gay, bisexual rights. See, for example, Eric Heinze, *Sexual Orientation: A Human Right—an Essay on International Human Rights Law* (Boston: Martinus Nijhoff, 1995); Rachel Rosenboom, ed., *Unspoken Rules: Sexual Orientation and Women's Human Rights* (London: Cassell, 1996); Robert Wintemute, *Sexual Orientation and Human Rights* (Oxford: Clarendon, 1997); Barry D. Adam, Jan Willem Druyvendah, and Andre Kronwel, eds., *The Global Emergence of Gay and Lesbian Politics: National Imprints of a Worldwide Movement*, 2nd ed. (Philadelphia: Temple University Press, 1999); International Gay and Lesbian Human Rights Commission, *The International Tribunal on Human Rights Violations against Sexual Minorities* (San Francisco: International Gay and Lesbian Human Rights Commission, 1995); David M. Donahue, *Lesbian, Gay, Bisexual, and Transgender Rights: A Human Rights Perspective* (Minneapolis: Minneapolis Human Rights Resource Center, University of Minnesota, 2000).

2. Giovanna Borradori, "Autoimmunity: Real and Symbolic Suicides: A Dialogue with Jacques Derrida," in *Philosophy in a Time of Terror: Conversations with Jürgen Habermas and Jacques Derrida* (Chicago: University of Chicago Press, 2003), 133.

3. Obviously, I do not intend to suggest that "humanism" (even in the West) is a monolithic tradition. The house of humanism contains many mansions. For a discussion of the many varieties and uses of the concept, see Martin Halliwell and Andy Mousley, *Critical Humanisms: Humanist/Anti-Humanist Dialogues* (Edinburgh: Edinburgh University Press, 2003).

4. I take the term from Paul Gilroy, *Against Race* (Cambridge, MA: Belknap Press of Harvard University Press, 2000).

5. Judith Butler, *Precarious Life: The Powers of Mourning and Violence* (New York: Verso, 2004), 34.

6. In addition to the contributions to this volume see, for example, Riki Wilchins, Emilia Lombardi, and Dana Priesing, GENDERPAC First National Survey of Transgender Violence, http://www.gpac.org/archive/news/notitle.html?cmd=view& msgnum=0089 (1997) (accessed August 23, 2005).

7. See Jacqueline Rose, "Margaret Thatcher and Ruth Ellis," in *Why War? Psychoanalysis, Politics, and the Return to Melanie Klein* (London: Blackwell, 1993), 45.

8. Borradori, "Autoimmunity," 133.

9. Riki Wilchins, *Read My Lips: Sexual Subversion and the End of Gender* (Ithaca, NY: Firebrand Books, 1997), 67.

10. Susan Stryker, "My Words to Victor Frankenstein above the Village of Chamounix: Performing Gender," *GLQ* 1, no. 3 (1994): 237, 251n2.

11. Giorgio Agamben, *Remnants of Auschwitz: The Witness and the Archive* (New York: Zone Books, 1999), 55.

12. Kevin Rothstein, "Travesty of Justice: When Is a Murder Not a Murder? When the Victim Is Transsexual," *Boston Phoenix,* May 1997, http://www.bostonphoenix .com/archive/1in10/97/05/MURDER.html (accessed August 24, 2005) (emphasis added).

13. The description of the victim as "it" also figured in the trial of the killers of Gwen Araujo, a young transgender woman who was brutally murdered in Northern California in the fall of 2002. For an excellent recent article on the trial, see Victoria L. Steinberg, "A Heat of Passion Offense: Emotions and Bias in 'Transpanic' Mitigation," *Boston College Third World Law Journal* 25 (2005): 1. I discuss the Araujo case at greater length below. See note 21 and accompanying text.

14. Rey Chow, *The Protestant Ethnic and the Spirit of Capitalism* (New York: Columbia University Press, 2002), 7.

15. See Kendall Thomas, "Ain't Nothin' Like the Real Thing: Black Masculinity, Gay Sexuality, and the Jargon of Authenticity," in *Representing Black Men,* ed. George Cunningham and Marcellus Blount (New York: Routledge, 1996), 55, 58. I call this founding myth of gender "fictional" because the human infant has to be taught to be human, as the gendered infant has to be educated into his or her gender.

16. Butler, *Precarious Life,* 33.

17. Giorgio Agamben, *State of Exception* (Chicago: University of Chicago Press, 2005), 2.

18. Leslie Feinberg, *Trans Liberation: Beyond Pink and Blue* (Boston: Beacon, 1998), 69 (emphasis added).

19. Hannah Arendt, *The Origins of Totalitarianism* (New York: Harcourt Brace Jovanovich, 1973), 301. The original sentence reads in full: "It seems that a man who is nothing but a man has lost the very qualities which make it possible for other people to treat him as a fellow man."

20. The dynamic I am trying to describe here closely resembles the account Judith Butler offers in this volume of the relationship between gender identity and the "diagnosticizing" discourse of GID.

21. Steinberg, "Heat of Passion Offense."

22. Ibid., 4 (footnotes omitted).

23. Ibid., 16 (footnotes omitted) (citing Memorandum of Law from Michael P. Thorman to Alameda Super. Ct. in Support of Motion to Set Aside Hate Clause Allegation and Information Pursuant to Penal Code § 995, Points and Authorities in Support Thereof at 9, People v. Magidson, No. H-33728C [Super. Ct. Cal. Filed June 25, 2003]). The trial judge was forced to schedule a retrial after concluding that the jury which heard the case had become deadlocked.

24. Universal Declaration of Human Rights, G.A. Res. 217 A (III), U.N. GAOR, 3d Session, U.N. Doc. A/810 (1948) ("No one shall be subjected to torture or to cruel, inhuman or degrading treatment or punishment"); Convention against Torture or Other Cruel, Inhuman, or Degrading Treatment or Punishment (CAT), opened for signature Dec. 10, 1984, G.A. Res. 39/46, 1465 U.N.T.S. 85, U.N. GAOR 3d. Comm. opened for signature Dec. 10, 1984, 1465 U.N.T.S. 85 (entered into force June 26, 1987). See also International Covenant on Civil and Political Rights (ICCPR), opened for signature Dec. 19, 1966, art. 7, 999 U.N.T.S. 171, art. 7 (entered into force March 23, 1976) ("No one shall be subjected to torture or to cruel, inhuman or degrading treatment or punishment").

25. I also don't mean to imply that Gwen Araujo's killers should not have been found guilty and punished under the criminal law.

26. Jean-François Lyotard, *The Inhuman: Reflections on Time* (Stanford, CA: Stanford University Press, 1991), 2.

27. Agamben, *Remnants of Auschwitz*, 121.

28. For a disestablishment argument with respect to sex, sexuality, and sexual orientation, see Janet R. Jakobsen and Ann Pellegrini, *Love the Sinner: Sexual Regulation and the Limits of Religious Tolerance* (New York: New York University Press, 2003), 103–26; for an application of the disestablishment concept to the problem of heteronormativity, see Lisa Duggan, "Queering the State," *Social Text*, no. 39 (1994): 9; for an analysis of disestablishment regarding race, see Neil Gotanda, "A Critique of 'Our Constitution Is Color-Blind,'" *Stanford Law Review* 44 (1991): 1.

29. Emphasis added.

30. Jamison Green, *Becoming a Visible Man* (Nashville, TN: Vanderbilt University Press, 2004), 81 (emphasis added)

31. Shane Phelan, *Sexual Strangers: Gays, Lesbians, and Dilemmas of Citizenship* (Philadelphia: Temple University Press), 137.

32. Kate Bornstein, *Gender Outlaw: On Men, Women, and the Rest of Us* (New York: Routledge, 1994), 114.

33. Patrick Califia, *Sex Changes: The Politics of Transgenderism*, 2nd ed. (San Francisco: Cleis, 2003), 275.

34. Jacqueline Stevens, *Reproducing the State* (Princeton, NJ: Princeton University Press, 1999), 212.

35. Riki Wilchins, "A Note from the Editrix," *In Your Face*, spring 1995, 4.

36. Roberto Unger, *Politics: The Central Texts* (New York: Verso, 1997), 387–91; see also William H. Simon and Charles F. Sabel, "Destabilization Rights: How Public Law Litigation Succeeds," *Harvard Law Review* 117 (2004): 1015.

37. Califia, *Sex Changes*, 277 (emphasis added).

38. Sandy Stone, "Split Subjects, Not Atoms; or, How I Learned to Fall in Love with My Prosthesis," in *The Cyborg Handbook,* ed. Chris Hables Gray (New York: Routledge, 1995), 393.

39. See, for example, Michael Daniels, *Woof! Perspectives on the Care and Training of the Human Dog* (Las Vegas, NV: Nacza Plains Corporation, 2003); see also Michael Daniels, *GRRR!* (Las Vegas, NV: Nacza Plains Corporation, 2004).

Appendix:
The International
Bill of Gender Rights

Preface by Phyllis Randolph Frye

The International Bill of Gender Rights (IBGR), adopted July 4, 1996, in Houston, Texas, is derived from two earlier documents, both of which sought to articulate basic human rights for transgender people. JoAnn Roberts had drafted and disseminated a "Bill of Gender Rights" in 1991. Working independently and without knowledge of Roberts's efforts, Sharon Stuart published a proposal for a "Gender Bill of Rights" in the 1991 annual meeting newsletter of the International Foundation for Gender Education. Following the first annual meeting of the International Conference on Transgender Law and Employment Policy in August 1992, Stuart began the work of drafting an expanded Gender Bill of Rights that incorporated her proposal as well as Roberts's work. A first draft presented in August 1993 at ICTLEP's second annual meeting was extensively revised and refined in committee. Major contributors to the 1993 committee's efforts included Susan Stryker, Jan Eaton of Virginia, Martine Rothblatt, and Phyllis Frye. The IBGR was reviewed and amended at subsequent annual meetings of ICTLEP in 1994, 1995, and 1996. The IBGR was reviewed and amended, led by Stuart, at subsequent annual meetings of ICTLEP in 1994, 1995, and 1996.

The IBGR strives to express fundamental human and civil rights from a gender perspective. However, the ten rights enunciated below are not to be viewed as special rights applicable to a particular interest group, that is, transgender people. Nor are these rights limited in application to persons for whom gender identity and role issues are of paramount concern. All ten sections of the IBGR are universal rights that can be claimed and exercised by every human being regardless of sex or gender.

327

The IBGR is a theoretical expression that has no force of law absent its adoption by legislative bodies or recognition of its principles by courts of law, or by administrative agencies and international structures such as the United Nations.

In recent years the IBGR's principles have been embodied in various legislative initiatives designed to protect the rights of transgender people. Municipalities in widely scattered sections of the United States have adopted several of these initiatives. Meanwhile, the rights of transgender people are gaining increased recognition and protection in countries such as Canada, South Africa, Australia, Great Britain, and throughout Western Europe.

The International Bill of Gender Rights

1. The Right to Define Gender Identity

All human beings carry within themselves an ever-unfolding idea of who they are and what they are capable of achieving. The individual's sense of self is not determined by chromosomal sex, genitalia, assigned birth sex, or initial gender role. Thus, the individual's identity and capabilities cannot be circumscribed by what society deems to be masculine or feminine behavior. It is fundamental that individuals have the right to define, and to redefine as their lives unfold, their own gender identities, without regard to chromosomal sex, genitalia, assigned birth sex, or initial gender role.

Therefore, all human beings have the right to define their own gender identity regardless of chromosomal sex, genitalia, assigned birth sex, or initial gender role.

2. The Right to Free Expression of Gender Identity

Given the right to define one's own gender identity, all human beings have the corresponding right to free expression of their self-defined gender identity.

Therefore, all human beings have the right to free expression of their self-defined gender identity; and further, no individual shall be denied Human or Civil Rights by virtue of the expression of a self-defined gender identity.

3. The Right to Secure and Retain Employment and to Receive Just Compensation

Given the economic structure of modern society, all human beings have a right to train for and to pursue an occupation or profession as a means of providing shelter, sustenance, and the necessities and bounty of life, for themselves and for those dependent upon them; further, all human beings have the right to secure and retain employ-

ment and to receive just compensation for their labor regardless of gender identity, chromosomal sex, genitalia, assigned birth sex, or initial gender role.

Therefore, individuals shall not be denied the right to train for and to pursue an occupation or profession, nor be denied the right to secure and retain employment, nor be denied just compensation for their labor, by virtue of their chromosomal sex, genitalia, assigned birth sex, or initial gender role, or on the basis of a self-defined gender identity or the expression thereof.

4. The Right of Access to Gendered Space and Participation in Gendered Activity

Given the right to define one's own gender identity and the corresponding right to free expression of a self-defined gender identity, no individual should be denied access to a space or denied participation in an activity by virtue of a self-defined gender identity which is not in accord with chromosomal sex, genitalia, assigned birth sex, or initial gender role.

Therefore, no individual shall be denied access to a space or denied participation in an activity by virtue of a self-defined gender identity which is not in accord with chromosomal sex, genitalia, assigned birth sex, or initial gender role.

5. The Right to Control and Change One's Own Body

All human beings have the right to control their bodies, which includes the right to change their bodies cosmetically, chemically, or surgically, so as to express a self-defined gender identity.

Therefore, individuals shall not be denied the right to change their bodies as a means of expressing a self-defined gender identity; and further, individuals shall not be denied Human or Civil Rights on the basis that they have changed their bodies cosmetically, chemically, or surgically, or desire to do so as a means of expressing a self-defined gender identity.

6. The Right to Competent Medical and Professional Care

Given the individual's right to define one's own gender identity, and the right to change one's own body as a means of expressing a self-defined gender identity, no individual should be denied access to competent medical or other professional care on the basis of the individual's chromosomal sex, genitalia, assigned birth sex, or initial gender role.

Therefore, individuals shall not be denied the right to competent medical or other professional care on the basis of chromosomal sex, genitalia, assigned birth sex, or initial gender role, when changing their bodies cosmetically, chemically, or surgically.

7. The Right to Freedom from Involuntary Psychiatric Diagnosis and Treatment

Given the right to define one's own gender identity, individuals should not be subject to involuntary psychiatric diagnosis or treatment.

Therefore, individuals shall not be subject to involuntary psychiatric diagnosis or treatment as mentally disordered, dysphoric, or diseased, on the basis of a self-defined gender identity or the expression thereof.

8. The Right to Sexual Expression

Given the right to a self-defined gender identity, every consenting adult has a corresponding right to free sexual expression.

Therefore, no individual's Human or Civil Rights shall be denied on the basis of sexual orientation; and further, no individual shall be denied Human or Civil Rights for expression of a self-defined gender identity through private sexual acts between consenting adults.

9. The Right to Form Committed, Loving Relationships and Enter into Marital Contracts

Given that all human beings have the right to free expression of self-defined gender identities, and the right to sexual expression as a form of gender expression, all human beings have a corresponding right to form committed, loving relationships with one another, and to enter into marital contracts, regardless of their own or their partner's chromosomal sex, genitalia, assigned birth sex, or initial gender role.

Therefore, individuals shall not be denied the right to form committed, loving relationships with one another or to enter into marital contracts by virtue of their own or their partner's chromosomal sex, genitalia, assigned birth sex, or initial gender role, or on the basis of their expression of a self-defined gender identity.

10. The Right to Conceive, Bear, or Adopt Children; the Right to Nurture and Have Custody of Children and to Exercise Parental Capacity

Given the right to form a committed, loving relationship with another, and to enter into marital contracts, together with the right to express a self-defined gender identity and the right to sexual expression, individuals have a corresponding right to conceive and bear children, to adopt children, to nurture children, to have custody of children, and to exercise parental capacity with respect to children, natural or adopted, without regard to chromosomal sex, genitalia, assigned birth sex, or initial gender role, or by virtue of a self-defined gender identity or the expression thereof.

Therefore, individuals shall not be denied the right to conceive, bear, or adopt children, nor to nurture and have custody of children, nor to exercise parental capacity with respect to children, natural or adopted, on the basis of their own, their partner's, or their children's chromosomal sex, genitalia, assigned birth sex, initial gender role, or by virtue of a self-defined gender identity or the expression thereof.

Contributors

Kylar W. Broadus is a professor, attorney, and transgender advocate in central Missouri. He teaches business law at Lincoln University of Missouri and has a general practice of law. He does advocacy for the transgender community as well as for gays and lesbians. He has served on the Human Rights Commission of Columbia, Missouri, has been a board member of PROMO, the statewide GLBT organization, and is a board member of the Transgender Law and Policy Institute.

Judith Butler is Maxine Elliot Professor in the departments of rhetoric and comparative literature at the University of California, Berkeley. She is the author of *Subjects of Desire: Hegelian Reflections in Twentieth-Century France* (1987); *Gender Trouble: Feminism and the Subversion of Identity* (1990); *Bodies That Matter: On the Discursive Limits of "Sex"* (1993); *The Psychic Life of Power: Theories of Subjection* (1997); *Excitable Speech* (1997); *Antigone's Claim: Kinship between Life and Death* (2000); *Hegemony, Contingency, Universality,* with Ernesto Laclau and Slavoj Žižek (2000); *Undoing Gender* (2004); and *Precarious Life: Powers of Violence and Mourning* (2004). *The Judith Butler Reader,* edited by Sara Salih, was published in 2004. Her most recent book, *Giving an Account of Oneself* (2005), considers the partial opacity of the subject, and the relation between critique and ethical reflection. She is also the author of numerous articles on cultural and literary theory, philosophy, psychoanalysis, feminism, and sexual politics.

Mauro Cabral (A. I. Grinspan) is a PhD candidate in philosophy at National Córdoba University in Argentina, where he also is a teacher and researcher at the Center of Research on Literature and Humanities. He works as a program consultant on trans and intersex issues in the Latin American office of the International Gay and Lesbian Human Rights Commission.

Paisley Currah teaches political science at Brooklyn College of the City University of New York and is executive director of the Center for Lesbian and Gay Studies (CLAGS). He is a founder and board member of the Transgender Law and Policy Institute.

Dallas Denny is a writer and activist in Pine Lake, Georgia, population 610. She is editor of IFGE's *Transgender Tapestry Journal* and director of Fantasia Fair, an annual conference held in October at the tip of Cape Cod, Massachusetts. She is the author of *Gender Dysphoria: A Guide to Research* and *Current Concepts in Transgender Identity*.

Taylor Flynn is an associate professor at Western New England College School of Law and formerly was an attorney with the American Civil Liberties Union of Southern California. She has focused her work in the areas of gender identity and sexual orientation discrimination, and has litigated trans rights cases in areas including family law, employment, and political asylum. Her publications have appeared in the *Columbia Law Review, Stanford Law and Policy Review,* and *Iowa Law Review.* She has spoken widely on trans and gay rights issues and has appeared on CNN's *Crossfire, Good Morning, America,* and National Public Radio.

Phyllis Randolph Frye, Esq., has been an activist in the transgender movement for more than twenty years. She was a founder of the Transgender Law Conference in 1991 and has authored numerous articles on the legal issues affecting transgender people. She has received the Creator of Change Award from the National Gay and Lesbian Task Force and the Virginia Prince Lifetime Contribution Award from the International Foundation for Gender Education.

Julie A. Greenberg is a professor of law at Thomas Jefferson School of Law, where she teaches classes related to sexuality, gender, and sexual orientation. Her scholarship primarily focuses on the legal issues affecting intersex and transgendered persons. Her work has been quoted in more than one hundred and fifty books and articles and has been instrumental in expanding the approaches taken by courts in the United States and other countries in sex determination rulings.

Morgan Holmes is assistant professor of sociology at Wilfrid Laurier University in Canada. She has been working on intersex issues since 1993, when she joined ISNA as a founding member. Her interests have broadened to assess the treatment of many different forms of stigmatized bodies; she is now conducting research with families of children with disabilities. She continues to work and publish in the overlapping areas of medicine, law, and discourses of normalcy.

Richard M. Juang cochairs the advisory board for the National Center for Transgender Equality (NCTE) in Washington, DC. He has taught at Oberlin College and Susquehanna University. He is the lead editor of NCTE's *Responding to Hate Crimes: A Community Resource Manual* and coeditor of *Transgender Justice*, which explores models of activism.

Bennett H. Klein has been the AIDS Law project director at Gay and Lesbian Advocates and Defenders (GLAD) since 1994. He was a litigation associate at the Boston law firms of Kotin, Crabtree, and Strong and Gaston and Snow. He has been involved in several Boston-area community organizations, including serving as a "buddy" for the AIDS Action Committee of Massachusetts, a board member of the Massachusetts Lesbian and Gay Bar Association, and a founding member of the Boston Alliance of Gay and Lesbian Youth.

Jennifer L. Levi is assistant professor at Western New England College School of Law. She is affiliated with Gay and Lesbian Advocates and Defenders (GLAD), a nonprofit legal organization whose mission is to end discrimination based on sexual orientation, gender identity and expression, and HIV status. She served as lead attorney in a number of cases representing transgender individuals who have faced discrimination, including *Pat Doe v. Yunits*, defending a transgender youth's right to wear clothing to school consistent with her gender identity; *Rosa v. Park West Bank*, establishing that the scope of federal sex discrimination law includes transgender people; and *Beger v. Division of Medical Assistance*, defending a transgender person's right to state insurance coverage for health care.

Shannon Price Minter is the legal director for the National Center for Lesbian Rights, one of the nation's leading advocacy organizations for lesbian, gay, bisexual, and transgender people. He was NCLR's lead attorney on Sharon Smith's groundbreaking wrongful death suit and has litigated many other impact cases in California and other states. He is the lead attorney in *Woo v. Lockyer*, the case that will determine whether same-sex couples are able to marry in California. He serves on the boards of Equality California, the Transgender Law Center, and the Transgender Law and Policy Institute.

Ruthann Robson is professor of law at the City University of New York School of Law. She is the author of numerous works that develop a lesbian legal theory, including the books *Sappho Goes to Law School* and *Lesbian (Out)Law: Survival under the Rule of Law,* as well as many articles in such journals as *New York Law School Journal of Human Rights, Albany Law Review, Women's Rights Law Reporter, Hastings Law Journal, Australian Feminist Law Journal,* and *Yearbook of New Zealand Jurisprudence.* She has given many presentations on women and sexuality and the law in the United States, South Africa, Canada, Great Britain, Australia, and New Zealand. A frequent contributor to *Out Magazine,* she has also published three novels, numerous short stories, and poetry. In 2003 her article "Notes from a Difficult Case" won a creative nonfiction best essay award from *Creative Nonfiction Magazine.*

Nohemy Solórzano-Thompson is assistant professor of Spanish at Whitman College. She teaches seminars in U.S. Latino/a, Latin America, and Spanish theater and film. Her research focuses on portrayals of masculinity in contemporary Mexican and Chicano film, performance, and culture.

Dean Spade is a transgender activist and attorney. He founded the Sylvia Rivera Law Project in August 2002, a collective organization that provides free legal services to low-income people facing gender identity discrimination. His writing has appeared in the *Chicano-Latino Law Review,* the *Harvard Lesbian and Gay Review,* and the *Berkeley Women's Law Journal.* He is coeditor of the online journal Makezine.org.

Kendall Thomas is Nash Professor of Law and founding codirector of the Center for the Study of Law and Culture at Columbia University in the City of New York.

Paula Viturro studied law at Buenos Aires University and is now a PhD candidate in human rights and development at Pedro de Olavide University in Seville, Spain. She teaches at the law school of Buenos Aires University and coordinates the Area "Technologies of Gender" of the Centro Cultural Ricardo Rojas. She is a member of the feminist group Ají de Pollo.

Willy Wilkinson, MPH, is a third-gendered writer and public health consultant who conducts transgender and LGBT trainings for various health and social service providers. He assists organizations in better serving the needs of their populations through research, evaluation, and technical assistance, and has worked on a number of public health research projects and community programs serving the transgender community in San Francisco. Willy was a qualitative data analyst for San Francisco's Transgender Focus Group Study and served on the community advisory board of the Transgender Community Health Project. He launched the Trannyfags Project in San Francisco, as well as a support group in Berkeley for people of color on the FTM spectrum. In 2004 Willy conducted a needs assessment of FTMs of color and their partners, and launched the Health Care Access Project at Transgender Law Center in San Francisco. Willy's writing has appeared in numerous anthologies and periodicals.

Index

Transgender
RIGHTS